FIELD GUIDE TO
PATTERN GLASS

Mollie Helen McCain

D0684396

COLLECTOR BOOKS

A Division of Schroeder Publishing Co., Inc.

Searching for a Publisher?

We are always looking for knowledgeable people considered to be experts within their fields. If you feel there is a real need for a book on your collectible subject and have a large comprehensive collection, contact Collector Books.

Cover design by Beth Summers
Book design by Ben Faust

Collector Books
P.O. Box 3009
Paducah, Kentucky 42002-3009

www.collectorbooks.com

DEDICATION

Dedicated to
The Harrington Girls,

Fern and Lillian,
Margaret and Katharine,
Doris and Helen,

Who have all been
dearly loved.

Contents

Acknowledgments 6
Introduction 6
References 8
Glass Companies 484
Index 487

Animals
Plates 1 – 10
Page 10

Circles
Plates 11 – 33
Page 30

Diamonds
Plates 34 – 71
Page 78

Facets
Plates 72 – 112
Page 156

Flowers
Plates 113 – 131
Page 238

Fruit
Plates 132 – 139
Page 276

Hobnails and Beads
Plates 140 – 153
Page 292

Panels
Plate 154 – 168
Page 320

People
Plates 169 – 174
Page 350

Plain
Plates 175 – 180
Page 362

Plants
Plates 181 – 194
Page 374

Ribs and Columns
Plates 195 – 205
Page 402

Ropes
Plates 206 – 207
Page 424

Shells
Plate 208
Page 428

Squares and Rectangles
Plates 209 – 218
Page 430

Stars
Plates 219 – 223
Page 450

Swirls
Plates 224 – 231
Page 460

Odds and Ends
Plates 232 – 235
Page 476

ACKNOWLEDGMENTS

My heartfelt thanks to the members of the Early American Pattern Glass Society for their interest and assistance in compiling this book. Bob Burford sent not only illustrations but the actual pieces of glass for me to draw; he also spent many hours sharing his expertise by compiling information on new patterns. John Gregory shared his knowledge of patterns with wine goblets accumulated over years of collecting, with manufacturers, dates, references, and other valuable information, and copied many references for me from his extensive library. He and Jim Pollard sent along a privately printed book of references that proved to be of immense value. Dr. Charles Marlin not only sent information, but also volunteered to be my "leg man," and his help included insights and encouragement at times when I needed it.

Thanks are due to Lisa Stroup and Della Wyatt for their fine work at Collector Books.

Perhaps the most important person in the production of this book has been my daughter-in-law, Gail McCain. Without her, this book would never have been written. At every turn of the road she was there, assisting with computer problems, making sure I had whatever supplies that were necessary, and encouraging me with lots of hugs. To her I owe a debt of gratitude that can never be repaid.

Finally, thanks to all you lovers of pattern glass — you have made sure that this wonderful part of American history will never be lost and will always be appreciated.

Mollie Helen McCain
Jacksonville, Florida

INTRODUCTION

This guide is planned to allow easier identification of early American pressed glass patterns when you are collecting in the field. Most books on pattern glass are organized alphabetically or have no organization at all. This is fine when one knows the pattern name, but very time-consuming when looking for an unknown pattern, and impossible to do in the field. In this guide the categories are grouped according to molded characteristics — circles, stars, plants, flowers, etc. Intricately detailed examples are called "faceted." Some patterns have more than one motif, so I have tried to use the dominant characteristic — although in some cases it was a toss-up. Sometimes I have shown more than one example in different categories.

Most of these patterns came in crystal clear glass; many came in colored glass, opaque glass, flashed or stained with color, decorated with enamels or decals, and gilded. They date from the middle 1800s to about 1915. The earliest patterns often featured flint glass, fine, clear glass with lead content. These items have a lovely "ring" when tapped. Later glass could be filled with imperfections, bubbles, and rough mold lines, or they could be gleaming and flawless, depending on who made them. Some patterns were made by more

6

than one company, the molds themselves having been sold; these patterns may have examples of both fine and poorer glass. But all of it is delightful and collectible.

I have described patterns as made in either basic table service — sugar, creamer, butter, and spooner; or extended table service — basic plus pitchers, celery vases, bowls, syrups, toothpick holders, and many other pieces. When more unusual pieces are known, I will mention them, wine goblets or sugar shakers, for example. Of course, new pieces are surfacing all the time, so do not take my listings as the final word! I have also made an attempt to note colors other than crystal, when known. Your book will have even greater value if you note your own observations in it.

As the first researchers of pressed glass described patterns, they named them, and sometimes each writer assigned another name regardless of any earlier ones. I have tried to include all known names for each pattern and to use the most well-known one as the primary name. I have cross-indexed each name for your convenience. For the most part, I have used the names given by Minnie Watson Kamm whenever possible. Her research and detailed drawings are a marvel, and she made a real effort not to ignore other researchers. Only in very special cases have I actually given a new name to any pattern, and then only because there seemed to be no earlier documentation.

Prices for pattern glass fluctuate wildly according to the pattern, the rarity of the piece or color, the geographic location involved, and the kind of sale, estate, auction, garage, antique store, etc. The best way to learn prices is to buy an annual price guide such as that published by Collector Books. These guides contain prices noted in real sales and can give you an idea of the rarity or abundance of each piece. A recent goblet sold for $10,000, yet you can find nice goblets for as little as $20.

People are usually concerned with reproductions, but knowing your pattern and the look and feel of old glass will usually be a sufficient guide. Find dealers you can trust, and have the sales slip document what you are buying so that, if you find you have purchased a reproduction, you can return it for a refund. If the dealer won't allow such a return, pay only a minimum price. Some reproductions from earlier years are now themselves collectible.

When you decide on a pattern or type of glass you wish to collect, read everything you can find about it. Included here with each pattern are codes assigned to books describing that pattern. Some of these books are only found in libraries, but many are available now, some as reprints. Knowledge will increase your enjoyment in a field of collecting that is truly American, representing our own history, and the tastes of earlier generations. To many of our ancestors, pattern glass was the first really beautiful glass they could afford for their homes. A pattern glass pitcher was kept proudly in the middle of the dining room table by many a farm wife who cherished it. The patterns reflect the tastes of those early people, whether fancy ones pretending to be cut glass, those that featured garden flowers or animals, politics, or secret jokes. (Take a good look at the Currier and Ives tray...) The best of luck to you in your collecting!

REFERENCES

To those new to the lure of pattern glass, there is a vast amount of literature, much out of print but available at some libraries. When collecting pattern glass became popular in the 1930s, Ruth Webb Lee and Minnie Watson Kamm vied for prominence in presenting and naming patterns. Kamm illustrated eight spiral-bound booklets that began with large, detailed drawings of pitchers and progressed to printing original glass company ads; her contribution to the field was enormous. William Heacock republished her books in a hardbound form with notes. Ruth Webb Lee was considered at the time to be the most professional researcher, and her little blue handbook of tiny line drawings was very popular among collectors, as were her scholarly volumes on pattern glass. Many others contributed to the field with books about salt shakers, goblets, toy sets, salt dishes, and special collections.

Of later publications, no one is as prolific as William Heacock, with many richly illustrated books and magazines. He was thorough and unending in his research, and his death has left a great void in the pattern glass field.

There are many valuable research tools listed below that were used in this book. I have included references to early books because they are the sources of information that are part of the history and mystique of pattern glass. New books are now being published that will earn their places in pattern glass history. This identification field guide should be the starting point for a collector, who can then go on to learn from others about the individual intricacies and peculiarities of their particular pattern glass interests.

Each book entry begins with a code that you will see among appropriate pattern listings.

ABC – Drepperd, Carl W., *ABC'S of Old Glass.* Award Books, New York, 1944.

Archer – Archer, M. & D., *Imperial Glass.* Collector Books, Paducah, KY, 1978.

Barret – Barret, Richard C., *Popular American Ruby-Stained Glass.* Crown Publishers, Inc., New York, NY.

Batty – Batty, Bob H., *A Complete Guide to Pressed Glass.* Pelican Publishing Co., Gretna, LA, 1978.

Bond – Bond, Marcelle, *The Beauty of Albany Glass.* Publishers Printing House, Berne, IN.

Bones – Bones, Frances, *The Book of Duncan Glass.* Wallace-Homestead, Des Moines, IA, 1973.

Boul – Boultinghouse, Mark, *Art and Colored Glass Toothpick Holders.*

Bred – Bredehoft, Neila and Tom and J. & B. Sanford, *American Glass Companies Vol. I Findlay Glass.* Cherry Hill Publications, St. Louisville, OH, 1994.

Burns – Burns, M. L., *Heisey's Glassware of Distinction.* By author.

Duncan – Bredehoft, N. M., G. A. Fogg, and F. C. Maloney (editors), *Early Duncan Glassware, 1874 – 1892.* By authors, 1987.

Edwards – Edwards and Carwile, *Standard Encyclopedia of Pressed Glass 1860 – 1930.* Collector Books, Paducah, Ky., 1999.

Gob – Millard, Dr. S. T., *Goblets I and II.* Wallace-Homestead, Des Moines, IA, 1975.

Gorham – Gorham, C. W., *Riverside Glass Works of Wellsburg, West Va. 1879 – 1907.* By author, 1995.

Har – Hartung, *Carnival Glass in Color* (no page numbers). By author.

Hartley – Hartley, J. M., *Old American Glass.* Texas Christian University Press, Fort Worth, TX, 1975.

H – Heacock, William, *Victorian Colored Pattern Glass,* Books I, II, III, 4, 5, 6, 7. Antique Publications, Marietta, OH, 1976 – 1986.

HCG – Heacock, William, *Collecting Glass 1 – 3.* Antique Publications, Marietta, OH, 1984 – 1986.

HGC – Heacock, William, *The Glass Collector 1 – 6.* Peacock Publications, Columbus, OH, 1982 –

1983.

Herrick – Herrick, Ruth, *Greentown Glass*. By author.

Hobbs – Bredehoft, Neila and Tom, *Hobbs, Brockunier and Co. Glass*. Collector Books, Paducah, KY, 1997.

HPV – Heacock, William, *Pattern Glass Preview #1 – 6*. By author.

HTP – Heacock, William, *1,000 Toothpick Holders*. Antique Publications, Marietta, OH, 1977.

Innes – Innes, Lowell, *Pittsburgh Glass 1797 – 1891*. Houghton Mifflin, Boston, MA, 1976.

Jenks – Jenks, B. and Luna, J., *Early American Pattern Glass*. Wallace-Homestead Book Co., Radnor, PA, 1990.

K – Kamm, Minnie Watson, *Pressed Glass (Pitcher) Books 1 – 8*. Motschall Co., Detroit, MI 1939 – 1954.

Kerr – Kerr, Ann, *Fostoria: An Identification and Value Guide*. Collector Books, Paducah, KY, 1994.

Krause – Krause, G., *The Years of Duncan*. Heyworth Star, Heyworth, IL, 1980.

L – Lee, Ruth Webb, *Ruth Webb Lee's Handbook of Early American Pressed Glass Patterns*. By author, Framingham Centre, MA, 1931.

Lucas. Lucas, R. I., *Tarentum Pattern Glass*. By author, 1981.

LV – Lee, Ruth Webb, *Victorian Glass Specialties of the 19th Century*.

Lechler – Doris and Virginia O'Neill, *Children's Glass Dishes*.

LEAPG – Lee, Ruth Webb, *Early American Pressed Glass*. By author, Pittsford, NY, 1931.

Measell – Measell, J., *Greentown Glass, The Indiana Tumbler and Goblet Co.* Grand Rapids Public Museum, Grand Rapids, MI, 1979.

McKee – Innes, L. and J. S. Spillman, *M'Kee Victorian Glass*. Dover Publications, NY, 1981.

Metz – Metz, Alice H., *Early American Pattern Glass 1 & 2*. Heritage Antiques, South Orleans, MA,` 1977; Collector Books, 2000.

Miller – Miller, Robert W., *Price Guide to Antiques & Pattern Glass, 4th and 7th Editions*. Wallace-Homestead Book Company, Des Moines, Iowa, 1977, 1981.

Mugs – Adams, Walter and John Mordock, *Pattern Glass Mugs*. Collector Books, Paducah, KY, 1995.

Mur – Murray, Dean L. *Cruets Only* (1) and *More Cruets Only* (2), Kilgore Graphics Inc., Phoenix, AZ.

NM – Miller, Everett and Addie, *The New Martinsville Glass Story*. Richardson Publishing Co., Marietta, OH, 1972.

Oliver – Oliver, Elizabeth (and Merrilees, Rebecca, illustrator), *American Antique Glass*, Golden Press, New York, 1977.

PetPat – Peterson, Arthur, *Glass Patents and Patterns*. By author.

PetSal – Peterson, Arthur, *Glass Salt Shakers, 1,000 Patterns*. Wallace-Homestead Book Co., Des Moines, IA, 1970.

Revi – Revi, Albert C., *American Pressed Glass and Figure Bottles*. Thomas Nelson, Inc., Camden, NJ, 1964.

Salts – Heacock, William and Patricia Johnson, *5,000 Open Salts*. Richardson Printing Co., Marietta, OH, 1982.

Smith – Smith, Don E., *Findlay Pattern Glass*. Gray Printing Co., Fostoria, OH.

Stout – Stout, S. McP., *The Complete Book of McKee Glass*. Trojan Press, North Kansas City, 1972.

Swan – Swan, F. H., *Portland Glass Company*. Roger Williams Press, Providence, RI, 1939.

Taylor – Taylor, Ardelle, *Colored Glass Sugar Shakers and Syrup Pitchers*. By author.

Unitt – Unitt, Doris and Peter, *American and Canadian Goblets 1 & 2*. Clock House, Peterborough, Ont., 1977.

W – Warman, Edwin G., *Antiques and Their Prices* (several editions).

Welker – Welker, John and Elizabeth, *Pressed Glass in America*. Antique Acres Press, Ivyland, PA, 1985.

Wilson – Wilson, K. M. *New England Glass and Glassmaking*. Thomas Y. Crowell, NY, 1972.

Also used extensively:

Gregory, John D., *Pattern Glass Wines*. Private printing by author, Monkton, MD, 1997.

Lyle, Becky, *Early American Pattern Glass Reference Index*. Private printing by author, Ritzville, WA, 1998.

SECTION ONE — ANIMALS

Pattern glass animals – some of the most beautiful — and bizarre — pieces of glass a collector can prize. Clockwise from top right: Owl novelty, Beaver Band, Robin, Elephant novelty, Deer and Pine Tree, Jumbo.

PLATE 1. ANIMALS

CURRIER AND IVES (BALKY MULE; EULALIA), tray and syrup. Bellaire Glass Co., 1890; Co-operative Flint Glass Co. Extended table service including lamp, decanter, wine set, canoe-shaped bowls, cup and saucer. Only the trays have the balky mule scene; other pieces have only the "daisies" in a pattern. Crystal, canary (rare), amber, blue, opaque white, ruby-stained. See plate 78. *Ref. K3-117; LV-86; Metz 1-158; Unitt 1-268; H7-112; Mugs p. 65.*

PLATE 2. ANIMALS

DEER WITH LILY-OF-THE-VALLEY, goblet. Known in crystal goblet. *Ref. L-164 #17; Gob I-36.*

THREE DEER, goblet. Crystal goblet known. *Ref. K8-69; Metz 1-96.*

DEER AND OAK TREE, pitcher. National Glass Co. (Indiana Tumbler and Goblet Works) ca. 1900 – 03. Pitcher and mug known. Crystal, chocolate glass. *Ref. K3-122; K4-123; Mugs p. 13; Metz 2-80.*

DEER ALERT, pitcher. *Ref. K4-124.*

ALLIGATOR, match holder. A novelty.

HORSEHEAD MEDALLION, spooner. Made ca. 1885 – 1895 in extended table service including toy table set. Crystal; milk-white glass. *Ref. LV pl. 29.*

BEAR WITH BOOK, salt shaker. Novelty.

RACING DEER (DEER RACING), pitcher. Dalzell, Gilmore and Leighton, 1890s. Crystal pitcher known. *Ref. K6-60.*

DEER AND PINE TREE (DEER AND DOE), mug. Belmont Glass Co. ca. 1883; McKee Glass Co. ca 1886. Extended table service of over 25 pieces including waste bowl, jam jar, platter, miniature mug. Crystal, blue, amber, dark amber, lt. and emerald green, yellow-green, gilded. The goblet has been reproduced. *Ref. L-119; LEAPG-342; Metz 1-96; K4-31; HGC-1 p. 3; Mugs p. 16;* Schroy-47.

OWL HEAD, salt shaker. One of many delightful whimsies.

LOOP WITH ELK, goblet. *Ref. Gob II-144.*

WESTWARD HO! (PIONEER; TIPPECANOE), pitcher. Gillinder and Sons, 1879. Made in extended table service including covered candy dish, bread platter, jam jar, sherbet, wines, cordials, and rare champagne. Crystal, frosted. Mugs were also made in opalescent, opaque white, blue, and opaque blue; they are rare in color. The mug, which has a stag on one side and a bison on the other, has not been reproduced to date, although many of the pieces in this pattern have been. See the covered compote on Plate 171. *Ref. L-89; LEAPG-281; K1-16; Mugs p. 12, 13, 14; Gob II-40, 160; Metz 1-110; Unitt 1-94; Jenks p. 551;* Schroy-154.

A note about goblets: There is a whole range of goblet sizes, often confusing, and often hard to identify. In order of size downward, goblets are found in water goblets, champagnes, claret, wine, and smallest of all, cordials. All are very collectible, and many are rare.

12

*Deer with Lily-
of-the-Valley*   *Three Deer*   *Deer and Oak Tree*   *Deer Alert*

*Alligator
Match Holder*   *Horsehead
Medallion*   *Bear with Book*   *Racing Deer*

Deer & Pine Tree   *Owl Head*   *Loop with Elk*   *Westward Ho!*

PLATE 3. ANIMALS

LION AND BABOON, pitcher. Extended table service including a toy table set. *Ref. K3-57; Jenks p. 329; Metz 1-97; Schroy-160.*

GIRAFFE, goblet. A novelty. *Ref. Gob II-117; Schroy-160.*

JUMBO (ELEPHANT), compote. Canton Glass Co., 1883; Aetna Glass Co. 1883. Extended table service including a very rare spoon rack. Crystal. *Ref. L-94; LEAPG-308; K5-14; Metz 1-94; Schroy-85.*

CLEAR LION HEAD (ATLANTA; SQUARE LION'S HEAD; LATE LION), salt shaker. Fostoria Glass Co. #500, 1895; Westmoreland Specialty Glass, 1905. Extended table service of many and varied pieces including wine, cordials, champagne. Crystal, ruby-stained. *Ref. K5-83; Schroy-9; H7-69.*

MONKEY (MONKEY UNDER TREE), butter dish and pitcher. Duncan Glass made ca. 1880s in extended table service in many and varied pieces, but no goblet was made. Crystal, opalescent. A mug very similar to this pattern was made by Valley Glass Co. in about 1891 in crystal, amethyst, and possibly pale blue. *Ref. K4-81; Metz 1-07; Schroy-101; Jenks p. 374; Mugs p. 17.*

LION (LION'S HEAD), cologne bottle. Gillinder & Sons, 1876. Extended table service including rare frosted cheese dish, wine, cordials, champagne, toy table set. When frosted is called "Frosted Lion." Crystal, milk glass. The bread plate and goblet have been reproduced. *Ref. L-93; LEAPG-283; K1-44; Metz 1-96; Metz 2-192; Unitt 1-90; Jenks p. 327; Schroy-90.*

TINY LION (LION WITH CABLE), open sugar bowl, 1880s. Richard & Hartley; Tarentum Glass Co., and U. S. Glass Co. Made in extended table service including celery vase, compote, salt shaker (without lions). Crystal. The goblet has been reproduced. *Ref K2-35; Metz 2-82; Jenks p. 330.*

OASIS, pitcher. This design is acid etched. Made in extended table service including celery vase. *Ref. K8-1; Metz 1-99; Metz 2-92.*

Lion and Baboon

Giraffe

Jumbo

*Clear Lion
Head*

Monkey (two examples)

Lion

Tiny Lion

Oasis

PLATE 4. ANIMALS

PIG AND CORN, goblet. Made in goblet only, ca. 1875-85. *Ref K8-67; Gob I Pl. 36; Metz 1-96; Schroy-160.*

SQUIRREL-IN-BOWER, pitcher. Portland Glass Co., ca. 1870. Known in scarce water pitcher and very rare goblet. *Ref. K4-60; Metz 1-95.*

BRINGING HOME THE COWS, pitcher. Dalzell, Gilmore and Leighton, 1880s. Made in basic table service plus pitcher. Crystal. *Ref. K4-12; Schroy-160.*

DANCING GOAT, ale glass. Hobbs, Brockunier and Co., 1876. This was sent to the Centennial Exhibition in Philadelphia. *Ref. K7-74; Hobbs p. 51.*

EGYPTIAN (PARTHENON), 8" footed bowl. Boston and Sandwich Glass Co., 1870s. Extended table service including Cleopatra platter, Salt Lake Temple platter, large pyramids plate, pickle dish, bread tray. Crystal. Not all pieces depict all of its motifs, but always present is the stippled, stylized flower rim. *Ref. L-111; K1-31.*

SQUIRREL WITH NUT, pitcher. *Ref. K5-128; Metz 1-95.*

RABBIT IN TREE, salt shaker. A novelty. *Ref. PetSal 36K.*

BEAVER BAND, goblet. Known in goblet only; made in Canada for a church celebration. *Ref. Gob II-130; Metz 2-198.*

SQUIRREL, pitcher. Adams and Co., 1880s; U. S. Glass after 1891; Indiana Tumbler and Goblet Co., 1890s. Extended table service including rare goblet. Crystal. *Ref. L-100; LEAPG-534; Metz 1-94; Metz 2-82; Schroy-160; Jenks p. 489; Mugs p. 12.*

Pig and Corn   *Squirrel-in-Bower*   *Bringing
Home the
Cows*

Dancing Goat   *Egyptian*   *Squirrel with
Nut*

Rabbit in Tree   *Beaver Band*   *Squirrel*

PLATE 5. ANIMALS

FOX AND CROW, pitcher. Indiana Tumbler and Goblet Co. (National), late 1890s. Pitcher known. *Ref. K4-124; Schroy-160.*

DEER AND DOG (DOG AND DEER; DEER, DOG AND HUNTER; FROSTED DOG), pitcher and enlarged finial. Gillinder Glass Co., ca. 1880s in extended table service including mug, wine. Pieces with the dog finial are very expensive. *Ref. K1-52; L-101; Gob II-38: Metz 1-99; Metz 2-192; Unitt 1-171.*

DOG HUNTING, pitcher. National Glass Co., ca. 1902. *Ref. K4-125.*

SHELL AND TASSEL (ROUND), sugar bowl. George Duncan and Sons #555, 1880. Extended table service in both round and square forms including historical platters. The goblet has been reproduced. *Ref. L-157; K3-59; Metz 1-138; Metz 2-192; Schroy-130; Jenks p. 475.*

OWL AND POSSUM, goblet. *Ref. LEAPG-535; L-100; Metz 1-92; Schroy-160.*

BOAR, serving dish. A rare novelty in milk glass shown in *American Glass Vol. II, p. 86.*

POLAR BEAR (ICEBERG; ARCTIC; NORTH POLE), goblet. Crystal Glass Co., 1880s. Extended table service including finger bowl, oval tray. Crystal, frosted. *Ref. L-91; LEAPG-294; Metz 1-96; Schroy-113; K5-15.*

FISH, salt shaker. A novelty. *Ref. PetSal 28T.*

ST. BERNARD (CZAR), covered dish. Fostoria Glass Co. #450, 1895. Extended table service including jam jar, wine, champagne. Most pieces are in a diamond pattern, and the dog appears only as a finial. See Plate 64. The pattern LEAFLETS on Plate 55 (by Central Glass Co.) also has a similar reclining dog finial. *Ref. K4 Pl. 8; K5-61; Metz 1-148.*

Fox and Crow *Deer and Dog (and finial)*

Dog Hunting *Shell and Tassel* *Owl and Possum*

Boar *Polar Bear* *Fish* *St. Bernard*

PLATE 6. INSECTS & FISH

DOLPHIN, candlestick. Boston and Sandwich; Bakewell, Pears; 1850s; 1868; Hobbs, Brockunier and Co., 1880. Made in a number of dolphin-based pieces including compote. Hobbs made an extended table service including pickle jar and cover. Their pieces had dolphin finials and bases, in crystal and frosted. *Ref. L-143; Hobbs p. 59; K3-7; Metz 1-104; Schroy-160.*

BUTTERFLY EARS (ALARIC), mustard pot. Bryce, Higbee and Co., mid-1880s. Made in extended table service. See detail on Plate 58. *Ref. K8-131.*

GARDEN OF EDEN (LOTUS; TURTLE; FISH; LOTUS AND SERPENT), pitcher. McKee and Brothers, 1880. Extended table service including mug, platter, bread tray. Crystal. Some pieces do not have the strange "turtle head." See Plate 186. *Ref. Gob II-8; K3-58; Metz 2-205; Mugs p. 13; Jenks p. 240; Schroy-65.*

AQUARIUM, pitcher. U. S. Glass Co., after 1909. Pitcher known. Crystal, amber, emerald green. *Ref. K4-119; Schroy-161; H5-169.*

ELEPHANT, salt shaker. A novelty.

BUTTERFLY HANDLES (BUTTERFLY), sugar bowl. Extended table service. *Ref. LV-27; Metz 1-107; Metz 2-80.*

STIPPLED LEAF, FLOWER AND MOTH (STIPPLED LEAF AND FLOWER), pitcher. Made in the 1870s in extended table service including decanter. Crystal. *Ref. K1-47.*

LATE BUTTERFLY (MIKADO), pitcher. Indiana Tumbler and Goblet Co., 1907. Extended table service including tumbler. *Ref. Gob II-31; LV-28; Gob II-31; Metz 1-106; Unitt 1-204.*

BUTTERFLY WITH SPRAY (ACME), mug. Bryce, Higbee and Co., 1880s Extended table service including tumbler. Crystal, amber, blue, canary, painted. *Ref. K3-46; Mugs p. 22.*

BUTTERFLY, pitcher. U. S. Glass Co. #6406, 1908. Extended table service including covered mustard jar. Crystal; frosted handles. *Ref. K2-123; H5-179; Metz 1-107.*

FISH, pitcher. Cambridge Glass Co., 1915. Courtesy of Bob Burford.

Dolphin   Butterfly Ears   Garden of
                               Eden   Aquarium

Elephant   Butterfly Handles   Stippled Leaf,   Late Butterfly
                                  Flower and Moth

Butterfly with Spray   Butterfly   Fish

PLATE 7. ANIMALS

PARROT, pitcher. Dalzell, Gilmore and Leighton, 1889.

PARROT (PARROT AND FAN; OWL AND FAN), goblet. Possibly made ca. 1880s by Richards and Hartley in extended table service including rare wine. Crystal, ruby-stained. *Ref. K8-67; Gob I-95; Metz 1-92; Unitt 1-187; H7-137.*

DRAGON, footed compote. McKee Brothers, 1870. Extended table service. All pieces are rare; goblet is most often seen. Crystal. *Ref. Gob II-130; Welker-355; Revi-241; Metz 1-97; Metz 2-82.*

CHICK, (inset) sugar bowl finial. Extended table service including salt shaker. See Plate 158 for sugar bowl. *Ref. LV-20.*

BIRD-IN-RING (GRACE), spoon holder. Part of the pattern "JAPANESE" by Duncan Glass, 1881. The bird appears on the sugar bowl and spooner; a butterfly on the goblet (and called "Butterfly and Fan.") See Plate 171. *Ref. K2-16; K7-76; Metz 1-106.*

OWL, pitcher. Milk glass, blue slag in pitchers of various sizes. U. S. Glass made a pitcher and creamer in 1891. *Ref. K1-56; Metz 1-12; H5-176.*

LITTLE OWL, creamer. U. S. Glass Co. (Challinor), 1891. Made in toy basic service with bear sugar, fish spooner, turtle butter; the set called MENAGERIE. Crystal, opaque colors, amber. *Ref. K1-56.*

GRASSHOPPER WITH INSECT (LOCUST; LONG SPEAR), spoon holder. Made in the 1880s in extended table service in crystal. This pattern has to be one of the most delightful in the field; who thought of using crawling grasshoppers as handles? Check their wings for damage. *Ref. K1-88; Jenks p. 254; Schroy-68.*

PEACOCK AT THE FOUNTAIN (PEACOCK AND PALM), creamer. Northwood Glass Co. Extended table service including punch bowl, footed orange bowl, tumbler. Carnival glass in many colors. *Ref. K6-24; H4-57.*

STRUTTING PEACOCK, creamer. Imperial Glass, late 1880s Extended table service including decanter, tumbler. Crystal, blue, purple, green, carnival. *Ref. K6-13.*

Parrot Pitcher

Parrot

Dragon

Chick, finial

Bird-in-Ring

Owl

Little Owl

Grasshopper

Peacock at the Fountain

Strutting Peacock

PLATE 8. BIRDS

CARDINAL BIRD, spoon holder and sugar bowl. Possibly Ohio Flint Glass Co., 1870s. Extended table service including sauce. One can find a tiny caterpillar on the leaf. Crystal. *Ref. L-100; LEAPG-533; Metz 1-92; K1-31.*

BIRD AND STRAWBERRY (BLUEBIRD), pitcher. Beatty Glass Co., 1910; Indiana Glass Co. #157, 1914. Extended table service including punch set, wine, heart-shaped relish, tumbler, and goblet (which carries a high price.) Crystal, colors, decorated. *Ref. K2-85; Gob II-75; Metz 1-104; Unitt 1-186; Jenks p. 67; Schroy-21.*

BIRDS AT FOUNTAIN, goblet. Made ca.1880s in extended table service including toy mug in two variations, one with a single design, and one with designs both front and back. Crystal, milk glass, alabaster, and blue alabaster. This motif was a popular one in colonial America, symbolizing immortality and can be found on early gravestones. Courtesy of Dr. Charles Marlin. *Ref. Gob I-167; Metz 1-92; Unitt 1-191; Schroy-160.*

PANELLED CARDINAL, goblet. *Ref. Gob II-111; Metz 1-93.*

FLYING BIRDS, goblet. Made ca. 1870 and known in the goblet. *Ref. L-164-6; Metz 1-92.*

HUMMINGBIRD (FLYING ROBIN; BIRD AND FERN; THUNDERBIRD, HUMMINGBIRD AND FERN), pitcher. Northwood Glass, ca. 1888. Extended table service including water tray, cheese plate, covered bowl, open salt, wine. Marked with an underlined N trademark. Crystal, amber, blue. *Ref. K4-25; Metz 1-92; Unitt 1-186; Schroy-79; Jenks p. 287.*

BIRD AND TREE, pitcher. *Ref. L-190.*

SINGING BIRDS (THRUSH AND APPLE BLOSSOMS), mug. Northwood Glass Co., 1911 – 1920. Extended table service including wine. Crystal, carnival, custard glass, opalescent. *Ref K2-67; Gob II-30; Metz 2-84; Unitt 1-186; HGC6-40; Mugs p. 19.*

BIRDS AND INSECTS, mug. Made ca. 1850 in mug and goblet; clear, amber. *Ref. Mugs p. 24.*

Cardinal Bird (two examples)   *Bird and Strawberry*

Birds at Fountain   *Panelled Cardinal*   *Flying Birds*   *Hummingbird*

Bird and Tree   *Singing Birds*   *Birds and Insects*

PLATE 9. BIRDS

MOON AND STORK (OSTRICH LOOKING AT THE MOON; STORK LOOKING AT THE MOON), goblet. *Ref. K8-67; Metz 1-104.*

BLUE HERON, creamer. *Ref. K4-24; Metz 1-104.*

WADING HERON, pitcher. U. S. Glass #6404, ca. 1915. Crystal, green (rare). *Ref. K6-61; H5-169.*

FROSTED STORK (FLAMINGO; FROSTED CRANE), pitcher. Extended table service including jam jar, tray, finger bowl, pickle castor. All pieces are scarce. Finials are storks. *Ref. L-100; LEAPG-305; Metz 1-104; Schroy-64; Jenks p. 235.*

FLAMINGO, goblet. Basic table service plus goblet. Non-flint. *Ref. Metz 1 pl. 61; Metz 2-82.*

CLEAR STORK (CRANE; STORK), pitcher. 1890 – 1891. Extended table service including tumbler, compote. An oval relish dish has a ONE HUNDRED AND ONE border (see Plate 153). *Ref. K3-64; Metz 1-104.*

FLYING STORK, perfume bottle. Whitall-Tatum Glass Co.

FLYING STORK, goblet. Non-flint; different from the preceding. *Ref. Metz 2-86; Gob. II-117; Schroy-160; Jenks p. 226.*

OWL AND STUMP (OWL), toothpick holder. Central Glass Co., ca. 1890. Novelty. Crystal, colors. *Ref. Lee; HTP-89.*

HERON, pitcher. Indiana Tumbler and Goblet Co., 1890s. Extended table service including water tray. *Ref. Miller p. 316; Metz 1-104; Metz 2-90; Schroy-160.*

Moon and Stork   *Blue Heron*   *Wading Heron*

Frosted Stork   *Flamingo*   *Clear Stork*

Flying Stork   *Flying Stork*   *Owl and Stump*   *Heron*

PLATE 10. BIRDS

FLYING SWAN, pitcher. Challinor Glass Co., 1890s. Extended table service including toothpick holder. Crystal, slag. *Ref. K2-81.*

SWAN, pitcher. Canton Glass Co., 1882. Extended table service including jam jar. Crystal, amber, canary, cobalt blue. *Ref. K1-63; L-177; Gob I-17; Metz 1-104; Metz 2-86; Unitt 2-202; Schroy-149; LEAPG-513; Jenks p. 503.*

SWAN WITH TREE, pitcher. U. S. Glass Co. (Gas City factory), 1890s. Known in goblet and pitcher. *Ref. K5-127; Metz 2-86.*

BULLET EMBLEM (BULLET; SHIELD IN RED, WHITE AND BLUE; EAGLE AND ARMS), butter dish. U. S. Glass Co, 1898. A Spanish-American War commemorative. Made in basic table service. This piece with original decorations sold for $425 at the Green Valley Auction in Pittsburgh in 1998. *Ref. H5-1; Schroy-26.*

PANELLED SWAN, goblet. *Ref. Gob II-30; Metz 2-86.*

SWAN ON POND (SWAN TWO; WATERFOWL), pitcher. Bryce Brothers, 1880s; U. S. Glass Co. #3802, 1891; Federal Glass Co., 1914. Extended table service. Crystal, frosted, amber, milk glass, opaque white. *Ref K3-36; Mugs p. 18; H5-86.*

DOUBLE Y'S, relish dish (author's name). A strange piece with handles of seemingly dead birds.

LATE SWAN, creamer. Westmoreland Specialty Co., 1891 – 1892. Known in sugar and creamer. Opaque white and turquoise. *Ref. K1-92.*

FROSTED EAGLE, compote. Probably Crystal Glass Co., late 1870s. Extended table service including salt shaker, compote. The plain pitcher is pictured on Plate 180. *Ref. K6-62; Metz 1-94; Jenks p. 232.*

Flying Swan

Swan

Swan with Tree

Bullet Emblem

Panelled Swan

Swan on Pond

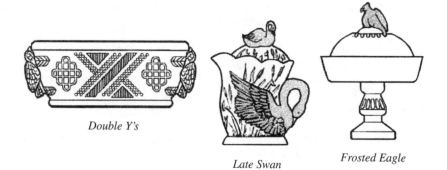

Double Y's

Late Swan

Frosted Eagle

PLATE 11. CIRCLES

OVAL THUMBPRINT BAND, pitcher. Made ca. 1850; flint. *Ref. K5-28.*

PANELLED "S," goblet. Made in 1880s in extended table service including wine. *Ref. Gob I-88; Metz 1-208; Unitt 1-62.*

ELECTRIC, creamer. U. S. Glass Co. #15038, 1891. Extended table service including cracker jar. Crystal, ruby stained. *Ref. K3-78, Mugs p. 72; Metz 2-1142; H7-110; Schroy-54.*

CANNONBALL (BULLET), pitcher. Made in 1889. Crystal, ruby-stained. *Ref. K2-15; Metz 1-144; H7-88.*

IMPERIAL'S CANDLEWICK, salt shaker. Imperial Glass Corp., 1889. Known in five types of shakers. *Ref. PetSal 156-G.*

ATLAS (CRYSTAL BALL; KNOBBY BOTTOM; BULLET; ORBED FEET; CANNON BALL), celery vase. Bryce Brothers, 1889; Adams and Co.; U. S. Glass Co., 1891. Extended table service including toothpick, open salt, wine, gill tumbler (very short and squat), cordial, champagne, claret. See the pitcher on Plate 178. Crystal, ruby-stained. *Ref. K2-15; LV26; Metz 1-144; HTP-52; H5-75; H7-70+; Jenks p. 29; Schroy-10.*

PRESSED BLOCK (EYEBROWS), pitcher. U. S. Glass Co. (Doyle #11), 1891. Extended table service including waste bowl, wine; flat tumbler lacks the "diamond" detail. Crystal, ruby-stained. See Plates 19 & 210. *Ref. K5-11; Gob II-97; Metz 2-18; H7-114+*

ANGELUS, creamer. Huntington Glass Co., 1892 – 1898. Extended table service including waste bowl, wine. Crystal, ruby-stained. *Ref. K5-54; K6-39, Pl. 27; PetPat-165; H7-131.*

BEADED LOBE (WINONA), finger bowl and salt shaker. Greensburg Glass Co. #200, ca. mid-1880s. Extended table service including wine, cordial, champagne, claret. Crystal, ruby-stained. *Ref. K3-135; K5-112; K8-163; H7-216.*

EYEWINKER (CRYSTAL BALL; WINKING EYE; CANNONBALL), pitcher. Dalzell, Gilmore and Leighton, 1889. Extended table service including wine and banana boat. No toothpick made originally. The goblet and wine have been reproduced as well as other pieces. Crystal. *Ref. K5-76; Metz 1-210; Unitt 1-54; Unitt 2-221; HTP-72 (repro); Jenks p. 198; Schroy-56.*

PILLAR BULLS-EYE (THISTLE), pitcher. Bakewell and Co., 1875. Extended table service including egg cup, decanter, wine, and champagne. Crystal. *Ref. L-190; Metz 1-26; Unitt 1-113; K5-142; LEAPG-163.*

Oval Thumb-
print Band

Panelled "S"

Electric

Cannonball

Imperial's
Candlewick

Atlas

Pressed Block

Angelus

Beaded Lobe (two views)

Eyewinker

Pillar Bulls-eye

PLATE 12. CIRCLES

QUESTION MARK (OVAL LOOP), pitcher. U. S. Glass Co. (Richards & Hartley #55), 1891. Extended table service including sugar shaker, wine, cordial. Crystal, ruby-stained. *Ref. K4-135; Metz 1-208; Jenks p. 429; Schroy-118; H5-114; H7-166, 181.*

BRYCE (RIBBON CANDY; FIGURE EIGHT; DOUBLE LOOP; CANDY RIBBON), creamer. Bryce Brothers, 1880s; U. S. Glass Co. #15010, 1880s; 1891. Extended table service including wine, cordial, and claret. Crystal, green. *Ref. K1-32; LV-32; Metz 1-154; Unitt 2-58; H5-76; Jenks p. 438; Schroy-120; Mugs p. 77.*

TEARDROP AND THUMBPRINT, pitcher. U. S. Glass Co. #15032 (Ripley), 1896. Extended table service including wine. Crystal, blue, ruby-stained, decorated. *Ref. K3-32; LV-69; Metz 1-144; H7-201+.*

TENNIS RACQUET (WINDSOR), goblet. U. S. Glass Co. #15102 (Ripley), 1907. Extended table service including wine. *Ref. Gob II-97; Metz 2-176; H5-174.*

ARCHED OVALS (CONCAVED ALMOND; OPTIC), creamer. Ripley and Co., 1880s U. S. Glass Co. #15091 (Ripley), 1905. Extended table service including wine. Crystal, ruby-stained, rose-flashed, emerald green. *Ref. K8-39; Gob II-80; Metz 1-220; Schroy-7; HI-13; HTP-56; H5-174; H6-96; H7-68+; Schroy-7.*

CRYSTAL WEDDING (COLLINS; CRYSTAL ANNIVERSARY), pint tankard. Adams and Co.; U. S. Glass Co., 1880s, 1891. Extended table service including fruit basket, vase, wine, claret. Crystal, ruby-stained, cobalt blue (scarce). *Ref. K3-74; Metz 1-144; Schroy-40; H5-47, 64; H7-97.*

LONG TEARDROP AND THUMBPRINT (TEARDROP AND THUMBPRINT VARIANT), pitcher. Extended table service including lamp, water tray. *Ref. K3-103.*

LOWER MANHATTAN, toothpick holder. Crystal, colored "eyes." *Ref. HTP-84.*

ASHBURTON WITH CONNECTED OVALS (DOUBLE FLUTE; BARREL ASHBURTON; LARGE THUMBPRINT), goblet. Boston and Sandwich; McKee and Brothers; New England Glass Co, 1850s. Extended table service including bitters bottle, ale glass, cordials, wines, champagne, claret, mug, lamp, egg cup, rare covered toddy jar. The wine, cordial, and claret have been reproduced. *Ref. L-3; Metz 1-16; Metz 2-24;; Unitt 1-29, 31; Jenks p. 26; LEAPG-10; Schroy-9.*

MANHATTAN, pitcher. U. S. Glass Co. #15078 (Glass Port), 1902 – 1910. Extended table service including tall covered jar, cracker jar, lamp. Reproduced in the 1950s. See Plate 82. Crystal, rose-flashed, green-flashed. *Ref. K6-44; Schroy-94; HTP-56, 82; H5-144; H7-148.*

RIBBED THUMBPRINT (CANADIAN HORSESHOE), pitcher. Jefferson Glass Co. #221, ca. 1905 – 1919. Extended table service including shot glass, wine. Crystal, apple green, blue, ruby-stained, some custard. *Ref. K8-190; Revi-207; HGC4-37; HI-37; H4-54; H6-39; H7-185.*

Question Mark   *Bryce*   *Teardrop and Thumbprint*

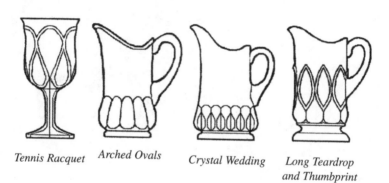

Tennis Racquet   *Arched Ovals*   *Crystal Wedding*   *Long Teardrop and Thumbprint*

Lower Manhattan   *Ashburton*   *Manhattan*   *Ribbed Thumbprint*

U. S. GLASS CO. STATE SERIES

The U. S. Glass Co. issued patterns named for various states, calling them their STATE SERIES. These are some of the loveliest collectibles one can find.

Above is the MICHIGAN pattern, found in maiden's blush, flashing, enameling, and decal decorations. See Plate 203.

MORE STATE SERIES PATTERNS: Clockwise from top: MISSOURI, KENTUCKY, OREGON, DAKOTA, VIRGINIA, TENNESSEE, KANSAS. Center: MINNESOTA

PLATE 13. CIRCLES, THUMBPRINTS

SERRATED TEARDROP, pitcher. Dalzell, Gilmore & Leighton, 1903. *Ref. HGC2-44.*

DAKOTA (BABY THUMBPRINT), creamer and pitcher. Ripley and Co., 1880s; U. S. Glass Co. (Ripley), 1891; 1898. A State Series pattern. Extended table service including castor set, rare cake cover, six sizes pitchers, wine. Crystal, ruby-stained, rare cobalt, etched. *Ref. K4-8; LV67; Metz 1-99; Unitt 1-171; Mugs p. 77 (mis-numbered); H5-120; H7-35; Jenks p. 163; Schroy-46.*

DOUBLE THUMBPRINT BAND, syrup. Made in about 1880. Only syrup known. *Ref. HIII-23.*

CAT'S-EYE (THUMBPRINT ON SPEARHEAD), goblet. Extended table service including salt shaker. *Ref. PetSal 175P; Gob II-141; Metz 2-146.*

BAR AND FLUTE (CORSET AND THUMBPRINT; RUBY BAR AND FLUTE), pitcher. Probably U. S. Glass Co., 1893. Extended table service including syrup. Crystal, ruby-stained. *Ref. K2-106; HIII-21; H5-30; H7-17.*

ARGUS (THUMBPRINT; CONCAVE ASHBURTON), tumbler. McKee Glass Co., 1859; Bakewell, Pears and Co., 1870. Made in extended table service including ale glass, champagne, wines, cordials, champagnes, claret, handled whiskey (scarce), egg cup, decanters. Flint, crystal. The wine has been reproduced. See Plate 24. *Ref. L-11; Metz 2-42; Unitt 1-34; Jenks p. 20; Mugs p. 45.*

BIGLER (FLUTE AND SPLIT), tumbler. Boston and Sandwich, 1850s. Extended table service including bar tumbler, bitters bottle, wine, cordial, champagne, 33 items in all. Crystal, canary, amethyst. *Ref. K7-39; LEAPG-44; Metz 1-20; Unitt 1-32; Mugs p. 147; Jenks p. 66; Schroy-21.*

COLONIAL, creamer. Boston and Sandwich, 1850 – 1860. Extended table service in flint glass including whiskey tumbler which is a mug with an applied handle. Crystal, rare opalescent. See Plate 17. *Ref. K8-9; LEAPG-44; Metz 1-18; Mugs p. 41; Welker p. 243.*

U. S. THUMBPRINT, pitcher. U. S. Glass Co. #15013 (Nickle Plate), 1891. Extended table service. Crystal, ruby-stained. *Ref. K5-5; Metz 2-178; H7-208.*

CELTIC (MIRROR PUNTY), creamer. McKee and Brothers, 1894. Extended table service including wine. *Ref. K3-116; K6-35; Welker p. 235; Metz 1-194.*

CAROLINA (INVERNESS; MAYFLOWER), covered sugar bowl. Bryce Brothers, 1880s; U. S. Glass Co. #15083 (Bryce), 1903 – 1910. A State Series pattern. Made in extended table service in many pieces including wine. The row of thumbprints is pressed on the **inside** of the glass. Crystal, ruby-stained, purple-stained, decorated by etching through the stain. *Ref. K2-28; Gob II-53; Metz 2-130; Mugs p. 69; Jenks p. 109; Schroy-32; H5-167; H6-48; H7-89.*

Serrated
Teardrop

Dakota (two views)

Double
Thumbprint
Band

Cat's-Eye

Bar and Flute

Argus

Bigler

Colonial

U.S. Thumbprint

Celtic

Carolina

PLATE 14. CIRCLES, THUMBPRINTS

LINED PANEL (MADISON VARIANT), celery. Shown in the same advertisement with the James B. Lyon pattern, "Madison." A beautiful flint glass pattern known in celery, spooner, covered sugar, and covered compote. Only the celery is easily found. *Welker; Innes p. 309; Metz 1-22* (Information from Dr. Charles Marlin).

MADISON, spill holder. Made by James B. Lyon and called in an old advertisement "Crystal." Extended table service in flint glass. *Ref. K6-75.*

KING'S CROWN (RUBY THUMBPRINT; RUBY CROWN, EXCELSIOR; "XLCR"), pitcher. Adams and Co.; U. S. Glass Co. (Adams factory), 1891. Very extended table service including pickle castor set, fruit basket, footed orange bowl, mustard, individual open salt, claret, wine, champagne, cordial. Crystal, rare emerald green, rare cobalt blue, ruby-stained, amber-stained, engraved. Known to have been extensively reproduced. *Ref. K1-104; L-162; Metz 1-144; Schroy-86; HI-39; H5-58; H7-114, 136.*

MARIO, salt shaker. U. S. Glass Co. (Hobbs #341), 1891. Extended table service. Crystal, ruby-stained, amber-stained, etched. *Ref. K6-31; LV 43: HIII-32; H7-86+, Hobbs p. 126.*

EYELET (NEARCUT #25008), creamer. Cambridge Glass Co., 1906. Extended table service including tumbler, compote, bowls. *Ref. K7 Pl. 73.*

TARENTUM THUMBPRINT (TINY THUMBPRINT), creamer. Tarentum Glass Co., 1904. Extended table service including wine. Crystal, green, ruby–stained, green and yellow custard. *Ref. K5-83; PetPat 189; H4-46; H7-200; Mugs p. 63.*

OVAL THUMBPRINT, creamer. Central Glass Co. #610, ca. 1880. Extended table service. *Ref. K2-26.*

FOUR THUMBPRINTS, creamer. U. S. Glass Co. #05012 (Richards and Hartley), 1892. Extended table service. *Ref. K5-57.*

APOLLO (CANADIAN HORSESHOE; THUMBPRINT AND PRISMS; SHIELD BAND; FROSTED FESTAL BALL), creamer. Adams and Co., 1875; U. S. Glass Co., 1891 – 1899. Extended table service including rare cake stand, egg cup, tray, wine, sugar shaker. Crystal, scarce ruby-stained. *Ref. K3-6; Metz 1-146; Gob I-149; Gob II-70; LV Pl. 62; Unitt 1-245; Unitt 2-50; Schroy-6; H5-65; H6-18, 76; H7-67.*

THUMBPRINT WINDOWS, creamer. Made ca. 1890s in basic table service. *Ref. K2-14.*

Lined Panel   *Madison*   *King's Crown*

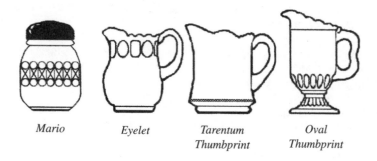

Mario   *Eyelet*   *Tarentum Thumbprint*   *Oval Thumbprint*

Four Thumbprints   *Apollo*   *Thumbprint Windows*

PLATE 15. CIRCLES

ROBIN HOOD, creamer. Fostoria Glass Co., 1898. Extended table service including scarce syrup. *Ref. K7-7; H6-87; Schroy-121.*

WEDDING RING (DOUBLE WEDDING RING), syrup. Made in the 1870s in extended table service including champagne, wine, cordial, decanter. No toothpick holder originally made. Flint and non-flint. *Ref. Gob I-2; Metz 1-36; Unitt 2-222; HTP-72 (repro); Schroy-153; Jenks p. 550.*

DOUBLE GREEK KEY, pitcher. Nickel Plate Glass Co., 1890s. Extended table service. Crystal, stippled, opaque white, opalescent blue. See other Greek Key patterns on Plate 218. *Ref. H1-47; H2-19+; Metz 1-37; Metz 2-198.*

IDAHO (SNAIL; COMPACT; SMALL COMET), plate. George Duncan and Sons #360, 1880s; U. S. Glass Co., 1898. Commonly known as the State Series pattern for Idaho, although Heacock shows another one in his Book 5, *U. S. Glass*, p. 121; see my Plate 176. Extended table service including individual salt and sugar, rose bowl, scarce goblet, covered cheese dish, banana stand, wine, berry set. Crystal, ruby-stained (scarce). See Plate 230. *Ref. K7-123; LV-46; H5-48; Metz 1-209; Metz 2-169; K2-69; K5-93; Jenks p. 484; Schroy-132; H6-42; H7-194.*

CHAIN WITH STAR (FROSTED CHAIN), goblet. Bryce Brothers #79, 1882; U. S. Glass Co. (Bryce), 1891. Made in extended table service including wine, cordial. *Ref. L–132; Gob I-175; Metz 1-116; Unitt 1-102; K8-12; Schroy-33; LEAPG-552; Jenks p. 113.*

CHAIN, goblet. Made ca. 1880s in extended table service including wine, cordial. Crystal. *Ref. L-132; LEAPG-551; K1-24; Gob I-175; Metz 1-132; Unitt 1-102; Schroy-33.*

SCROLL WITH STAR (WYCLIFF), cup. Challinor, Taylor and Co., ca. 1890; U. S. Glass Co. (Challinor), 1891. Extended table service. Crystal. *Ref. LV-28; Gob II-6; H5-94; H6-74; Metz 1-36; Mugs p. 74.*

DOUBLE CIRCLE, salt shaker. Jefferson Glass Co. #231, ca. 1905. Made in cruet, toothpick holder, salt shaker, and tray. Apple green, "electric" blue, rare crystal. *Ref. K7-155; PetSal 156R; HI-21; HIII-58; H6-26.*

BELFAST, goblet. *Ref. Gob II-60; Metz 1-213.*

Robin Hood

Wedding Ring

Double Greek Key

Idaho

Chain with Star

Chain

Scroll with Star

Double Circle

Belfast

41

PLATE 16. CIRCLES, BULLS-EYE

YORK COLONIAL (CURLING COLONIAL; EARLY COLONIAL; LATE WAY COLONIAL; EMPIRE COLONIAL; KNOB STEM COLONIAL), sugar base. Curling, Robertson and Co., 1856; Central Glass Co., ca. 1870s. Extended table service including ale glass, wine, champagne, claret. Some flint glass; crystal, opalescent, amethyst, blue. *Ref. Miller 7th Ed. p. 586; Metz 1-18; Metz 2-16; Unitt 1-22; LEAPG-44; Gob I-7.*

BULLS-EYE AND BAR, covered egg cup. Pieces known include bitters bottle, bar tumbler, goblet, wine. Flint glass. *Ref. Gob II-144; Metz 1-22; Unitt 1-56.*

BROOKLYN (GIANT PRISM WITH THUMBPRINT BAND; LONG-PETALLED THUMBPRINT), ale glass. Made ca. 1870 in extended table service including decanter, wines. See Plate 28. *Ref. L154-12; LEAPG-63; K7-3; Gob I-131; Gob 2-99; Metz 1-48; Unitt 2-63.*

TULIP AND OVAL, creamer. This pattern has been confused with TULIP. The maker is unknown, but Dr. Charles Marlin of Knox, PA, a collector of this pattern, says that some pieces appear to date from the 1850s, and others from the 1860s. He can verify that the following pieces were made: ale, footed tumbler, creamer, perfume bottle, syrup with applied handle, castor set, celery, flat tumbler with rayed base, pickle jar with rayed stopper, bitters bottle, 1-qt. pitcher, open compote on high standard. *Ref. K7-4.*

EXCELSIOR EARLY, goblet. Boston and Sandwich, 1850s; Ihmsen & Co., 1851; McKee and Brothers, 1868; Bryce Brothers. Extended table service including decanters, ale glass, bitters bottle, egg cups, wine cordial, claret. *Ref L-4; Jenks p. 197; LEAPG-21; Schroy-56.*

BULLS-EYE AND LOOP, goblet.

MIRROR AND LOOP, goblet. Wine is also known, *Ref. Gob II-2; Metz 1-18.*

PENDLETON, goblet. Known in goblet, syrup, and tumbler. Courtesy of Dr. Charles Marlin. *Ref. Unitt 1-23; Metz 1-124.*

COMET, goblet. Boston and Sandwich Glass Co., 1850s. Extended table service including whiskey tumbler. Crystal, canary, blue. Flint. *Ref. L-49; LEAPG-155; Metz 1-12; Mugs p. 147; Jenks p. 128.*

BULLS-EYE AND BROKEN COLUMN, goblet. *Ref. Gob II-30; Metz 2-8, 12.*

BARREL EXCELSIOR, spoon holder. Boston and Sandwich; McKee; 1850s and 1860s. Extended table service including ale glass, decanters, mugs, wine, bottle. *Ref. Miller 7th Ed. p. 369; Metz 1-16; Metz 2-28.*

BULLS-EYE AND PRISM (BULLS-EYE AND BAR), goblet. Made ca. 1840s. Flint glass. *Ref. Gob II-4; Metz 2-12; Miller 7th Ed. p. 392.*

HOURGLASS (EXCELSIOR WITH DOUBLE-RINGED STEM; EGG AND DART; EXCELSIOR VARIANT), spoon holder. Made in 1868; 1880s in extended table service including wine. Crystal, canary, amber, blue. See Plate 39. *Ref. Gob I-58; Gob II-2; K2–8; Metz 1-128; LV-173; Unitt 1-299.*

York Colonial   *Bulls-Eye and Bar*   *Brooklyn*   *Tulip and Oval*

Excelsior   *Bulls-Eye*   *Mirror and*   *Pendleton*   *Comet*
Early   *and Loop*   *Loop*

Bulls-Eye and   *Barrel Excelsior*   *Bulls-Eye*   *Hourglass*
Broken Column   *and Prism*

43

PLATE 17. CIRCLES, BULLS-EYE

LEE, goblet. Named in honor of Ruth Webb Lee. Extended table service including whiskey tumbler, decanter, wine, cordial, champagne. *Ref. Gob I-143; Metz 1-10.*

HALLEY'S COMET (ETRURIA), goblet. Made in extended table service including wine. Crystal, ruby-stained. *Ref. Gob I-164; Metz 1-208; Unitt 1-63; H7-112; 151; Jenks p. 256.*

TONG, creamer. Made ca. 1860s in extended table service. *Ref. K5-24; LV Pl. 25; Metz 11-7; Metz 2-28; Schroy-161.*

RUNNING BULLS-EYE, 8 oz. tumbler. Crystal, stained, gilded. Courtesy of Bob Burford.

COLONIAL, ale glass. See Plate 13.

BULLS-EYE (LAWRENCE), goblet. New England Glass Co. #1121, 1131, & 1142; 1860s; Boston and Sandwich. Very extended table service including bitters bottle, castor bottle, water bottle, decanter, cologne bottle, rare covered egg cup, wine, cordials, champagne, lamp, pomade jar, and open salt. Crystal, milk glass, rare opalescent, rare opaque white. *Ref. L49; LEAPG-156; Gob I-87; Metz 1-12; Unitt 1-42; Schroy-27; Mugs p. 43.*

EYE BAND, salt shaker. *Ref. PetSal 160L.*

OVAL MITRE, goblet. McKee Brothers, ca. 1865. Extended table service including open and covered sugar bowls. *Ref. L-12; LEAPG-48; Metz 1-26.*

FRAMED CIRCLES, wine. Made ca. 1840s in flint glass, and known in goblet and wine. *Ref. Miller 7th Ed. p. 447; Metz 2-10.*

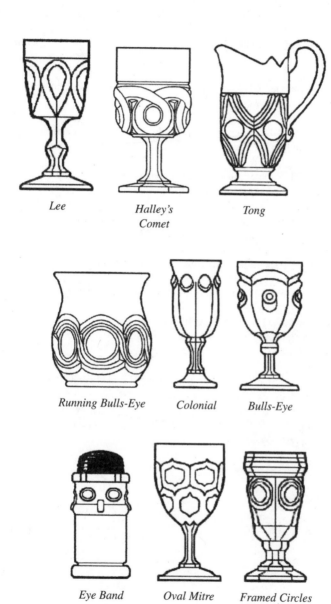

Lee

*Halley's
Comet*

Tong

Running Bulls-Eye

Colonial

Bulls-Eye

Eye Band

Oval Mitre

Framed Circles

PLATE 18. CIRCLES

TEXAS BULLS-EYE (BULLS-EYE VARIANT; FILLEY; NOTCHED BULL'S-EYE), goblet. Bryce Brothers #1221, 1875; A. J. Beatty and Sons #1221, 1888; U. S. Glass Co. (Bryce factory), 1891. Made in extended table service including wines, cordials, tumblers, castor set. *Ref. L-50; K7-72; Gob I-156; Metz 1-208; Jenks p. 511; Schroy-141; H5-86.*

MONROE, spill holder. Made in 1850s in extended table service including rare lamp. Crystal, cobalt blue. *Ref. K6-75.*

EIGHT-O-EIGHT (INDIANA), creamer. Model Flint Glass Co. #808, 1896. Extended table service including lamp, wine. *Ref. K4-78; Metz 1-148.*

DIVIDED HEARTS, goblet. Boston and Sandwich Glass Co., 1860s. Extended table service including syrup and lamp. *Ref. Gob II-68; Metz 1-28.*

FOSTORIA'S ROCOCO, spoon holder. Fostoria Glass Co. #234, 1891. Basic table service. Crystal, ruby-stained. *Ref. K6 Pl. 59; H7-119.*

LINCOLN DRAPE, spoon holder. Boston and Sandwich, 1860s. Extended table service including wine, egg cup, decanter, tumbler, spill holder, lamp. Crystal, milk glass, sapphire blue. *Ref. L-46; Gob I–118; Metz 1-12; Unitt 1-276; Jenks p. 326.*

LINCOLN DRAPE WITH TASSEL, goblet. Boston and Sandwich, 1865. Extended table service including tall lamp, miniature lamp, egg cup, cordial, wine. *Ref. L-46; Metz 1-12; Unitt 1-276; Schroy-90.*

BULLS-EYE WITH FLEUR-DE-LIS (BULLS-EYE AND PRINCESS FEATHER), goblet. Boston and Sandwich, 1860s; Union Glass Co. Extended table service including rare ale glass, decanter, lamp, rare pitcher, mug, footed master salt, wine, and cordial. Crystal, rare amber. Flint glass. *Ref. L-51; Gob I-34; Metz 1-12; Metz 2-192; K8-46; Jenks p. 91; Schroy-27; Mugs p. 147.*

HAMMOND, goblet. *Ref. Gob II-39; Metz 2–66.*

Texas Bulls-Eye   Monroe   Eight-O-Eight

Divided
Hearts   Fostoria's
Rococo   Lincoln Drape

Lincoln Drape
with Tassel   Bulls-Eye with
Fleur-de-lis   Hammond

PLATE 19. CIRCLES

BLOCK WITH THUMBPRINT, LATE, goblet. Extended table service. *Ref. L–101.*

BEADED THUMBPRINT BLOCK, salt shaker. U. S. Glass Co., ca. 1893. Extended table service. Crystal, ruby-stained. See also Plate 210. *Ref. PetSal 154-R; H7-74; Mugs p. 67.*

McKEE'S VIRGINIA, pitcher. McKee and Brothers, 1900 – 1915. Made in extended table service. *Ref. K4-85.*

PRISM AND CRESCENT (PANEGYRIC), cup. Boston and Sandwich, 1850s. Extended table service including wine, champagne, whiskey tumbler, lamp. *Ref. Gob I-101; Metz 11-8; LV-53; Mugs p. 49.*

MELTON (FRETTED VAULT; BLOCK AND OVAL; RECESSED OVALS), spoon holder. Wine also known. *Ref. Gob I–108; Gob II–65; Metz 1-216.*

WASHINGTON EARLY (LEAFY PANEL AND THUMBPRINT), decanter. New England Glass Co., 1869. Extended table service including wine, cordial, champagne, claret, syrup, egg cup, pedestalled butter dish. *Ref. L-10; Gob I-1; Metz 1-18; Unitt 1-23; Mugs p. 49.*

THUMBPRINT ON SPEARPOINT (TEARDROP AND CRACKED ICE), mug. Dalzell, Gilmore and Leighton, ca. 1889; Cambridge Glass Co., 1903. Crystal. *Ref. PetSal 175Q; Mugs p. 71.*

ELLIPSES, toothpick holder. Beaumont Glass co. #106, 1901. Extended table service including wine, cordial. Crystal, cranberry flashed. *Ref. Boul Pl. 93; HI-21; HGC2-18.*

THUMBPRINT ROW, salt shaker. *Ref. PetSal 175T.*

PRESSED BLOCK, salt shaker. The shaker has a more ornate pattern that the rest of the set. See Plates 11 and 210.

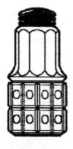

Block with Thumbprint, Late

Beaded Thumbprint Block

McKee's Virginia

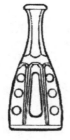

Prism and Crescent

Melton

Washington Early

Thumbprint on Spearpoint

Ellipses

Thumbprint Row

Pressed Block

PLATE 20. CIRCLES

OVAL WINDOWS, salt shaker. *Ref. PetSal 34-O.*

JAM JAR, creamer. Jenkins Glass Co., ca. 1920. Extended table service. *Ref. K8-28.*

MELLOR (BLOCK AND CIRCLE), spoon holder and pitcher. Gillinder and Sons, 1874; Jenkins Glass Co., ca. 1920. Extended table service including wine, miniature lamp. The wine has been reproduced. *Ref. Gob I -113; Metz 1-208; Unitt 1-253; Unitt 2-126.*

NAIL (RECESSED PILLAR), pitcher (etched). Bryce Brothers; Ripley Glass Co.; U. S. Glass Co. #15002, 1890 – 1896. Made in extended table service including finger bowl, water tray, vases, wine, cordial, claret. Crystal, ruby-stained. *Ref. K2-87; Metz 1-150; Metz 2-142; Mugs p. 99; H3-71; H5-121; H6-35; H7-155; Jenks p. 377; Schroy-23.*

BLOCKED ARCHES (BERKELEY), pitcher. U. S. Glass Co. #15020 (Bryce, Gas City), 1891. Extended table service including finger bowl, wine, syrup, cup, and saucer. Crystal, ruby-stained, frosted. *Ref. K6-25; Metz 1-216; H5-51; H7-75; Schroy-23.*

GOTHIC (CATHEDRAL), pitcher. Boston and Sandwich; Union Glass Co.; McKee and Brothers, 1860s. Extended table service including compote, egg cup, fruit bowl, champagnes, cordials, wine, castor bottle. Flint glass. *Ref. L-55; LEAPG-175; Gob I-125; Metz 1-20; Unitt 1-80; Schroy-67; Jenks p. 249.*

ELLIPSE ONE, creamer. *Ref. K7-17.*

ROMOLA, pitcher. Robinson Glass Co., 1894; Model Flint Glass, 1901. Extended table service including tray, sugar shaker, wine, cordial. *Ref. K6 Pl. 38; K8-77.*

PANEL, RIB AND SHELL, pitcher. General Glass Co., 1885. Extended table service including salt shaker. Has been found with a Daisy and Button design in the large oval. Crystal. *Ref. K4-118.*

Oval Windows   Jam Jar   Mellor (two examples)

Nail   Blocked Arches   Gothic

Ellipse One   Romola   Panel, Rib and Shells

PLATE 21. CIRCLES

TOKYO, toothpick holder and creamer. Jefferson Glass Co. #212, ca. 1904. Extended table service including doughnut stand, salt shaker. Crystal, opalescent colors. *Ref. K7-147; HI-43; HII-32+; H6-44; Schroy-145.*

SNAKESKIN WITH DOT, pitcher. Made ca. 1870s in extended table service. Crystal, amber, cobalt blue. *Ref. K3-69; L-74.*

BULLS-EYE AND DAISY (NEWPORT), goblet. U. S. Glass Co. #15117, 1909. Extended table service including wine. Crystal, ruby-stained, emerald green, decorated. See Plate 131. *Ref. Metz 1-214; Gob I-166; Schroy-27; H5-44; H7-160.*

TWO HANDLE, creamer. Basic table service. Crystal, blue. *Ref. K5-150.*

EUGENIE, celery holder. McKee and Brothers, 1859. Extended table service including egg cup, cordial, wine, champagne, rare covered sugar bowl with dolphin finial. Crystal; flint. *Ref. L-5; LEAPG-58; Metz 1-20; Schroy-55; Jenks p. 193.*

BLOCK AND ROSETTE, sugar bowl. Duncan Glass, ca. 1902. Extended table service including toy table service (rare). Crystal, ruby-stained. *Ref. Gob II-91; HI-50; H7-78.*

TARGET, cruet. Richards and Hartley #545, 1885; U. S. Glass Co., 1891. Made in wine set; crystal, ruby-stained. *Ref. H5-117.*

BEADED OVAL BAND, syrup. U. S. Glass Co. (Nickel Plate #2), 1891. Extended table service including bitters bottle. Crystal. *Ref. PetSal 154P.*

Tokyo (two examples)   *Snakeskin with Dot*

Bulls-Eye   *Two Handle*   *Eugenie*
and Daisy

Block and   *Target*   *Beaded Oval*
Rosette   *Band*

PLATE 22. CIRCLES

RAYED WITH LOOP, plate. Sandwich-type glass. Extended table service. Flint. *Ref. L-37.*

GEORGIA (PEACOCK FEATHER; PEACOCK EYE), pitcher. U. S. Glass Co. #15076 (Richard and Hartley), 1902; Federal Glass Co., 1910. A State Series pattern. Made in extended table service including 7" and 9" lamps, plate. U. S. Glass pieces are most often seen. Crystal, blue (scarce), amber (rare), ruby-stained. See Plate 149. *Ref. L-106; K1-77; Jenks p. 242; Mugs p. 75; H7-122; Schroy-66.*

OVAL MEDALLION (ARGYLE; BEADED OVAL WINDOW), goblet. Bryce Brothers, 1885; U. S. Glass Co., 1892. Extended table service including wine. *Ref. K2-39; Gob I-91; Metz 1-158; Unitt 2-156.*

OVAL PANEL (OVAL SETT), creamer. U. S. Glass Co. (Challinor #23), 1892. Extended table service including wine, but no spoon holder known. Crystal, purple slag, opaque white. *K2-120.*

DUNCAN PANEL, etched creamer. George Duncan and Sons, 1890s. Extended table service including rare covered honey dish with handles. Has crosshatched bottom. Clear, canary, amber, blue. *Ref. K3-110.*

ALMOND THUMBPRINT (ALMOND; POINTED FINGERPRINT; POINTED THUMBPRINT; FINGERPRINT), tumbler. Bakewell, Pears & Co.; Bryce Brothers. Extneded table service including wine, cordials. *Ref. L-154 #14; Gob I-157; Metz 1-44; Unitt 1-47; Jenks p. 11; Schroy-4.*

JOB'S TEARS, goblet. Made in the mid-1880s in extended table service including wine, cordial. Crystal (non-flint.) *Ref. Unitt 2-41; Metz 1-142, Pl. 101; Gob I-101; K3-78.*

PANNIER, goblet. *Ref. Gob II-103; Metz 1-216.*

KALONYAL, pitcher. A. H. Heisey Co.'s #1776, 1905. Marked with H-in-diamond trademark. Made in extended table service including clarets, egg cup, cordials, wines, champagnes, water bottle (81 items in all). Crystal, ruby-stained (rare), gilded. *Ref. K7-55, 142; HTP-87; Burns p. 27; H7-171.*

Rayed with Loop

Georgia

Oval Medallion

Oval Panel

Duncan Panel

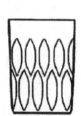

Almond
Thumbprint

Job's Tears

Pannier

Kalonyal

PLATE 23. CIRCLES

BOWLINE, salt shaker. *Ref. PetSal 23H.*

CO-OP'S ROYAL (BULBOUS BULLS-EYE), toothpick holder. Co-operative Flint Glass Co., 1894 – 1915. Extended table service including wine. Crystal, opaque white, ruby-stained. *Ref. K6-23; HTP-53, 56; HI-38; H7-53+.*

CORRIGAN, salt shaker. Extended table service including wine. *Ref. Gob II-39; Metz 2-140; Unitt 1-317.*

SPECIALTY, pitcher. Specialty Glass Co. #100, 1891. Basic table service. Crystal, ruby-stained. *Ref. K5-80; H7-89, 100, 195.*

FLOWERED OVAL, goblet. Made in extended table service including egg cup.

U. S. #156, cruet. U. S. Glass Co., 1909. *Ref. HIII-88.*

THOUSAND EYE BAND (BEAD BAND), salt dish. Made ca. 1880, 1903 in clear, chocolate (rare). The creamer is very plain, with only the band of beads across the base. A wine is also known (courtesy of John Gregory.) *Ref. Salts p. 103; K8-43; Gob II-151; Metz 1-145; Metz 2-130.*

GIANT BULLS-EYE (BULLS-EYE AND SPEARHEAD, EXCELSIOR; CONCAVE CIRCLE), cracker jar and cruet. U. S. Glass Co. #157, 1898; Belmont Goblet Co., Findlay, Ohio, 1890 – 1907. made in extended table service including castor set, decanter, lamp, wine, perfume bottles. Crystal. *Ref. K2-101; Gob II-149; Metz 2-8; Unitt 1-52; Jenks p. 244; Schroy-66.*

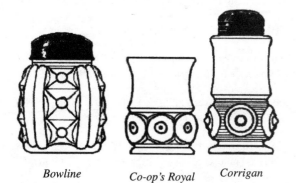

Bowline   *Co-op's Royal*   *Corrigan*

Specialty

Flowered Oval   *U.S. #156*

Thousand Eye Band

Giant Bulls-Eye (two views)

PLATE 24. CIRCLES

MIRROR, McKEE (LOOP AND MOOSE EYE; BULLS-EYE AND LOOP), goblet. McKee Brothers, 1864. Primarily made in drinking pieces, ale glass, champagne, cordial, wine, tumbler; also known: compote, spooner, pickle jar. *Ref. Gob I-108; Unitt 1-39.*

ARGUS, (THUMBPRINT), pitcher. See Plate 13.

LONG OPTIC (TYCOON), creamer. Columbia Glass Co., 1890; U. S. Glass Co., 1891. Extended table service including mug. Crystal. *Ref. K4-66; H5-129; Mugs p. 75, 76.*

BRYCE ELIPSE, wine. Bryce Brothers, 1880s; U. S. Glass, 1891. (Yes, the U. S. Glass catalog spelled the name with one "L.") *Ref. Revi-88; H5-86.*

PILLAR, goblet Bakewell, Pears and Co., 1875. Extended table service including ale glass, decanter, bar bottle, cordial (scarce), wine, claret. Flint. *Ref. L-28; LEAPG-37; Metz 1-24; K5-48; Mugs p. 41, 42.*

COIN AND DEW DROP, goblet. *Ref. Gob II-62; Metz 1-188.*

EGG BAND, goblet. Made ca. 1880s. *Ref. K7-71.*

EGG IN SAND (BEAN; STIPPLED OVAL), pitcher. Extended table service including tray, cordial, wine, bread platter, jam jar. *Ref. K3-71; LV-67; Metz 1-180; Gob I-141; Jenks p. 189; Schroy-54.*

ORION THUMBPRINT, goblet. Canton Glass Co., 1894. Extended table service. Crystal, milk glass, black glass, colors. *Ref. Metz 1-202.*

INVERTED THUMBPRINT (COIN SPOT; POLKA DOT), cruet. George Duncan and Sons, 1884; Hobbs, Brockunier and Co., 1884. A blown pattern. Made in extended table service including biscuit jar, finger bowl, several types of goblet, mustard jar, bitters bottle, wines, cordials, clarets. Crystal, old gold, sapphire, marine green, canary, ruby (cranberry), rubina, rubina verde, ruby amber, opalescent colors. Hobbs called their pattern "Polka Dot." *Ref. LV-28; LEAPG-501; Herrick p. 276 Pl. 2; HIII-28; HI-27; H6-53, 63; Hobbs p. 68.*

INVERTED THUMBPRINT OVAL, creamer. King, Son, and Co. Made in water set and odd pieces. *Ref. K1-87; HTP-44.*

ROPE AND THUMBPRINT (INVERTED ROUND), syrup. Central Glass Co. #796, 1885. Extended table service, but no cruet or toothpick holder. Crystal, amber, blue, canary. *Ref. K1-119; HIII-59.*

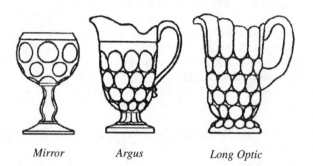

Mirror   *Argus*   *Long Optic*

Bryce Elipse *Pillar* *Coin and Dewdrop* *Egg Band* *Egg in Sand*

Orion Thumbprint *Inverted Thumbprint* *Inverted Thumbprint Oval* *Rope and Thumbprint*

PLATE 25. CIRCLES

THOUSAND EYE (DAISY), Adams, 1874, cruet and pitcher, and Richards and Hartley pitcher (1888). Made by several glass companies over a number of years: Richards and Hartley Flint Glass Co. (#103, 1880); New Brighton Glass Co.; Adams and Co.; U. S. Glass Co., 1891. Very extended table service. Richards and Hartley produced salt shakers in a holder, rare twine holder, little hat, wine, cordials, and the more common pieces as well. The Adams and Co. #130 cruet was part of a two-cruet-in-holder set. They used the three knobs as finials and stems, and produced pieces in canary, crystal, blue, vaseline, apple green, and some scarce pieces in opalescent white. They made square plates in 1891. Richards and Hartley used plain stems, scalloped bases, and patterned finials. Heacock shows a top hat toothpick holder. There are many reproductions in new pieces and colors, so know your glass when you buy. *Ref. L-137; K1-18; Metz 1-184; Schroy-142; Jenks p. 514; Mugs p. 65; H5-39; HTP-86; HI-42; HII-35; HIII-44, 57; H7-44.*

HUNDRED EYE, goblet. Extended table service including wine. *Ref. PetSal 31M; Gob II-106; Metz 1-184; Unitt 1-44.*

PANELLED THOUSAND EYE (DAISY SQUARE), pitcher. Richards and Hartley. Extended table service with a woman's face modeled as a finial. *Ref. K2-66; Metz 2-100.*

BARRELED THUMBPRINT (CHALLINOR THUMBPRINT), pitcher. Challinor, Taylor and Co. #312; U. S. Glass Co., ca. 1891. Extended table service including wine, square bowls, tankard pitcher. Crystal. *Ref. K1-103; LV-58; Metz 1-44; Gob II-40.*

MIDGET THUMBPRINT, goblet. Made in extended table service. *Ref. Gob II-95.*

CRYSTAL #12, rose bowl. Crystal Glass Co., 1891 – 92. Extended table service. *Ref. K6 pl. 42.*

DOT, creamer. Doyle & Co., 1880s; U. S. glass Co. (Doyle), 1891. Extended table service. This pattern is also called RAINDROP and shown on Plate 141. *Ref. K8-99.*

YALE (CROWFOOT), spooner. McKee and Brothers, 1894. Extended table service including cordial. Very similar to PLUME AND FAN on Plate 51, except Yale fans lean and Plume fans are upright. *Ref. LV-19; K3-126; Gob I-68; Schroy-158; Jenks p. 564.*

Thousand Eye (three examples)

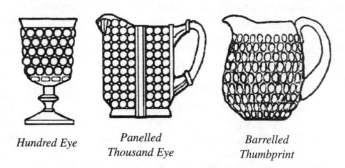

Hundred Eye   *Panelled*   *Barrelled*
                       Thousand Eye   *Thumbprint*

Midget   *Crystal #12*   *Dot*   *Yale*
Thumbprint

PLATE 26. CIRCLES

SAWTOOTHED HONEYCOMB (CHICKENWIRE; SERRATED BLOCK AND LOOP; RADIANT), creamer. Steiner Glass Co.; Union Stopper Co., ca. 1906 – 1908. Extended table service including wine. Crystal, ruby-stained, rose-flashed. *Ref. K1-115; Gob II-94; Metz 1-218; HTP-55; HIII-40; H6-85; H7-182; Jenks p. 465; Schroy-127.*

HEXAGONAL BULLS-EYE (CREASED HEXAGON BLOCK; DOUBLE RED BLOCK), goblet and pitcher. Dalzell, Gilmore and Leighton, 1890s. Extended table service including wine. *Ref. K1-114; Gob II-50; Metz 1-165; Unitt 1-104; Unitt 2-171.*

SUNK HONEYCOMB (CORONA), syrup. Greensburg Glass Co.; McKee and Brothers, ca. 1903. Extended table service including decanter, wine, rare jelly compote. Crystal, ruby-stained. *Ref. K2-57; Revi-172; Mugs p. 84; H6-43; H7-95.*

U. S. #341, syrup. U. S. Glass Co., ca. 1908. *Ref. HIII-80.*

HEXAGON BLOCK, celery vase. Hobbs, Brockunier & Co. #335, 1890; U. S. Glass Co. (Hobbs #335), ca. 1891. Extended table service including tankard pitcher, covered pickle jar. Crystal, ruby-stained, amber-stained; etched through stain; engraved. *Ref. PetSal 30T; HIII-26, 70; H5-126; H7-97+; Metz 1-46; Metz 2-144; Hobbs p. 119.*

BLOCK AND HONEYCOMB, pitcher. McKee and Brothers, 1860s. Known in goblet, butter dish, sugar bowl, and pitcher. *Ref. K5-38; Metz 1-46.*

THOUSAND HEXAGONS, bowl. Duncan Glass, ca. 1890. Extended table service including two sizes butter dish. *Ref. HPV#2, p. 5.*

PANELLED HEXAGONS, jelly stand. McKee Glass Co., ca. 1886. *Ref. HGC1 p. 3.*

NIAGARA, creamer. Fostoria Glass Co. #793, 1900. Made in extended table service including tankard pitcher, berry set. *Ref. K8-195.*

Sawtoothed Honeycomb

Hexagonal Bulls-Eye (two examples)

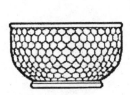

Sunk Honeycomb   *U.S. #341*   *Hexagon Block*   *Block and Honeycomb*

Thousand Hexagons   *Panelled Hexagons*   *Niagara*

63

PLATE 27. CIRCLES

HONEYCOMB AND ZIPPER, salt shaker. *Ref. PetSal 163L.*

HONEYCOMB OBI, salt shaker. *Ref. PetSal 163N.*

NEW YORK HONEYCOMB, etched open salt. New England Glass Co., 1869; U. S. Glass Co., 1895. A State Series pattern for New York; always has three rows of honeycomb. Extended table service including cordials, wines, champagne, claret. Crystal, ruby-stained. *Ref. L-60; Metz 1-42; Metz 2-84; H4-52; H5-52; H7-160.*

FRONTIER (COLONIAL AND MITRE; BOGALUSA), sugar bowl. New Martinsville Glass Co., 1912. Extended table service including wine. Crystal, ruby-stained. *Ref. HTP-120; H7-120.*

BEVELLED WINDOWS (ST. REGIS), syrup. U. S. Glass Co. (Glassport) #15107; 1907. Extended table service including wine. Crystal. *Ref. H5-146.*

HONEYCOMB (VERNON; THOUSAND FACES; CINCINNATI HONEYCOMB), decanter. New England Glass Co., 1860s; Bakewell, Pears and Co.; McKee Brothers, 1880. Made in extended table service including spill holder, finger bowl, egg cups. Flint and non-flint glass. *Ref. L-60; LEAPG-193; K6-13; Schroy-77; Jenks p. 278; Mugs p. 41.*

TULIP AND HONEYCOMB, toy covered bowl. Federal Glass Co., 1914 in toy set. Crystal. *Ref. HGC4 p. 20; HTP-88.*

DUNCAN #77, tumbler. George Duncan and Sons, ca. 1900. *Ref. Bones.*

LOOP AND HONEYCOMB, goblet. *Ref. Gob II-2; Metz 1-38.*

*Honeycomb
and Zipper*   *Honeycomb
Obi*   *New York
Honeycomb*

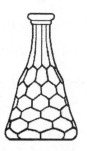

Frontier   *Bevelled Windows*   *Honeycomb*

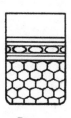

Tulip and Honeycomb   *Duncan*   *Loop and
Honeycomb*

PLATE 28. CIRCLES

PIONEER #21 (BULLS-EYE AND ARROWHEAD), pitcher. Pioneer Glass Co., ca. 1892. Extended table service including castor set, cracker jar. Crystal, ruby-stained. *Ref. K3-81; H6-37; H7-84.*

CAT'S-EYE AND FAN (ROMAN), creamer. George Duncan & Sons, early 1880s. Extended table service. *Ref. K1-25.*

FINECUT AND FAN, sauce. Bryce, Higbee and Co., 1910. Extended table service including toy service, wine. The pitcher shows greatly elongated fans and more diamond point. *Ref. HPV1-6; HPV3-7.*

MIRROR AND FAN, goblet. U. S. Glass Co. #5601 (Bryce), 1891. Wine set including decanter, tray. Two types of wine: one with upper and lower fans; one with no upper fans. Crystal, emerald green, ruby-stained. *Ref. H5-73; H7-33, 153.*

BOW TIE, spoon holder. Thompson Glass Co, 1889. Made in extended table service. *Ref. K6-50; Gob II-5; Metz 1-211; Metz 2-116; Schroy-24.*

FEDERAL #1605, wine. Federal Glass Co., 1914. *Ref. HGC4 p. 19.*

BROOKLYN, pitcher. See Plate 16.

ELLIPSE TWO, pitcher. *Ref. K6-20.*

Pioneer #21

Cat's-Eye and Fan

Finecut and Fan

Mirror and Fan

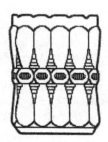

Bow Tie

Federal #1605

Brooklyn

Ellipse Two

PLATE 29. CIRCLES

HEART WITH THUMBPRINT (BULLS-EYE IN HEART; HARTFORD), cup. Tarentum Glass Co., 1898. Extended table service including vases, wine, cordials, 8" lamp, finger lamp. Crystal, ruby-stained, green-stained, custard, opaque green, and rare in rose pink. *Ref. K2-103; K6 Pl. 51; Metz 1-214; Mugs p. 104-5; Gob I-63; Unitt 1-54; LV-59; H4-45+; H7-48; Schroy-71; Jenks p. 266.*

PEACOCK EYE, mug. Boston and Sandwich, 1840. Clear, opalescent, cobalt, amethyst. *Ref. Mugs p. 38.*

PUNTY AND DIAMOND POINT, bitters bottle. A. H. Heisey Glass Co. #305, 1889 – 1907. Extended table service including decanter, sugar shaker. *Ref. K7-138; HTP-87.*

WAFFLE AND THUMBPRINT (PALACE; BULLS-EYE AND WAFFLE; TRIPLE BULLS-EYE), pitcher. Curling, Robertson & Co., 1856; James B. Lyon and Co., Pittsburgh, 1861; New England Glass Co., 1869. Extended table service including mug, cordial, champagne, wine, claret, decanters, egg cup. Flint glass. *Ref. L-26; K3-29; Gob I-80, 125; LEAPG-54; Unitt 1-157; Metz 1-22; Jenks p. 544; Schroy-141; Mugs p. 47.*

FAMOUS (PANELLED THUMBPRINT; THUMBPRINT PANEL; THUMBPRINT SERRATED BAR), syrup. Co-operative Flint Glass Co. #317, 1899. Extended table service including scarce syrup, wine, lamp. Crystal, green, ruby-stained, deep blue. *Ref. K1-114; PetSal 175R; Gob II-115; Metz 2-149; HI-22; HIII-23; HGC1-87; HTP-27; H7-93.*

HEART IN SAND (VINCENT'S VALENTINE; LOVERS), toothpick holder. New Martinsville Glass Co. #724, ca. 1910. Toothpick is rare; a wine is known. Crystal, decorated, ruby-stained. *Ref. HTP-100; HI-50/51; H7-126.*

TRIPLE THUMBPRINTS, creamer. Extended table service. *Ref. K8-34.*

TWIN LADDERS, creamer. Cambridge Glass Co. #2503, 1903. Extended table service. *Ref. K7-30.*

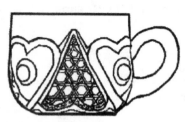
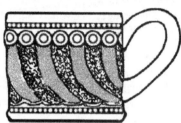

Heart with Thumbprint *Peacock Eye*

Punty and Diamond Point *Waffle and Thumprint* *Famous*

Heart in Sand *Triple Thumbprints* *Twin Ladders*

PLATE 30. CIRCLES

LARGE STIPPLED CHAIN, pitcher. Extended table service including wine. *Ref. Gob II-63; Metz 2-182.*

CHAIN AND SHIELD (SHIELD AND CHAIN), pitcher. Made in the 1870s in extended table service including platter, wine, cordial. *Ref. K1-21; Gob I-168; Metz 1-132; LEAPG-323; Unitt 1-103; Schroy-33.*

BELLAIRE (BELLAIRE #2), pitcher. Made ca. 1879. *Ref. K7-14.*

STIPPLED CHAIN, open salt. Gillander and Sons, 1870s. Extended table service. *Ref. K8-74; L-190; LV Pl. 22; Metz 1-182; Jenks p. 494; Schroy-136.*

YOKE AND CIRCLE (ERA), sauce. J. B. Higbee Co., 1912. Extended table service including wine. *Ref. Gob II-124; Metz 1-37; HGC2 p. 22.*

LOOP AND CHAIN BAND, goblet. *Ref. Gob II-122.*

CHAIN, EARLY, pitcher. McKee Brothers, 1864. Extended table service including platter, wine. *Ref. K1-24; McKee p. 67.*

TAPE MEASURE (SHIELDS), pitcher. Portland Glass Co. in the early 1870s. Extended table service. *Ref. K5-9; Metz 2-124; Schroy-161.*

TWO BAND, creamer. Made ca. 1890 in extended table service including toy table set. Crystal, ruby-stained. *Ref. K1-64; HTP-88; Metz 2-208+.*

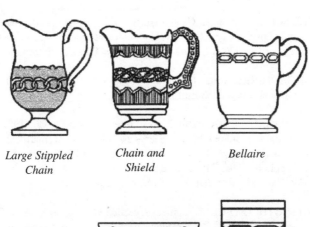

*Large Stippled
Chain*

*Chain and
Shield*

Bellaire

Stippled Chain

Yoke and Circle

*Loop and
Chain Band*

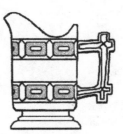

Chain, Early

Tape Measure

Two Band

PLATE 31. CIRCLES

TOP AND BOTTOM SCROLL, salt shaker. Opaque glass. *Ref. PetSal 171T.*

FOSTORIA #1008, syrup. Fostoria Glass Co. Painted milk glass. *Ref. HIII-49.*

MULTIPLE SCROLL, creamer. Canton Glass Co., ca. 1890 – 1919. Basic table service plus mug, square plates. Crystal, amber, blue; black opaque, opal milk glass. *Ref. K5-77; K6 Pl. 27; Mugs p. 65; Glass Collector's Digest Vol. XII #4 (Dec./Jan. 1999) p. 20.*

CAMBRIDGE CURLY, wine. Cambridge Glass Co. (author's name). Identified by Charles Upton; courtesy of Bob Burford.

CAPITAL (FILIGREE; ESTATE), mug. Westmoreland Specialty Co., 1907. Made in novelty items including toothpick holder in crystal, color flashed, marigold carnival glass, gilded gold or silver. This small mug is inscribed "Harold 1908"; I have seen a light green creamer with gold inscribed "1915" as a souvenir of an exposition. Mug courtesy of Bob Burford. *Ref. Har; HTP-73; HGC2 p. 66; Mugs p. 108.*

ESTHER (TOOTH AND CLAW), cruet. Riverside Glass Works, 1896. Extended table service including castor set, jam jar, lamp, wine, rare syrup. Crystal, ruby and amber-stained, emerald green, gilded. *Ref. K5-54; LV-40; Metz 1-220; Schroy-55; Jenks p. 192; HI-22; HIII-55; H7-111.*

SCROLL (STIPPLED SCROLL; LILLY), sauce. Duncan Glass Co., ca. 1880s. Extended table service including cordials. *Ref. K7-71; L-140; Gob I-86; Metz 1-148; Unitt 2-34.*

OVALS AND FINE PLEAT, goblet. *Ref. Gob II-152.*

BUTTRESSED LOOP, creamer. Adams and Co. #16, 1874. Crystal, yellow, amber, blue, green. *Ref. K2-114.*

*Top and
Bottom Scroll*

*Fostoria
#1008*

Multiple Scroll

*Cambridge
Curly*

Capital

Esther

Scroll

*Ovals and
Fine Pleat*

*Buttressed
Loop*

PLATE 32. CIRCLES

TIEBACK, salt shaker. Milk glass. *Ref. PetSal 176D.*

TRELLIS SCROLL, salt shaker. McKee Glass Co. *Ref. PetSal 38V; Stout p. 212.*

SCROLL IN SCROLL, salt shaker. Milk glass. *Ref. PetSal 171R.*

SPIRAL AND MALTESE CROSS, creamer. Made ca. 1870s in extended table service. Crystal, amber. *Ref. K1-30; Metz 1-172.*

DOUBLE SCROLL, salt shaker. Fostoria Glass Co. #233, 1891. Extended table service. See Plate 230. *Ref. K6 Pl. 58.*

SCROLL AND CHAIN, salt shaker. Milk glass. *Ref. PetSal 171P.*

MOSAIC SCROLL, salt shaker. Milk glass. *Ref. PetSal 171S.*

CROESUS, salt shaker. Riverside Glass Co. #484; McKee and Sons, ca. 1897 – 1901. Extended table service including berry set, castor set, jam jar. Crystal, emerald green, amethyst, ruby-stained, gilded. Reproduced extensively. See pitcher on Plate 71. *Ref. K4-112; HI-19; HIII-58; H6-24, 77; H7-5; Metz 1-221; Metz 2-144; Schroy-39; Jenks p. 135.*

TOSSED SCROLLS, creamer. Milk glass. *Ref. K8-39.*

SCROLL BAND, pitcher. *Ref. K5-125.*

Tieback

Trellis Scroll

Scroll in Scroll

*Spiral and
Maltese Cross*

Double Scroll

*Scroll and
Chain*

Mosiac Scroll

Croesus

Tossed Scrolls

Scroll Band

PLATE 33. CIRCLES

EAGLE'S FLEUR-DE-LIS, syrup. Eagle Glass and Mfg. Co., 1901. *Ref. HIII-85.*

FLEUR-DE-LIS AND TASSEL (FLEUR-DE-LIS AND DRAPE), mustard jar. Adams and Co., 1880s; U. S. Glass Co. #15009 (Adams; Ripley), 1891. Extended table service including tray, cup and saucer, finger bowl, cordial, wine, claret, champagne. Crystal, milk glass, emerald green, gilded. The wine has been reproduced. *Ref. K3-50; LV-59; Gob II-14; Metz 1-138; H5-61.*

BANDED FLEUR-DE-LIS (STIPPLED FLEUR-DE-LIS DIAMOND BAND), pitcher. Imperial Glass Co. #5, 1890s. Extended table service including wine (courtesy of John Gregory.) *Ref. K2-44; Gob II-164.*

ARCHED FLEUR-DE-LIS (LATE FLEUR-DE-LIS), creamer. Bryce Higbee and Co., 1898 –1907; J. B. Higbee Co. after 1907. Extended table service including wine. Crystal; ruby-stained; gilded. *Ref. PetSal 161D; Mugs p. 89; HPV1 p. 5; HPV6 p. 21; H7-68+; Schroy-6.*

ROCOCO, creamer. Central Glass Co., 1891; Imperial Glass Co., 1906. Made in extended table service. *Ref. K3–105.*

FLEUR-DE-LIS (FROSTED FLEUR-DE-LIS; STIPPLED FLEUR-DE-LIS), pitcher. King, Son and Co., 1885; U. S. Glass Co., 1891. extended table service including wine. Crystal, amber, blue, green, milk glass, ruby-stained. *Ref. K1-84; Gob I-173; Metz 1-138; Unitt 1-149; H7-103.*

DRAPED GARLAND, syrup. Made ca. 1900 in extended table service. Crystal, ruby-stained. *Ref. PetSal 159Q; HIII-23; H7-108.*

STIPPLED MEDALLION, goblet. Union Glass Co., 1860s. Extended table service including egg cup, plates. *Ref. L-28; K8-13; Metz 1-126.*

BAROQUE, creamer. Made in the 1850s. *Ref. K3-31.*

*Eagle's Fleur-
de-Lis*

*Fleur-de-Lis
and Tassel*

*Banded Fleur-
de-Lis*

*Arched Fleur-
de-Lis*

Rococo

Fleur-de-Lis

Draped Garland

*Stippled
Medallion*

Baroque

PLATE 34. DIAMONDS/SCALES

SMOCKING (DIVIDED DIAMONDS), goblet and tumbler. Boston and Sandwich, 1840s. Extended table service including 9" lamp, rare creamer, egg cup, water and whiskey tumblers, 10" vase, wine, bar bottle, berry set, champagne. *Ref. K6-12; Gob II-6, 27; Metz 1-44; Metz 2-52; Jenks p. 483; Schroy-132.*

SPEARHEADS (ALLIGATOR SCALE WITH SPEARPOINT), pitcher. McKee Glass Co., 1880s. Extended table service. *Ref. K1-112; Metz 1-208.*

SEELY (FOSTORIA), creamer. U. S. Glass Co. (Nickel Plate), 1891. Extended table service. Crystal. *Ref. K6-76; K8-35; Gob II-27; H5-136.*

FRISCO, creamer. Fostoria Glass Co. #1229, 1904. Extended table service including bar tumbler, bitters bottle, flared-rim bowls, 33 items in all. *Ref. K7-39.*

WARD'S NEW ERA (CO-OP 20TH CENTURY), pitcher. Co-operative Flint Glass Co., 1901. Was sold by Montgomery Ward in 1901 and 1903; the four–piece table set cost 42 cents. Extended table service including cruet, jelly compote, wine. Kamm says the diamonds are formed of tiny notches. *Ref. K5-80; HGC4 p. 37; H7-205, 213.*

SUNKEN ARCHES, creamer. Riverside Glass Works #370, 1891. Extended table service. *Ref. K5-58.*

CONCAVED ARROWHEADS (GOTHIC), creamer. King Glass Co., 1875. Extended table service including wine. *Ref. K8-10; Revi-211; Innes p. 366.*

DUNCAN #904, cup. George Duncan and Sons, ca. 1900. *Ref. Bones p. 109.*

ALLIGATOR SCALES, goblet. Made ca. 1870s in flint glass. *Ref. Gob II-12; Metz 2-166.*

LOOP AND PETAL, goblet. This goblet is shown on Plate 196 for comparison to similar patterns. *Ref. Gob II-1; Metz 1-10/11.*

ARTICHOKE (VALENCIA), creamer. Fostoria Glass Co., 1891. Extended table service. No goblet made originally. Crystal, opalescent, satin, colors. See Plate 181. *Ref. K7-78; Schroy-9; Jenks p. 24.*

Smocking (two examples)   Spearheads   Seely

Frisco   Ward's
New Era   Sunken Arches   Concaved
Arrowheads

Duncan #904   Alligator
Scales   Loop and
Petal   Artichoke

PLATE 35. DIAMONDS

BAND, goblet. Extended table service including footed tumbler. *Ref. L-61; Metz 1-18.*

BULLS-EYE AND WISHBONE, goblet. *Ref. Gob II-F; Metz 1-32.*

BULLS-EYE WITH DIAMOND POINT, goblet. Extended table service. *Ref. L-27; LEAPG-161; K3-100; Metz 1-12; Schroy-27.*

BUCKLE WITH ENGLISH HOBNAIL, creamer. Extended table service. *Ref. K2-75.*

HIGH HOB, sherbet cup. Westmoreland Glass Co. #550, 1915. Extended table service including wines. Crystal, ruby-stained. *Ref. K3-147; HII-89; H7-129; Revi-323.*

DIAMOND POINT DISCS (DIAMOND SPLENDOR; CRESCENT), mug and creamer. Bryce, Higbee and Co., 1898; J. B. Higbee Glass Co. after 1907; New Martinsville Glass Co. after 1916. Extended table service. Crystal, ruby-stained. *Ref. K3-90; Mugs p. 66; H7-105.*

COLONIAL WITH DIAMOND BAND, goblet. *Ref. Gob II-29; Metz 1-18.*

REVERSE TORPEDO (BULLS-EYE BAND; BULLS-EYE WITH DIAMOND POINT; POINTED BULLS-EYE), celery vase. Dalzell, Gilmore and Leighton #49, 1891. Extended table service including banana dish, fruit basket, wine. Crystal, ruby-stained. *Ref. K3-100; Gob II-76; Unitt 1-79; Unitt 2-105; H7-84+; Jenks p. 426; Metz 1-152; Schroy-119.*

CANE MEDALLION, pitcher. Westmoreland Glass Co., 1896. Extended table service. *Ref. K1-93; Metz 2-164.*

Band *Bulls-Eye and Wishbone* *Bulls-Eye with Diamond Points* *Buckle with English Hobnail*

High Hob *Diamond Point Discs (two views)*

Colonial with Diamond Band *Reverse Torpedo* *Cane Medallion*

PLATE 36. DIAMONDS

BEADED DIAMOND, creamer. *Ref. K7-37.*

DUNCAN MIRROR (OVAL LENS; KAMM'S MIRROR; LATE MIRROR), cologne bottle. Duncan Glass Co. #352, 1891. Known in salt shaker, covered mustard, condiment set, botttles. The ovals are very deeply set. *Ref. PetSal 154J; Krause, Glass Review, Sept., 1984 p. 10; K6 Pl. 98; Welker-357.*

BROKEN BAR AND THUMBPRINT, salt shaker. *Ref. PetSal 155Q.*

VICTORIA, footed bowl. Bakewell, Pears and Co., 1870s. Extended table service including scarce sugar bowl. *Ref. L-18; Metz 2-18; LEAPG-77; K5-73; Schroy-150.*

BUCKLE, goblet. Boston and Sandwich; Gillinder and Sons; 1870s – 1880s. Extended table service including compote, cordials, egg cup, open salt, champagne, wine. *Ref. L-102; LEAPG-311; Gob I-110; Metz 1-122; Metz 2-112; K5-8; Jenks p. 80.*

NET AND SCROLL, salt shaker. Opaque glass. *Ref. PetSal 34D.*

PANELLED OVAL, spoon holder. Made ca. 1860 in extended table service including egg cup, champagne, wine. *Ref. LV-84; Metz 1-26; Unitt 1-60.*

DIAMOND WITH CIRCLE, mug. Made in the 1880s in clear, amber, blue, apple green. *Ref. Mugs p. 81.*

BANDED BUCKLE, spoon holder. Doyle & Co., 1870; King, Son & Co., 1875 – 1880. Extended table service including high and low compotes, cordials, egg cup, tumbler, wine. *Ref. K4-9; Gob I-110; Metz 1-122; Unitt 2-12; Schroy-12; Jenks p. 42.*

HORN OF PLENTY (COMET; PEACOCK TAIL), egg cup. Boston and Sandwich; Bryce Brothers; McKee & Brothers; 1830s, 1850s. Extended table service including lamp, wine, decanters, whiskey tumbler, claret, cordials, champagnes, handled mug, spill holder. Crystal, amber, blue, cobalt, amethyst, opalescent, stained. At the Green Valley Auction in Pittsburgh in 1998, a rectangular honey dish with cover and matching tray sold for $14,000. *Ref. L-47; Metz 1-12; Unitt 1-42; Unitt 1-220; Jenks p. 282; Mugs p. 40.*

DICKINSON, goblet. Sandwich Glass, 1860s. Extended table service including wine, open salt. *Ref. Gob I-12; Gob II-6; Metz 2-36; Unitt 1-152; Schroy-52.*

TOOTHED MEDALLION, creamer (etched). *Ref. K7-6.*

Beaded Diamond

Duncan Mirror

Broken Bar and Thumbprint

Victoria

Buckle

Net and Scroll

Panelled Oval

Diamond with Circle

Banded Buckle

Horn of Plenty

Dickinson

Toothed Medallion

PLATE 37. DIAMONDS

DUNCAN #2001, tumbler. George Duncan's Sons and Co., 1891. Extended table service including tray, finger bowl. Crystal, ruby-stained. *Ref. K7-21.*

STRATFORD, pitcher. Cambridge Glass Co., 1906. Extended table service including 20 vases, 12 bowls, mustard and pickle jars, and 15 open sugar bowls with varying rims. *Ref. K7-65.*

ROANOKE (SAWTOOTH; LATE SAWTOOTH), creamer. Gillinder and Sons, 1885; U. S. Glass Co. (Ripley), 1891. Extended table service including wine, rose bowl. Crystal, green, ruby-stained. *Ref. K2-99; K8-168; LV-135; Jenks p. 446; Schroy-121; H5-122; H7-187.*

RICHMOND, pitcher. Richards and Hartley #190, 1888; U. S. Glass Co, 1891. Extended table service including half-gallon and quart pitchers, wine. Crystal. It is hard to depict the squareness of this pitcher. *Ref. LV-61; K1-77; H5-116.*

STEPPED DIAMOND POINT, pitcher. A variation of Diamond Point made in the 1860s. *Ref. K7-5; Jenks p. 177.*

PANELLED SAWTOOTH (FLUTED DIAMOND POINT), pitcher. Duncan Glass, ca. 1880s. Extended table service including wine. *Ref. K1-37; Metz 1-174.*

PRISM AND SAWTOOTH, goblet. An early flint pattern made in extended table service. *Ref. Gob II-152.*

DIAMOND BAND, pitcher. Indiana Glass Co. #169, 1915. Extended table service including wine, cordials, champagne. *Ref. K4-137; LEAPG-320; Metz 1-212.*

HINOTO (DIAMONDPOINT WITH PANELS; BANDED DIAMOND POINT), goblet. Boston and Sandwich, 1850s. Extended table service including champagne, cordials, wines, rare covered sweetmeat, open salt. The mug is a whiskey tumbler with an applied handle. Crystal, rare canary. *Ref. L-153 #11; Metz 1-28; Unitt 1-130; Unitt 2-52; Jenks p. 275; Schroy-74; Mugs p. 39.*

PRISM AND FLATTENED SAWTOOTH (RIBBED PINEAPPLE), spill. Made in the 1850s in extended table service including lamp, wine. *Ref. Gob II-19; Metz 1-184; Unitt 1-87.*

84

Duncan #2001　　Stratford　　Roanoke

Richmond　　Stepped Diamond
Point　　Panelled Sawtooth

Prism and
Sawtooth　　Diamond Band　　Hinoto　　Prism and
Flattened Sawtooth

PLATE 38. DIAMONDS

SAWTOOTH AND WINDOW, salt shaker. *Ref. PetSal 171M.*

HEAVY DIAMOND (DIAMOND BLOCK), pitcher. Imperial Glass Co., ca. 1925 – 1935. *Ref. K1-99.*

HECK (DOUBLE PRISM; *TEARDROP ROW – in error*), creamer. Model Flint Glass Co., 1893. Extended table service including wine. *Ref. K1-97; PetSal 41Q; Unitt 2-104.*

ADAMS DIAMOND, creamer. Adams and Co., ca. 1880s. *Ref. K7-8.*

GIANT SAWTOOTH, lamp and tumbler. Made in the 1830s and known in lamp, spill, and tumbler. *Ref. Gob II-103; Metz 1-8; Metz 2-40.*

SAWTOOTH, celery vase and salt shaker. Boston and Sandwich; Union Glass Co; U. S. Glass Co. (Bryce; Gillinder), 1891. Extended table service including spill, tumbler, wine, champagne, claret, goblet, and toy table service. Crystal, ruby-stained. *Ref. L-40; LEAPG-585; Metz 1-118; Unitt 1-82; K5-46; K8-14; H6-163; H7-67.*

STIPPLED DIAMONDS, toy spoon holder (toothpick holder). Toy table service, ca. 1891. This is the STIPPLED FORGET-ME-NOT pattern without the flowers. *Ref. Lechler 167; HTP-89.*

Sawtooth and Window

Heavy Diamond

Heck

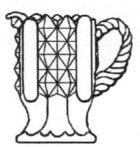

Adams Diamond

Giant Sawtooth (two examples)

Sawtooth (two examples)

Stippled Diamonds

PLATE 39 DIAMONDS

ENGLISH QUILTING, creamer. *Ref. K2-5.*

FLATTENED SAWTOOTH, pitcher. George Duncan and Sons, ca. 1880. Extended table service including finger bowl, wines, cordials. *Ref. L-65; LEAPG-138.*

LENS AND BLOCK, creamer. Made ca. 1870. *Ref. K6-8.*

OPPOSING PYRAMIDS (GREENSBURG'S FLORA; TRUNCATED PRISMS; FLORA), salt shaker. Greensburg Glass Co., 1889. Extended table service including wine, cordial. *Ref. K8-31; Gob II-82; Metz 1-162; Unitt 2-23.*

SUPERIOR (DIAMOND POINT BAND), creamer. U. S. Glass Co. #15031 (Ripley), 1896. Extended table service including wine. Crystal, ruby-stained, engraved. *Ref. Metz 2-46; K3-78; H5-172; H7-233.*

AMAZON (SAWTOOTH BAND), salt shaker and creamer. U. S. Glass Co. (Bryce), ca. 1890. Very large table service including waste, champagne, wine, cordial, claret, flared bowls, toy table set, lion-head handled bowls. Crystal, amber, vaseline, blue, ruby-stained. *Ref. K3-9; LV-42; Metz 1-34; Jenks p. 12; Schroy-5; H5-78; H6-18; H7-67.*

BIG DIAMOND, creamer. Dalzell, Gilmore and Leighton, 1885. Extended table service. *Ref. K6-30.*

HOURGLASS (EGG AND DART), creamer. See Plate 16.

PANEL WITH DIAMOND POINT BAND, creamer. Central Glass Co. #439; Crystal Glass Co., 1881. Extended table service. *Ref. K1-35.*

SQUARED STAR, creamer. Ripley & Co.; U. S. Glass Co., ca. 1885 – 1891. Extended table service. *Ref. K6-2.*

English
Quilting

Flattened
Sawtooth

Lens and Block

Opposing
Pyramids

Superior

Amazon (two examples)

Big Diamond

Hourglass

Panel with
Diamond
Point Band

Squared Star

PLATE 40. DIAMONDS

LACE BAND (IMPERIAL #4), pitcher. Imperial Glass Co., 1902. Extended table service including wine. This pattern is identical with the following one except for the vertical panels. Crystal, ruby-stained. *Ref. K7-183; Metz 2-140; Gob II-3; H7-138.*

OPTIC FLUTE, creamer. Imperial Glass Co. #6, ca. 1902. extended table service including wine, lemonade set with no base pattern on the tumblers. Crystal, ruby-stained. *Ref. K7-45; Batty p. 225; H7-138.*

TULIP WITH SAWTOOTH (TULIP), pitcher. Bryce, Richards and Co., ca. 1854; Bryce, McKee and Co., 1860; U. S. Glass Co., 1891 (in non-flint). Extended table service including decanter, powder jar, wine set, cordial, champagne, cruets. Crystal, opaque white, opalescent. The wine has been reproduced. *Ref. L-53; Metz 1-32; Unitt 1-194; Mugs p. 48; Schroy-147; Jenks p. 529.*

TULIP, decanter. Bryce, Richards and Co., 1860; McKee Brothers later. Extended table service including high and low compotes, several sizes decanters, pint and quart jugs, tumbler, cordials, champagne, wine. The cordial has been reproduced. Flint glass. *Ref. L-53; LEAPG-166; K3-28; Mugs p. 47.*

SPECIALTY #6, creamer. Specialty Glass Co., 1892. This piece was used as a container for condiments. *Ref. K8-181.*

SPECIALTY PATTERN E (SPEARPOINT WITH DAISY BAND), wine. Specialty Glass Co., 1892. Extended table service. *Ref. K8-180; Gob II-107; Metz 2-150; Unitt 1-109.*

PANELLED SMOCKING, creamer. U. S. Glass Co.; Bartlett-Collins in the late 1920s. Basic table service. Crystal, decorated. *Ref. K2-88.*

PAVONIA (PINEAPPLE STEM), spoon holder and goblet. Ripley and Co., 1885; U. S. Glass Co., 1891. Extended table service including tray, finger bowl, wine, cordial. Crystal, ruby-stained, etched. *Ref. K3-15; K4-142; Metz 1-146; Unitt 1-285; Mugs p. 81; H5-43; H7-169+; Jenks p. 400; Schroy-109.*

CUT BLOCK (SQUARE IN DIAMOND POINT), syrup. A. H. Heisey Glass Co. #1200 ca. 1900. Extended table service including wine. Crystal, ruby-stained. *Ref. LV-40; HI-19; H4-41; H6-12; H7-98.*

PIONEER'S VICTORIA, pitcher. Maker unknown; Pioneer Glass Co. decorated it 1885 – 1902. Extended table service including egg cup, wine set, cordial, champagne. Crystal, ruby-stained. *Ref. K3-83; K8 Pl. 77; Metz 2-138; Unitt 2-134; Mugs p. 80; H6-45, 48; H7-210+.*

TRIPLE TRIANGLE (PILLAR AND CUT DIAMOND), pitcher. Doyle and Co., 1880s; U. S. Glass Co. (Doyle #76), 1891. Extended table service including wine. Crystal, ruby-stained. *Ref. K8-104; Metz 2-142; Mugs p. 81; H5-42; H7-205; Jenks p. 527; Schroy-146.*

90

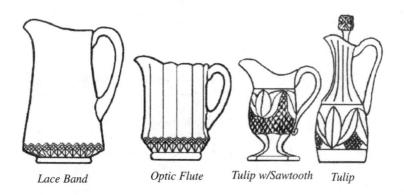

Lace Band   *Optic Flute*   *Tulip w/Sawtooth*   *Tulip*

Specialty #6   *Specialty Pattern E*   *Panelled Smocking*   *Pavonia (two examples)*

Cut Block   *Pioneer's Victoria*   *Triple Triangle*

PLATE 41. DIAMONDS

PRISM WITH DIAMOND POINTS, goblet. Boston and Sandwich, early; Bryce Brothers; U. S. Glass Co., 1891. Extended table service including wines, cordial, two types goblet. *Ref. K3-28; Gob I-73; Metz 1-50; Unitt 1-136.*

PRISM AND DIAMOND, creamer. Extended table service. *Ref. K6-9.*

PRISM WITH BALL AND BUTTON, creamer. *Ref. K1-111.*

BEAUTY, pitcher. Pioneer Glass Co., 1891. Extended table service including wine. Crystal, ruby-stained. *Ref. K8-176; Revi-280; H7-74.*

DIAMOND SIDE, salt shaker. Crystal, ruby-stained. *Ref. PetSal 159A; H7-79.*

LADDER TO THE STARS, covered sugar bowl. Cambridge Glass Co. #2626, ca. 1907; Federal Glass Co., ca. 1914; originally called "Radium." Extended table service including wine, cordial, milk jar. *Ref. PetSal 164Q.*

PRISM WITH BLOCK (ESTHER), creamer. Westmoreland Glass Co., 1896. Extended table service. Crystal, ruby-stained. *Ref. K1-109; H7-111.*

BALL AND BAR, pitcher. Probably Westmoreland Glass Co., 1896. *Ref. Kamm.* Extended table service. *Ref. K7-20.*

PANELLED FLATTENED SAWTOOTH, tumbler. *Ref. Gob II-143; Metz 2-160.*

STARS AND STRIPES (BRILLIANT; CLIMAX), creamer. Kokomo and Jenkins Glass Co., 1899; Federal Glass Co. #209, 1914. Extended table service including toy table service, wine, cordial. There are some reproductions. Crystal, milk glass, ruby-stained, opalescent and green. *Ref. K2-70; Metz 11-198; HGC4-17; H7-91; Mugs p. 94; Schroy-135; Jenks p. 492.*

TARENTUM'S LADDER WITH DIAMONDS (FINE CUT AND RIBBED BARS), goblet. Tarentum Glass Co., 1903. Extended table service. Crystal, ruby-stained. *Ref. K8-42; PetSal 164Q; H7-46+.*

LADDER WITH DIAMONDS (FINE CUT AND RIBBED BARS; MOBILE), goblet. Duncan and Miller Glass Co. #52, 1904. Extended table service including decanter, wine, champagne, bud vase. Crystal, ruby-stained. *Ref. PetSal 32C; K8-43; H7-138.*

*Prism w/Diamond
Points*

*Prism and
Diamond*

*Prism with Ball
and Button*

Beauty

Diamond Side

*Ladder to the
Stars*

*Prism with
Block*

Ball and Bar

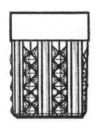

*Panelled Flattened
Sawtooth*

Stars and Stripes

*Tarentum's
Ladder with
Diamonds*

*Ladder with
Diamonds*

PLATE 42. DIAMONDS

CADMUS, goblet. Beaumont Glass Co., 1902; Dugan Glass Co., 1915. The wine is also known. *Ref. Gob II-83; Metz 2-160; Unitt 1-134; Schroy-30.*

SUNBURST AND BAR, half-gallon pitcher. Hobbs, Brockunier and Co., 1891. Extended table service including master salt, lamp shades. The tumbler lacks the "fan" and can be found with "White River Flour" in the base. Crystal, canary, sapphire, amber-stained. *Ref. LV-58; H6-61.* (The Bredehoft's call this pattern "Maltese & Ribbon" in their book, *Hobbs, Brockunier and Co. Glass,* p. 92.)

IMPERIAL'S #80, pitcher. Imperial Glass Co., 1901. *Ref. K7-66.*

DIAMOND BRIDGES, pitcher. U. S. Glass Co. #15040, 1896. Extended table service. Crystal, emerald green, ruby-stained. *Ref. H5-51; H7-104.*

ENGLISH, creamer. McKee Glass Co. Extended table service. Westmoreland also made a pattern called "English" (K2-109), but it is now called "Diamond with Diamond Point," and is quite different. *Ref. Stout p. 210.*

AUSTRIAN (FINE CUT MEDALLION; PANELLED OVAL FINE CUT), pitcher. Indiana Tumbler and Goblet #200, 1897 – 1898; Federal Glass Co. #110, 1914. Made in extended table service including handled sauce, toy basic service, wine cordial, banana dish, punch cup, rose bowls. Crystal, canary, green, chocolate, opaque white, rare amethyst, ruby-stained. *Ref. Gob II-8; K2-43; Unitt 1-296; Herrick p. 50; Mugs p. 83; HI-50; H7-153; Jenks p. 33; Schroy-10.*

HUNGARIAN, salt shaker. *Ref. PetSal 163S.*

O'HARA DIAMOND (SAWTOOTH AND STAR; RUBY STAR), syrup. O'Hara Glass Co., 1880s; U. S. Glass Co. #15001, 1885 – 1896. Extended table service including banana stand, plain tray, wine, champagne, claret, finger bowl. Crystal, ruby-stained. See the pitcher on Plate 52. *Ref. K5 Pl. 32; K8-14; Metz 1-118; Unitt 1-82; Mugs p. 80; H5-51; H7-163.*

PRESSED DIAMOND (BLOCK AND DIAMOND; ZEPHYR), syrup. Central Glass Co. #775, ca. 1885; U. S. Glass Co., 1891. Extended table service including pickle castor, wine. The syrup is very rare. No toothpick holder was made. Crystal, amber, canary, blue (scarce), vaseline, apple green (rare). *Ref. K8-33; LV-70; Gob II-113; Metz 1-162, 182; Metz 2-18; H7-114, 176.*

KOKOMO (BAR AND DIAMOND; R & H SWIRL; ZIPPERED SWIRL; SWIRL BAND), syrup. Richards and Hartley, 1885; U. S. Glass Co. (Richards and Hartley), 1891; Kokomo Glass Co. (Jenkins), 1901. Extended table service including decanter, trays, hand lamp, toy table set, wine set. On some pieces the swirls reverse. Crystal, ruby-stained. See celery vase on Plate 229. *Ref. LV-62; LEAPG-38; PetSal 174R; Gob I-142; Unitt 1-112; H5-116; H7-71, 137; Jenks p. 316; Schroy-87; Metz 1-212.*

Cadmus

Sunburst and Bar

Imperial's #80

Diamond
Bridges

English

Austrian

Hungarian

O'Hara
Diamond

Pressed
Diamond

Kokomo

PLATE 43. DIAMONDS

LATTICE WITH BARS, spill (author's name). Courtesy of Bob Burford. *Ref. Lee, Rarities in Pattern Glass (Antiques Magazine, March, 1935.)*

DIAMOND IN POINTS, creamer. Made ca. 1860. *Ref. K4-81.*

SERRATED RIB AND FINECUT, creamer. Made ca. 1901 in extended table service including wine, tumblers, flared rim bowls. Crystal, gilded. *Ref. Gob II-153; Metz 2-1-64; Unitt 2-135; HPV #6 p. 15.*

DIAMOND POINT, spill holder. Sandwich Glass; New England Glass Co.; Bryce, Richards and Co., and others, 1830 – 1870s; 1890s. Extended table service including egg cup, wines, cordials, champagnes, claret, plates. Some in flint glass. *Ref. L-43; LEAPG-130; K4-134; Metz 1-174; Schroy-51; Jenks p. 177; Gob II-72; Unitt 2-120; Mugs p. 40.*

DIAMOND SWAG (FANDANGO), creamer. A. H. Heisey Glass Co. #1201, ca. 1898 – 1909. Extended table service including jelly compote, triangular jelly dish, wine, spoon tray, cracker jar, vases, banana compote, sugar shaker. Crystal. See Plate 108. *Ref. K5-117; LV-40; K6 Pl. 62.*

HARTFORD, creamer. Fostoria Glass Co., 1900s. Extended table service. Crystal, canary, amber, ruby-stained. *Ref. K8-193; Schroy-70; H7-125.*

FLAT DIAMOND (LIPPMAN; PILLAR), goblet. Richards and Hartley, 1885; U. S. Glass Co., 1891. Extended table service including wine, cordial. Crystal, ruby-stained. Courtesy of John Gregory. *Ref. Gob II-59; Metz 1-198; LV Pl. 32; H7-116; Schroy-61. Millard also shows the goblet in Book 1-89 and calls it PANELLED DIAMOND, RED TOP. Metz shows a similar pattern in 1-198 called CLEAR AND DIAMOND PANELS. Unitt shows a goblet with wider space at the top in 2-53 called SHORT PANELLED DIAMONDS. Similar patterns in this book are DIAMOND QUILTED Pl. 49, and PANELLED DIAMOND POINT Pl. 47.*

CHALLINOR #314, creamer. Challinor, Taylor and Co.; U. S. Glass Co., 1891. Basic table service. Milk glass. *Ref. K4-84.*

LATE DIAMOND POINT BAND (SCALLOPED DIAMOND POINT; PANEL WITH DIAMOND POINT BAND; DIAMOND POINT WITH FLUTES), pitcher. Central Glass Co., 1870s Extended table service including covered cheese dish, mustard dish, wine, claret. *Ref. K5-3; Gob II-24; Metz 1-128; Unitt 2-188; Schroy-127.*

Lattice with
Bars

Diamond in
Points

Serrated Rib
and Finecut

Diamond
Point

Diamond
Swag

Hartford

Flat Diamond

Challinor
#314

Late Diamond
Point Band

PLATE 44. DIAMONDS

AMBOY, goblet. *Ref. Gob II-27; Metz 2-164.*

BUCKLE AND SHIELD, goblet. *Ref. Gob II-64.*

HAND (PENNSYLVANIA; PENNSYLVANIA HAND), pitcher. O'Hara Glass Co., 1880. Extended table service including wine, jam jar, cordial, champagne, claret, platter. Rare mug is a tumbler with applied handle. The compotes are rather plain with only the grasping hand in the base. See Plate 171. Crystal. *Ref. K3-9; L-107; LEAPG-324; Metz 1-162; Gob I-120; Mugs p. 76; Schroy-69; Jenks p. 260, 402.*

CORAL GABLES, goblet. The wine is also known. *Ref. Gob II-15; Unitt 2-162.*

DOUBLE DIAMOND PANELS, goblet. *Ref. Gob II-14; Metz 2-162.*

BULLS-EYE AND BUTTONS, syrup. Made ca. 1895 – 1900 and known in syrup, cruet, and toothpick holder. Green, crystal. *Ref. Mur-2; HIII-17; H6-21.*

TIPTOE (RAMONA; HOGAN'S SALT SHAKER), salt shaker. McKee Glass Co. after 1900. Extended table service. *Ref. PetSal 42H.*

PANEL AND RIB, creamer. Made ca. 1885 in extended table service. Crystal, yellow, vaseline, amber. *Ref. K4-17.*

DIAMOND PANELS, toothpick holder. Made ca. 1895 in toy basic table service. Crystal, green, blue. *Ref. HTP-30.*

BULLS-EYE IN DIAMOND, salt shaker. *Ref. PetSal 156C.*

DIAMOND POINT AND PUNTY, salt shaker. Do not confuse with PUNTY AND DIAMOND POINT. *Ref. PetSal 27L.*

NEW ENGLAND PINEAPPLE (LOOP AND JEWEL), tumbler. New England Glass Co.; Boston and Sandwich; ca. 1860s. Extended table service including wines, cordials, champagnes, decanter. Flint, crystal, rare opalescent. A wine and cordial have been reproduced. *Ref. L-53; LEAPG-164; Metz 1-12; Unitt 1-284; K4-54; Mugs p. 48; Jenks p. 381; Schroy-102.*

Amboy

*Buckle and
Shield*

Hand

Coral Gables

*Double Diamond
Panel*

*Bulls-Eye
and Buttons*

Tiptoe

Panel and Rib

*Diamond
Panels*

*Bulls-Eye in
Diamond*

*Diamond-
Point and
Punty*

*New England
Pineapple*

PLATE 45. DIAMONDS

HOLLIS (DIAMOND BAR AND BLOCK), pitcher. U. S. Glass Co. (O'Hara), ca. 1900. Crystal, ruby-stained. *Ref. K2-68; H7-104.*

NAILHEAD (GEM), pitcher. Boston and Sandwich; Bryce, Higbee and Co., ca. 1880s Extended table service including cordial, wine, round and square plates. Crystal, aquamarine, decorated. *Ref. K4-41; K8-19; L-108/158; LEAPG-539; Metz 1-150; Jenks p. 379; Schroy-102.*

NICKEL PLATE'S RICHMOND (BLOCK AND DOUBLE BAR; BAR AND BLOCK; BARS AND BUTTONS; AKRON BLOCK), creamer. Nickel Plate Glass Co. #76, 1889; U. S. Glass Co., 1891. Extended table service including wine. This pattern has pieces where the pattern appears in a vertical block; the tankard pitcher is called "BAR AND BLOCK." Crystal, ruby-stained. *Ref. K1-76; K6 p. 16; H5-136; H7-71, 72.*

BROOCH BAND, goblet. *Ref. Gob II-120.*

WORLD'S PATTERN, pitcher. Bryce, Walker and Co., 1880s. Made in extended service. *Ref. K8-145.*

ART (TEARDROPS AND DIAMOND BLOCK), creamer. Adams and Co.; U. S. Glass Co.; 1870s; 1891. Extended table service including cracker jar, banana dish, fruit basket, wine, cordial. Crystal, ruby-stained. for a different look, see Plate 46; the pattern could be hard to recognize without knowledge of both forms. Compotes are fluted, with teardrops but no diamonds. *Ref. K3-77; Gob I-101; Metz 1-210; Unitt 1-54; H5-66; H7-33, 68, 201; Mugs p. 81; Jenks p. 22; Schroy-8.*

REGAL BLOCK (CO-OP #190), creamer. Co-operative Flint Glass Co. #190, 1892. Extended table service including wine set, cordial. Crystal, ruby-stained. *Ref. K5-65; K6 Pl. 47; Gob II-97; Metz 2-166; Unitt 1-254; HGC3 p. 72; H7-184+.*

QUILT AND FLUTE, creamer. Known in creamer, mustard jar and sugar bowl. *Ref. K1-71.*

DIAMOND WEB, salt shaker. *Ref. PetSal 27P.*

ALL-OVER DIAMOND (DIAMOND BLOCK; DIAMOND SPLENDOR), cruet. Duncan #356, 1890; U. S. Glass #15011 (Gillinder; Duncan), 1891. Extended table service including condensed milk jar, egg cup, wine, cordial. Crystal, ruby-stained. *Ref. K3-134; K6 Pl. 16; Metz 1-164; Jenks p. 9; Schroy-4; H5-103; H7-67+.*

BEVELLED DIAGONAL BLOCK (CROSSBAR), creamer. U. S. Glass Co. (Challinor #311), 1891. Extended table service including jam jar, cordial, wine. Crystal, ruby-stained. *Ref. LV-59; K2-19; H5-93; H7-75.*

Hollis

Nailhead

Nickel Plate's Richmond

Brooch Band

World's Pattern

Art

Regal Block

Quilt and Flute

Diamond Web

All-Over Diamond

Bevelled Diagonal Block

PLATE 46. DIAMONDS

COACHMAN'S CAPE, goblet. Bellaire Goblet Co., 1880s; U. S. Glass, 1891. The wine is also known (courtesy of John Gregory.) *Ref. Gob I-106; Metz 1-194; Unitt 1-160.*

PEQUOT, goblet. Extended table service including jam jar, wine, champagne, castor set. *Ref. Gob II-127; Metz 1-194; Unitt 2-93; Schroy-110.*

LOUISIANA (SHARP OVAL AND DIAMOND; GRANBY), spooner and creamer. Bryce Brothers, 1880s; U. S. Glass Co. #15053 (Bryce), 1898. A State Series pattern. Very extended table service including cordial, mug, bread tray, wine, three types sugar bowl. Crystal, frosted. *Ref. K1-59; K6 Pl. 93; Gob I-92; Unitt 1-312; Mugs p. 76; H5-164; Jenks p. 343; Schroy-93.*

HEISEY #150, creamer. A. H. Heisey Co., 1897. Extended table service. *Ref. K4-90.*

FLAT DIAMOND BOX, creamer. Fostoria Glass Co. #301, 1892. Extended table service, but no toothpick or cruet known. This piece is **square**, with the prisms on the corners. Crystal, ruby-stained. *Ref. K3-94; Metz 2-132; HIII-24; H7-116.*

ART, pitcher. See Plate 45.

OVAL DIAMOND PANEL (OVAL PANEL), goblet. *Ref. L-62.*

BULLS-EYE AND DIAMOND QUILTED, goblet. *Ref. Gob II-118; Metz 2-146.*

FLAT DIAMOND AND PANEL (LATTICE AND OVAL PANELS), egg cup. Sandwich Glass. Extended table service including tumbler, decanter, claret, wine, champagne, lamp. Crystal, opaque. *Gob I-81; Metz 1-29; Unitt 1-157; Oliver p. 53.*

SUNK PRISM (PITCAIRN), pitcher. King, Son and Co. #14, ca. 1880. Extended table service including wine. *Ref. K3-36; Gob II-52; Metz 2-150; Unitt 1-133.*

Coachman's
Cape

Pequot

Louisiana (two views)

Heisey #150

Flat Diamond Box

Art

Oval Diamond
Panel

Bulls-Eye and
Diamond
Quilted

Flat Diamond
and Panel

Sunk Prism

PLATE 47. DIAMONDS

DIAMOND POINT LOOP, creamer. Made ca. 1890s in extended table service. Crystal, amber, canary, apple green, blue, engraved. *Ref. K2-111.*

SLEWED DIAMOND, pitcher. *Ref. K4-119.*

SUNK DIAMOND AND LATTICE, pitcher. McKee Glass Co. at the National factory, ca. 1901, and numbered their #900. Extended table service. *Ref. K2-126.*

FEDERAL #1607 (CO-OP #296), wine. Co-operative Flint Glass Co., 1900; Federal Glass Co., ca. 1914. The cordial is also known. Federal #1605 (Plate 28) lacks the diamond point, but does have big diamonds with its large ovals; it might be confused with this one. *Ref. HGC4 p. 20; Welker p. 342.*

PANELLED DIAMOND POINT, spoon holder. Richards and Hartley, 1885. Extended table service including wine, champagne. *Ref L-104; LEAPG-321; Gob I-123; Metz 1-198.* Bryce, Higbee and Co. also made this pattern in 1890 – 1905 in crystal, crystal with blue and red top. Probably they made no goblets, although the wine is known. *Ref. PGP 1-6.* The King Glass Co. made a version in the 1880s, their #204, reissued by U. S. Glass in 1891. Its diamonds are flat-topped with a tiny dot or cross centered on each. *Ref. Revi-223.* Gillinder's version was #411, 1880s; and U. S. Glass, 1891. It has narrower plain panels. *Ref. LEAPG Pl. 86; Metz 1-34; Revi-168* (courtesy of John Gregory).

HARVARD YARD (CRYSTAL), cruet. Tarentum Glass Co., 1896. Extended table service including wine, cordial set, egg cup. Crystal, green, pink, ruby-stained. *Ref PetSal 162S; PetPat 187; H6-95; H7-125; Jenks p. 265; Schroy-71; Mugs p. 89.*

CARMEN (PANELLED DIAMONDS AND FINECUT), cruet. Fostoria Glass #575, 1896. Extended table service including wine. Crystal, yellow-flashed. *Ref. K5-121; LV-37; Gob II-116; Metz 2-164; H3-18; H6-87.*

SWIRL-ATOP-DIAMOND, salt shaker. *Ref. PetSal 174-P.*

DIAMOND ROSETTES, goblet. Date of manufacture uncertain, but made in extended table service. Crystal, canary, amber. *Ref. Metz 1-122; Metz 2-114.*

CRISS-CROSS BAND, goblet. Extended table service including toy set, wine. *Ref. Gob II-85; Unitt 2-124.*

DIAMOND WITH DIAMOND POINT (ENGLISH), creamer. Westmoreland Glass Co., 1894. Extended table service. Crystal, opalescent. *Ref. K2-109; Schroy-55.*

Diamond
Point Loop

Slewed
Diamond

Sunk Diamond
and Lattice

Federal #1607   *Panelled Diamond*   *Harvard Yard*   *Carmen*
                   Point

Swirl-Atop-   *Diamond*   *Criss-Cross*   *Diamond with*
Diamond   *Rosettes*   *Band*   *Diamond*
                                                       Point

PLATE 48. DIAMONDS

STAR AND DIAMOND, salt shaker. This may be a blown piece. *Ref. PetSal 173D.*

LONG STAR (IHC; TEUTONIC), pitcher. McKee Glass Co., 1894 – 1898. Extended table service. Crystal. Note: A plain oval pickle dish featuring a cross and the letters IHS in **not** part of this pattern. *Ref. K3-133; K7-43; PetSal 175G.*

SQUARED DAISY AND DIAMOND (ARGYLE), pitcher. Jones, Cavitt and Co, (Pittsburgh), 1888. *Ref. K6 Pl. 19.*

FANCY DIAMONDS (FINECUT AND BLOCK; DIAGONAL BEAD BANDS), pitcher. Model Flint Glass Works, 1890. Extended table service including wine. *Ref. Metz 2-148; Unitt 2-25; Metz 1-212.*

BARRED STAR (SPARTAN), creamer. U. S. Glass Co. (Gillinder), 1891. Extended table service. *Ref. LV-49; Metz 1-120.*

STAR IN DIAMOND, creamer. U. S. Glass #414, 1891. *Ref. K1-62.*

PATTERN F, goblet. Specialty Glass Co., 1892. Known in goblet and wine. *Ref. K8-180.*

CAMBRIDGE #2700, butter dish. Cambridge Glass Co., 1910 – 1917. Courtesy of Bob Burford.

DEEP STAR (DIAMOND WALL; DIAMOND BAR AND BLOCK), creamer. Model Flint Glass Works #851, ca. 1890. Extended table service including wine, toy table service. Crystal, ruby-stained. *Ref. K4-77; Mugs p. 78; Bond p. 21, 50 et al; H7-105.*

*Star and
Diamond*

Long Star

*Squared Daisy
and Diamond*

Fancy Diamonds

Barred Star

Star in Diamond

Pattern F

*Cambridge
#2700*

Deep Star

PLATE 49. DIAMONDS

DIAMOND LATTICE (CHESTERFIELD; DIVIDED SQUARES), creamer. Cambridge Glass Co. #2500, ca. 1903. Extended table service including wine. *Ref. K2-77; Gob II-4; Metz 2-170; Unit 1-262.*

OVERALL DIAMOND (SYLVAN; ENGLISH HOBNAIL VARIANT), salt shaker and creamer. Fostoria Glass Co. #1119, 1902. Extended table service including punch set, rose bowls, carafe, cologne bottle. *Ref. K7-32; K4-100.*

WESTMORELAND (SWIRLED BLOCK), cruet and toy pitcher. Gillinder and Sons #420, 1888; U. S. Glass Co. #15011, 1892. (Not Westmoreland — this is a clear case of overzealous naming!) Extended table service of 75 pieces including toy table set, wine, champagne, honey jar, nut bowl, ice tub, decanter, covered cheese plate. Crystal, ruby-stained. *Ref. K1-117; LV-148; Mugs p. 80; Unitt 1-255; H6-45; H7-67; Schroy-154.*

DOUBLE SPEAR, pitcher. McKee and Brothers, 1880s. Extended table service. *Ref. K1-21; L-132; LEAPG-442; Metz 1-142.*

CHEVRONED DIAMONDS, salt dish (author's name). Known in amber salt dish. Courtesy of Bob Burford.

BAKEWELL BLOCK, wine goblet. Bakewell, Pears and Co., ca. 1850s. Extended table service including champagne, two sizes of tumbler, cordials, decanter. Flint glass. This representation has been verified by Henry Bakewell, grandson of the president of Bakewell, Pears Glass Co., and Charles A. Bakewell, also a descendant, to Bob Burford of the Early American Pattern Glass Society. Lee's drawing was incorrect. *Ref. Metz 1-24; Unitt 1-282; Mugs p. 46.*

DIAMOND QUILTED, celery vase. Made ca. 1880s in extended table service including wine, cordials, champagnes, claret, water tray, footed tumbler. Crystal, canary, amber, blue, amethyst, purple. *Ref. L-104; Gob I-151; Metz 1-140; Jenks p. 180; Schroy-51; Mugs p. 80.*

Diamond Lattice   *Overall Diamond (two examples)*

Westmoreland (two examples)   *Double Spear*

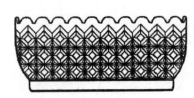  

Chevroned Diamonds   *Bakewell
Block*   *Diamond
Quilted*

PLATE 50. DIAMONDS

ENGLISH HOBNAIL, pepper shaker. Westmoreland Glass Co. #555, 1910. Extended table service including wine, toy condiment set. *Ref. L-85; LEAPG-278; Metz 2-98; Gob II-72; Unitt 2-268, 207.*

MASCOTTE (MINOR BLOCK; DOMINION; ETCHED FERN AND WAFFLE), goblet. Ripley and Co., 1884; U. S. Glass Co. (Ripley), 1891. Extended table service including several sizes of tall compotes, wine, cookie stand. Often etched. Crystal, ruby-stained. *Ref. LV-42; K1-17; Gob II-132; Metz 1-150; Jenks p. 358; Schroy-97; H5-123; H7-149.*

DIAMOND IN DIAMOND (DIAMOND), creamer. Extended table service. *Ref. K3-14.*

LINED DIAMONDS, salt dish. Base has a "starburst." *Ref. Salts, addendum.*

HAMILTON (CAPE COD), tumbler. Boston and Sandwich; Cape Cod Glass Co., 1860s. Extended table service including castor set, decanter, egg cup, whiskey (scarce), wines, cordials, champagne. Flint; crystal, rare deep blue, rare opalescent. *Ref. L-56; LEAPG-177; Gob I-117; Unitt 1-134; Metz 1-26; Jenks p. 257; Schroy-69; Mugs p. 40.*

CHECKERS, goblet. Note: Millard named this pattern "Checkerboard," but as there is already a pattern by that name, I suggest shortening it to "Checkers." *Ref. Gob II-12.*

DIAMOND WITH FAN, salt shaker. *Ref. PetSal 159E.*

BLOCK AND PANEL, salt shaker. Extended table service. *Ref. LV-60.*

TRIPLE X, salt shaker. A similar pattern is "Tacoma" on Plate 65. *Ref. PetSal 176-I.*

THREE PLY PANEL, salt shaker. McKee Brothers, ca. 1904, known in condiment set and syrup. *Ref. K4 Pl. 10; PetSal 42E.*

English
Hobnail

Mascotte

Diamond in
Diamond

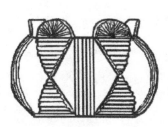

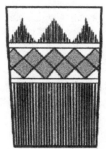

Lined Diamonds

Hamilton

Checkers

Diamond with
Fan

Block and Panel

Triple X

Three Ply
Panel

PLATE 51. DIAMONDS

CROSS IN DIAMOND (CRUSADER CROSS; STAR; DIAMOND), pitcher. U. S. Glass Co. (Challinor #9), 1891. Extended table service. Crystal. *Ref. K5-51; Gob II-44; H5-90.*

PLUME AND FAN, creamer. Findlay Flint Glass Co. ca. 1891; Dalzell, Gilmore and Leighton ca. 1893. This pattern can be compared to YALE, which has little fans leaning in circles, not upright as in this pattern. *Ref. HGC1 p. 86.*

HOBNAIL-IN-SQUARE (VESTA; AETNA'S #335), pitcher. Aetna Glass and Mfg. Co., 1887. Extended table service. Crystal, opalescent, amber, blue, apple green, canary. *Ref. K5 Pl. 24; Mugs p. 68; HII-21.*

NONPAREIL, spoon holder.

BLOCK BAND DIAMOND (DIAMOND; SQUARE AND DIAMOND BAND), syrup. Duncan Glass Co. #27, 1890s. Extended table service including wine. *Ref. K3-132; Unitt 2-161; H7-79.*

DIAMOND IN SPACE, salt shaker. *Ref. PetSal 158R.*

THOUSAND DIAMONDS, syrup. George Duncan and Sons #317, ca. 1890. Has raised quilting. Known in water set and syrup. Crystal, blue, apple green. *Ref. HIII-44.*

MERRIMAC, salt shaker. McKee and Brothers, 1898. Extended table service. *Ref. K6 Pl. 96.*

LADY HAMILTON (PEERLESS), goblet. Richards and Hartley, 1875; U. S. Glass, 1891; odd dresser pieces made by Heisey and marked with their H-in-diamond logo. Extended table service including mustard jar, bread plate, two creamers, 22 compotes, pickle jar, wine, champagne, individual salt. *Ref. K4-127; K7-64; Gob I-49; Metz 1-168; Unitt 1-132.*

SQUARED DAISY AND DIAMOND, pitcher. Extended table service. *Ref. K2-99.*

GRAND (NEW GRAND; DIAMOND MEDALLION; FINECUT MEDALLION; FINE-CUT AND DIAMOND), pitcher. Bryce, Higbee and Co., 1885. Extended table service including finger bowl, wine, cordial. *Ref. K1-23; K8-119; LV-31; Gob II-108; Unitt 1-315; Jenks p. 251; Schroy-67.*

Cross in Diamond

Plume and Fan

Hobnail-in-Square

Nonpareil

Block Band Diamond

Diamond in Space

Thousand Diamonds

Merrimac

Lady Hamilton

Squared Daisy and Diamond

Grand

113

PLATE 52. DIAMONDS

HAWAIIAN LEI (GALA), sugar bowl. Bryce, Higbee and Co. after 1900. Extended table service including handled basket, wine, champagne, toy set. Crystal. *Ref. Gob I-46; Metz 1-150; Schroy-71.*

STAR-IN-SQUARE, creamer. Duncan and Miller Glass Co. #75, ca. 1904. Extended table service. Crystal, ruby-stained. *Ref. K8-48; H6-79; H7-41.*

INDIANA (FEATHER; PRISON WINDOW), butter dish. U. S. Glass Co. #15029 (Gas City), 1896 – 1897. A State Series pattern. Extended table service. Crystal, ruby-stained. See "Prison Window" on Plate 212. *Ref. LV-39; PetSal 169J; Jenks p. 291; Schroy-80; K4-105; H7-132.*

BOX PLEAT (O'HARA'S CRYSTAL WEDDING), creamer. Adams and Co., 1875. Extended table service. All pieces have three "feet." *Ref. K6-53; K8-110.*

STAR BAND (BOSWORTH), creamer. Indiana Glass Co., 1915. Extended table service including wine, open footed salt. Crystal, opalescent. *Ref. K1-13; Gob II-19; Metz 1-137; Metz 2-178.*

ARCHED TRIPOD (TRIPOD STEM), creamer. Made ca. 1885 in extended table service including lamp. *Ref. Gob II-17; K3-6.*

O'HARA DIAMOND, pitcher. See Plate 42.

SEMI-OVAL, salt shaker. *Ref. PetSal 39B.*

ICICLE WITH CHAIN BAND, goblet. *Ref. Gob II-52; Metz 1-153; Metz 2-48.*

FAN AND STAR, celery vase. Challinor, Taylor and Co. #304, 1880s; U. S. Glass Co., 1891. Extended table service. *Ref. Metz 1-148; Metz 2-104; H5-91.*

DICE AND BLOCK, cruet. Belmont Glass Co., ca. 1885. Only the cruet was made. Crystal, amber, blue, canary. *Ref. HIII-55; H6-26.*

PETTICOAT, mug. Riverside Glass Co., ca. 1899. Extended table service including three sizes of hats. Two similar "petticoat" patterns are shown on Plate 77. Crystal, canary, gilded. *Ref. PetSal 35J; Mugs p. 79; HI-35; HIII-56; H6-37.*

Hawaiian Lei

Star-in-Square

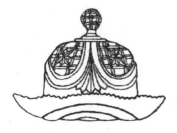
Indiana

Box Pleat

Star Band

Arched Tripod

O'Hara Diamond

Semi-Oval

Icicle with
Chain Band

Fan and Star

Dice and Block

Petticoat

PLATE 53. DIAMONDS

PILLOW-IN-OVAL, creamer. *Ref. K8-37.*

HERO (RUBY ROSETTE), etched creamer. West Virginia Glass Co. #700, 1894. Extended table service including hand lamp. Crystal, ruby-stained, cobalt blue. See next pattern. *Ref. K5-59; H7-127.*

PILLOW ENCIRCLED (MIDWAY), pitcher. Model Flint Glass Co., 1889; National Glass Co., 1901. Extended table service including tray, cruet, wine. Crystal, ruby-stained, etched. This pattern has a groove above the diamonds; HERO does not. *Ref. K2-129; K5-79; Metz 1-148; Heacock, Antique Trader article Sept. 9, 1981 p. 85; H7-151.*

PATTEE CROSS (GEORGIA; BROUGHTON), goblet. U. S. Glass Co. #15112 (Richards and Hartley; Bryce), 1909. Made in very extended table service including toy set, crimped vase, wine, ruffled bowl. Crystal, emerald green, rose-flashed, amethyst stained. (Not a State Series pattern). *Ref. K2-121; Gob II-79; Metz 1-218; Mugs p. 92; H5-43, 150 & 167; H7-169.*

CORNELL, pitcher. Tarentum Glass Co., 1898. Extended table service including wine, cordial, rose bowl. *Ref. K7-37; HI-19.*

PILLOW AND SUNBURST (ELITE), pitcher. Westmoreland Glass Co., 1891, 1896, 1917. Extended table service. Crystal, ruby-stained. *Ref. K1-100; Metz 1-218; H7-110, 172.*

PILLOWS, creamer. A. H. Heisey Co. #325, ca. 1900 – 1912. Extended table service of 45 pieces. Crystal, ruby-stained. *Ref. K2-96; H7-172.*

UNIQUE, syrup. Co-operative Flint Glass Co., 1898. Extended table service. *Ref. K7-38.*

FOUR PETAL, sugar bowl. McKee and Brothers, ca. 1850s. Extended table service. *Ref. L-12; LEAPG-43; Metz 1-33; Metz 2-50; K5-26.*

SYDNEY, pitcher and salt shaker. Fostoria Glass Co. #1333, 1905. Extended table service including decanter, carafe. Crystal. *Ref. K7-38.*

Pillow-in-Oval

Hero (etched)

*Pillow
Encircled*

Pattee Cross

Cornell

*Pillow and
Sunburst*

Pillows

Unique

Four Petal

Sydney (two examples)

PLATE 54. DIAMONDS

HEART PLUME (MARLBORO; RAYED DIVIDED DIAMOND HEART), salt shaker. U. S. Glass Co. #14105 (Bryce), 1907. Extended table service including wine. Crystal, rose-flashed. See creamer on Plate 95. *Ref. PetSal 30-O; Revi-317; Unitt 2-201; H5-150.*

FLAT IRON, pitcher. Columbia Glass Co., 1888; U. S. Glass Co., 1898. The wine is also known. *Ref. K4-101; Hartley p. 72.*

TWIN TEARDROPS (ANONA), quart pitcher. Bryce, Higbee and Co., ca. 1905; Federal Glass Co., ca. 1914. Extended table service including wine. Crystal, ruby-stained. *Ref. K4-76; Gob I-162; Unitt 2-140; HGC4-22; H7-67.*

X LOGS (PRISM ARC; DIAMONDS IN OVAL), pitcher. Possibly made by T. G. Cook and Co., 1892 – 1895; or Cooperative Flint Glass Co., ca. 1893. Extended table service including wine. Crystal, opaque white, ruby-stained. *Ref. K5-134; Gob II-47; Metz 1-142; Mugs p. 78; H7-176.*

PALMETTE, footed salt. Made ca. 1870s in extended table service including rare creamer, 10" lamp, footed tumbler, wine, cordials, champagne, relish with scoop. *Ref. K4-20; L-95; Metz 1-126; Unitt 1-213; Jenks p. 392; Schroy-106.*

HELENE, spoon holder. Co-operative Flint Glass Co. Crystal, ruby-stained. *Ref. H7-127.*

SNOWSHOE, creamer. Basic table service known. *Ref. K4-48; Metz 1-194.*

KAYAK, pitcher. Imperial Glass Co. Extended table service including tray, wine. *Ref. K2-95.*

CAMBRIDGE #2511, butter dish. Cambridge Glass Co., 1910 – 1915. Courtesy of Bob Burford.

LACY HEART, mug. Boston and Sandwich, ca. 1835. *Ref. Mugs p. 37.*

PRINCESS FEATHER (ROCHELLE; LACY MEDALLION), spooner. Boston and Sandwich; Bakewell, Pears; U. S. Glass Co., 1890s. Extended table service including egg cup, wine. Crystal, opaque white. *Ref. L-19; LEAPG-464; K3-31; Gob I-25; Metz 1-126; Unitt 1-266; Schroy-115; Jenks p. 419.*

BEVELLED DIAMOND AND STAR (DIAMOND PRISMS; ALBANY), creamer. Tarentum Glass Co., ca. 1898. *Ref. Heacock.* Extended table service including bread plate, wine. Crystal, ruby-stained. *Ref. K2-74; Gob II-25; Metz 2-174; H5-48; H7-65, 75.*

Heart Plume   *Flat Iron*   *Twin
Teardrops*   *X Logs*

Palmette   *Helene*   *Snowshoe*   *Kayak*

*Cambridge
#2511*   *Lacy Heart*   *Princess
Feather*   *Bevelled Diamond
and Star*

PLATE 55. DIAMONDS

FLORAL DIAMOND BAND, syrup. Bryce Brothers #900, ca. 1900. Only syrup made. Crystal, blue. *Ref. HIII-24.*

LEAFLETS, pitcher. Central Glass Co. #585, 1881. Extended table service. Plates and trays have a birds in tree motif; covered pieces have a reclining dog finial. *Ref. K3-46.*

CONNECTICUT, covered compote. U. S. Glass #15068 (King factory), 1898. A State Series pattern. Made in extended table service including belled bowls, cruet, wine. Crystal, ruby-stained. *Ref. K4-65; K5-68; Jenks p. 128; Schroy-37; H5-166; H7-93.*

SPIREA BAND (SQUARE AND DOT; SQUARED DOT; EARL), goblet. Bryce, Higbee and Co., 1885. Extended table service including wine, cordial, claret, platter, sugar shaker. Crystal, amber, blue. *Ref. K4-34; K8-17; Gob I-177; Metz 1-136; H5-41; Jenks p. 487; Schroy-134.*

HOME (SQUARE AND DIAMOND BANDS), creamer. Pioneer Glass Co.; McKee Brothers, 1880s; 1894. extended table service. Crystal, ruby-stained. *Ref. K1-59.*

PRISMATIC, creamer. *Ref. K3-13.*

CROSS BANDS, creamer. Made ca. 1878. *Ref. K4-36.*

WAVERLY, individual creamer. U. S. Glass Co. (Bryce #140), 1891. Extended table service. Crystal. Note: "Waverly" is the spelling in the original catalog. *Ref. K4-107; H5-80.*

FOSTORIA'S #226, creamer. Fostoria Glass Co., 1891. Extended table service. Crystal, opaque colors. *Ref. K6 p. 58.*

BROKEN BANDS, creamer. U. S. Glass Co. (Doyle #65), 1892. Extended table service. Crystal, amber, blue. *Ref. K3-48.*

120

Floral Diamond
Band

Leaflets

Connecticut

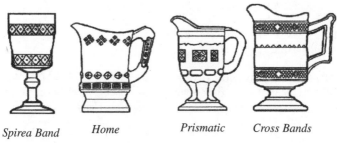

Spirea Band

Home

Prismatic

Cross Bands

Waverly

Fostoria's
#226

Broken Bands

PLATE 56. DIAMONDS

TANDEM DIAMONDS AND THUMBPRINT, goblet. *Ref. Gob II-4.*

RUBY DIAMOND, pitcher. Made ca. 1893 in extended table service. Crystal, ruby-stained. *Ref. K2-93; H7-189.*

LATTICE (DIAMOND BAR; DIAMOND LATTICE), pitcher. King, Son and Co., 1880; U. S. Glass Co., 1891. Made in extended table service including platter, egg cup, wine, cordial. *Ref. K4-40; L-78; LEAPG-542; Gob I-97; Metz 1-160; Unitt 1-146.*

LATTICE AND LENS, creamer. Made ca. 1880. *Ref. K8-24; Metz 2-152.*

TARENTUM'S MANHATTAN, butter dish. Tarentum Glass Co., 1896 – 1900. Extended table service including wine. Crystal, ruby-stained. An old catalog spells the name "Manhatton," but Heacock believed that was a misprint. *Ref. Lucas p. 292, 297; H7-148+; Pet-Pat-188.*

DIAMOND RIDGE, salt shaker. George Duncan and Sons #48, 1901. Extended table service including toy table set, carafe, bar tumbler, pickle jar, wine, champagne. Crystal, ruby-stained, gilded. *Ref. PetSal 158W; PetPat-57; Mugs p. 78; HTP-79; H7-79, 88.*

INVERTED PRISM AND DIAMOND BAND, creamer. Extended table service. Kamm believed this to be of English origin. *Ref. K2-4.*

PRISM AND DIAMOND BAND (STAR AND DIAMOND; CENTRAL #438), creamer. Central Glass Co. #438, 1881. Extended table service including eight covered compotes, three low compotes, pickle dish, wine, cordial, champagne, claret. *Ref. K3-50; Gob I-100; Metz 1-192; Metz 2-116.*

DIAMOND SPEARHEAD, toothpick holder. National Glass Co. (Indiana, PA), ca. 1900, which was operating the Northwood Glass Works; this is considered a Northwood pattern. Extended table service including wine. Cobalt, opalescent, crystal. *Ref. H1-19; H2-37; H3-23; PetSal-159; Schroy-52; Mugs p. 89.*

PANEL AND CANE, pitcher. Made ca. 1890 in extended table service. *Ref. K4-12.*

DROPPED DIAMONDS, pitcher. Imperial Glass Co. #75, ca. 1902. *Ref. K7-186.*

THREE-IN-ONE (FANCY DIAMONDS), creamer. Imperial Glass Co., late 1880s. Extended table service including wine set, syrup, covered biscuit jar. Crystal, ruby-stained. The name Kamm gave it refers to the fact that the large diamonds are divided into four smaller diamonds, and each smaller one is divided into four tiny ones. *Ref. K4-74; K7-80; Metz 1-212; Unitt 2-124; H7-201.*

*Tandem Dia-
monds and
Thumbprint*

Ruby Diamond

Lattice

Lattice and Lens

*Tarentum's
Manhattan*

*Diamond
Ridge*

*Inverted Prism
and Diamond
Band*

*Prism and
Diamond
Band*

*Diamond
Spearhead*

Panel and Cane

*Dropped
Diamonds*

Three-in-One

PLATE 57. DIAMONDS

LOZENGES, spooner. Made ca. 1880s. *Ref. K8-74.*

QUATREFOIL, pitcher. Made ca. 1880s in extended table service including rare goblet, open and covered sugar bowls. A tumbler would be very rare. Crystal, apple green. *Ref. Metz 1-146.*

VIRGINIA (BANDED PORTLAND; MAIDEN'S BLUSH; PORTLAND WITH DIAMOND POINT BAND), footed dish and cruet. U. S. Glass Co. #15071 (Gillinder; Gas City; Richards and Hartley), 1901. A State Series pattern. Extended table service including vase, wine set, water bottle, jam jar, relish boat, puff box, candlesticks, tray, cologne bottles, sardine dish. Crystal, green-flashed, rose-flashed; ruby-stained. *Ref. K2-89; Gob II-9, 98; Metz 1-196; Unitt 1-36; HI-58; H5-44, 50; H6-45; H7-212.*

SISTER KATE, pitcher. Found as a ruby-stained souvenir, ca. 1890. *Ref. K2-46; H7-194.*

PANTAGRAPH BAND, goblet. Crystal, ruby-stained. *Ref. Gob II-24; Metz 2-188; H7-194.*

ANGORA, goblet. Made ca. 1890 in extended table service in crystal. *Ref. Gob II-27; Metz 1-152.*

FAN WITH DIAMOND (SHELL), pitcher. McKee and Brothers, 1880. Extended table service including wine, egg cup, cordials. *Ref. K3-18; Gob I-64; Metz 1-154; Unitt 1-212; LEAPG-541; Schroy-57; Jenks p. 201.*

LAKEWOOD, goblet. Extended table service. *Ref. Gob II-75; Metz 1-146.*

BEAUMONT'S COLUMBIA, salt shaker. Beaumont Glass Co. #100, 1898. Extended table service including vases. Crystal, vaseline, gilded, ruby-stained (rare). *Ref. K7-168; HI-59; H3-20; H7-7.*

ACORN DIAMONDS, syrup. U. S. Glass Co. (Bryce), 1891. Syrup only known. *Ref. HIII-51.*

GEM STAR, cruet. West Virginia Glass Co., 1894. Extended table service. *Ref. K6-38.*

Lozenges   *Quatrefoil*   *Virginia (two examples)*

Sister Kate   *Pantagraph Band*   *Angora*   *Fan with Diamond*

Lakewood   *Beaumont's Columbia*   *Acorn Diamonds*   *Gem Star*

PLATE 58. DIAMONDS

BUTTERFLY EARS (and detail), mustard pot shown for comparison. See Plate 6.

BUCKLE AND DIAMOND, pitcher. McKee and Brothers, ca. 1880. Extended table service. *Ref. K1-51; L-154 #18.*

GALLOWAY (VIRGINIA; MIRROR; WOODROW), toy pitcher. Jefferson Glass Co., 1900 – 1925; U. S. Glass Co. #15086 (Gas City; Glassport), 1904. Extended table service including toy set, decanter, cracker jar, tall vase, water bottle, wine, champagne. Crystal, rose-flashed, ruby-stained, gilded. Note: Galloway should not be called "Virginia" because the State Series pattern for Virginia is BANDED PORTLAND. *Ref. K3-89; Gob I-218; Metz 1-218; Mugs p. 78; HI-43; H5-145, 154; H7-152; Jenks p. 236; Schroy-64.*

HARVARD (QUIXOTE), salt shaker. Tarentum Glass Co., 1898 – 1912. Extended table service including wine, punch cup, finger bowl. Crystal, green, ruby-stained, custard. *Ref. K6-51; Gob II-89; Metz 2-140; HI-25; H7-92.*

LOOP AND BLOCK WITH WAFFLE BAND, goblet. *Ref. Gob II-83; Metz 1-168.*

ALBANY, butter dish and detail. U. S. Glass Co. (Bryce #140), 1891. Crystal, ruby-stained. *Ref. K8-138; H7-48+.*

POINTED ARCHES, toy pitcher. The mug is also known. Crystal, ruby-stained. *Ref. K8-54; Mugs p. 81.*

KING ARTHUR, pitcher. Duncan and Miller Glass Co. #68, ca. 1908. Extended table service. *Ref. HGC5 p. 42; H6-80.*

IVANHOE, toothpick holder. Dalzell, Gilmore and Leighton, ca. 1890. Extended table service. The toothpick holder is scarce. *Ref. LV-108; Schroy-82.*

AURORA (DIAMOND HORSESHOE), tumbler. Brilliant Glass Works; Greensburg Glass Co.; 1888 – 1902. Extended table service including plate ringed with plain diamonds, water set, cordial, wine set. Crystal, ruby-stained, etched. *Ref. K2-110; K3-18; K8-59; Metz 1-194; Schroy-10; Mugs p. 78; H7-70.*

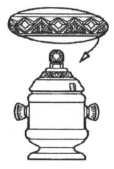

Butterfly Ears
(and detail)

Buckle and
Diamond

Galloway

Harvard

Loop and
Block with
Waffle Band

Albany (and detail)

Pointed Arches

King Arthur

Ivanhoe

Aurora

PLATE 59. DIAMONDS

RIVERSIDE'S VICTORIA (DRAPED RED TOP; DRAPED TOP), pitcher. Riverside Glass Co., ca 1900. Extended table service. Crystal, ruby-stained. *Ref. K6 Pl. 63; Jenks p. 541; H6-3-45; H7-58, 187, 211.*

LOOP AND BLOCK (DRAPED RED BLOCK), creamer. Pioneer Glass Co. #23, 1890s. Extended table service including decanter, wine set, berry set. Crystal, ruby-stained. *Ref. K8-178; Gob II-18; Unitt 1-255; H7-143.*

WASHINGTON CENTENNIAL (CHAIN WITH DIAMONDS), goblet and pitcher. Gillinder and Sons, 1876 – 1889. Extended table service including fish-shaped pickle dish, platter with various motifs, champagne, wine. Crystal, milk glass. *Ref. Gob II-20; K2-124; Jenks p. 548; Metz 1-112; Schroy-152.*

MITRED DIAMOND (CELTIC; NEW MARTINSVILLE), goblet. New Martinsville Glass Co., 1903. The wine is also known. *Ref. Gob II-15; Metz 1-194; Unitt 2-140; Schroy-101.*

PITTMAN, goblet. *Ref. Gob II-20.*

PANELLED LATTICE, goblet. Wine also known. *Ref. Gob II-85; Metz 2-160.*

WIMPOLE, sugar bowl. Extended table service including ketchup jug. Crystal, ruby-stained. *Ref. HPV #2-14; H6-17; H7-63, 15, 215.*

MT. VERNON (PRISM), sugar bowl. Imperial Glass Co. #699, 1912. Extended table service. *Ref. Archer p. 153.*

KING'S #29 (ADAMS), creamer. King Glass Co., 1890. Extended table service including wine. *Ref. K5-74; LV-54.*

SPIRALLED TRIANGLE, creamer. Beatty-Brady Glass Co. #106, 1898. Extended table service. *Ref. K4-70.*

Riverside's
Victoria

Loop and
Block

Washington
Centennial

Mitred Diamond

Pittman

Panelled
Lattice

Wimpole

Mt. Vernon

King's #29

Spiralled Triangle

PLATE 60. DIAMONDS

SANBORN (IRON KETTLE), creamer. U. S. Glass Co. (Challinor #83), 1891. Extended table service. Crystal. *Ref. LV-62; H5-91.*

ZIG-ZAG BAND, pitcher. Made during the 1870s in extended table service. *Ref. K4-10.*

WIGWAM (TEEPEE), pitcher. Iowa Glass Co., late 1880s. Extended table service. Crystal. Has tiny Maltese crosses between the "wigwams." *Ref. K8-11; Gob I-23.*

THUMBPRINT AND DIAMOND, goblet. *Ref. K7-70.*

RUBY, creamer. LaBelle Glass Co., 1878. Extended table service. Crystal. *Ref. K3-102.*

DART, creamer. Made ca. 1880 in extended table service. *Ref. K3-4; Jenks p. 166; Schroy-47; Metz 1-216.*

ZIG-ZAG (MITRED BARS; MITRED DIAMOND POINTS), salt shaker. Bryce Brothers #126, 1880s; U. S. Glass Co., ca. 1898; McKee Brothers, 1900. Extended table service including wine, cordial. Crystal, amber. *Ref. K2-33; Gob I-68; W-130; Metz 1-172; Unitt 1-292; Unitt 2-158; H5-80.*

RIBBON BAND WITH PENDANTS, goblet. *Ref. Gob II-60; Metz 2-126.*

STIPPLED DIAMOND BAND, goblet. *Ref. L-164 #8; Metz 2-146.*

DOYLE, goblet. Doyle and Company, ca. 1870s; U. S. Glass Co., ca. 1891. *Ref. K7 Pl. 14.*

Sanborn

Zig-Zag Band

Wigwam

*Thumbprint
and Diamond*

Ruby

Dart

Zig-Zag

*Ribbon Band
with Pendants*

*Stippled
Diamond
Band*

Doyle

PLATE 61. DIAMONDS

LEAF AND DART, pitcher and celery vase. Richards and Hartley Glass Co., 1875; U. S. Glass Co., 1891. Extended table service including finger lamp, wine, cordial, master salt, rare cruet. *Ref. L-149; Welker p. 235, 244, 403; Jenks p. 318; K1-11; LEAPG-440; Schroy-87; Metz 1-178.*

ARABESQUE, pitcher. Bakewell, Pears and Co., 1860s. Extended table service. Crystal. *Ref. L-155; LEAPG-471; K1-10; Metz 1-180; Schroy-6.*

LOOP AND DART (PRIDE), goblet. Boston and Sandwich; Richards and Hartley; Portland; 1860s. Extended table service including egg cup, rare 6" plate, wine, cordial. *Ref. L-148; Gob I-42; K8-4; LEAPG-435; Metz 1-178; Schroy-91; Jenks p. 337.*

DOUBLE LOOP AND DART, goblet. *Ref. L-148; LEAPG-440; Metz 1-178.*

SHIELD AND SPIKE, goblet. *Ref. Gob II-22; Metz 2-116.*

TIDY (STAYMAN; DRAPERY VARIANT; RUSTIC), creamer. McKee and Brothers, 1880. Extended table service. *Ref. Gob II-68; K4-22; Metz 1-134.*

DOUBLE LOOP (STIPPLED DOUBLE LOOP), creamer. Made in the 1880s in extended table service including wine. *Ref. L-101; LEAPG-441; Metz 1-178; Unitt 2-26.*

LOOP AND DART WITH DIAMOND ORNAMENT (LOOP AND JEWEL), tumbler. Boston and Sandwich; Richards and Hartley; Portland; 1860s. Extended table service including wine, cordials. *Ref. L-148; Gob I-41; Jenks p. 339; Metz 1-178; Unitt 1-150; Schroy-92.*

LOOP AND DART WITH ROUND ORNAMENT (LOOP AND JEWEL), footed tumbler. Boston and Sandwich; Richards and Hartley; Portland Glass Co., ca. 1869. Extended table service including egg cup, butter pat, cordials, wine, champagne. *Ref. L-149; Gob I-142; Jenks p. 338; Metz 1-178; Unitt 1-150; Schroy-92.*

Leaf and Dart (two views)   *Arabesque*

Loop and Dart   *Double Loop
and Dart*   *Shield and
Spike*   *Tidy*

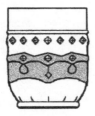

Double Loop   *Loop and Dart
with Diamond
Ornament*   *Loop and Dart
with Round
Ornament*

PLATE 62. DIAMONDS

DIAGONAL BAND WITH FAN (GREEK), goblet. Ripley & Co., 1880s; U. S. Glass Co. (Ripley), 1891. Extended table service including wine, cordial, champagne. Crystal. *Ref. L-156; Gob I-140; Metz 1-172; Unitt 1-292.*

JACOB'S COAT, creamer. Extended table service including berry set. Crystal, amber. *Ref. L-115; LEAPG-515; Metz 2-112.*

COARSE ZIG-ZAG (HIGHLAND), pitcher. Bryce, Higbee and Co., 1908; New Martinsville Glass Co., 1917. Extended table service including wine, plate, berry set. Crystal, ruby-stained. *Ref. K2-28; PetSal 157; H7-10.*

HERRINGBONE, creamer. Made ca. 1890s in extended table service including wine. *Gob 1-82; Metz 1-176; LEAPG-543; K7-75.*

LACY SPIRAL (COLOSSUS), pitcher. Made in the 1880s in extended table service. *Ref. K4-57; Metz 1-176.*

MAYPOLE (SILVER SHEEN; SCROLL AND DOTS), pitcher. National Glass Co. (McKee factory), 1901. Made in extended table service including wine. *Ref. K2-126; Gob I-102; Unitt 2-130; H6-69.*

JACOB'S LADDER (MALTESE), goblet. Bryce, Walker and Co., 1876; U. S. Glass Co., 1891. Extended table service including wine, cordials, open salt, rare mug. Some pieces were reproduced ca. 1988 in red and green. Crystal; rare in amber, blue, vaseline, amethyst-stained. *Ref. K1-20; Metz 1-140; Mugs p. 80; H5-33, 85; H6-32; Jenks p. 297; Schroy-83; LEAPG-344.*

SMOOTH DIAMOND (DOUBLE ICICLE; EARLY DIAMOND; OPPOSING ICICLE; DOUBLE BLAZE), goblet. Indiana Tumbler and Goblet Co., ca. 1880s. Extended table service including wine. *Ref. Gob 2-74; Metz 1-533; Unitt 2-112; K8-20.*

PANELLED DIAMONDS AND ROSETTES, goblet. *Ref. Gob II-61; Metz 2-126.*

ENGLISH HOBNAIL AND THUMBPRINT, creamer. Extended table service including flared fruit bowl. *Ref. L-14; LEAPG-279; Metz 2-102.*

Diagonal Band
with Fan

Jacob's Coat

Coarse Zig-Zag

Herringbone

Lacy Spiral

Maypole

Jacob's Ladder   Smooth Diamond

Panelled
Diamonds
and Rosettes

English Hob-
nail and
Thumbprint

PLATE 63. DIAMONDS

FAN AND FEATHER, salt shaker. *Ref. PetSal 160M.*

TEASEL (SHORT TEASEL), plate. Bryce Brothers #87, 1880s; U. S. Glass Co., 1891. Extended table service including wine. *Ref. L-96; LEAPG-300, 418; Gob I-92; Metz 1-68; Unitt 1-208.*

TEXAS (LOOPS WITH STIPPLED PANELS), cruet. U. S. Glass Co. #15067 (Ripley; Bryce), 1900. A State Series pattern. Extended table service including wine, rare ruby-stained. There are reproductions in colors, so beware. *Ref. K2-58; H1-48; H5-173; H7-201; Jenks p. 509; Schroy-141; Metz 1-212.*

QUILTED FAN TOP (DIAMOND WITH DUAL FAN), salt shaker and goblet. Extended table service including 10" plate, wine. *Ref. PetSal 162S; Metz 2-160; Gob II-56.*

CZARINA, pitcher. Fostoria Glass Co. #444, 1895. Made in extended table service including vases, berry sets. Crystal, ruby-stained. *Ref. K1-101; K5-91; H1-28; H5-43; H7-136; Jenks p. 307.*

PINEAPPLE AND FAN (HOLBROOK; SHEPHERD'S PLAID; CUBE WITH FAN; PSEUDO-CZARINA; CUBE AND DIAMOND; DIAMOND BLOCK AND FAN; MILTON CUBE AND FAN), creamer. Adams and Co., 1880s; U. S. Glass Co. #15041 (Gillinder; Adams), 1894 – 1910. Extended table service. The "Pineapple and Fan" version has 5-rayed fans; "Holbrook" has 7-rayed fans. Crystal, ruby-stained, emerald green. This pattern must have been named by just about everyone who wrote about pattern glass. The creamer sold for $1.50 per dozen in 1909. *Ref. K3-79; K4-68; K5-60; Gob II-84; Metz 1-212; Unitt 1-124; Schroy-111; Mugs p. 78; H5-143; H7-201.*

KENTUCKY, salt shaker and goblet. U. S. Glass Co. #15051 (King), 1897. A State Series pattern. Extended table service including wine. Crystal, emerald green, cobalt blue (scarce). A very similar pattern but without the diamond point is MILLARD (Plate 163), also made by U. S. Glass. Crystal, ruby-stained. *Ref. K4-68; LV-39; HI-28; H5-43; H7-136; Jenks p. 307; Schroy-85.*

Fan and Feather   *Teasel*

Texas

Quilted Fan Top (two views)   *Czarina*

Pineapple and Fan   *Kentucky (two views)*

PLATE 64. DIAMONDS

HOBBS DIAMOND AND SUNBURST, pitcher. Hobbs, Brockunier, 1880. Extended table service. Crystal. However, the Bredehofts believe this pattern does not meet the quality of Hobbs pieces, and that Kamm's identification is mistaken. *Ref. K3-22; Hobbs p. 165.*

EDGERTON, goblet. *Ref. Gob II-67; Metz 2-172.*

DIAMOND AND SUNBURST, EARLY, plate. Made ca. 1864 in extended table service including egg cup, wine. *Ref. L-12.*

ILEX, goblet. *Ref. Gob II-104; Metz 2-104.*

PITTSBURGH FAN, goblet. Extended table service. *Ref. Gob II-47; Metz 2-166.*

DIAMONDS WITH DOUBLE FANS, goblet. Indiana Glass Co., ca. 1907 in extended table service. Crystal, ruby-stained. *Ref. Gob II-88; H7-105.*

ST. BERNARD, creamer. See Plate 5.

DIAMOND SUNBURST, plate and pitcher. Made ca. 1860s in extended table service including lamp, wine, egg cup, decanter. *Ref. L-78.*

TARENTUM'S VIRGINIA (MANY DIAMONDS), compote. Tarentum Glass Co., 1894. Made in extended table service of some 44 pieces including wine, cordial. Crystal, green, ruby-stained. *Ref. K6 Pl. 73; Metz 1-228; H7-211+.*

*Hobbs Diamond
and Sunburst*

Edgerton

*Diamond and
Sunburst,
Early*

Ilex

*Pittsburgh
Fan*

*Diamonds
w/Double
Fans*

St. Bernard

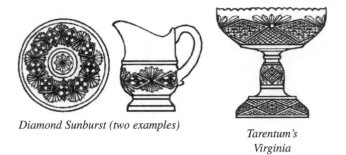

Diamond Sunburst (two examples)

*Tarentum's
Virginia*

PLATE 65. DIAMONDS

DIAMOND MIRROR, spooner. Fostoria Glass Co., 1880s. Made in extended table service. Crystal. *Ref. Gob II-53; Metz 2-148.*

BELMONT DIAMOND, cruet. Belmont Glass Co., ca. 1885. Only cruet known. *Ref. HIII-54.*

BOLING, goblet and plate. U. S. Glass Co. (Bryce), 1891. Extended table service. *Ref. Gob II-138; Metz 1-156.*

TACOMA (JEWELLED DIAMOND AND FAN), cruet. Greensburg Glass Co., 1894; Model Flint Glass Co. #907, 1900 – 1903; McKee. Extended table service including jam jar, decanter, wine. Crystal, ruby-stained. *Ref. K6 Pl. 46; H6-44; H7-200; Jenks p. 504; Schroy-139.*

DOUBLE FAN, pitcher. Dalzell, Gilmore and Leighton, ca. 1890. Extended table service. *Ref. K1-39; H5-90; Metz 2-148.*

CAVITT (MIKADO FAN), pitcher. Jones, Cavitt and Co. #128, 1887; Bryce Brothers, 1889; U. S. Glass, 1891. Extended table service including tray, wine, pickle jar. *Ref. K5-143; Gob I-128; Metz 2-148; Unitt 1-280.*

DIAMONDS AND CROSSBARS, goblet. *Ref. Gob II-13.*

BELMONT'S REFLECTING FANS (BLOCKADE), cruet. McKee; Belmont; ca. 1885. Only cruet known. *Ref. HIII-54.*

KING'S CURTAIN, pitcher. Made in the 1880s in extended table service including wine. *Ref. Gob I-90; Metz 1-156; Unitt 1-281.*

CHALLINOR DOUBLE FAN, creamer. U. S. Glass Co. (Challinor #305), 1891. Extended table service. *Ref. LV-57; H5-90.*

Diamond
Mirror

Belmont
Diamond

Boling (two examples)

Tacoma

Double Fan

Cavitt

Diamonds and
Crossbars

Belmont's
Reflecting
Fans

King's Curtain

Challinor
Double Fan

PLATE 66. DIAMONDS

SPIDER FANS, wine. Known in wine goblets *(author's name)*. Courtesy of Bob Burford.

FEDERAL #1608 (CO-OP #295), wine. Co-operative Flint Glass Co., 1900; Federal Glass Co., ca. 1914. *Ref. HGC4 p. 20; Welker p. 342.*

PILGRIM, pitcher. National Glass Co.; McKee, ca. 1901. Extended table service. This pattern is identical to MAJESTIC (below) except for poorer quality of glass, and the shape of pieces. Some pieces were interchangeable with MAJESTIC. Crystal, ruby-stained. *Ref. K5-27; HCG1 p. 86; H7-147, 172.*

MARYLAND (LOOP AND DIAMOND; LOOP AND FAN; INVERTED LOOPS AND FAN), pitcher. U. S. Glass Co. #15049 (Bryce), 1897. A State Series pattern made in extended table service including wine, cup, bread plate, two types salt shaker. Crystal, ruby-stained. *Ref. K1-60; Metz 1-154; Gob I-139; H7-149; Jenks p. 356; Schroy-96.*

MAJESTIC KIN, salt shaker. *Ref. PetSal 165S.*

PARACHUTE (RABBIT TRACKS), pitcher. McKee Glass Co., ca. 1901. Extended table service. *Ref. K4-130.*

RIVERSIDE (DARBY), pitcher. Riverside Glass Co., ca. 1897. Extended table service including berry set; a goblet would be rare. Crystal, vaseline. *Ref. K8-35; LV-37.*

MAJESTIC (DIVIDED BLOCK WITH SUNBURST; CUBE AND DOUBLE FAN; PURITAN), pitcher. McKee and Brothers Glass Co., National factory, 1893; Cambridge Glass Co. #669, 1903 (not U. S. Glass as once believed). See note on PILGRIM (above). Extended table service. Crystal, purple slag, ruby-stained, rare green, cobalt, yellow-green. *Ref. K2-71; K6 Pl. 70; Gob II-159; Unitt 2-131; Mugs p. 101; HI-30; HIII-32; H6-34, 68, 78; H7-147+.*

HEISEY'S PINEAPPLE AND FAN, mug. A. H. Heisey Glass Co. #1255, ca. 1897 – 1907. Extended table service including water jug, rose bowl. Crystal, green, gilded, scarce ruby-stained. *Ref. K2-93; K7-136; H1-36, 56; H2-70, 81; H4-41; H6-37; H7-172; Jenks p. 405; Schroy-111; Mugs p. 88.*

PRINCETON, salad bowl. McKee Glass Co., ca. 1886. Extended table service including wine. Crystal, ruby-stained. *Ref. PetPat 188; HGC1 p. 3.*

TARENTUM'S ATLANTA (SHINING DIAMONDS; ROYAL CRYSTAL; DIAMOND AND TEARDROP), pitcher. Tarentum Glass Co., 1894. extended table service including wine, cordial, cologne bottle. Crystal, ruby-stained. *Ref. K5-78; K6-31; LV-57; Gob I-165; Metz 2-144; Jenks p. 456; Mugs p. 79; H7-200.*

Spider Fans

Federal #1608

Pilgrim

Maryland

Majestic Kin

Parachute

Riverside

Majestic

Heisey's Pineapple and Fan

Princeton

Tarentum's Atlanta

PLATE 67. DIAMONDS

CAMBRIDGE #2504, butter dish. Cambridge Glass Co., 1910 – 1915. Courtesy of Bob Burford.

SHEAF AND DIAMOND, bowl. Bryce, Higbee and Co., ca. 1905. Extended table service including wine. *Ref. Metz 2-172; Gob I-128; Unitt 1-279; HCG1-89.*

ANTWERP, goblet. *Ref. Gob II-118; Metz 2-172.*

DIAMOND AND SUNBURST ZIPPERS (DIAMOND AND SUNBURST VARIANT), creamer. U. S. Glass Co. #15018, 1893. Extended table service including square bowl. Crystal, ruby-stained. *Ref. K6 Pl. 30; H5-164; H7-104.*

JABOT, pitcher. *Ref. K8-27.*

FINECUT AND BLOCK, cordial. King, Son and Co. #25, 1890; Model Flint Glass Co.; U. S. Glass Co., 1891. Extended table service including lamp, wines, cordial, champagnes, claret. Crystal, amber-stained, sapphire blue; canary, painted, stained blocks. *Ref. K1-42; L-161; Unitt 1-294; Gob I-28; Metz 1-160; Jenks p. 209; LEAPG-525; Mugs p. 80; H5-52.*

GRATED DIAMOND AND SUNBURST, creamer. George Duncan and Sons #20, ca. 1895. Extended table service including individual salt dip, water bottle. Crystal. *Ref. K1-105; Mugs p. 78.*

DIAMOND AND SUNBURST, creamer. Bryce, Walker and Co., 1894. Made in extended table service. Crystal, ruby-stained. *Ref. K1-12, 105; K3-94; Metz 1-192; LEAPG-557; Metz 1-192; Jenks p. 182; Schroy-50; H7-104.*

Cambridge #2504

Sheaf and Diamond

Antwerp

*Diamond and
Sunburst
Zippers*

Jabot

*Finecut and
Block*

*Grated Diamond
and Sunburst*

*Diamond and
Sunburst*

PLATE 68. DIAMONDS

SHEAF AND BLOCK (FICKLE BLOCK; ALDEN), goblet. Co-operative Flint Glass Co., 1893. Extended table service. Crystal, ruby-stained. *Ref. Gob II-88; K6-16; Revi p. 129; Metz 2-172; H7-66, 116, 192, 238.*

WESTMORELAND'S PRISCILLA, creamer. Westmoreland Glass Co. #15, ca. 1890. *Ref. HGC1 p. 87.*

OKLAHOMA, sugar bowl and creamer. Imperial Glass Co. 3281A. Crystal, carnival glass. Tumblers in this pattern were found in their original box marked with the logo of a Mexican firm. They may have been made by Imperial for export, or the molds themselves sold. *Ref. HGC3 p. 45.*

DIAMOND FAN, toy creamer. Made in extended table service in milk glass including punch cup. The milk glass toy creamer shown is in a time capsule in Paducah, Kentucky, due to be opened in the next century *Ref. Author.*

PANELLED DIAMOND BLOCKS (QUARTERED BLOCK), creamer. George Duncan and Sons #24, 1894. Extended table service including wine, champagne, ice tub. Crystal, ruby-stained. *Ref. K3-96; K6 Pl. 56; Gob II-146; Metz 2-172; Unitt 2-52; Jenks p. 426; H7-39, 108, 167.*

FAN WITH SPLIT DIAMOND, creamer. Made ca. 1885 in extended table service including vase, toy table set, cordial, pickle dish. *Ref. K2-54.*

FLATTENED DIAMOND AND SUNBURST, creamer. Made ca. 1890 in extended table service. *Ref. K2-80.*

FEDERAL'S IMPERIAL, creamer. Federal Glass Co., ca. 1914. Extended table service. *Ref. HGC4 p. 20.*

MELROSE (DIAMOND BEADED BAND), etched creamer. Bryce, Walker & Co., 1887; Greensburg Glass Co., 1889; McKee Brothers, 1901; J. B. Higbee Co., 1907; Northwood Glass Co., 1915; New Martinsville Glass Co., 1916. Extended table service including tray, finger bowl. Crystal, ruby-stained. *Ref. K3-128; K8-164; Metz 2-134; H7-13, 57, 149; Jenks p. 355; Schroy-99.*

Sheaf and Block *Westmoreland's Priscilla*

Oklahoma (two views)

Diamond Fan *Panelled Diamond Blocks* *Fan with Split Diamond*

Flattened Diamond and Sunburst *Federal's Imperial* *Melrose*

147

PLATE 69. DIAMONDS

CHAMPION (SEAGIRT; FAN WITH CROSSBARS; GREENTOWN #11; DIAMOND AND LONG SUNBURST), goblet. McKee Glass Co., 1896; Indiana Tumbler and Goblet; 1894 – 1917. Extended table service including decanter, carafe, tray, wine set. Crystal, ruby-stained. *Ref. K1-106; Gob II-113; Metz 1-228; HI-17; H4-18; H6-22; H7-89; Jenks p. 114; Schroy-34.*

PANAMA (FINE CUT BAR; VIKING), pitcher. U. S. Glass Co. #15088, 1904. Extended table service including wine. Crystal, but a milk glass wine is known; courtesy of John Gregory. *Ref. K2-49; Metz 1-220; Gob I-142; Schroy-107; Mugs p. 91; H5-179.*

PLEATED OVAL, creamer. New Martinsville Glass Co. #700, ca. 1910. Extended table service. *Ref. K8-34.*

NAPOLEON, bowl. McKee Brothers, 1896. Extended table service. *Ref. K-6 Pl. 61.*

FEDERAL #102, tumbler. Federal Glass Co., 1914. Extended table service including two sizes of tumblers. *Ref. HGC5 p. 41.*

HICKMAN (EMPIRE; LA CLEDE), creamer. McKee and Brothers, 1894 – 1904; Federal Glass Co., 1914. Extended table service including three types of salt shaker, toy condiment set, wine, cordial, champagne. crystal, green, rare ruby-stained. *Ref. Gob I-57; Metz 1-214; Unitt 1-308; Schroy-73; HI-46; HIII-55; H7-129.*

JOSEPHINE'S FAN, open salt. Robinson Glass Co.; Cambridge Glass Co., ca. 1900 – 1903. Extended table service including cracker jar, mustard pot. *Ref. Salts p. 135.*

BEADED FAN (DEWDROP AND FAN), pitcher. Made 1875 – 1880 in extended table service. *Ref. K1-65; HII-62.*

TEPEE (NEMESIS; WIGWAM; ARIZONA), spoon holder. George Duncan and Sons #28; U. S. Glass Co., 1897. Extended table service including wine, cordial, champagne, claret, rare green toothpick holder, rare covered cheese dish. *Ref. K2-78; Gob II-128; Unitt 1-306; HI-50; Jenks p. 508; Metz 1-154.*

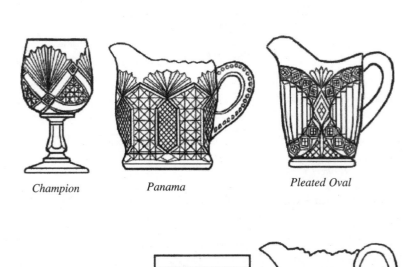

Champion   Panama   Pleated Oval

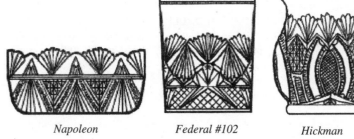

Napoleon   Federal #102   Hickman

Josephine's Fan   Beaded Fan   Tepee

PLATE 70. DIAMONDS

MALVERN (IMPERIAL #9; PECORAH), pitcher. Imperial Glass Co., 1904. Extended table service including cracker jar, pickle jar, wine, bottle, sugar shaker, egg cup. *Ref. K7-184; Gob I-150; Metz 2-178; Unitt 1-285; Batty-229.*

FEATHERED OVALS, creamer. *Ref. K7-13.*

BEAUTIFUL LADY, pitcher. Bryce, Higbee and Co., ca. 1905. Extended table service including wine, toy cake stand. Crystal, ruby-stained. *Ref. K2-47; H7-10; Jenks p. 59; Schroy-20.*

PERSIAN (CROWN AND SHIELD), salt shaker. Fostoria Glass Co. #576, 1897. Extended table service including claret, wine, cheese dish, finger bowl, carafe. *Ref. K7-35; Gob II-85; Unitt 1-296.*

NATIONAL'S EUREKA, creamer. National Glass Co., 1901. Extended table service. Crystal, ruby-stained. *Ref. K5-69; H7-15.*

MAGNA, salt shaker and creamer. Made in 1898 in extended table service including wine. Crystal, ruby-stained. *Ref. K7-36; Unitt 2-141; Revi-129; Welker p. 259; HI-39; H7-190.*

SCALLOPED SIX-POINT (DIVIDED MEDALLION WITH DIAMOND CUT), cup. George Duncan and Sons #30, 1897. Extended table service including two types toothpick holder, wine, carafe. Crystal, ruby-stained. *Ref. K7-125; HI-39; H7-190; Schroy-127; Jenks p. 468.*

CIRCLE X, open sugar bowl, author's name.

Malvern

*Feathered
Ovals*

*Beautiful
Lady*

Persian

*National's
Eureka*

Magna (two examples)

Scalloped Six-Point

Circle X

PLATE 71. DIAMONDS

NATIONAL STAR, pitcher. National Glass Co., 1900. Extended table service. Ruby-stained, vaseline, and crystal. *Ref. H6-70; H7-63+.*

DIAGONAL BAND (DIAGONAL BLOCK AND FAN), pitcher. Made in the 1880s in extended table service including wine. Crystal, apple green (scarce). In the stippled bands are small diamonds. *Ref. K1-140; K7-8; LEAPG-575; Gob II-71; Unitt 1-292; Jenks p. 176; Schroy-50.*

CROESUS, pitcher. See Plate 32.

BEACON LIGHT, salt shaker. Beatty-Brady Glass Co., ca. 1904. Extended table service. *Ref. PetSal 22B.*

INNA (CLASS ACT), tall celery. Paden City Glass Mfg. Co. #199, ca. 1915. Extended table service. Heacock named this pattern CLASS ACT, not realizing that it had been named INNA by Barnett in his Paden City book. Crystal, ruby-stained. *Ref. H6-92; H7-133.*

STERLING (PINWHEELS; BLAZING STAR), creamer. Westmoreland Glass Co., 1896; 1917. Extended table service including toy set, punch bowl and cups, wine. Crystal, ruby-stained. *Ref. K1-102; Metz 2-222; H7-296+.*

DUCHESS, toothpick holder and cruet. Riverside Glass Co., 1899. Extended table service. Crystal, emerald green, amethyst-flashed, opalescent. *Ref. HII-19; HIII-55; H6-26.*

BLOCKED THUMBPRINT, creamer. Made ca. 1870. Extended table service. *Ref. K8-9; Metz 2-24.*

SHOSHONE (BLAZING PINWHEELS; FLORAL DIAMOND; VICTOR), cruet. U. S. Glass Co., 1896 (#15046) (King, Glassport factories). Extended table service including claret jug, mustard jar, ice tub, punch bowl, wine. Crystal, ruby-stained. *Ref. K4-71; Gob II-88; Unitt 1-295; HI-140; HII-57; H5-50; H7-209.*

National Star

Diagonal
Band

Croesus

Beacon Light

Inna

Sterling

Duchess (two views)

Blocked
Thumbprint

Shoshone

VARIETY — that is what Pattern Glass offers, from colors, gilding, and staining to crystal and flint glass, and every motif imaginable. From top, PARIAN SWIRL and RED BLOCK; WILD ROSE WITH SCROLLING and WOODEN PAIL; and a PADDLEWHEEL bowl. All have charm and beauty unequaled in any other kind of glass.

The Chicago World's Fair of 1893 sold ruby-stained pattern glass with etching, often with the patron's name or souvenir Fair data. Ruby-stained glass is a delight to own and display. Shown are (left) SCALLOPED SWIRL, (upper right) NAIL, and (lower right) BLOCK AND ROSETTE.

PLATE 72. FACETS

Note: There is a very fine line between diamond and facet patterns. Diamond point patterns have all-over diamonds; in fine cut patterns, the diamonds are intersected into facets. "Mirror Star" and "Sandwich Star" are examples of fine cut on a large scale.

GREEK CROSS BAND, goblet. Known in goblet and wine. *Ref. Gob II-53; Metz 1-121; Metz 2-168.*

SANDWICH STAR, spill holder. Boston and Sandwich Glass Co., 1850. Extended table service including wine, champagne, dolphin-based compote, cordial, decanter. All pieces are rare; the goblet is very rare. At the Green Valley Auction in Pittsburgh in 1998, a goblet sold for $1,500. Flint glass; crystal, amethyst (rare). *Ref. L-14; LEAPG-42; Gob I-74; Unitt 1-288; Metz 1-10; Jenks p. 461; Schroy-126.*

NEW ERA (ERA), pitcher. Bryce, Higbee and Co., mid 1880s to 1891. Extended table service including bread plate, honey dish, square olive jar, square plate, tray. Crystal, ruby-stained. *Ref. K8-64; H7-158.*

MIRROR STAR (OLD GLORY), pitcher. New Martinsville Glass Co., ca 1910 – 1915. Crystal, ruby-stained. *Ref. K4-138; H7-153+.*

GROGAN, goblet. Extended table service including wine. *Ref. L-164 #10; Gob II-98; Metz 1-175.*

HANOVER (BLOCK WITH STARS; BLOCKHOUSE), mug. Richards and Hartley, 1888; U. S. Glass Co., 1891. Extended table service including cheese plate and cover, puff box with stars, wine. Crystal, amber, blue, canary. *Ref. K1-113; Metz 1-156; Gob I-133; Unitt 1-104; Jenks p. 261; Mugs p. 100; H5-40, 109.*

JASPER (ELEANOR; LATE BUCKLE; BELT BUCKLE), creamer. Bryce Brothers, 1880; U. S. Glass Co., 1891. Extended table service including open salt, wines. Called "Eleanor" in blue glass. *Ref. K2-13; L-72; Metz 1-222; Gob I-109; Unitt 1-153; H5-84.*

PANELLED DIAMOND CROSS (PRISM AND DAISY BAR), goblet. U. S. Glass Co., 1891. Extended table service including wine. This pattern is part of the HEAVY PANELLED FINE CUT group. *Ref. K2-24; Gob I-128; Metz 1-174; Metz 2-160; Unitt 1-243; H5-105; Jenks p. 300.*

NEWPORT, sauce and pitcher. U. S. Glass Co. (Richards and Hartley #65), 1891. This pattern was known only in pitchers, but Bob Burford has found a matching sauce. More pieces are probably out there, well worth collecting. Crystal, ruby-stained, etched. *Ref. H5-118; H7-84+.*

Greek Cross
Band

Sandwich
Star

New Era

Mirror Star

Grogan

Hanover

Jasper

Panelled Diamond Cross

Newport (two examples)

PLATE 73. FACETS, FINE CUT

STAR AND FEATHER, goblet. *Ref. L-135; LEAPG-529; Metz 1-117.*

ACANTHUS SCROLL, creamer. U. S. Glass #15036, 1895. Extended table service. Crystal. *Ref. K5-105.*

FINE CUT AND RIB, pitcher. Probably Doyle and Co. *Ref. Kamm.* Extended table service. *Ref. K6-60.*

HARTLEY (DAISY AND BUTTON WITH OVAL PANELS; DAISY AND CUBE WITH OVAL PANELS; PANELLED DIAMOND CUT AND FAN), etched pitcher. Richards and Hartley #900, 1888; U. S. Glass Co., 1891. Extended table service including bread plate, platter, wine. Crystal, amber, canary, blue. *Ref. K1-69; LV-42; Gob I-34; Unitt 1-156; Metz 1-222; H5-110; Jenks p. 254; Schroy-70.*

SQUARED FINE CUT, pitcher. Jones, Cavitt and Co., 1886. *Ref. K5-32.*

GOTHIC WINDOWS (GOTHIC ARCH; SILVER BAND), creamer. Indiana Glass Co. #166, ca. 1920s. Extended table service including wine. *Ref. K1-112; Gob II-116; Metz 2-178.*

PANELLED FINE CUT, salt shaker. Extended table service. *Ref. PetSal 161A.*

VALENCIA WAFFLE (BLOCK AND STAR; HEXAGONAL BLOCK), syrup. Adams and Co. #85, 1885; U. S. Glass Co., 1891. Extended table service including rectangular bowls, pickle jar, wine. Crystal, blue, amber, apple green, ruby-stained. *Ref. K1-43; Gob I-71; Metz 1-164; Unitt 1-300; HIII-44; H5-71; H7-78+; Jenks p. 535; Schroy-149.*

BEADED FINE CUT, pitcher. Dalzell, Gilmore and Leighton. Extended table service. *Ref. K3-45.*

Star and Feather

*Acanthus
Scroll*

*Fine Cut and
Rib*

Hartley (etched)

Squared Fine Cut

Gothic Windows

*Panelled
Fine Cut*

*Valencia
Waffle*

*Beaded
Finecut*

159

PLATE 74. FACETS, FINE CUT

SIX PANEL FINE CUT (DAISY WITH AMBER STRIPES; D & B WITH CLEAR STRIPE), syrup. Extended table service including wine. Crystal, amber-stained, ruby-stained. *Ref. Smith-72; Gob II-66; HGC1 p. 16; HIII-41; H7-194.*

McKEE'S COMET, pitcher. McKee and Brothers, 1887. Extended table service including gas globe. *Ref. K4-13.*

HEAVY PANELLED FINECUT (SEQUOIA; PARAGON; PANELLED DIAMOND CROSS; DORIC; BAG WARE), tumbler and creamer. Adams and Co., 1880s; U. S. Glass Co. (Duncan #800), 1891. Extended table service including wine set, claret, champagne, cordial, finger bowls, tray, decanter, pickle jar, straight and flared spooner, canoe-shaped bowl. Only some of the pieces are panelled; those that are not are called "Sequoia." A U. S. Glass Co. catalog shows both this pattern and "Heavy Fine Cut" (Plate 75) pieces as the same pattern, #800. Crystal, blue, amber, vaseline, ruby-stained. *Ref. K2-24; Mugs p. 78; HIII-74; H6-67; H7-168; Metz 2-160; Schroy-73.*

TINY FINECUT (PARISIAN), goblet. U. S. Glass Co., 1900. Made in wine set only in crystal, emerald green, ruby-stained. *Ref. Gob II-134; Metz 2-134; H5-45, 49; H7-202.*

WATERFALL, pitcher. O'Hara Glass Co., 1880s. Extended table service. Crystal, light blue, canary. *Ref. K5-125.*

FEATHER (FINE CUT AND FEATHER; INDIANA SWIRL; SWIRL; DORIC; CAMBRIDGE FEATHER; FEATHER AND QUILL; FEATHER SWIRL; PRINCE'S FEATHER), syrup. McKee and Brothers, 1896 – 1905; Cambridge Glass Co., 1902. Extended table service including wine, champagne, square sauce, cordial. Crystal, green, amber, red, chocolate, ruby-stained. *Ref. K1-73; LV-57; Gob I-30; Metz 1-140; K4-105; Jenks p. 202; Schroy-57; HI-22; HIII-23; H5-23, 84; H7-116.*

PANELLED STRAWBERRY CUT (PANELLED DIAMOND), spoon holder. Extended table service.

*Six Panel
Fine Cut*

*McKee's
Comet*

Heavy Panelled Fine Cut (two examples)

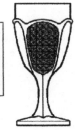
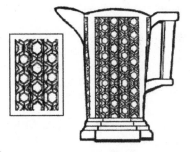

*Tiny Finecut and
enlargement*

*Waterfall and
enlargement*

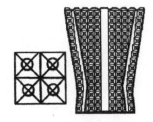

Feather and enlargement

*Panelled Strawberry Cut
and enlargement*

PLATE 75. FACETS, FINE CUT

AETNA #300, creamer. Aetna Glass and Mfg. Co., 1886. *Ref. K5-55.*

OREGON (BEADED LOOP; BEADED OVALS), goblet and pitcher. U. S. Glass Co. #15053 (Bryce), 1907. A State Series pattern made in extended table service including wine, cordial. Crystal, rare green, rare ruby-stained. *Ref. K8-163; LV-44; H5-164; H7-165; Jenks p. 391; Metz 1-154; Metz 2-156; Mugs p. 62.*

CATHEDRAL (ORION), creamer. Bryce Brothers, 1880s; U. S. Glass Co. (Bryce), 1891. Extended table service including wine, rounded pitcher, cordial. The "Cathedral" creamer, rather short and squat, is called WAFFLE AND FINE CUT and lacks the arched portion that gave this pattern its name. Crystal, amber, blue, amethyst, canary, ruby-stained (only by U. S. Glass.) *Ref. K1-19; K2-98; Metz 1-158; Gob I-18; LEAPG-499; Mugs p. 101; H5-49, 51; H6-21; H7-27.*

HEAVY FINECUT (BAG WARE), celery vase. George Duncan and Sons, ca. 1885; U. S. Glass Co., 1891. Extended table service including individual butter, finger bowl. Crystal, amber blue, vaseline. This pattern and "Heavy Panelled Fine Cut" on Plate 74 are shown as part of the #800 pattern in a U. S. Glass Co. catalog. *Ref. K2-24; H5-102; H6-18.*

TWO PANEL (DAISY IN PANEL; DAISY IN SQUARE), pitcher. Richards and Hartley #25, 1880s; U. S. Glass Co., 1891. Extended table service including lamp, wine set, cordial set. The "daisies" are a smaller version of Heavy Fine Cut. Crystal, apple green, amber, blue, canary. *Ref. L-159; LEAPG-499; K3-45; Gob I-53; Metz 1-158; Unitt 2-114; Jenks p. 531; Schroy-147; Mugs p. 101.*

FLATTENED FINE CUT, pitcher. Extended table service. Has horizontal ridges on the front of the pitcher (see arrow). *Ref. K2-24.*

FINECUT (FLOWER IN SQUARE), creamer. Bryce Brothers, 1870s; U. S. Glass Co., 1891. Extended table service including tray, finger bowl, wine, lamps. Crystal, amber, blue, vaseline, canary. *Ref. K8-21; Metz 1-160; Unitt 1-262; Jenks p. 208; LEAPG-510.*

Aetna #300   Oregon (two examples)

Cathedral

Heavy Finecut

Two Panel

Flattened Fine Cut   Finecut and enlargement

PLATE 76. DAISY AND BUTTON

DAISY AND BUTTON OVAL MEDALLION (OVAL PANELLED DAISY AND BUTTON; PANELLED DAISY; DAISY AND BUTTON WITH RIMMED PANEL; DAISY AND BUTTON WITH SCROLL PANEL), spooner. Cooperative Flint Glass Co., 1880s. Extended table service including wine. Crystal. *Ref. L-154-3; K4-44; Gob II-98; Metz 1-222; Mugs p. 83.*

PANELLED DAISY AND BUTTON (ELLROSE), spooner. U. S. Glass Co. (Richards and Hartley), 1891. Extended table service. Crystal, ruby, amber and blue stained, amber, vaseline, blue. *Ref. K1-80; H5-50, 104; H7-110.*

CLOVER (R & H), spooner. Richards and Hartley Glass Co., 1880s; U. S. Glass Co., 1891. Extended table service. Crystal, emerald green, ruby-stained. Do not confuse with Duncan's "Clover" on Plate 78. *Ref. K4-98; H5-117; H7-110.*

DAISY AND BUTTON WITH THIN BARS, pitcher. U. S. Glass Co. (Gillinder), 1891. Note: the tumblers lack the thin bars. Crystal, vaseline. *Ref. H5-124.*

DAISY AND BUTTON, cup. Hobbs, Brockunier; Gillander; U. S. Glass Co.; 1888; ca. 1891. Made in extended table service including many novelities such as slippers, wine, canoes, and vases. Crystal, ruby-stained (red dots). Hobbs used colors of old gold, sapphire, marine green, canary, amberina, ruby. Hobbs' pattern was almost identical to that of Gillinder and Sons except that Hobbs used glass finials and Gillinder, metal ones; Hobbs' set was round, Gillinder's, oval. Although many companies made versions of Daisy and Button, there are perhaps more reproductions than the real glass around. Try to learn the difference between the old and new, or pay a minimum price. *Ref. L-169; K8-13; Metz 1-222; Hobbs p. 73, 168; HII-92; HIII-22; H5-102; H7-100+; Jenks p. 149; Schroy-43.*

AETNA, etched pitcher. Aetna Glass and Mfg. Co. #325, 1886. Made in water set: pitcher, tumblers, waste bowl, tray. *Ref. K5-130.*

LITTLE BAND, creamer. Made ca. 1880. *Ref. K2-40.*

DAISY AND BUTTON, mustard bottle. See above.

DAISY AND BUTTON WITH THUMBPRINT, tumbler. Adams and Co. #86, 1885; U. S. Glass Co., 1891. Extended table service including wine, champagne, claret. All colors made, ruby-stained. *Ref. K3-73; L-161; Metz 1-122; HIII-22; H5-33, 41, 52, 70; H7-101.*

DAISY AND BUTTON BAND, salt shaker. O'Hara Glass Co., ca. 1885. Extended table service. *Ref. K6-20.*

CLIO (DAISY AND BUTTON WITH ALMOND BAND), pitcher. U. S. Glass Co. (Challinor), 1891. Extended table service including bowls with fan corners. Crystal, blue, vaseline, green. *Ref. Metz 2-156; H5-89.*

164

D & B Oval Medallion

Panelled Daisy and Button

Clover

D and B with Thin Bars

Daisy and Button

Aetna

Little Band

Daisy and Button

D and B with Thumbprint

D and B Band

Clio

PLATE 77. FACETS, DAISY & BUTTON

BELMONT, sugar bowl. Belmont Glass Works #100, 1886. *Ref. K6-38; Metz 2-156.*

HOBBLESKIRT (RADIANT), pitcher. National Glass Co., 1901. *Ref. K5 Pl. 5.*

DAISY AND BUTTON PETTICOAT, etched creamer. Extended table service in clear and canary. *Ref. K6-54.*

DAISY AND BUTTON "V" (D & B WITH V ORNAMENT), tumbler. Beatty and Sons #555, 1885; U. S. Glass Co., 1892; Federal Glass Co., ca. 1914. Extended table service including wine (which may lack the "V".) Crystal, amber, blue, canary. *Ref. Gob II-73; L-161; Metz 1-223; HGC4 p. 18; Mugs p. 84.*

GLOBE AND STAR, creamer (engraved). Made ca. 1890 in extended table service. Crystal, colors. *Ref. K2-23.*

QUEEN (SUNK; POINTED PANEL; PANELLED DAISY AND BUTTON), pitcher. McKee and Brothers #2, 1894; and others. Extended table service including wine, claret. Crystal, canary, amber, apple green, blue, ruby-stained. *Ref. K3-38; Gob I-34; Metz 1-224; Jenks p. 427; Schroy-117; H7-110.*

DAISY AND BUTTON WITH CROSSBAR, POINTED, tumbler. Extended table service. *Ref. L-168.*

DAISY AND BUTTON WITH PRISMS, pitcher. Extended table service. *Ref. K7-22; Metz 1-225.*

DAISY AND BUTTON WITH CROSSBAR (MIKADO; DIAMOND AND THUMBPRINT CROSSBAR), cruet (rare). Burlington Glass Works, 1880s; Richards and Hartley #99, 1885; U. S. Glass Co., 1891. Extended table service including lamps, wine set, cordial, open and covered sugar bowls, tray. Crystal, amber, blue, yellow. *Ref. K3-53; L-167; Metz 1-222; Unitt 1-206; Gob I-129; Jenks p. 155; Schroy-44; Mugs p. 85; HIII-22; H5-39, 50, 112.*

Belmont *Hobbleskirt* *D and B Petticoat*

D and B "V" *Globe and Star* *Queen*

D and B with
Crossbar,
Pointed

D and B with
Prisms

D and B with
Crossbar

PLATE 78. FACETS

DUNCAN'S CLOVER, tumbler. Duncan & Miller Glass Co. #58, 1904; Union Stopper Co., 1911. Extended table service including wine, finger bowl. See "Clover" by Richards and Hartley on Plate 76. *Ref. K8-44; Metz 2-6.*

GREENSBURG'S PILLAR, pickle jar. Greensburg Glass Co. #42, 1880s. Extended table service including wine, banana stand. *Ref. K8-75.*

CURRIER AND IVES, decanter. See Plate 1.

KING'S BLOCK, cruet. King, Son & Co. #312, 1880; U. S. Glass Co., 1907. Extended table service including wine. Crystal, vaseline. *Ref. H5-132; H6-80; Revi-216.*

HEISEY'S SUNBURST, salt shaker. A. H. Heisey Glass Co. #343, 1904 – 1920. There is considerable variation in this line; two different creamers, and a line called #343½, are shown on Plates 96 and 104. The tumbler has large ovals just above the sunbursts, and the goblet has the sunbursts located in a circle. Extended table service including wine. Crystal, ruby-stained. *Ref. K7-50; H7-160.*

FUNNEL ROSETTE, pitcher. Made in the 1890s. *Ref. K2-129.*

CHECKERBOARD (BRIDLE ROSETTES; WESTMORELAND #500; BLOCK AND FAN; SQUARE BLOCK; OLD QUILT), pitcher. Westmoreland Glass Co., 1910. Extended table service including wine, ice tea. Crystal, ruby-stained. Reproduced in opaque white. "Bridle" refers to decorations on a horse's bridle, not a bride's bouquet. Note: Earlier researchers made a hash of this pattern. Kamm named it *Checkerboard* in K2-130. Metz showed a *Checkerboard* plate in Book 1 p. 218 and called it *Bridle Rosettes*, a name Millard had given it. Heacock called it *Bridal Rosettes* in Book III p. 84, and confused it with CAMBRIDGE RIBBON (below); he discussed its true identity in *The Glass Collector 1* p. 15. *Ref. K2-130; HGC1-15; H7-81, 157; Schroy-24; Metz 1-218.*

FLAT PANELLED STAR, salt shaker. *Ref. PetSal 173J.*

CAMBRIDGE RIBBON, creamer. Cambridge Glass Co. #2653, ca. 1908. Extended table service including cracker jar, trays, carafe, wine. Crystal, ruby-stained. The big difference between this pattern and CHECKERBOARD is that the "ribbons" are crossed over in this pattern and are plain on CHECKERBOARD. *Ref. H7-88; HPV6-20 (wrong name); HGC1-15 (discussion only).*

*Duncan's
Clover*

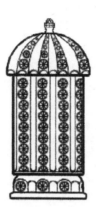

*Greensburg's
Pillar*

Currier and Ives

King's Block

*Heisey's
Sunburst*

Funnel Rosette

Checkerboard

Flat Panelled Star

Cambridge Ribbon

PLATE 79. FACETS

CANE COLUMN (PORTLAND; JEWEL; PANELLED CANE), pitcher. Portland Glass Co., 1870. Extended table service including wine. *Ref. K4-11; Gob I-32; Metz 1-158; Unitt 1-120; H4-55.*

SUNKEN BUTTONS (MITRED DIAMOND; PYRAMIDS), syrup. Made in the 1880s in extended table service including platter, wine, cordial, berry set. Crystal, vaseline, blue, canary, amber. *Ref. K4-129; LV-31; Gob II-35; Metz 1-216.*

FINE CUT AND PANEL, pitcher. Bryce Brothers, late 1880s; U. S. Glass Co. (Bryce #260), 1891. Extended table service including wine set, cordial, tobacco jar, platter. Crystal, amber, blue, canary, vaseline. *Ref. L-61; Gob I-89; Metz 1-160; Mugs p. 83; H5-49, 80.*

THREE PANEL, pitcher. Richards and Hartley Glass Co. #25, 1888; U. S. Glass Co., 1891. Extended table service including mug, tumbler. The alternating circles feature little "stars" (*). Crystal, amber, yellow, blue. *Ref. K3-115; L-96, 159; LEAPG-511; Metz 1-160; H5-113; Jenks p. 212; Mugs p. 65.*

TUXEDO, tumbler. Fostoria Glass Co. #1578, 1907. Extended table service including vase. *Ref. K6 Pl. 75.*

RAINBOW, pitcher. McKee and Brothers, 1898 – 1927+; Kemple Glass Co., 1951. Extended table service including carafe, cigar jar, wine sets. Marked "Pres-Cut." Crystal, ruby-stained, rose-pink, gilded. *Ref. K6-89; Mugs p. 83; H7-183.*

JEWEL, sugar bowl. King, Son and Co. Extended table service including wine. *Ref. Revi p. 219; Mugs p. 85.*

HEISEY'S PANELLED CANE, pitcher. A. H. Heisey #315, 1900 – 1904. Extended table service including wine, cordial. Crystal, ruby-stained. *Ref. K7-31; H4-55; H7-78.*

PANELLED CANE (BRILLIANT), creamer. Fostoria Glass Co., ca. 1901 – 1904. Extended table service including wine, scarce toothpick holder. *Ref. K1-96; K8 Pl. 99; Metz 1-158.*

Cane Column *Sunken Buttons* *Fine Cut and Panel*

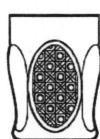

Three Panel   *Tuxedo*   *Rainbow*

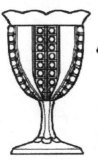

Jewel *Heisey's*   *Panelled Cane*
   Panelled
   Cane

PLATE 80. FACETS, BUTTONS

BEVELLED BUTTONS, pickle jar. U. S. Glass Co. (Duncan #320), 1891. Extended table service. Crystal, ruby-stained. *Ref. H5-99; H7-75.*

RED BLOCK (BLOCK; BARRELED BLOCK; AMBER BLOCK; GEM; MODEL GEM; HEXAGONAL BLOCK; DOUBLE RED BLOCK; CLEAR BLOCK), pitcher. Produced from about 1885 to 1907 by many companies: Fostoria Glass Co. #140, 1889; Model Flint Glass Works, 1893 – 1902; Bryce Brothers; Central Glass; Doyle and Co. #250; and U. S. Glass (Doyle version) in 1892 and 1898. It is very difficult to differentiate the various companies' patterns. Extended table service including mustard and saucer, lamp, wine set, round and rectangular bowls. Crystal, ruby-stained. *Ref. K1-105; K2-83; L-162; LEAPG-523; Mugs p. 84; Gob I-136; Gob II-93; Metz 1-165; HGC5-34; H7-121+; Jenks p. 432; Schroy-119.*

HEXAGONAL BLOCK BAND, pitcher. Made in about 1880 in extended table service. *Ref. K5-13.*

HENRIETTA (BIG BLOCK; DIAMOND BLOCK), creamer. U. S. Glass Co. (Columbia), 1891. Extended table service including individual creamer, mustard jar, sugar shaker, rose jar, wine. Crystal, ruby-stained. *Ref. K1-110; LV-70; Metz 1-210; Schroy-73; H5-128; H6-90; H7-127+.*

PANELLED HEXAGONS, jelly compote. McKee Glass Co., ca. 1886. *Ref. HGC1 p. 3.*

DIAMOND BLOCK WITH FAN (BLOCKADE), pitcher, U. S. Glass Co. (Challinor #309), 1891. Extended table service including finger bowl, wine. Crystal. *Ref. LV-65; Gob I-136; Metz 1-164; H5-93.*

OVERALL HOB, creamer. Westmoreland Glass Co. #444, ca. 1915. Extended table service. Crystal. *Ref. K5-13.*

BLOCK AND LATTICE (BIG BUTTON; RED BLOCK AND LATTICE; BLOCK AND STAR), pitcher. Pioneer Glass Co. #9, ca. 1891. Extended table service including cracker jar, wine. Crystal, ruby-stained. *Ref. K4-75; K8-172; Metz 2-144; Gob II-165; H7-76+.*

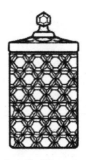

Bevelled Buttons

Red Block

*Hexagonal
Block Band*

Henrietta

*Panelled
Hexagons*

*Diamond Block
with Fan*

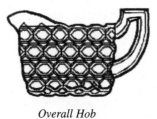

Overall Hob

Block and Lattice

173

PLATE 81. FACETS, BUTTONS

BUTTON AND BUTTON, creamer. Belleaire Goblet Co., ca. 1890. Extended table service *Ref. K1-96.*

NOVA SCOTIA DIAMOND, mug. Nova Scotia Glass Co.; Burlington Glass Works, 1880s. *Ref. Mugs p. 80.*

LACY DAISY, NEW MARTINSVILLE, mustard base (mug). J. B. Higbee Glass Co., 1908; New Martinsville after 1919. *Ref. Mugs p. 83.*

BLOCK AND TRIPLE BARS, goblet. *Ref. Gob II-88; Metz 1-161.*

LACY DAISY, creamer. U. S. Glass Co. #9525, 1918. Extended table service including jam jar, rose bowl, puff box, three-legged bowls, wine, individual salts, toy pieces. On some pieces the pattern runs diagonally in diamond shape. Crystal, color (scarce). *Ref. K2-73; Metz 1-86; Metz 2-62; H5-162.*

STRAWBERRY AND FAN VARIANT, pitcher. Fostoria Glass Co. #402, ca. 1900. *Ref. K5-139.*

ENGLISH CANE, salt shaker. McKee Brothers #98. *Ref. PetSal 156-i.*

DAISY-IN-SQUARE, creamer. U. S. Glass Co. (Duncan #330), 1891. Extended table service. *Ref. PetSal 158M.*

WHEELING BLOCK, creamer. Cambridge Glass Co., ca. 1904. Extended table service including candy tray. *Ref. K3-96.*

Button and Button

Nova Scotia Diamond

Lacy Daisy, New Martinsville

Block and Triple Bars

Lacy Daisy

Strawberry and Fan Variant

English Cane

Daisy-in-Square

Wheeling Block

PLATE 82. FACETS, CANE

BUTTON BLOCK, salt shaker. *Ref. PetSal 24D.*

FLUTE AND CANE (HUCKABEE), pitcher. Imperial Glass Co. #666, 1920s. Extended table service. *Ref. K2-72.*

CANE (McKEE HOBNAIL), pitcher. Boston and Sandwich; Gillinder and Sons; McKee and Brothers; 1875 – 1885. Extended table service including jam jar, water tray, finger bowl, wine, cordial, pickle dish, waste bowl. *Ref. L-132; LEAPG-509; Gob I-222; Metz 1-158; K3-39; Jenks p. 105; Schroy-31.*

CANE AND FAN, salt shaker. *Ref. PetSal 24G.*

CANE AND CABLE, salt shaker. *Ref. PetSal 24F.*

MANHATTAN, sauce. See Plate 12.

UNION (BULLS-EYE WITH DIAMOND POINT; OWL; BULLS-EYE DIAMOND), carafe. New England Glass Co., 1869. Extended table service including wines, cordials, champagne. *Ref. Gob I-161; Metz 1-12; Unitt 1-576; K3-100.*

CANE AND ROSETTE (JEWEL; FLOWER PANELLED CANE), goblet. George Duncan & Son, 1877; King, Son & Co., 1885; U. S. Glass, 1891. Extended table service including wine, cordial, champagne, claret. *Ref. LV p. 61; Gob II-162; Metz 1-159.*

SCROLL WITH CANE BAND, creamer. West Virginia Glass Co., 1895 – 1900. Extended table service. Crystal, ruby-stained. *Ref. K3-92; Metz 2-144; HIII-140+; H6-41; H7-5+.*

Button Block   *Flute and Cane*   *Cane*

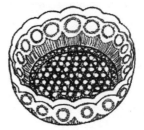

*Cane and
Fan*   *Cane and
Cable*   *Manhattan*

Union   *Cane and
Rosette*   *Scroll with
Cane Band*

177

PLATE 83. FACETS

RAINBOW VARIANT, salt shaker. Probably the same pattern as BUTTON PANEL below. *Ref. PetSal 36L.*

BUTTON PANEL WITH BARS, toothpick holder. Extended table service but scarce; toothpick holder is rare. Crystal, ruby-stained. *Ref. HI-16; H7-7.*

BUTTON PANEL (DIAMOND CRYSTAL; RAINBOW VARIANT), toothpick holder. Duncan #44, ca. 1900. Extended table service including toy service, wine. Crystal, ruby-stained. *Ref. PetPat 58; K5-60; HIII-54; H6-21+; H7-86+.*

SEDAN (PANELLED STAR AND BUTTON), pitcher. made ca. 1900 in extended table service including open and covered sugar bowls, wine. Crystal, rare purple slag. *Ref. K1-17; Gob II-19; Metz 1-174; Jenks p. 473; Schroy-129; Mugs p. 82.*

MASONIC (PRISM WITH DOUBLE BLOCK BAND; INVERTED PRISMS), creamer. U. S. Glass Co. #15100 (Gas City), 1907. Extended table service including wine. Crystal, emerald green (rare), ruby-stained. *Ref. K2-21; Gob II 84; Metz 2-158; H6-74; H7-149; Schroy-97.*

COARSE CUT AND BLOCK, creamer. Model Flint Glass Co., ca. 1890. Extended table service. *Ref. K1-110.*

BIG LEAF AND BUTTON, bowl. U. S. Glass Co. (Duncan #1002), 1891. Made in bowls only. Crystal, amber-stained. *Ref. H5-97.*

FINDLAY'S PILLAR, creamer. Findlay Glass Co., 1890. Extended table service including wine. *Ref. K6-48; Bred p. 21.*

CHESTNUT, tumbler. Crystal, amber, blue, canary, ruby-stained. *Ref. Gob I; Metz 2-166; H7-89.*

Rainbow Variant   *Button Panel with Bars*   *Button Panel*

Sedan   *Masonic*   *Coarse Cut and Block*

Big Leaf and Button   *Findlay's Pillar*   *Chestnut*

PLATE 84. FACETS

MASSACHUSETTS (ARCHED DIAMOND POINT; CANE VARIANT; GENEVA), salt shaker, vase, and rum jug. A State Series pattern. U. S. Glass Co. #15054 (King), 1898. Extended table service including cordial, several creamers, candy dish, shot glass, wine set, cordial, champagne, claret, decanter, table lamp. The "rum jug," a flask-shaped syrup with spout that does not pour, was reportedly used to transport liquor into "dry" states in the guise of syrup. It came in several sizes. This pattern is being reproduced in apple green, blue, rose pink, and crystal in very good copies; get a history on pieces you wish to buy. (Heacock shows a repro apple green butter dish in *The Glass Collector 4,* p. 46.) Crystal, green (dark), ruby-stained, rare cobalt. *Ref. K2-136; Gob II-59; K4-95; Mugs p. 82; H5-144; H7-149+; Jenks p. 361; Schroy-97.*

BUTTON AND STAR (RED BLOCK AND LATTICE), salt shaker. Extended table service. Crystal, ruby-stained. *Ref. PetSal 24A; H7-78.*

RAYED FLOWER, pitcher. Indiana Glass Co., ca. 1920. Extended table service including wine. Crystal, decorated. *Ref. K7-52.*

FLOWER WITH CANE (DIAMOND GOLD), pitcher. U. S. Glass Co. #15141 (Glassport), 1895 – 1912. Extended table service including toothpick holder on a fancy base, custard cup, wine. Crystal, green-stained, ruby-stained. See Plate 127. *Ref. K7-29, Unitt 2-81; H5-164; HTP-53.*

MODEL PEERLESS (SUNBURST DIAMOND), toothpick holder. Model Flint Glass Works (Albany, IN), 1893 – 1901. Extended table service including wine, cordial. This is Heacock's depiction; Kamm describes the creamer as being "composed of three horizontal rows of ...blocks...upper and lower rows alike and covered with coarse diamond point, the middle row...covered with a fine cut pattern somewhat coarser." Crystal, green. *Ref. K3-91; HTP-51, 82; HI-50.*

HOBSTAR BAND, cruet. Crystal, carnival glass. *Ref. HPV#6 p. 14.*

STAR MEDALLION (AMELIA), pitcher. Imperial Glass Co., ca. 1925. Extended table service. Crystal, carnival glass. *Ref. K4-82; HPV#1 (Kamm updates).*

Massachusetts (three examples)

Button and Star

Rayed Flower

Flower with Cane

Model Peerless

Hobstar Band

Star Medallion

PLATE 85. FACETS

CANE INSERT (ARCHED CANE AND FAN), powder jar. Tarentum Glass Co., 1898 – 1906. Extended table service including rare celery vase, wine. No known toothpick holder or salt shaker. Crystal, green, custard, gilded. Ref. *K6-51; PetPat 188; H4-46; Mugs p. 82.*

SWEET HEART, toy pitcher. Cambridge Glass Co., ca 1910. Extended table service including toy set, lamp. *Ref. K2-103.*

STYLE (ARROWHEAD IN OVAL; MADORA; BEADED OVAL AND FAN; MEDALLION FAN; RAMONA), creamer. Higbee Glass Co. ca. 1870 with bee trademark; Bryce, Higbee and Co.; Jefferson Glass Co., ca. 1915 – 1925. Extended table service including toy table service, wine, cordial, champagne, claret. Crystal, ruby-stained. *Ref. K8-43; K6-46; Unitt 1-309; H7-147.*

NEW JERSEY (LOOPS AND DROPS; RED LOOP AND FINECUT), plate, toothpick holder, and creamer. A State Series pattern. U. S. Glass Co. #15070 (Glassport), 1900. Extended table service including individual creamer and sugar, wine set. Crystal, ruby-stained. *Ref. PetSal 34E; Metz 2-162; H5-49, 144, 148; H6-88; H7-159+; Schroy-104.*

BUCKLE AND STAR (LATE BUCKLE; ORIENT), celery vase. Bryce Walker and Company, 1875; U. S. Glass Co., 1891. Extended table service including wine, cordial. Crystal. *Ref. L-166; K1-20; Metz 1-122; H5-85; Mugs p. 82.*

ROTEC, creamer. McKee Glass Co., 1894. Extended table service. This is one of McKee's "Tec" series, all of which are very collectible. Crystal, ruby-stained. *Ref. K6 Pl. 23; H7-188.*

Cane Insert   *Sweet Heart*

Style

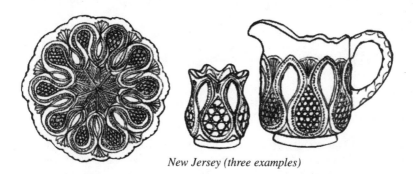

New Jersey (three examples)

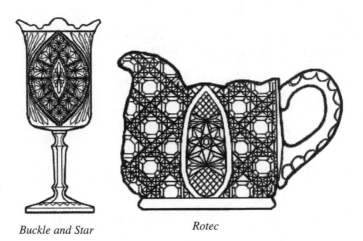

Buckle and Star   *Rotec*

PLATE 86. FACETS

PRISCILLA (ALEXIS; SUN AND STAR; CROWN JEWEL; STEELE), toothpick holder. Dalzell, Gilmore and Leighton Co., 1896 – 1910. Extended table service including individual creamer, plate, rose bowl, wine, cracker jar, square bowl. Pieces were shown in Montgomery Ward's catalog of 1896, called "Crown Jewel." Crystal, ruby-stained (rare). This pattern was reproduced by L. G. Wright in crystal and colors. *Ref. K4-92; LV-72; Gob I-141; Metz 1-210; Unitt 2-167; H7-66, 176.*

BOX-IN-BOX, (FACETED ROSETTE BAND), toothpick holder. Riverside Glass Co., 1898 – 1902. Extended table service iincluding wine. Crystal, etched, ruby-stained, emerald green. *Ref. K6-65; Metz 2-140; HPV#5 p. 12; HPV#6 p. 7; HI-15; H7-17+; Mugs p. 84.*

ROYAL, syrup. Perfection Glass Co. #250, Washington, PA. Courtesy of Bob Burford.

BLOCK AND DENT, salt shaker. *Ref. PetSal 155G.*

COLUMNED THUMBPRINTS, creamer. Westmoreland Glass Co., 1900. Extended table service. Crystal, ruby-stained. *Ref. K5-71.*

GLORIA, creamer. Ohio Flint Glass Co., 1906. Extended table service. Crystal, ruby-stained. *Ref. K6 Pl. 41; H7-123.*

FEATHER DUSTER (ROSETTE MEDALLION; HUCKLE), salt shaker. U. S. Glass Co. #15043, 1895. Extended table service including egg cup, tray, waste bowl, wine; rare McKinley Gold Standard bread plate, wine. Crystal, emerald green. *Ref. K2-42; LV-64; Gob II-77; Metz 2-174; Unitt 1-311; Jenks p. 205; Schroy-58; Mugs p. 107.*

STAR AND DIAMOND POINT, salt shaker. *Ref. PetSal 173E.*

TREMONT, spoon holder. Richards and Hartley, 1888; U. S. Glass, 1891. Extended table service. Crystal. *(Original mfg. name.) Ref. H5-113.*

FANCY ARCH, cruet. National Glass Co., 1901 – 1906. Extended table service including wine. Crystal, ruby-stained. *Ref. PetSal 21H; H7-45+.*

Priscilla

Box-in-Box

Royal

Block and Dent

Columned
Thumbprints

Gloria

Feather
Duster

Star and
Diamond
Point

Tremont

Fancy Arch

PLATE 87. FACETS

CROSSBAR AND CANE, salt shaker. *Ref. PetSal 26F.*

BANDED FINE CUT, goblet. *Ref. Gob II-147.*

DOUBLE CROSSROADS, salt shaker. Extended table service including wine. *Ref. PetSal 26G.*

BIG X, pitcher. Cambridge Glass Co., 1901. Extended table service. *Ref. K4-130.*

MEMPHIS (DOLL'S EYE), Northwood Glass Co. (Ref. Miller), 1908 – 1910. Extended table service including rare toothpick holder, fruit bowl on base. Crystal, carnival glass, colors. *Ref. Gob I; Miller 7th Ed. p. 495.*

PLUTEC, pitcher. McKee Glass Co., 1900. Extended table service including nut bowl, wine. Pieces are marked "Pres-cut." This is one of McKee's "Tec" series. Crystal, ruby-stained. *Ref. K3-87; H7-175; Schroy-112.*

LOG AND STAR (MILTON; CUBE AND DIAMOND; CUBE AND DAISY; CUT BLOCK AND DAISY), salt shaker and pitcher. Bellaire Goblet Co. #373, 1890; U. S. Glass, 1891. Extended table service including two cruets, tray, wine, cordial, claret. No toothpick holder or syrup known. Some pieces, like the shaker, are totally covered with the squared pattern. Crystal, amber, blue. *Ref. K5-140; Gob II-15; Gob I-67; HIII-58; H5-52; H6-34; Mugs p. 103.*

MAJESTIC CROWN (FLUTED), pitcher. U. S. Glass Co. (Challinor), 1891. Extended table service including trays, ice cream dish, rare pickle jar, waste bowl. Crystal, purple slag. *Ref. H5-52, 88; Heacock, Antique Trader article March 18, 1981 p. 94.*

Crossbar and Cane

Banded Fine Cut

Double Crossroads

Big X

Memphis

Plutec

Log and Star (two examples)

Majestic Crown

PLATE 88. FACETS

ARCH AND SUNBURST, salt shaker. *Ref. PetSal 21G.*

STAR AND RIB, creamer. Made ca. 1890 in extended table service. Clear, vaseline, blue. *Ref. HGC6 p. 44.*

DAISY IN DIAMOND, pitcher. O'Hara Glass Co. #725, 1886; U. S. Glass Co. Extended table including service ice cream tub, decanter, waste bowl. Crystal, scarce in amber, rose, and blue. *Ref. K3-77; Mugs p. 87.*

STAR-WITH-HANDLE, individual creamer. *Ref. K8-53.*

GLOVED HAND (COAT OF ARMS), creamer. U. S. Glass Co. #15100 (Gas City), 1907. Extended table service. Crystal. This mish-mashed pattern owes its charm to the name given it by early researchers, a point to be remembered when considering a change of name to one recently discovered. GLOVED HAND is a name and design remembered by all collectors with amusement. *Ref. K6-59; H5-164.*

TOLTEC, creamer. A McKee "Tec" pattern made in 1894 in 55 items including carafe, three syrups, wine, claret, rose bowl, spoon tray. Crystal, ruby-stained. *Ref. K6 Pl. 10; Unitt 2-130; Stout p. 217; HTP-29; H7-203.*

TEN-POINTED STAR, pitcher. Bryce, Higbee and Co. before 1907; J.B. Higbee Glass Co., 1907 – 1910. Extended table service. Crystal. *Ref. K2-62; HPV 1-6.*

NORTHWOOD NEARCUT (HOBSTAR; LOCKET), punch bowl. Northwood Glass Co. #12, 1905. Extended table service including wine. Crystal, ruby-stained (rare), carnival glass. *Ref. Hartung; HPV#5 p. 20; H7-61; PetSal 165K; Batty-210.*

Arch and Sunburst   *Star and Rib*   *Daisy in Diamond*

Star-with-Handle   *Gloved Hand*

Toltec

Ten-Pointed Star   *Northwood Nearcut*

PLATE 89. FACETS

BUTTON ARCHES (RED TOP; SCALLOPED DAISY), mug. Duncan Glass Co. #39, 1885; Duncan and Miller, ca. 1900. (U. S. Glass did **not** make it); Oriental Glass, 1906; Jefferson Glass Co. Extended table service including wine, mustard jar, toy mug. Crystal, ruby-stained, frosted, a scarce blue, and decorated custard glass. *Ref. K1-111; K6 Pl. 9; Metz 2-132; Unitt 1-181; Mugs p. 81; HI-16; HIII-18; H6-21+; H7-85+; Schroy-28; Jenks p. 94.*

DIAMOND WITH PEG, toothpick holder. McKee Glass Co., ca. 1894; Jefferson Glass Co., after 1900. Pieces found with "Krys-tol" mark were made after 1913. Extended table service including wine. Crystal, ruby-stained. *Ref. PetSal 27R; K4 Pl. 10; K6-65; HI-21; H4-52; H7-106.*

DIAMOND BAND WITH PANELS, creamer. Cooperative Flint Glass Co. #1908, 1908. Extended table service including wine. Crystal, ruby-stained. *Ref. K5-61; Metz 2-142; H7-104+.*

NEW HAMPSHIRE (BENT BUCKLE; MODISTE), mug, toothpick holder, and creamer. U. S. Glass Co. #15084, 1903. A State Series pattern. Extended table service including bud vase, wine, square bowls, champagne. Crystal, ruby-stained. *Ref. K3-97; Unitt 1-162; H5-35; H7-159+; Schroy-102; Jenks p. 382.*

STARTEC, creamer. McKee Glass Co., ca. 1900. One of their "Tec" series. Extended table service. *Ref. K3-137.*

RADIANT (DYNAST; COLUMBIA RADIANT), tumbler. Columbia Glass Co.; U. S. Glass Co., 1891. Extended table service including wine. Crystal, ruby-stained. *Ref. LV-70; Gob II -50; Metz 1-194; H5-129; H7-6, 182.*

HEART BAND, pitcher. McKee and Brothers, 1897. Limited table service. Crystal, green, gilded, decorated, carnival, ruby-stained. *Ref. K4-96; HI-50; H7-125; Mugs p. 107.*

JERSEY (THE KITCHEN STOVE), pitcher. McKee and Brothers, 1894. Extended table service. *Ref. K2-108.*

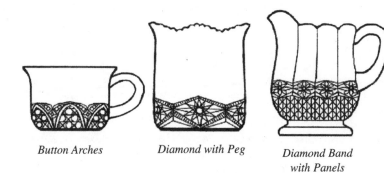

Button Arches   *Diamond with Peg*   *Diamond Band
with Panels*

New Hampshire (three examples)

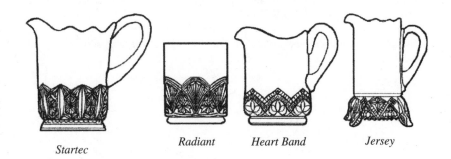

Startec   *Radiant*   *Heart Band*   *Jersey*

PLATE 90. FACETS

GRAND REPUBLIC, creamer. Union Stopper Co. #99, 1908. Extended table service including footed punch bowl and cups. *Ref. HPV #2 p. 4.*

HEAVY GOTHIC (WHITTON), goblet. U. S. Glass #15014 (Columbia), 1891. Extended table service including wine, claret, egg cup. Crystal, ruby-stained. *Ref. K2-109; Gob II-13; Metz 2-144; H5-131; H7-126+; Schroy-72; Jenks p. 268.*

POINTED JEWEL (LONG DIAMOND; SPEAR POINT), creamer. Columbia Glass Co., 1880s; U. S. Glass Co. #15006 (Nickel Plate; Columbia), 1891. Extended table service including toy table service called "Long Diamond," wine. Crystal, scarce opaque white, ruby-stained. Two Specialty patterns on Plate 40 are similar to this one. *Ref. K1-97; K8-54; Gob I-40; Metz 1-216; Mugs p. 80; Schroy-113; H5-131; H7-143+.*

FOSTORIA #956, creamer. Fostoria Glass Co., 1901. Extended table service. *Ref. K8-198.*

STAR BASE, salt shaker. *Ref. PetSal 173H.*

POINTED GOTHIC, toothpick holder. It was thought that this was a pattern ca. 1900, but it was actually made in about 1930 by Indiana Glass Co., their #453. Extended table service. *Ref. K6-32.*

FRINGED DRAPE (CRESCENT), spooner. McKee Glass Co., 1901; National Glass Co. Extended table service including cordial. Crystal, ruby-stained. *Ref. K6-32; Stout p. 217; H7-96.*

PENDANT (NOGI; AMULET), salt shaker. Indiana Glass Co., 1906. Extended table service. Crystal, ruby-stained. Note: Kamm (K5-48) misidentified the creamer in this pattern as "Heisey's Sunburst;" Heacock was at a loss to explain why. "Heisey's Sunburst" is highly variable, as you can see on Plates 78, 96, and 104. Heacock also calls a U. S. Glass Co. liquor set (H5-163) as "Pendant," although it seems to bear no resemblance to this pattern. *Ref. PetSal 168J; Gob I-150; HPV #2 p. 10.*

FAGOT (VERA), creamer. Robinson Glass Co., 1893. Extended table service. Crystal, ruby-stained. *Ref. K4-74; K6 Pl. 37; LV-62; H7-17+.*

Grand Republic

Heavy Gothic

Pointed Jewel

Fostoria #956

Star Base

Pointed Gothic

Fringed Drape

Pendant

Fagot

PLATE 91. FACETS

SUNBEAM, pitcher. McKee and Brothers, 1898 – 1902. Extended table service including carafe, wine, champagne. Crystal, emerald green, ruby-stained. *Ref. K4-76; H1-41; H6-43, 71; H7-198.*

ROCKET, pitcher. Indiana Glass Co., 1915 – 1925. *Ref. K5-148.*

CRYSTAL QUEEN, creamer. Northwood Glass Co., 1897. Extended table service including 125 items. A similar pattern, FANCY LOOP, is on Plate 215. *Ref. K6 Pl. 25; Mugs p. 86.*

TWIN SNOWSHOES (SUNBEAM), creamer. U. S. Glass Co. #15139 (Gas City), ca. 1918. Extended table service including wine, toy table set. Crystal. *Ref. K8-54; HTP-88; H5-156.*

GLENTEC, creamer. McKee Glass Co., ca. 1894 – 1914. One of McKee's "Tec" series. Extended table service including a bowl with three precious feet, handled spooner. Crystal, ruby-stained. *Ref. McCain, Schroeder's Insider Vol. 2 #4 p. 8; Stout p. 264; H7-123.*

REXFORD (EUCLID; BOYLAN; ALPHA), custard cup. J. B. Higbee Co., ca. 1910; New Martinsville Glass Mfg. Co., after 1918. Extended table service including wine, ruffle-edged bowl. Crystal, rare ruby-stained. *Ref. Gob II 63, 94, 113; Metz 1-228; Unitt 2-158; Mugs p. 86.*

GRENADE, creamer. Crystal, ruby-stained. *Ref. K6-29; Metz 2-70; H7-123+.*

Sunbeam 　　　　　　　　　　*Rocket*

Crystal Queen 　　　*Twin Snowshoes* 　　　　*Glentec*

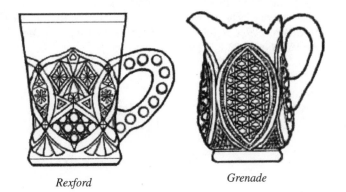

Rexford 　　　　　　　　　*Grenade*

PLATE 92. FACETS

OVAL STAR, toy pitcher. Indiana Glass Co. #300, ca. 1910. Made in toy table service including toy water tray (scarce). The toy spooner is used as a toothpick holder by collectors. *Ref. K6-47.*

ARROWSHEAF, pitcher. Made ca. 1900. *Ref. K3-120.*

DALTON (CRADLED DIAMONDS), pitcher. Tarentum Glass Co., 1904. Extended table service including wine. Crystal, ruby-stained, gilded. Courtesy of Bob Burford. *Ref. HTP-82; PetPat p. 190; Lucas p. 336, 340; Unitt 2-162; H7-47+.*

INTERLOCKED HEARTS (WISHBONE), goblet. Made ca. 1900 in extended table service including wine. *Ref. Gob II-80; K5-69; Metz 1-33.*

CROSSED SHIELD, pitcher. Fostoria Glass co. #1303, 1890s. Extended table service including cordial. *Ref. K5-100.*

V-IN-HEART, pitcher. *Ref. K6-26.*

BORDERED ELLIPSE, pitcher. McKee Glass Co., 1890s; Lancaster Glass Co., ca. 1896; Cambridge Glass Co., ca. 1904. Extended table service. Crystal, blue, ruby-stained. *Ref. K4-99; Mugs p. 77; H7-45+.*

SQUARED SUNBURST (STELLAR), creamer. U. S. Glass Co. #15103, ca. 1907. Extended table service. Crystal. *Ref. K7-48; H5-162, 177.*

ZIPPERED HEART, tumbler. Imperial Glass Co. #292, ca. 1904 – 1920s. Extended table service including basket-shaped handled spoon tray, lemonade set. Crystal, carnival glass (berry sets and vases only). *Ref. Archer p. 50.*

MEDALLION (SPADES; HEARTS AND SPADES), pitcher. U. S. Glass Co., ca. 1891. Extended table service including wine, mug. Crystal, blue, vaseline, apple green, amber. *Ref. L-102; LEAPG-500; Gob I-35; K5-19; H5-41, 42; Jenks p. 363; Metz 1-126; Metz 2-138; Schroy-98; Mugs p. 92.*

Oval Star

Arrowsheaf

Dalton

*Interlocked
Hearts*

Crossed Shield

V-in-Heart

*Bordered
Ellipse*

Squared Sunburst

Zippered Heart

Medallion

PLATE 93. FACETS

PLYTEC (RADIANT PETAL), salt shaker. McKee and Brothers, a "Tec" pattern. Extended table service. Crystal, ruby-stained. *Ref. PetSal 169C; H7-175, 185.*

ONEATA (CHIMO), pitcher. Riverside Glass Co., 1907. Extended table service including wine. *Ref. K6 pl. 75; Revi-34; Unitt 1-318.*

NEARCUT, creamer. Cambridge Glass Co. #2636, ca. 1906. Extended table service including basket, wine, vase. Crystal, ruby-stained. *Ref. K7-169; H7-161.*

VALTEC, creamer. McKee Glass Co., ca. 1894 – 1914. A "Tec" pattern. Extended table service including a stocky vase called a "sweet pea vase," and a tall, stretched out version of the same piece. *Ref. McCain, Schroeder's Insider Vol. 2 #4 p. 8.*

GLADIATOR, tumbler. McKee Brothers. Extended table service including tobacco jar. Crystal, ruby-stained. *Ref. K6 Pl. 60; Stout p. 211; H7-35, 122.*

WHEAT SHEAF (NEAR CUT #2260), creamer. Cambridge Glass Co., 1908. Extended table service including decanter, basket, celery vase and tray, punch bowl, wine, rose bowl, toy punch set. *Ref. K7-176.*

INVERTED FEATHER (NEAR CUT #2651; FEATHER CUT), creamer. Cambridge Glass Co., 1906. Extended table service including vases, sherbet, basket, water bottle, pickle tray, decanter, whiskey jug, bonbon, wine, berry set. *Ref. K8-106.*

CENTIPEDE (NORTEC), creamer. McKee and Brothers, another "Tec" pattern. Those who collect "Tecs" may want to call this Nortec, but I love the inspired name Peterson gave it and do not want to lose it. Extended table service including vase, punch bowls, brush holder, card tray, covered horse radish, tumbler. *Ref. PetSal 24P; Stout p. 271.*

PALM LEAF FAN, pitcher. Bryce, Higbee and Co., 1904. Extended table service including vase, wine, water bottle, square cake plate. Crystal, rare ruby-stained. It appeared in the 1905 Montgomery Ward catalog. *Ref. K2-63; Metz 1-74; Unitt 1-294; Mugs p. 92.*

Plytec

Oneata

Nearcut

Valtec

Gladiator

Wheat Sheaf

Inverted Feather

Centipede

Palm Leaf Fan

PLATE 94. FACETS

FINE CUT BAND, butter dish. Made ca. 1895 – 1905. Crystal, gilded. Courtesy of Bob Burford. *Ref. Gob II-153; Metz 1-152; Metz 2-174.*

PENNSYLVANIA (BALDER; KAMONI), syrup. U. S. Glass Co. #15048 (Central; Gillinder), 1898. A State Series pattern. Extended table service in every piece imaginable including toy sets, carafe, covered cheese dish, wine set, champagne, claret, round and square sauces. The toy spooner doubles as a toothpick holder and is rare in green. Crystal, ruby-stained, emerald green, custard. *Ref. K2-103; Metz 1-228; Jenks p. 402; Schroy-110; Mugs p. 86; H6-36; H5-49, 50, 143, 166; H7-171.*

CANE HORSESHOE (PARAGON), cruet. U. S. Glass Co. #15118 (Ripley), 1909. Extended table service including wine. Crystal, rare amber-stained, ruby-stained, gilded. *Ref. K1-100; Unitt 1-162; Mugs p. 86; H5-151+; H7-88; Jenks p. 106.*

MINNESOTA (MUCHNESS), bowl and goblet. U. S. Glass Co. #15055 (Ripley; Glassport), 1898. A State Series pattern. Extended table service including square fruit compote, individual creamer, wine, mug. Crystal, scarce ruby-stained, emerald green, gilded. *Ref. K8-205; Unitt 1-162; Mugs p. 90; HI-46; HIII-33; H5-49, 144; H7-152; Jenks p. 370; Schroy-100.*

MARTEC, tumbler and pitcher. McKee Glass Co., ca. 1894 – 1914, a "Tec" pattern. Extended table service including triangle olive, carafe, spoon tray, rose bowl, and many other pieces. There is considerable variation in different pieces; the pitcher could almost be an entirely different pattern from the tumbler, with its large bevelled diamonds not found on the tumbler. *Ref. McCain, Schroeder's Insider Vol. 1 #7 p. 7.*

RISING SUN (SUNRISE; SUNSHINE), cruet. U. S. Glass Co. #15110 (Ripley; Glassport), 1908. Extended table service including three shapes sugar bowls, wine set. Crystal, decorated, carnival glass, gilded, ruby-stained. *Ref. K2-61; Unitt 1-307; H5-142; H6-39; H7-186; Jenks p. 444.*

Fine Cut Band

Pennsylvania

Minnesota (two views)

Cane Horseshoe

Martec (two examples)

Rising Sun

201

PLATE 95. FACETS

BLAZING CORNUCOPIA (PAISLEY WITH PURPLE DOTS; GOLDEN JEWEL), creamer. U. S. Glass Co., 1913. Extended table service including a toothpick holder with handles, wine. Crystal, purple or pink stained circles. *Ref. K6-29; Gob II-83; Metz 1-214; HGC1 p. 13.*

RADIUM (CAMBRIDGE #2626), butter dish. Cambridge Glass Co., 1905 – 1915. Courtesy of Bob Burford.

STAR AND CRESCENT (FESTOONS AND SUNBURSTS), cruet. U. S. Glass Co. #15108 (King; Ripley), 1908. Extended table service including two handled spooner, wine. Crystal. *Ref. Gob I-50; Unitt 2-116; H5-151; H6-48.*

HEART PLUME, creamer. See Plate 54.

BEVELLED STAR (PRIDE), pitcher. Model Flint Glass Co., 1890 – 1897. Extended table service of 26 pieces. Crystal, amber, emerald green, cobalt blue. *Ref. K2-70; LV-79; HI-15; H6-20.*

SLEWED HORSESHOE (RADIANT DAISY; U. S. PEACOCK), creamer. U. S. Glass Co. #15111 (Glassport), 1908. Extended table service including ice cream tray, wine, toy table service. Crystal. *Ref. K8-15; Gob II-87; H5-155.*

IVERNA, cracker jar. Ripley and Co. #303, 1911. Extended table service including punch bowl and pedestal, biscuit jar, vases, handled sherbet, spoon tray. No goblet is known. *Ref. HPV#4 p. 6.*

HOBSTAR (PATHFINDER; OMNIBUS; KEYSTONE), creamer. U. S. Glass Co. #15124 (Glassport and Central factories), 1915. Extended table service including covered candy dish, handled spooner, wine. Crystal. *Ref. PetSal 31F; Metz 2-135; Gob II-135; H5-168; Mugs p. 85.*

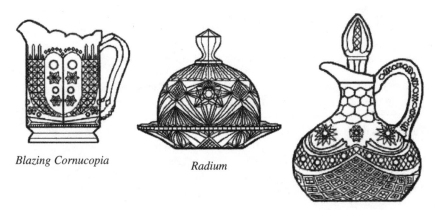

Blazing Cornucopia

Radium

Star and Crescent

Heart Plume

Bevelled Star

Slewed Horseshoe

Iverna

Hobstar

203

PLATE 96. FACETS

DAISY IN OVAL, goblet. Extended table service.

HEISEY #343½, creamer. Part of the **Heisey's Sunburst** set, pictured on Plates 78, 104, and the next piece.

HEISEY'S SUNBURST, creamer. See above and Plates 78 and 104.

PENTAGON (FIVE-FOOTED OVAL), creamer. Extended table service including wine. Crystal, ruby-stained. *Ref. K3-101; Metz 2-108; H7-63+.*

COTTAGE (DINNER BELL; FINE CUT BAND; ADAMS), pitcher. Adams and Co., 1874; U. S. Glass, 1890s. Extended table service including tray, finger bowl, wine, champagne, claret, three sizes covered compotes, cup and saucer, plates. Crystal, amber, dark green (rare), light blue, amethyst, ruby-stained. Note the hands holding the handle. *Ref. K1-38; LV-64; Metz 1-152; LV-206; Jenks p. 134; Schroy-39; Mugs p. 73; H5-51, 63.*

FROSTED MEDALLION (SUNBURST ROSETTE), syrup. Extended table service including wine. *Ref. K4-120; Gob II-163; Metz 1-124.*

SUNBURST IN OVAL, creamer. Duncan and Miller Glass Co. #67, ca. 1905. Extended table service. *Ref. HPV #2 p. 3; H6-79.*

BRITANNIC, creamer. McKee Glass Co., 1880s National Glass Co., after 1899. Extended table service including banana boat, wine, rose bowl, fruit basket, ice-cream tray, cologne bottles, carafe, cracker jar, lamps, castor set. Crystal, green, amber and ruby-stained. *Ref. K4-71; Metz 2-142; Schroy-25; Mugs p. 106; H7-82+.*

LENS AND STAR (STAR AND OVAL), creamer. U. S. Glass Co. (O'Hara), 1891. Extended table service. Crystal, frosted, etched. *Ref. K2-36; LV-75; Metz 1-118; Schroy-88.*

BIG STAR, salt shaker. *Ref. PetSal 173-i.*

FORMAL DAISY, creamer. *Ref. K2-101.*

STARS AND BARS (DAISY AND CUBE; EVANGELINE), pitcher. Bellaire Goblet Co., 1890; U. S. Glass, 1891. Extended table service including wine, jam jar, night lamp, toy table set, tray. No goblet originally made but has been reproduced. Some pieces have a large leaf in the clear sections. Any piece with an etched moose (yes, **moose**) is a reproduction. Crystal, amber, blue. See Plate 185 for pitcher with leaf. *Ref. K1-64; LV-69; HI-46; HIII-59; H6-42; Mugs p. 102.*

   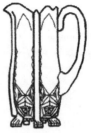

Daisy in Oval   *Heisey #343½*   *Heisey's Sunburst*   *Pentagon*

Cottage   *Frosted
Medallion*   *Sunburst
in Oval*   *Britannic*

Lens and Star   *Big Star*   *Formal Daisy*   *Stars and Bars*

205

PLATE 97. FACETS

SUNBURST (WHEAT), salt shaker. Jenkins Glass Co., 1900; Federal Glass Co. #600, 1914. Extended table service including cordial, egg cup, wine. *Ref. K3-63; LEAPG-326; Metz 1-192; Schroy-138; HGC5-p. 41.*

KENNETH, dish. Ohio Flint Glass Co., 1906; Central Glass Co. later. Extended table service. Often signed "Krystol." Crystal, ruby-stained. *Ref. HGC4p. 34; H7-16.*

FASHION, pitcher. Imperial Glass Co. #412½, 1914. Extended table service of 32 pieces. Crystal, carnival, ruby-stained; reproduced in colors. *Ref. K6-46; H7-101.*

BRILLIANT (PETALLED MEDALLION), syrup. Riverside Glass Co. #436, ca. 1895. Extended table service including wine. The mug becomes a mustard dish when a slotted lid is added. Crystal, ruby-stained, amber-stained. *Ref. K6 Pl. 65; Metz 1-20; Metz 2-154; Unitt 2-73; HI-16; HIII-16; Mugs p 88; H7-82.*

DIXIE BELLE, goblet. Extended table service. *Ref. Gob II-38; Unitt 2-166.*

DOTTED LOOP, pitcher. Extended table service including wine. *Ref. K6-16; Unitt 1-296; Metz 2-164.*

STARRED SCROLL (CRESCENT AND FAN), creamer. Made ca. 1900 in extended table service including rose bowl, wine, champagne. Crystal. *Ref. K8-30; Gob II-128; Metz 2-116; Unitt 1-304.*

McKEE'S STARS AND STRIPES, salt shaker. McKee and Brothers, 1898. Extended table service, all pieces scarce. *Ref. K6 Pl. 96.*

ROBINSON'S PURITAN (RADIANT DAISY), etched creamer. Robinson Glass Co., 1894. Extended table service including cracker jar, punch bowl. Crystal, ruby and amber stained. *Ref. K6-39; H7-178; Mugs p. 92.*

Sunburst   *Kenneth*   *Fashion*

Brilliant   *Dixie Belle*   *Dotted Loop*

Starred Scroll   *McKee's Stars*   *Robinson's*
                     and Stripes   *Puritan*

PLATE 98. FACETS

ROANOKE STAR (IMPERIAL STAR; STAR; HOB STAR), creamer. Imperial Glass Co. #282, ca. 1904. Extended table service in every imaginable piece including tray, cracker jar, wine set, whiskey tumbler, handled spoon tray, liquor bottles, oil bottle, decanter, handled bonbon, banana dish, covered milk jar. Crystal, carnival glass, ruby-stained. *Ref. Gob II-38; PetSal 40L; Unitt 1-306; H7-187.*

FERN BURST, cruet. Made ca. 1905 in extended table service including wine. *Ref. Gob II-67; Metz 2-176.*

SNOWFLOWER (FLOWER FAN), creamer. U. S. Glass Co. #35135 (Bryce), 1912. Extended table service including wine. Crystal. *Ref. PetSal 151-0; H5-169.*

RIVERSIDE'S AURORA, sugar bowl. Riverside Glass Co., ca. 1904. Extended table service. Crystal. *Ref. Metz 1-120; HPV #2 Pl. 6.*

ETTA, custard cup. Paden City Glass Mfg. Co., ca. 1915. Extended table service including wine. *Ref. H6 p. 93.*

SHIMMERING STAR (BEADED STAR), pitcher. Kokomo (Jenkins) Glass Co., ca. 1905. Extended table service. *Ref. K2-55.*

ELLIPSE AND STAR, salt shaker. *Ref. PetSal 160F.*

GEORGIA BELLE (WESTERN STAR), goblet. U. S. Glass Co. #15097, 1906. Extended table service. *Ref. Metz I-228; Gob I-56.*

STARRED LOOP, cup and tumbler. Duncan Glass Co., 1899; Duncan & Miller, 1900. Extended table service including wine, champagne. Notice that the tumbler has a narrow band of cane under the "sheafs." Crystal, ruby-stained. *Ref. K6 Pl. 57; H7-41+.*

Roanoke Star

Fern Burst

Snowflower

Riverside's Aurora

Etta

Shimmering Star

Ellipse and Star

Georgia Belle

Starred Loop (two examples)

PLATE 99. FACETS

POSTSCRIPT, plate and salt shaker. Tarentum Glass Co., 1905. Extended table service including wine. Crystal, ruby-stained. *Ref. Gob II-58; Unitt 2-167; H7-175.*

NAVARRE (PRINCE ALBERT), creamer. McKee Glass Co., 1901. Extended table service including carafe, cologne bottle, sugar shaker. Crystal, ruby-stained. *Ref. H6-70; H7-156.*

STAR AND NOTCHED RIB, salt shaker. *Ref. PetSal 173G.*

SEXTEC, tall creamer. McKee Glass Co., 1984. A "Tec" pattern. Extended table service including berry creamer, pickle jar, orange bowl, plates, cup, handled nut bowl, punch bowl. *Ref. K6 Pl. 24.*

SUNBURST ON SHIELD (DIADEM), pitcher. Northwood Glass Co., ca. 1905. Extended table service including water set. Crystal, opalescent. *Ref. K8-52; HII-23.*

X-BULL'S EYE (SUMMIT), salt shaker. Thompson Glass Co., 1890s. Extended table service including wine, tankard pitcher. *Ref. PetSal 177F.*

STAR AND FAN, salt shaker. *Ref. PetSal 173F.*

BEADED PANEL AND SUNBURST (CHRYSANTHEMUM; PANELLED SUNBURST WITH CANE), toothpick holder. A. H. Heisey Glass Co. #1235, ca. 1898 – 1903; probably U. S. Glass Co. a little earlier. Extended table service including wine. Crystal, color-stained. *Ref. K7-135; HI-14; H4-37, 41; H7-90+.*

AIDA, etched creamer. Belmont Glassworks, 1883. Extended table service. (Kamm says the area under the lip is very ornate.) *Ref. K5 Pl. 1; Metz 2-70.*

Postscript (two views)

Navarre

*Star and
Notched Rib*

Sextec

Sunburst on Shield

X-Bull's Eye *Star and Fan* *Beaded Panel* *Aida*

PLATE 100. FACETS

ROSETTE AND PALMS, salt shaker. Bryce, Higbee & Co., 1905; J. B. Higbee Co., ca 1910. Extended table service including wine, banana stand. The goblet has only one row of rosettes and taller palms. Crystal, ruby-stained. *Ref. LV-21; Gob I-167; Metz 1-125; Metz 2-68; Unitt 1-294; LV-55; H7-89.*

ORNATE STAR (DIVIDED STAR; LADDERS AND DIAMONDS WITH STAR), creamer. Tarentum Glass Co., 1907. Extended table service including cordial, wine. Crystal, ruby-stained. *Ref. K6-21; H7-165+.*

MOON AND STAR (STAR AND PUNTY; BULLS-EYE AND STAR; PALACE), pitcher. Boston and Sandwich, 1870; Pioneer Glass Co.; Wilson Glass Co.; Cooperative Flint Glass Co., 1900 – 1937; Adams and Co.; U. S. Glass Co, 1891; Phoenix Glass Co. to 1942; and others even later. Light green is modern; frosted is probably a reproduction. Made in very large extended table service including egg cup, claret, wine, champagne. No toothpick holder made originally. Many reproductions. Crystal, ruby-stained (which was made by Pioneer). *Ref. L-69 & 103; LEAPG-537; K1-80; Metz 1-210; Unitt 1-54; Unitt 2-220; HIII-91+; H5-51; H7-153, 167; HTP-72 (repro); Jenks p. 375; Schroy-101.*

KNOBBY BULLS-EYE (CROMWELL), creamer. U. S. Glass Co. #15155 (Glassport), 1915. Extended table service including two types salt shaker, wine, decanter. Crystal, decorated, ruby-stained. *Ref. Gob I-166; Metz 1-214; H5-159; H7-137+.*

THE STATES (CANE AND STAR MEDALLION), spoon holder. U. S. Glass Co. #15093, 1908. Extended table service including wine, punch bowl and cups. Crystal, green. *Ref. K5-142; Gob II-69; Metz 1-214; Unitt 2-116; Mugs p. 70; H5-145.*

BULLS-EYE AND ROSETTE, tumbler. Extended table service including spill holder. *Ref. Metz 1-32.*

STAR-IN-BULL'S-EYE, creamer. U. S. Glass Co. #15092 (Glassport factory), 1905; New Martinsville #147, ca. 1918. Extended table service including wine. Crystal, rose-flashed, ruby-stained, gilded. *Ref. K1-100; Gob I-99; H5-42, 49; Gob II-18; Unitt 1-164; HTP-52, 86; Mugs p. 66.*

LOTUS, open sugar bowl. Cambridge Glass Co., 1906. Courtesy of Bob Burford. *Ref. Metz 1-77.*

Rosette and Palms

Ornate Star

Moon and Star

Knobby Bulls-Eye

The States

*Bulls-Eye
and Rosette*

Star in Bulls-Eye

Lotus

213

PLATE 101. FACETS

CHILSON, goblet. Flint glass and rare. *Ref. Gob II-4; Metz 1-32.*

FEATHERED POINTS, creamer. Federal Glass Co., 1913 – 1914. Extended table service. *Ref. K4-120.*

CURTAIN TIE-BACK, creamer. Made in the mid-1880s in extended table service including wine, bread plate. *Ref. K3-118; Gob I-35; Metz 1-130; Unitt 1-260.*

FROSTED CIRCLE (HORN OF PLENTY), goblet. Bryce Brothers, 1876; Nickel Plate, 1890; U. S. Glass Co. #15007 (Columbia; Nickel Plate), 1891. Extended table service including pickle jar, wine, claret, plates. Crystal, ruby-stained. *Ref. K4-19; K6-30; LEAPG-297; Metz 1-138; Schroy-64; Jenks p. 230; H7-171.*

LENOX, creamer. McKee Glass Co., 1898 – 1915. Extended table service including individual salt dip, two types salt shaker, tobacco jar. Some pieces have more diamondpoint above the large "stars." Crystal, ruby-stained. *Ref. K6 Pl. 97; Stout p. 211; HTP-53; H6-74; H7-142.*

LOUISE (SUNK JEWEL; STARRED JEWEL), cracker jar. Fostoria Glass Co. #1121, ca. 1901. Extended table service. Crystal, ruby-stained. *Ref. K3-80; HTP-82; H6-13, 94; H7-145+.*

ICICLE WITH STAR, pitcher. Imperial Glass Co., 1902. *Ref. K4-121; K7 Pl. 86.*

CRAZY PATCH, goblet. Non-flint. *Ref. Gob II-71; Unitt 1-279; Metz 1-158; Metz 2 Pl. 71.*

FROST CRYSTAL (PEERLESS), creamer. Tarentum Glass Co. #1906, 1905 – 1910. Made in extended table service including wine, claret. Crystal, ruby-stained. *Ref. K6 Pl. 51; Mugs p. 72; H6-28; H7-171.*

WHEEL IN BAND (CORCORAN), pitcher. Made in the 1870s in extended table service including jam jar, wine. Crystal. *Ref. K2-45; Gob I-81; Metz 1-56; Unitt 1-100.*

Chilson   *Feathered Points*   *Curtain Tie-back*

Frosted Circle   *Lenox*   *Louise*   *Icicle with Star*

Crazy Patch   *Frost Crystal*   *Wheel in Band*

PLATE 102. FACETS

KEYSTONE, cruet. McKee and Brothers, 1901. Extended table service. Crystal, milk glass, ruby-stained, etched. *Ref. K1-114; HTP-82; H6-78; H7-136+.*

PRINCE OF WALES PLUMES (FLAMBEAUX), creamer. A. H. Heisey Glass Co. #335, 1900. Extended table service of 60 items. Crystal, green, ruby-stained, gilded. *Ref. K1-115; K8-185; HI-36; H7-176; Mugs p. 92.*

ROSE WINDOWS, pitcher. Fostoria Glass Co. #1660, ca. 1900 – 1905. *Ref. K4-138.*

BUTTRESSED SUNBURST, creamer. Tarentum Glass Co., 1910. Extended table service including berry set; wine; condiment items would be rare. Crystal, ruby-stained. *Ref. K1-114; H7-87; Schroy-29.*

RIBBED ELLIPSE (ADMIRAL), mug. Bryce, Higbee & Co., 1905. Extended table service including wine. Courtesy of John Gregory. *Ref. K5-70; HPV#1 p. 6, 7.*

MARDI GRAS (PANELLED ENGLISH HOBNAIL; EMPIRE; SIAMESE NECKLACE), creamer. George Duncan and Sons #42, 1894. Extended table service including champagnes, claret, wine, flared-rim sherry, cocktail, egg cup, toy table set, pomade jar with silver lid, carafe, salt dips, rose bowl, vases, cordial, punch cup, bitters bottle. Note: some pieces have a row of thumbprints around the top. Crystal, ruby-stained. For a similar pattern, see "Groove and Slash" on Plate 202. *Ref K3-77; Gob I-111; K5-70; K7 Pl. 17; Jenks p. 352; Schroy-95; H7-40.*

BUTTON AND STAR PANEL, salt shaker. Bryce, Higbee and Co., ca. 1902. Extended table service including toothpick holder. *Ref. PetSal 24B; HTP-82.*

LIBERTY (CORNUCOPIA), creamer. McKee and Brothers, 1892; Cambridge Glass Co., 1903. Extended table service including wine, champagne, cordial, tankard pitcher. *Ref. K4-72; Gob II-69; Metz 1-214; Unitt 1-160; Schroy-89.*

BULLS-EYE AND FAN (DAISIES IN OVAL PANELS), pitcher. U. S. Glass Co. #15090, ca. 1900s. Extended table service including wine, champagne. Crystal, two shades of green, sapphire blue, stained, gilded. *Ref. K1-58; Gob II-115; Metz 1-214; HTP-50; H5-33+; H7-101; Jenks p. 89; Mugs p. 65.*

Keystone

*Prince of
Wales Plumes*

Rose Windows

Buttressed Sunburst

Ribbed Ellipse

Mardi Gras

*Button and
Star Panel*

Liberty

Bulls-Eye and Fan

PLATE 103. FACETS

WEBB, mug. J. G. Higbee Glass Co., 1910; Paden City Glass Mfg. Co. #203, after 1918. Extended table service. Crystal. *Ref. Mugs p. 86; H6-93.*

FANCY CUT (REX), toy pitcher. Cooperative Flint Glass Co., ca. 1905. Made in toys, water set and punch set. Crystal. *Ref. K2-103; HTP-88.*

BRAZEN SHIELD, creamer. Central Glass Co. #98; Cambridge Glass Co. #2510, after 1904; Indiana Tumbler and Goblet Co. Extended table service. *Ref. Gob II-75; K7-13.*

NUCUT #526, creamer. Imperial Glass co., 1915. There are tiny stars within the circles. *Ref. K8-52.*

STAR IN OCTAGON, creamer. *Ref. K7-51.*

FEDERAL #1910, pitcher. Federal Glass Co., ca. 1914. Extended table service including wine. *Ref. HGC4 p. 11; HGC5 p. 41.*

CAMBRIDGE #2579, bowl. Cambridge Glass Co., early; Federal Glass Co., 1914. *Ref. HGC4 p. 22.*

DUNCAN #40 (BASSETTOWN), mug. George Duncan and Sons, 1898. Extended table service including wine. Crystal, ruby-stained. *Ref. Bones-109; K7 Pl. 94; H7-108.*

CO-OP REX, creamer. Cooperative Flint Glass Co., 1907. Extended table service *Ref. K6 Pl. 49.*

Webb

Fancy Cut

Brazen Shield

Nucut #526

Star in Octagon

Federal #1910

Cambridge
#2579

Duncan #40

Co-op Rex

PLATE 104. FACETS

PADDLES AND STARS, rectangular dish. Author's name, courtesy of Bob Burford.

JUBILEE (ISIS; NELLIE; RADIANT), pitcher. McKee and Brothers #132, 1894. Extended table service including wine. Crystal, ruby-stained. *Ref. K3-41; Gob I-27; Gob II-84; Metz 2-174; Unitt 1-200; Miller 4th Ed. p. 326: H7-134.*

STAR OCTAD, salt shaker. *Ref. PetSal 173P.*

FOSTORIA'S #600, individual creamer. Fostoria Glass Co., 1905. Extended table service. Crystal, ruby-stained. *Ref. K7-43; H7-119.*

TWIN FEATHERS (TOGO; BISMARC STAR; NEBRASKA; NEBRASKA STAR), creamer. Beatty Brady Glass Co.; Indiana Glass Co., 1907. Extended table service including wine. Crystal, ruby-stained. The goblet has been known as BISMARC STAR. *Ref. K7-54; Gob I-152; Unitt 2-128; H7-203+.*

ATLANTA, salt shaker. Westmoreland Glass Co., 1905. Extended table service including wine. Crystal, ruby-stained. *Ref. Gob II-63; Metz 1-096; Schroy-9; HPV3-10; HPV6-3; HI-13; H6-87; H7-69.*

SHELTON STAR, salt shaker. *Ref. PetSal 173U.*

HEISEY'S #343½ (HEISEY'S SUNBURST), creamer. Another version of the "Sunburst" line by Heisey. See Plates 78 and 96.

Paddles and Stars

Jubilee

Star Octad

Fostoria's #600

Twin Feathers

Atlanta

Shelton Star

Heisey's #343½

PLATE 105. FACETS

ILLINOIS (STAR OF THE EAST; CLARISSA), pitcher, butter dish, and syrup. U. S. Glass Co. #15052 (Glassport), 1897. A State Series pattern. Extended table service including vase, candlestick, celery tray and vase, covered cheese dish, lamp, ice cream tray, sugar shaker. Crystal, emerald green (scarce), ruby-stained. The quality of this glass is such that I once saw, featured on a velvet-draped pedestal in a gift shop, an Illinois vase marked "early flint glass." *Ref. PetSal 163U; HTP-84; H5-40, 143; H7-132; Schroy-79; Jenks p. 289.*

BRAZILIAN (CANE SHIELD), pitcher. Fostoria Glass Co. #600, ca. 1898. Extended table service including pickle jar, finger bowl, carafe, cracker jar, sherbet, rose bowl. *Ref. K5-138; K7-33; HI-15; HIII-54; H6-20.*

STAR OF DAVID (KING'S BREAST PLATE; PIMLICO; WETZEL), pitcher. New Martinsville Glass Co. #500. Extended table service including wine. Crystal, ruby-stained. *Ref. K5-133; Gob II-57, 112; Unitt 2-202, 222; H7-16.*

OXFORD, bowl. McKee and Brothers, 1897. Several sizes of bowls are shown in an old ad; probably made in extended table service. *Ref. K6 Pl. 60.*

DIAMOND FLUTE (JEANETTE; FLAMBOYANT), pitcher. McKee and Brothers, 1885. Extended table service including wine. Crystal; very rare in emerald green. *Ref. K4-93; Gob II-176; HPV1-22; H6-78; Mugs p. 78.*

Illinois (two examples, another below)

Illinois   *Brazilian*   *Star of David*

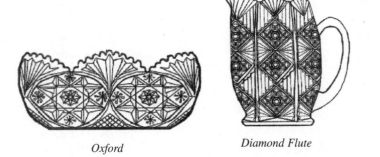

Oxford   *Diamond Flute*

PLATE 106. FACETS

FERRIS WHEEL (PROSPERITY), creamer. Indiana Glass Co., 1909. Extended table service including wine. *Ref. K4-27; Gob I-50.*

CARLTEC, creamer. McKee and Brothers, 1894; and 1917. A "Tec" pattern. Extended table service including oval and square creamers, spoon tray, rose bowl, basket. *Ref. K6-49.*

STAR AND LADDERS, creamer, author's name. Known in creamer and sugar bowl.

STARDUST, salt shaker. The possibility exists that this is actually FENTEC by McKee Glass Co. See Plate 107. *Ref. PetSal 40K*

DUNCAN HOMESTEAD, syrup. Duncan #63, ca. 1900. Extended table service including punch bowl, two types salt shaker, finger bowl, vases. Crystal, ruby-stained. *Ref. Bones 108; H7-130.*

BUCKINGHAM (CROSBY), creamer. U. S. Glass Co. #15106 (Glassport factory), 1907. Extended table service including wine. Crystal, rose-stained, gilded. *Ref. K6 Pl. 33; Gob II-108; Revi-310; Unitt 1-307; HTP-89; H5-146; Mugs p. 89.*

MEDALLION SUNBURST, mug. Bryce, Higbee and Co., ca. 1905. Extended table service including wine, butter pat. Crystal. *Ref. Gob II-114; Metz 1-228; Unitt 1-287; Unitt 2-138; HTP-83; Jenks p. 364; Schroy-98; Mugs p. 72.*

Ferris Wheel   *Carltec*

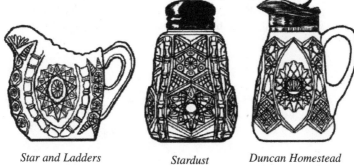

Star and Ladders   *Stardust*   *Duncan Homestead*

Buckingham   *Medallion Sunburst*

PLATE 107. FACETS

TWIN SUNBURSTS, pitcher. *Ref. K1-99.*

FENTEC, pitcher. McKee Glass Co., ca. 1894 – 1914. One of their "Tec" patterns. Extended table service with a huge variety of pieces. *Ref. McCain, Schroeder's Insider Vol. 2 #4 p. 7.*

SHIELD, creamer. Westmoreland Glass Co. #160. Extended table service. Crystal, ruby-stained. *Ref. K8-40; Metz 2-106; H7-192.*

LACY CABLE, creamer. Made ca. 1866. *Ref. K1-76.*

HORSESHOE CURVE, pitcher. *Ref. K1-149.*

SNOWFLAKE (SNOWFLAKE AND SUNBURST; FERNLAND), butter dish. Cambridge Glass Co. #2635, 1906. Extended table service including bread plate, wine, condiment set on tray, vases, toy table service. The toy spooner is collected as a toothpick holder. Crystal, yellow-green, cobalt blue, ruby-stained. *Ref. K2-104; K4-141; K7-174; HTP-55; H7-116, 194.*

Twin Sunbursts   *Fentec*

Shield   *Lacy Cable*

Horseshoe Curve   *Snowflake*

PLATE 108. FACETS

PYRAMID AND SHIELD, creamer. *Ref. HGC6 p. 13.*

ADA, creamer. Cambridge Glass Co.; Ohio Flint Glass Co, 1898; National Glass Co., 1903. Extended table service of over 100 pieces. Crystal, ruby-stained. *Ref. K7-199; H7-16.*

DIAMOND SWAG, toothpick holder. See Plate 43.

BONTEC, two pitchers. McKee Glass Co., ca. 1900, a "Tec" pattern. Extended table service including bonbon. *Ref. K3-139.*

INDIAN SUNSET, creamer. Made ca. 1905 in extended table service. *Ref. HTP-89.*

DIAMOND LACE, creamer. Extended table service. In Kamm 2 p. 70, this piece is identified as being made by A. H. Heisey Co. and called "Hobstar" in a Montgomery Ward catalog for 1914 with 20 items in the set. In Heacock's *Pattern Glass Preview #1,* he says it is not Heisey, it is Imperial, ca. 1905.

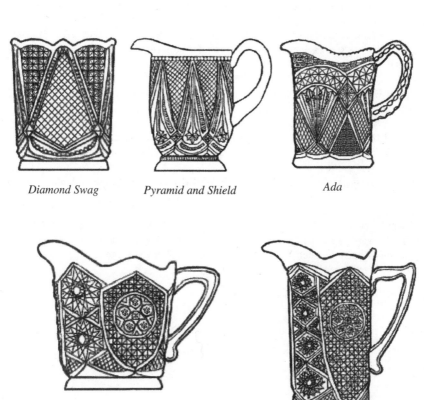

Diamond Swag   Pyramid and Shield   Ada

Bontec (two examples)

Indian Sunset   Diamond Lace

PLATE 109. FACETS

CANE PINWHEEL, pitcher. Known in pitcher only, author's name.

BUZZ STAR (COMET; WHIRLIGIG), pitcher. U. S. Glass #15101 (Bryce), 1907. Extended table service including wine, toy table service which is called WHIRLIGIG. Crystal. *Ref. K2-103; K4-140; H5-150, 174; HTP-74.*

PADDLEWHEEL SHIELD, creamer and goblet. Westmoreland Glass Co. #575, 1912. Extended table service, author's name.

DOUBLE PINWHEEL (STAR WHORL; JUNO), pitcher. Indiana Glass Co. after 1915. Extended table service. *Ref. K4-141; Gob II-90; Metz I-228; Unitt 2-116.*

PADDLEWHEEL (FERN WHEEL; FERN WHIRL), bowl, Westmoreland Glass Co., ca. 1907. Extended table service. *Ref. K8-41; Unitt 1-308; HGC 2-12.*

WILTEC, creamer. McKee Glass Co., 1894. A "Tec" pattern. Extended table service including vases, cigar jar, punch bowl, spoon tray, bonbon. The snowflake is reversed on some pieces, and the pitcher has two snowflakes, one above the other, with diamondpoint and small star beneath. *Ref. K8 Pl. 109; Stout p. 319.*

Cane Pinwheel

Buzz Star

Paddlewheel Shield (two examples)

Double Pinwheel

Paddlewheel

Wiltec

PLATE 110. FACETS, PINWHEELS

FEATHER SWIRL (SOLAR), goblet. U. S. Glass Co. #15116 (Bryce; Gas City), 1908. Extended table service including tray, wine, tall stretched vase. Crystal. *Ref. Gob II-153; Metz 2-176.*

WHIRLED SUNBURST IN CIRCLE, creamer. Beatty-Brady Glass Co., 1908. Basic table service. *Ref. K2-37.*

TEXAS STAR (SNOWFLAKE BASE), plate. Steiner Glass Co., 1905. Extended table service including wine. This star appears only on the bases of pieces; the body of the piece is very plain. To further confuse things, the salt shaker is a plain swirled column. Crystal, ruby-stained. See Plates 179 and 224. *Ref. K5-149; PetSal 41i; HTP-74; H7-182; Schroy-141.*

NEARCUT #2697, toy creamer. Cambridge Glass Co., 1909. Toy basic table service including handled spooner. *Ref. K7-175.*

CIRCULAR SAW (ROSETTA), creamer. Beaumont Glass Co., 1904. Extended table service including punch bowl, cracker jar. *Ref. K5-146.*

WHIRLWIND, salt shaker. *Ref. PetSal 43-0.*

SPINNING STAR (ROYAL), creamer. U. S. Glass Co. #15099. Extended table service including wine. Crystal. *Ref. H5-146.*

CANNONBALL PINWHEEL (CALEDONIA; PINWHEEL), creamer. U. S. Glass Co. #15094, 1906; Federal Glass Co., 1914. Extended table service. Federal made handled jelly, wine, square olive, and salt shaker, among other pieces. *Ref. K4-140; Gob I-100; Metz 1-194; Unitt 1-158; HGC4 p. 16.*

Feather Swirl

Whirled Sunburst in Circle

Texas Star

Nearcut #2697

Circular Saw

Whirlwind

Spinning Star

*Cannonball
Pinwheel*

PLATE 111. FACETS, PINWHEELS

McKEE'S SUNBURST (AZTEC SUNBURST), spooner. McKee Brothers, ca. 1910. Extended table service. *Ref. PetSal 174E; Stout p. 217.*

DAISY AND SCROLL (BUZZ SAW IN PARENTHESIS; U. S. VICTORIA), syrup. U. S. Glass Co. #15104 (Glassport), 1907. Extended table service including wine. Crystal, green. *Ref. H5-146; Gob II-114; Unitt 2-66.*

COMET IN THE STARS, pitcher. U. S. Glass Co. #15150 (Glassport), 1914. Extended table service. Crystal. *Ref. HPV #2 p. 6.*

FERNETTE, toothpick holder. Evansville Glass Co. (in Indiana), 1905. *Ref. HGC2 p. 12.*

RAMBLER, creamer. U. S. Glass Co. #15136 (Gas City), 1912. Extended table service including pickle dish, handled jelly, bonbon. Crystal. *Ref. H5-169.*

DIAMOND WHIRL, pitcher. U. S. Glass Co. #15109, 1915. Extended table service. Crystal. *Ref. H5-162.*

TWIN CRESCENTS, creamer. *Ref. K2-60.*

AZTEC (SPINNER DAISY; NEW MEXICO), creamer. McKee Brothers, 1903 – 1927. A "Tec" pattern. Extended table service including water bottle, punch bowl, wines, cordials, champagnes, claret. Crystal, ruby-stained. *Ref. K7-43; K8 Pl. 110; Stout p. 217; Jenks p. 35; Schroy-11; H7-70.*

234

McKee's Sunburst

Daisy and Scroll

Comet in the Stars

Fernette

Rambler

Diamond Whirl

Twin Crescents

Aztec

235

PLATE 112. FACETS

ROSBY, cracker jar base. Fostoria Glass Co. #1704, 1910 – 1928. Extended table service including open and covered cracker jars, flower bowl, molasses can. No goblet listed. Crystal, gold decorated. Some items were reproduced in the 1950s in milk glass; and in 1965 as part of the Centennial II collection. Punch bowl and cups were produced for an extended period. Courtesy of Bob Burford. *Ref. Kerr p. 134*

QUINTEC, salt shaker. McKee Glass Co. as one of their "Tec" series; reproduced by Kemple. Extended table service including bonbon, cigar jars. Crystal, ruby-stained. *Ref. PetSal 169L; Stout p. 219; H7-64.*

YUTEC, salt shaker. McKee Brothers, 1909, one of the "Tec" patterns. Reproduced by Kemple Glass Co. in colors. Extended table service including wine, champagne, cordial. *Ref. PetSal 177H; HTP-72 (Repro).*

SUNBURST AND STAR, salt shaker. *Ref. PetSal 174D.*

WHEEL OF FORTUNE, salt shaker. *Ref. PetSal 43N.*

U. S. REGAL, creamer. U. S. Glass Co. (Glassport), 1906. Extended table service including flare-bottom toothpick holder, sugar shaker, decanter, basket. Crystal, ruby-stained. There seems to be some speculation that U. S. Regal was the State Series for Oklahoma. The original catalog names it "U. S. Regal." Heacock and others say there was no U. S. Glass pattern for Oklahoma. Imperial Glass Co. made one for Oklahoma, however, and it is pictured on Plate 68. *Ref. K6 Pl. 35; Schroy-147; H5-145; HTP-86; H7-79.*

STIPPLED FANS, cruet. Lancaster Glass Co, 1912. Known in cruet, celery vase, toothpick and holder; probably made in basic table service, water and berry sets. Crystal, gilded. *Ref. Heacock, Antique Trader article May 26, 1982 p. 96.*

SQUAT PINEAPPLE (LONE STAR; GEM), creamer. McKee and Brothers, 1898; U. S. Glass, 1892; Federal Glass, 1914. Extended table service including two types salt shaker, wine. Crystal, emerald green. *Ref. K2-76; HGC4 p. 2; Schroy-134.*

DAISY AND CANE, pitcher. Known in water pitcher, author's name.

Rosby   *Quintec*   *Yutec*

Sunburst   *Wheel of*   *U. S. Regal*
and Star   *Fortune*

Stippled Fans   *Squat Pineapple*   *Daisy and Cane*

PLATE 113. FLOWERS

CURLED LEAF, pitcher. Bryce, Walker and Co., 1869. *Ref. K3-21; Metz 1-60.*

PRESSED SPRAY, pitcher. the pattern is impressed on the **inside** of the bowl. *Ref. K4-133.*

CARNATION, pitcher. Lancaster Glass Co., 1911. Extended table service. Crystal, decorated. *Ref. K2-130.*

FLOWER AND PLEAT (MIDWESTERN POMONA), salt shaker. Made ca. 1895 in extended table service. Crystal, frosted, color-washed, and rare in ruby-staining. *Ref. Pet-Sal 161K; HI-23.*

TARENTUM'S VICTORIA (QUESTION MARK), salt shaker. Tarentum Glass Co., 1900. Extended table service including dresser tray. Crystal, colors, opaque, decorated. *Ref. K2-53.*

FLOWER AND BUD (BLOOMS AND BLOSSOMS), salt shaker. Northwood Glass Co., ca. 1908. Made in novelties in crystal, opalescent, emerald green, carnival, decorated. *Ref. PetSal 29D; HII-63, 86.*

FLOWER AND HONEYCOMB, creamer. U. S. Glass Co., ca. 1915. *Ref. K7-28.*

BLEEDING HEART (KING'S FLORAL WARE; NEW FLORAL), tumbler. King, Son and Co. #85, 1875+; Boston and Sandwich; Burlington Glass Works; U. S. Glass Co., 1898. Extended table service including waste bowl, wines, cordial, egg cups, handled mug, flat and footed tumblers, oval and footed salts. Crystal, opaque, gilded. *Ref. K1-8; L-128; LEAPG-385; Gob II-43; Gob II-91; Metz 1-58; Metz 2-74; Jenks p. 71; Schroy-22; Mugs p. 28.*

PAMPAS FLOWER, creamer. Extended table service. *Ref. K8-2; Metz 2-64.*

CRANESBILL, pitcher. Made ca. 1890 in basic table service; all pieces scarce. *Ref. K1-62; Metz 2-60.*

Curled Leaf   *Pressed Spray*   *Carnation*

Flower and Pleat   *Tarentum's*   *Flower and*   *Flower and*
                     Victoria   *Bud*   *Honeycomb*

Bleeding Heart   *Pampas Flower*   *Cranesbill*

PLATE 114. FLOWERS

LILY-OF-THE-VALLEY (MAY FLOWER), creamer. Richard and Hartley, 1870s. Extended table service including rare master salt, wine, cordial, champagne. Some pieces have three fragile-looking legs. *Ref. L-126; Metz 1-58; K1-118; K4-4.*

STIPPLED WOODFLOWER, creamer. Extended table service. *Ref. L-136; LEAPG-393; Metz 1-77; Metz 2-62.*

FLOWER AND QUILL (PRETTY BAND), pitcher. Made ca. 1880s in extended table service including pickle castor, square plate. *Ref. K3-52; Metz 2-54.*

LEAF AND FLOWER, celery vase. Hobbs #339, 1891; U. S. Glass Co., 1891. Extended table service including rare celery basket, finger bowl, castor set with plain bottles; condiment set on leaf-shaped tray, celery basket. Crystal, satin finish, etched, ruby-stained, amber-stained. *Ref. LV-50; H7-140; Hobbs p. 123.*

FORGET-ME-NOT, tumbler. Fostoria Glass Co. #240, 1891. Extended table service. *Ref. K6 Pl. 58.*

LEE'S LILY-OF-THE-VALLEY, goblet. This is an unnamed piece in *L-153 #13.*

THISTLE, goblet. Bryce McKee & Co., 1872; Bakewell, Pears and Co., 1875. Extended table service including wine, cordial. The egg cup is scarce. Crystal, ruby-stained. *Ref. L-140; LEAPG-406; Gob I-132; Metz 1-68; Unitt 1-209; Jenks p. 512; Schroy-142; Mugs p. 28.*

FUCHSIA, mug. Boston and Sandwich, 1865. Basic table service, goblet and mug. *Ref. K8-5; Mugs p. 28.*

PANSY AND MOSS ROSE (PANSY, MOSS ROSE AND LILY-OF-THE-VALLEY), pitcher. Extended table service. *Ref. K1-61.*

CLEMATIS, creamer. Made ca. 1876 in extended table service including a 12" lamp with an iron base and a glass stem with a picture of a pink cat in it. *Ref. L-75; LEAPG-405; K3-25; Metz 1-54; Metz 2-66; Jenks p. 124; Schroy-36.*

Lily-of-the-Valley

*Stippled Wood-
flower*

*Flower and
Quill*

Leaf and Flower

Forget-Me-Not

*Lee's Lily-of-
Valley*

Thistle

Fuchsia

*Pansy and
Moss Rose*

Clematis

PLATE 115. FLOWERS

MARSH PINK (SQUARE FUCHSIA), open sugar bowl. Made in the 1880s in extended table service including jam jar, wine. This is a square dish. Crystal, amber (rare). *Ref. K2-30; Metz 1-66; Schroy-96.*

WATERLILY AND CATTAILS, pitcher. Northwood; Fenton; Diamond (Dugan) Glass Co., 1889. Extended table service. Crystal, opalescent, carnival (rare in lavender carnival). *Ref. K4-78; Schroy-153.*

MAGNOLIA (WATERLILY; FROSTED MAGNOLIA), pitcher. Dalzell, Gilmore and Leighton, 1890. Extended table service. Crystal, frosted. *Ref. K4-136.*

JAPANESE IRIS (REBECCA), creamer. New Martinsville Glass Co., ca. 1910. Extended table service. Crystal, ruby-stained. *Ref. K8-58; H7-49+.*

PANSY, pitcher. Made ca. 1910 in carnival glass. *Ref. K6-24.*

DANDELION, toothpick holder. Fostoria Glass Co. #1319, ca. 1911. *Ref. HTP-83.*

FLOWER WINDOWS, salt shaker. *Ref. PetSal 29M.*

NEW MARTINSVILE CARNATION, toothpick holder. New Martinsville Glass Co. after 1901. Crystal, rare in ruby-stained. *Ref. Miller-17; HI-46; H7-49, 88.*

FLORIDA (SUNKEN PRIMROSE), toothpick holder and square dish. Greensburg Glass Co., 1893. Extended table service. Crystal, ruby-stained. *Ref. K4-73; H5-38, 173; H6-29; H7-117; Jenks p. 222; Schroy-62.*

Marsh Pink

*Waterlily and
Cattails*

Magnolia

Japanese Iris

Pansy

Dandelion

Flower Windows

*New
Martinsville
Carnation*

Florida (two examples)

PLATE 116. FLOWERS

THE MOSAIC (DAISY AND BLUEBELL), creamer. Mosaic Glass Co. #51, 1891. Extended table service. *Ref. K1-93.*

PANELLED DAISY (BRAZIL), creamer. Bryce Brothers, 1880s; U. S. Glass Co. (Bryce), 1891. Extended table service including handled mug, sugar shaker, tray, finger bowl, decanter. Crystal, blue, milk glass, rare amber-stained. *Ref. L-95; LEAPG-395; Metz 1-62; K3-65; HIII-34, 78; H5-74; Mugs p. 32.*

PANELLED PRIMULA, pitcher. Made ca. 1900 in extended table service including lamp, cordial, decanter, cup and saucer, bread plate. *Ref. K3-117.*

DOLLY MADISON (JEFFERSON #271), tumbler. Jefferson Glass Co., 1903. Extended table service but limited. Crystal, blue, green, opalescent. *Ref. K7-152; HIII-19, 34; Schroy-52.*

TEARDROP FLOWER, creamer. Northwood Glass Co. ca. 1904. Extended table service including rare cruet. Crystal, colors. *Ref. K7-17.*

PANELLED HEATHER, pitcher. Indiana Glass Co. #126, 1911. Extended table service including wine. *Gob 1-152; Metz 1-67; Metz 2-178; Unitt 2-61; Schroy-108.*

NARCISSUS SPRAY, goblet. Indiana Glass Co., 1915 – 1930s. Extended table service. Crystal, decorated. *Ref. K4-137; L-153 #8. (There are differences in the drawings produced by Kamm and Lee; I saw a plate that favored Lee's rendition, so I have chosen to follow her lead.)*

DOUBLE DAHLIA WITH LENS, creamer. U. S. Glass Co., 1905. Extended table service including toothpick holder, wine set. Crystal, stained flowers and leaves, rose-flashed, emerald green. *Ref. K8-23; Unitt 2-72; HPV4-9; HI-21; H5-40.*

MADEIRA (RUBY TALONS), creamer. Tarentum Glass Co., ca. 1912. Extended table service. Crystal, ruby-stained. *Ref. HGC2-38; H7-146.*

244

The Mosaic

Panelled Daisy

Panelled Primula

Dolly Madison

*Teardrop
Flower*

*Panelled
Heather*

*Narcissus
Spray*

*Double Dahlia
with Lens*

Madeira

PLATE 117. FLOWERS

STIPPLED FORGET-ME-NOT (FORGET-ME-NOT IN SNOW; DOT), tumbler. Findlay Glass Co., 1899. Extended table service including wine, cordial, plates with baby, star or kitten motif. Crystal, blue, amber (rare), opalescent (rare). *Ref. L-128; LEAPG-370; K4-126; Metz 1-56; Unitt 2-80; Jenks p. 496; Schroy-136; Mugs p. 34.*

HORSESHOE. (GOOD LUCK; PRAYER RUG; PRAYER MAT), sauce and waste bowl. Adams and Co., 1881. Extended table service including jam jar, cordial, rare wine, platter, bread plate, rare master salt. Covered pieces have a horseshoe finial. A glass wheelbarrow with "branches" thought to be part of the BARLEY pattern may actually be part of HORSESHOE. The branches are identical to detail on HORSESHOE *(Steven D. Skeim, E.A.P.G. Newsletter, Volume 5 No 4, Winter, 1998.)* Crystal. Smaller pieces lack the horseshoe and "prayer rug." *Ref. L-112; K1-66; Metz 1-114; Gob I-54; Unitt 1-138; Schroy-78.*

ARCH AND FORGET-ME-NOT BANDS, pitcher. Made ca. 1885 in extended table service including jam jar. Has been found with advertising for "Henderson's Wild Cherry Beverage – Free.) *Ref. K2-82.*

FACETED FLOWER, pitcher. Made in the late 1800s in extended table service including water tray. *Ref. K2-82.*

GRASSHOPPER WITHOUT INSECT, pitcher. Beaumont Glass Co., 1898. Extended table service including celery vase on legs. See Plate 7 for insect. Crystal. *Ref. K1-88; Metz 1-94; Jenks p. 254; Schroy-68.*

PANELLED SAGEBRUSH, goblet. *Ref. Gob II-16.*

RIBBED FORGET-ME-NOT (PERT SET), creamer. Bryce Brothers, 1880s; U. S. Glass Co. (Bryce), 1890 – 1891. Extended table service including handled mustard with lid, toy table set. Crystal, amber (scarce), blue (scarce), amethyst, canary. *Ref. K1-67; LEAPG-375; Metz 1-56; H5-84; Mugs p. 32.*

FLOWER POT (POTTED PLANT), pitcher. Made in the 1880s in extended table service including two sizes salt shakers, bread tray. Crystal. *Ref. L-136; LEAPG-396; Metz 1-61; Metz 2-60; K1-87; Jenks p. 224; Schroy-62.*

HANGING BASKET, pitcher. National Glass Co. (Ohio Flint Glass Works), ca. 1902. Known in water pitcher and tumbler. Crystal, colors. *Ref. K6-61; EAPGS News Journal Vol. 6 #1 Spring, 1999 (by Bob Sanford).*

Stippled Forget-Me-Not

Horseshoe (two examples)

Arch and Forget-Me-Not Bands

Faceted Flower

Grasshopper Without Insect

Panelled Sagebrush

Ribbed Forget-Me-Not

Flower Pot

Hanging Basket

PLATE 118. FLOWERS, ROSES

OPEN ROSE, goblet. Made in the 1870s in extended table service including egg cup, master salt. Crystal. *Ref. L-222; LEAPG-361; Metz 1-54; Schroy-106; Jenks p. 390.*

DAHLIA, creamer. Portland Glass Co., 1865; Burlington Glass Works; Diamond Flint Glass Co.; Canton Glass Co.; 1865 – 1890. Extended table service including wine, cordial, egg cup, rare double egg cup, platter with grape handles, rare champagne. Crystal, amber, canary, blue, green. *Ref. K1-73; L-126; LEAPG-398; Metz 1-64; Gob I-18; Jenks p. 147; Schroy-42; Mugs p. 27.*

CABBAGE ROSE (ROSE), compote. Central Glass Co. #140 patent 1870. Extended table service including rare wine, rare milk pitcher, cordials, champagne, nineteen sizes of compotes, four sizes of cake stands, egg cup, footed salt. The finial is shaped like a rose bud. Crystal. *Ref. L-122; LEAPG-360; K3-40; K7-58; Metz 1-54; Unitt 1-199; Gob I-52; Mugs p. 28; Schroy-29; Jenks p. 98.*

AMERICAN BEAUTY (ROSE AND SUNBURSTS; LA FRANCE), creamer. Cooperative Flint Glass Co., ca. 1910 (**not** Northwood). Extended table service. Crystal, green, ruby-stained. *Ref. K2-98; HGC2-11; H7-102.*

ROSE-IN-SNOW, sugar bowl. Bryce Brothers, 1870s; U. S. Glass Co., 1891; Ohio Flint Glass Co., 1898. Extended table service including rare double relish dish, wine. Crystal, amber, canary, blue, gilded. *Ref. K4-43; LEAPG-358; Metz 1-54; Unitt 1-999; Gob I-17; Jenks p. 451; Mugs p. 31.*

PRIMROSE (STIPPLED PRIMROSE), pitcher. Canton Glass Co. #10, 1880s. Extended table service including card receiver in basket, wine, cordials, egg cup. Crystal, colors, slag, opaque, black. *Ref. L-136; Gob I-138; Metz 1-54; Unitt 2-70; K3-119.*

ROSE SPRIG, pitcher. Campbell, Jones and Co., 1886. Extended table service including water tray, handled mug, wine, cordial. Crystal, amber, canary, blue. The goblet has been reproduced. *Ref. L-125; LEAPG-387; Metz 1-54; Metz 2-62; Welker p. 235; Mugs p. 31; Schroy-123; Jenks p. 453.*

GARLAND OF ROSES, creamer. Made ca. 1900. Extended table service including footed open salt, egg cup, and very rare toothpick holder. All pieces are rare. Crystal, vaseline, chocolate. *Ref. K4-58; HTP-58.*

HUNDRED LEAVED ROSE, pitcher. Made ca. 1890s, possibly Model Flint Glass Co., in extended table service. Crystal, frosted. *Ref. K2-128; Miller 4th Ed. p. 321.*

Open Rose

Dahlia

Cabbage Rose

American Beauty

Rose-in-Snow

Primrose

Rose Sprig

Garland of Roses

Hundred Leaved
Rose

PLATE 119. FLOWERS

WREATH AND BARS, goblet. *Ref. Gob II-16.*

DAISY WHORL (DAISY WHORL WITH DIAMOND BAND), goblet. Made in the 1870s in extended table service. *Ref. Gob II-121; Metz 2-108; K4-8.*

LATE ROSETTE, mug. Kamm said this may have been a prize in packages of oatmeal, coffee, etc. Known in crystal, amber, blue, ruby-stained. *Ref. K1-35; H7-140+.*

ROMAN ROSETTE, syrup. Bryce, Walker and Co.; U. S. Glass Co.; #15030; 1875; 1891. Extended table service including mug, toy mug, bread plate, wine, cordial. Being reproduced; the stippling should have a pebbled look, not a pitted appearance. Crystal, ruby-stained (U. S. Glass produced the stained items.) *Ref. K1-34; L-157; LEAPG-482; Gob I-93; Metz 1-124; Unitt 1-302; Mugs p. 96; Schroy-122; Jenks p. 449; H5-33; H7-187+.*

FERN GARLAND (COLONIAL WITH GARLAND; OLD COLONY), creamer. McKee Glass Co., ca. 1894. Extended table service including wine. Pieces are marked "Pres-Cut." Also made without the impressed garland. Crystal, ruby-stained. *Ref. K4-106; Gob II-111; Metz 2-176; Unitt 2-77; H7-164+.*

SHASTA DAISY, creamer. Extended table service. Crystal, opaque glass. *Ref. K6-25.*

JUMBO, creamer. See Plate 3.

FLOWER BAND, WARMAN'S, salt shaker. Known in milk glass. *Ref. W-140.*

FANCY FANS, sugar shaker. Milk glass; may also be painted. *Ref. HIII-49.*

THISTLE AND CLOVER, salt shaker. It has a clover leaf on the other side. *Ref. PetSal 154M.*

DOUBLE DAISY (ROSETTE BANDS), pitcher. Possibly produced by Riverside; Heacock believed that this was produced by U. S. Glass, ca. 1893 (not found in his U. S. Glass book). Extended table service including wine; the compote is rare. Crystal, ruby-stained. *Ref. K7-23; Gob II-24; Metz 1-124; Unitt 1-303; H7-106+; Schroy-53; Jenks p. 185.*

Wreath and   *Daisy Whorl*   *Late Rosette*   *Roman Rosette*
Bars

Fern Garland   *Shasta Daisy*   *Jumbo*

Flower Band,   *Fancy Fans*   *Thistle*   *Double Daisy*
Warman's   *and*
                                 Clover

PLATE 120. FLOWERS

SPRIG IN SNOW, salt shaker. Known in shaker and salt dip, clear and in color. *Ref. Pet-Sal 40C.*

BELLFOWER, SINGLE VINE (RIBBED LEAF; R.L.), plate. Boston and Sandwich, 1840s; McKee Brothers, 1868; and others in both flint glass and non-flint. Extended table service including rare cake stand, rare castor set, rare decanter, rare handled mug, lamps, champagne, rare whiskey, wine, rare 6" plate. Crystal, cobalt blue (rare), amber (rare), opaque. At the Green Valley Auction in Pittsburgh in 1998 an unrecorded syrup pitcher sold for $1,300. *Ref. K6-6; L-30; LEAPG-95; Metz 1-30; Metz 2-54; Gob I-16; Unitt 1-62; K4-49; Jenks p. 60; Schroy-20.*

HEART STEM, pitcher. Made ca. 1890 in extended table service. *Ref. K4-7; Metz 2-184.*

DOUBLE BAND FORGET-ME-NOT, goblet. Kokomo-Jenkins Glass Co. #500, 1904. Wine is also known. *Ref. Gob II-47; Metz 1-56.*

STIPPLED FLOWER BAND (STARFLOWER BAND), goblet. *Ref. L-153 #2; Metz 1-64.*

STIPPLED STARFLOWER (STARFLOWER BAND), goblet. Made in the late 1880s in extended table service including footed salt, wine. *Ref. L-153 #7; Metz 1-64; Unitt 1-148.*

BELLFLOWER, DOUBLE VINE, pitcher. A variation on the above pattern.

FORGET-ME-NOT IN SCROLL, goblet. Made ca. 1870s in extended table service. *Ref. L-77.*

FLOWER BAND, goblet. Extended tale service. *Ref. L-107; LEAPG-374; K4-47; Metz 1-56.*

TULIP BAND, goblet. See similar patterns on Plate 40. *Ref. Gob II-104; Metz 1-32.*

Sprig in Snow

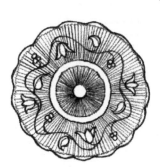

Bellflower, Single Vine

Heart Stem

*Double Band
Forget-Me-Not*

*Stippled
Flower Band*

*Stippled
Starflower*

*Bellflower,
Double Vine*

*Forget-Me-Not
in Scroll*

Flower Band

Tulip Band

PLATE 121. FLOWERS

PANELLED FLOWER AND FERN, mug. Made ca. 1835 in flint glass; there may possibly be a saucer to match. *Ref. Mugs p. 38.*

DELAWARE (FOUR PETAL FLOWER; NEW CENTURY), tumbler and covered pomade box. U. S. Glass Co. #15065 (Bryce), 1899. A State Series pattern. Extended table service including banana boat, rose bowl, berry set, bride's basket, two types toothpick holders, pin tray. Crystal, rose-flashed, emerald green, custard, milk glass (scarce). *Ref. K1-103; HI-19; H4-54; H5-34+; H6-25, 95; H7-102; Jenks p. 170; Schroy-48.*

DAHLIA AND LEAF, plate. Known in plate *(Author's name).*

ASTER AND LEAF (TAPERED VINE), syrup. Beaumont Glass Co. #217, 1895. Made in condiment items including sugar shaker. Found only in colors. *Ref. K7 Pl. 63; PetSal 21J; HIII-15.*

BEAUMONT'S FLORA, toothpick holder. Beaumont Glass Co. #399, 1898. Extended table service. Emerald green, opalescent colors, gilded. *Ref. K7-59; HTP-46.*

LACY FLORAL, creamer. Westmoreland Glass Co., 1904. Extended table service including wine. Crystal, milk glass, decorated. *Ref. K5-114; H3-50.*

DAISY AND PALM, goblet. This is Northwood glass made in an amethyst goblet; and in carnival glass a footed candy dish, open compote, rose bowl (stemmed), and rose bowl on three feet. Opalescent glass pieces with angular, ribbon feet have small holes close to the outer ends (Hartung, *Carnival Glass in Color.*) Carnival colors of marigold, purple, and green are known, and Hartung calls the pattern "Daisy and Plume." *Ref. Gob II-86.*

MAINE (PANELLED FLOWER STIPPLED), syrup and milk pitcher. U. S. Glass Co. #15066, 1899. A State Series pattern. Extended table service including rare green syrup, mug, wines. No goblets were made. Crystal, emerald green, decorated, stained. *Ref. K4-86; L-77; Metz 1-66; LV-158; H5-36+; Jenks p. 346; Schroy-94; Mugs p. 36.*

Panelled Flower and Fern

Delaware (two examples)

Dahlia and Leaf

Aster and Leaf

Beaumont's Flora

Lacy Floral

Daisy and Palm

Maine (two examples)

255

PLATE 122. FLOWERS

COSMOS (STEMLESS DAISY), syrup. Consolidated Lamp and Glass co., 1898 – 1905. Extended table service including condiment set, miniature lamp, perfume bottles, pickle castor, trays. Opaque and cased colors. *Ref. K5-53; HI-50; HIII-21.*

FISHNET AND POPPIES, syrup. Known in milk glass syrup. *Ref. HIII-24.*

ROSETTE ROW, salt shaker. *Ref. PetSal 38E.*

DIAGONAL ROSETTES, creamer. Non-flint, made in basic table service, at least. *Ref. Metz 1-125.*

BEADED FLOWER, salt shaker. Indiana Tumbler and Goblet Co. Extended table service. *Ref. PetSal 154M.*

FLOWER BAND BARREL, salt shaker. Milk glass. *Ref. PetSal 21U.*

HONEYCOMB WITH FLOWER RIM (INVERTED THUMBPRINT WITH DAISY BAND), pitcher. U. S. Glass Co. #15060, 1899; 1903. The honeycomb design is pressed from the inside. Extended table service including vase, waste bowl, pickle tray, card tray with handle on top, candlestick. Clear pieces have been reproduced. Crystal, blue, green. *Ref. K2-117; HI-43; Metz 1-202.*

VERMONT (VERMONT HONEYCOMB), pitcher. The same pattern as the preceding by U. S. Glass in opaque custard glass. A State Series pattern. Extended table service. The decorated custard glass does not show the honeycomb pattern which is on the inside. Heacock, in *U. S. Glass from A to Z*, shows 15 pieces of this scarce and beautiful pattern, including three sizes of card trays, a vase, and a master berry. The tumbler's ridged "feet" are pulled up close to the sides. *Ref. K6 Pl. 19; HTP-71, 72 (repros); HI-43; H4-51+; H5-53; Jenks p. 538; Schroy-150.*

PEARL FLOWERS, bowl. Made ca. 1905 – 1910 in various sized bowls. Crystal, carnival, and opalescent colors of white, blue, and green. *Ref. HII-70.*

STYLIZED FLOWER (FLOWER AND PANEL), spoon holder. Challinor, Taylor and Co., 1885; U. S. Glass Co, 1891. Basic table service and pitchers. Crystal, brown mosaic, opalescent, and rare in amber. *Ref. K2-127; H5-94.*

PERIWINKLE, salt shaker. *Ref. PetSal 35i.*

Cosmos

Fishnet and Poppies

Rosette Row

Diagonal Rosettes

Beaded Flower

Flower Band Barrel

Honeycomb with Flower Rim

Vermont

Pearl Flowers

Stylized Flower

Periwinkle

PLATE 123. FLOWERS

FLOWERED SCROLL, syrup. George Duncan and Sons #2000, 1893. Extended table service. Crystal, ruby-stained, amber-stained. *Ref. K8-183; Metz 1-220; HIII-25; H7-118.*

SIX PANSY (PANSY), salt shaker. Consolidated Lamp and Glass Co. Extended table service. Not made in crystal; opaque colors. *Ref. K6-78.*

COREOPSIS, syrup. Made ca. 1902, possibly by Consolidated Lamp and Glass in extended table service including stubby syrup, cracker jar, berry set. The butter has a metal base, and other pieces have metal rims and lids. Decorated milk glass; rare in red satin with white decoration; no crystal. *Ref. K5-52; HIII-21; H6-17.*

LITTLE FLOWER (PANELLED APPLE BLOSSOM), creamer. Probably ca. 1890 – 1910, and possibly Jenkins Glass Company. Extended table service including covered butter, goblet, compote, sugar, sauce, butter. A mold-blown pattern. Kamm thought it might have been a premium in some grocery product. *Ref. K7-53.*

SINGLE ROSE, salt shaker. Extended table service. Known as "Wild Rose" in carnival glass. Crystal, opaque white, decorated, carnival. *Ref. K3-86.*

APPLE BLOSSOMS, syrup. Northwood Glass Co., ca. 1896. Extended table service including sugar shaker, miniature lamp. Decorated milk glass. *Ref. HI-50; HIII-14.*

PANELLED DOGWOOD, sauce dish. U. S. Glass Co., after 1908. Made only in various-sized bowls in crystal, emeral green, rose-flashed, amethyst-flashed. *Ref. Metz 2-66; H5-45+; H7-68.*

ALBA BLOSSOMS, syrup. Dithridge and Co., 1895. Syrup and sugar shaker known. White opaque glass. *Ref. HIII-14.*

PRIMROSE AND PEARLS, syrup. Milk glass. *Ref. HIII-49.*

ART NOVO (PANELLED DOGWOOD; DOGWOOD; WILD ROSE), toothpick holder. Cooperative Flint Glass Co., 1905 – 1918+. Extended table service including miniatures, wine. Crystal, rose-flashed, ruby-stained, frosted, milk glass, decorated. *Ref. K1-69; Gob II-36; Metz 2-66; Unitt 1-203; HI-13; H7-52, 68; Schroy-161.*

Flowered Scroll

Six Pansy

Coreopsis

Little Flower

Single Rose

Apple Blossoms

Panelled Dogwood

Alba Blossoms

Primrose and Pearls

Art Novo

PLATE 124. FLOWERS WITH SCROLLS

DITHRIDGE #25, syrup. Dithridge and Co. Milk glass (may be painted). *Ref. HIII-49.*

LOUIS XV, cruet. Northwood Glass Co., 1899. Extended table service including rare toothpick holder, banana-boat shaped berry set. The pitcher has short, knobby feet. Most often found in green or custard glass; possibly crystal. *Ref. K2-199; HTP-46; HIII-56.*

FLORADORA (BOHEMIAN), creamer. U. S. Glass Co. #15063, 1899. Extended table service including straw jar, rare mug. Crystal, rose-flashed, emerald green, frosted, stained, gilded. *Ref. K6 Pl. 59; HI-15; Mugs p. 27.*

ROCK CRYSTAL (PURITAN; NOSTALGIA), creamer and salt shaker. McKee Glass Co., 1894. Extended table service including wines, cordial, champagne, claret, ice cream glass, sherbet, candlestick, finger bowl, pickle tray, punch bowl. Crystal, ruby-stained. *Ref. K3-136; K5-96; Unitt 1-298; Unitt 2-212; H7-178.*

BEADED BOTTOM, salt shaker. Dithridge and Co., 1898. Milk glass. *Ref. PetSal 22.*

WILD ROSE WITH BOW KNOT, syrup. McKee and Sons; National Glass Co., 1901. Extended table service including smoke set on tray. Crystal, colors, frosted, opaque, decorated. *Ref. K2-64; HTP 47, 55; H6-46+.*

WILD ROSE WITH SCROLLING (SULTAN), creamer. McKee Glass Co., ca. 1902 – 1910. Extended table service including rare double relish. The background is stippled. Crystal, amber, canary, blue. *Ref. K8-44; Stout p. 211.*

INTAGLIO (FLOWER SPRAY WITH SCROLLS; PANELLED FLOWERS), creamer. Northwood Glass Co., 1898. Extended table service including wine. Crystal, colors, custard glass. *Ref. K2-110; K7-200; Metz 1-76; HGC5-47; HIII-21; H6-31; Schroy-80.*

ROSE WREATH, pitcher. Pittsburgh Lamp, Brass & Glass Co., 1902. *Ref. K4-142.*

Dithridge #25   *Louis XV*   *Floradora*

Rock Crystal (two examples)   *Beaded Bottom*   *Wild Rose w/Bow Knot*

Wild Rose w/Scrolling   *Intaglio*   *Rose Wreath*

PLATE 125. FLOWERS

THISTLE AND FERN, salt shaker. *Ref. PetSal 42A.*

FLORICUT, pitcher. U. S. Glass Co. (Glassport), 1916. Extended table service including bowls with stubby feet, handled sauce, tall and medium tumblers, vases. Crystal; part pressed and part cut. *Ref. H5-160.*

TWO FLOWER, pitcher. U. S. Glass Co. #15138, 1918. Extended table service including tall shallow compotes, handled footed nut bowl. Crystal. *Ref. H5-170.*

FIELD THISTLE, creamer. U. S. Glass Co. (Gas City), 1912. Extended table service including open and covered sugar bowls (open with two handles; covered with no handles), castor set, crimped olive dish. Crystal, carnival. *Ref. Hartung; H5-157.*

SUNFLOWER PATCH, cruet. Duncan and Miller, ca. 1897. Extended table service. Rare in ruby-stained. *Ref. H6-81; H7-41+.*

WINDFLOWER, pitcher. Made in the 1870s in extended table service including egg cup, wine, cordials, footed salt. *Ref. L-139; LEAPG-391; K5-5; Gob I-25; Metz 1-62; Unitt 1-202; Jenks p. 558; Schroy-156; HIII-73.*

MORNING GLORY, egg cup. Boston and Sandwich, 1860s. Extended table service including individual salt dip, footed tumbler, creamer, wine, champagne. Flint glass; all pieces are rare. The goblet and wine have been reproduced. At the Green Valley Auction in Pittsburgh in 1998, a goblet sold for $1,850. *Ref. K6-3; Metz 1-14; Gob I-FP; Unitt 1-202; Unitt 2-220.*

PANELLED THISTLE (DELTA), creamer. J. B. Higbee Glass Co., 1908; Jefferson Glass Co. in Canada, 1910 – 1920. Extended table service including flared cup, wines, cordials, champagne. May have the "bee" trademark. The wine has been reproduced. Crystal, rare ruby-stained. *Ref. K1-83; L-114; Gob II-77; Metz 1-68; Unitt 1-208; Unitt 2-223; H7-103; HTP-86; Jenks p. 398; Schroy-109; Mugs p. 35; H7-10, 103, 168.*

LATE THISTLE (INVERTED THISTLE), sugar bowl. Cambridge Glass Co., ca. 1903. Marked "Near Cut" on inside of base in about 1906. Extended table service including covered honey dish. Crystal, ruby-stained. *Ref. K1-114; LEAPG-605; Metz 1-69; Metz 2-64; H7-133.*

INTAGLIO DAISY, pitcher. U. S. Glass Co. (Glassport) #15133, 1911. Extended table service. Crystal, decorated. *HTP-48; H5-170.*

CRYSTAL ROCK, pitcher. U. S. Glass Co., 1905. Extended table service. Crystal, decorated. *Ref. K6 Pl. 34; H5-175.*

Thistle and Fern   *Floricut*   *Two Flower*   *Field Thistle*

Sunflower Patch   *Windflower*   *Morning Glory*   *Panelled Thistle*

Late Thistle   *Intaglio Daisy*   *Crystal Rock*

PLATE 126. FLOWERS

PANELLED FORGET-ME-NOT, goblet. Bryce Brothers, 1880s; U. S. Glass Co., 1891; also Doyle and Co. Extended table service including bread tray, jam jar, cordial, wine. Crystal, amber, canary, blue, green. *Ref. K3-43; L-130; Metz 1-56; Unitt 1-140; Jenks p. 395; Schroy-107.*

PANELLED SUNBURSTS AND DAISY, pitcher. U. S. Glass Co. #15146, 1915. Extended table service. Crystal. *Ref. H5-170.*

GARDEN PINK (FLOWER MEDALLION), creamer. Indiana Glass Co. #167, 1913. Extended table service including wine. *Ref. K5-148.*

WILDFLOWER, pitcher. Adams and Co. #140, 1874; U. S. Glass Co., 1891. Extended table service including footed and flat butter dishes, wine. Crystal, amber, blue, green, amethyst, vaseline. The goblet and wine have been reproduced. *Ref. K1-36; LV-6; Metz 1-62; Gob I-53; Unitt 1-197; Unitt 2-223; HIII-46; H5-40, 70; Jenks p. 554; Schroy-155.*

GAELIC, pitcher. Indiana Glass Co., 1908. Extended table service including punch cup, pickle tray, heart-shaped dish, wine. Crystal, decorated. *Ref. K4-122; Gob II-64; HTP-85; H6-96.*

FLOWER AND DIAMOND, pitcher. U. S. Glass Co. #14147, 1913. Extended table service. *Ref. H5-170.*

ROSE POINT BAND (WATERLILY; CLEMATIS; FUCHSIA WITH DIAMOND BAND), creamer. Indiana Glass Co. #153, 1913. Extended table service including wine. Crystal. Kamm shows two creamers, one with feet, one without. The main flower on the footless creamer is very distinctive, with three petals turned up and the others turned down (see inset above creamer). My version of the faceted portion is fanciful, as Kamm seems to have given up on a detailed drawing, it being so ornate. She describes it, thankfully, as "composed of almost microscopic faceted figures, forming tiny rosettes and half-rosettes like a band of fine old rose-point lace." *Ref. K2-116; K7-28; Gob I-152; Metz 1-64; Schroy-123.*

THISTLEBLOW (PANELLED IRIS), pitcher. Jenkins Glass Co. #514, 1905. Extended table service including wine, punch cup. *Ref. K6-45; Gob II-48; Metz 1-230; Unitt 1-204.*

FLORAL OVAL (PITTSBURGH DAISY; BANNER; CANE AND SPRIG; SPRAY AND CANE), pitcher. John F. Higbee Glass Co., ca. 1910; New Martinsville Glass Co., 1916. Extended table service including wine. Crystal. It has been reproduced with the "bee" trademark in an amberina square plate; probably other pieces in color. *Ref. K5-97; Gob II-69; Metz 1-87; Unitt 2-66; Mugs p. 25.*

*Panelled
Forget-Me-
Not*

*Panelled Sunbursts
and Daisy*

Garden Pink

Wildflower

Gaelic

Flower and Diamond

Rose Point Band

Thistleblow

Floral Oval

265

PLATE 127. FLOWERS

DAISY AND BUTTON WITH NARCISSUS (CLEAR LILY), pitcher. Made in the 1880s; Indiana Glass Co. in the 1920s. Extended table service including wine, decanter, tray. Crystal, gold-flashed, decorated. *Ref. K4-139; LV-34; Gob I-152; Metz 1-66; Unitt 1-206; Schroy-45.*

STARRED COSMOS, pitcher. Indiana Glass Co. Crystal, decorated. *Ref. K4-131.*

SUNK DAISY (KIRKLAND; DAISY CO-OP), goblet. Cooperative Flint Glass Co., 1898. Extended table service including wine. Crystal, green, decorated, ruby-stained. *Ref. K3-89; Gob II-138; Metz 1-62; Unitt 1-200; HTP-83; H7-137.*

FLOWER WITH CANE, sugar bowl. See Plate 84.

POINSETTIA, pitcher. Imperial Glass Co. #74, 1904. Crystal, carnival. *Ref. K7-186.*

RED SUNFLOWER, sauce. Cambridge Glass Co. #2760, 1910. May be marked "Near-Cut." Called "Red Sunflower" even when not stained. Extended table service including rose bowl, lamp. Crystal, ruby-stained. *Ref. K2-116; H7-157.*

ROSETTE WITH PINWHEELS, pitcher. Indiana Glass Co. #171, 1915. Extended table service including wine. *Ref. K2-39.*

*Daisy and Button
with Narcissus*

Starred Cosmos

Sunk Daisy

Flower with Cane

Poinsettia

Red Sunflower

Rosette with Pinwheels

PLATE 128. FLOWERS

GARFIELD DRAPE (CANADIAN DRAPE), goblet and detail. Adams and Co., 1881 (the year President Garfield was assassinated.) Extended table service including memorial portrait bread plate "We Mourn Our Nation's Loss," cake stand, covered compotes, footed and flat sauces, pickle dish. A rare goblet has a low-relief rope drape instead of dewdrops. Campbell, Jones and Co. made a 10" stippled laurel leaf memorial bread plate; and several other portrait plates of Garfield exist, but are not part of the Garfield Drape pattern. See the milk pitcher on Plate 145. Courtesy of Bob Burford. *Ref. L-104; LEAPG-530; Metz 1-114; Schroy-65; Jenks p. 241.*

SCROLL WITH FLOWERS, pitcher. Central Glass Co., 1870s. Extended table service including egg cup, mustard jar, wine, cordial. Crystal. Kamm said this pattern "is the height of Victorian artlessness." *K1-65; Metz 1-58; Gob I-61; LEAPG-407; Schroy-138; Jenks p. 471.*

CHALLINOR'S TREE OF LIFE, cracker jar. Challinor, Taylor #313, 1885; U. S. Glass, 1893. Extended table service. Opaque colors, milk glass. *Ref. LV-80; HIII-64.*

PINS AND BELLS, creamer. Made ca. 1880 and scarce. *Ref. K4-38; Metz 2-198.*

ODD FELLOW, goblet. Adams and Co., early 1880s. Extended table service including platter. *Ref. L-153 #9; Metz 1-114; Schroy-161.*

DEWDROPS AND FLOWERS (STIPPLED VIOLET; QUANTICO; N.S. STARFLOWER), pitcher. Made ca. 1880 in extended table service including wine. *Ref. K1-49; Metz 1-56; Unitt 1-196; Unitt 2-180.*

DAISY PLEAT, mug. Made in the 1880s. *Ref. Mugs p. 25.*

TRIANGULAR MEDALLION, goblet. *Ref. K8-70; Metz 2-66.*

BARRED FORGET-ME-NOT, pitcher. Canton Glass Co., 1883. Extended table service including cordials, wine, square handled pickle dish. Crystal, canary, vaseline, amber, blue, apple green. *Ref. L-132; K4-34; Gob I-140; Metz 1-56; Unitt 1-140; Schroy-14.*

Garfield Drape and detail

Scroll with Flowers

Challinor's Tree of Life

Pins and Bells

Odd Fellow

Dewdrops and Flowers

Daisy Pleat

Triangular Medallion

Barred Forget-Me-Not

PLATE 129. FLOWERS

THE SUMMIT, toothpick holder. Thompson Glass Co., 1894; Cambridge Glass Co. #2505, 1903. Extended table service including wine. Crystal, ruby-stained. *Ref. K6-22; H7-56, 197.*

DIAPERED FLOWER, mustard jar. Westmoreland Glass Co. The diamonds have raised borders; those of "Quilted Phlox" are sunken. Opaque blue. *Ref. K6-44.*

BEADED ACANTHUS, pitcher. Imperial Glass Co. #78, 1904. To better show the pattern, artist did not depict stippled background, which is comprised of tiny daisies. *Ref. K3-123.*

QUILTED PHLOX, syrup. Hobbs Glass Co., 1898 – 1905. Extended table service including miniature lamp, rose bowl. Crystal, opaque colors; cased; milk glass; later production in emerald and apple greens, light blue, amethyst. Avon has reproduced a milk glass shaker. *Ref. PetSal 36H; HI-37; H6-11.*

PANELLED 44 (ATHENIA; REVERSE 44), pitcher. U. S. Glass Co. #15140 (Glassport factory), 1912. Extended table service including wine, champagne, footed tankard, mug, three-legged bonbon. May be marked with "U. S." trademark. Crystal; stained green or amethyst, decorated with silver or gold, ruby-stained. *Ref. Gob II-150; Metz 1-142; Unitt 1-251; HTP-84; H5-156; Schroy-108; Mugs p. 98.*

SPOTTED BOX, creamer. Opaque glass. *Ref. K4-111.*

FLOWER BASKET, salt shaker. *Ref. PetSal 29H.*

POSIES AND PODS, butter dish. Northwood Glass Co., 1905. Extended table service including berry set. Crystal, color-stained, opalescent. *Ref. HPV 4-16.*

LITTLE DAISY, creamer. Atterbury and Co., 1881. It has the same shape as "Sunflower" on Plate 131. *Ref. K5-50.*

The Summit

Diapered Flower

Beaded Acanthus

Quilted Phlox

Panelled 44

Spotted Box

Flower Basket

Posies and Pods

Little Daisy

PLATE 130. FLOWERS

BEADED TULIP (ANDES), goblet. McKee Glass Co., 1894. Extended table service including champagne, water tray, wine, cordials, bread plate. *Ref. L-116; LEAPG-376; K3-127; Gob I-124; Gob II-133; Metz 1-64; Unitt 1-194; Schroy-18; Jenks p. 58.*

WREATHED SUNBURST, pitcher. U. S. Glass Co. #150096, 1906. Extended table service. Crystal. *Ref. K8-23.*

RUFFLED EYE, pitcher. Indiana Tumbler and Goblet Co., 1890s. Extended table service including wine. Crystal, canary, amber, emerald green, caramel slag. *Ref. K6-58.*

SCROLLED SUNFLOWER, spoon holder. Known in basic table service. *Ref. K6-53.*

STIPPLED DAISY, tumbler. Made in the 1880s in extended table service including wine, open and covered sugar bowls. Crystal, clear, and stippled. *Ref. L-101; LEAPG-390; K3-85; Metz 1-62.*

PANELLED SUNFLOWER, mug. D. C. Jenkins Co., ca. 1920. *Ref. Mugs p. 38.*

DOLTEC, cake plate. McKee Glass Co., ca. 1894 – 1914. Extended table service. Very much like Sextec on Plate 99 but the cake plate for Sextec has five flowers and a five-pointed star effect.

DAISY MEDALLION (SUNBURST MEDALLION) spoon holder. Made in the 1880s in extended table service including wine, courtesy of John Gregory. Crystal. *Ref. K5-35; Gob II-52; Metz 1-128; Unitt 1-287.*

INTAGLIO SUNFLOWER, creamer. U. S. Glass Co. #15125 (Glassport), 1911. Extended table service including tall covered jar. Crystal, decorated. *Ref. K7-53; HTP-48, 85; H5-178.*

Beaded Tulip

Wreathed Sunburst

Ruffled Eye

Scrolled Sunflower

Stippled Daisy

*Panelled
Sunflower*

Doltec

Daisy Medallion

Intaglio Sunflower

PLATE 131. FLOWERS

JEWEL AND FLOWER (BEADED FLOWER AND LEAF), creamer. Made in extended table service. *Ref. K8-30; HII-22; H6-32; Schroy-84.*

WILLOW OAK (OAK LEAF; STIPPLED STAR; ACORN; THISTLE; WREATH), creamer. Bryce Brothers, 1880s; U. S. Glass Co., 1891. Extended table service including flanged sauce, waste bowl. Crystal, amber, blue, canary. *Ref. K1-36; Mugs p. 32; H5-42+; Jenks p. 556; LEAPG-506; Metz 1-62; Schroy-156.*

FLOWER FLANGE (DEWEY), pitcher. Indiana Tumbler and Goblet Co., 1898. Extended table service. This bears a slight resemblance to Vermont on Plate 122, kind of like the ugly duckling. *Ref. K1-84; Metz 1-220; Metz 2-106.*

SUNFLOWER (LILY), sugar bowl. Atterbury and Co., 1881. Extended table service. Crystal, amber, blue, opalescent, mosaic glass. *Ref. K1-55; LEAPG-409; Metz 1-60; Schroy-138; Jenks p. 502.*

ROSETTE (MAGIC), spoon holder. Bryce Brothers, 1880s; U. S. Glass Co. (Bryce), 1891. Extended table service including fish relish, handled plate, tray, wine, cordial. Crystal. *Ref. L-106; LEAPG-544; K4-46; K7-102; Gob I-77; Metz 1-124; Mugs p. 73; H5-79; Schroy-124; Jenks p. 455.*

PLEATED MEDALLION, creamer. New Martinsville Glass Co., ca. 1908. Extended table service. Crystal. *Ref. K3-91; HTP-83.*

PANELLED HONEYCOMB, pitcher. Bryce, Walker and Co., ca. 1885 – 1890. Extended table service. *Ref. K3-55; Metz 1-59.*

BULLS-EYE AND DAISY, syrup. See Plate 21.

PANELLED DIAMOND AND FLOWER, goblet. *Ref. L-164 #7.*

RUSTIC ROSE (BASKETWEAVE ROSE), wine. Lancaster Glass Co., 1913. Made in wine and decanter set in crystal and ruby-stained. *Ref. Unitt 1-197; HCG1 p. 97; H7-189.*

Jewel and Flower   *Willow Oak*   *Flower Flange*

Sunflower   *Rosette*   *Pleated Medallion*

Panelled Honeycomb   *Bulls-Eye and Daisy*   *Panelled Diamond and Flower*   *Rustic Rose*

275

PLATE 132. FRUIT

STRAWBERRY (FAIRFAX STRAWBERRY), covered compote. Bryce, Walker & Co., 1870. Extended table service including handled plate, egg cup, wine, cordial. Crystal, milk glass, ruby-stained. *Ref. L-151; LEAPG-451; Gob I-31; Metz 1-88; Unitt 1-231; H7-133; Schroy-137.*

STRAWBERRY AND CURRANT (THREE FRUITS), mug and goblet. Dalzell, Gilmore and Leighton #9, 1880s. There are different fruits on various pieces. Extended table service including wine, covered cheese dish. Crystal. The goblet and wine have been reproduced, courtesy of John Gregory. *Ref. L-141; Metz 1-82; Unit 1-232; Mugs p. 36.*

INVERTED STRAWBERRY (LATE STRAWBERRY VARIANT), tumbler. Cambridge Glass Co. #2780, 1915. Extended table service including salt dip, wine, toy table service. No toothpick holder was made originally. Crystal, ruby-stained. *Ref. Gob II-48; Metz 1-89; Metz 2-64; Unitt 2-87; HGC3-8; H7-133; HTP-89 (repro); H6-31; H7-133+; Schroy-81; Mugs p. 33.*

PANELLED STRAWBERRY, pitcher. Indiana Glass Co. #127, ca. 1913. Extended table service. Crystal, rose, decorated. *Ref. K4-89; Metz 1-89.*

STIPPLED STRAWBERRY; pitcher. U. S. Glass Co. (Gas City), after 1900. Extended table service. *Ref. K1-114.*

CORNUCOPIA (HORN AND FRUITS), pitcher. Westmoreland Glass Co., 1900. Extended table service including cordial, wine. The reverse side of pitcher has a spray of cherries. *Ref. K2-124/5.*

HEISEY'S PLANTATION (FLORIDA PINEAPPLE; PLANTATION), salt shaker. A. H. Heisey Co. Extended table service including sugar castor. *Ref. PetSal 169B.*

STRAWBERRY AND CABLE (FALMOUTH STRAWBERRY), goblet. Northwood Glass Co. Extended table service. *Ref. Gob II-39.*

STRAWBERRY WITH CHECKERBOARD, creamer. Jenkins Glass Co., ca. 1920. *Ref. K4-103.*

Strawberry

Strawberry and Currant (two views)

*Inverted
Strawberry*

*Panelled
Strawberry*

*Stippled
Strawberry*

Cornucopia

*Heisey's
Plantation*

*Strawberry
and Cable*

*Strawberry with
Checkerboard*

PLATE 133. FRUIT

GRAPE BAND (GRAPE VINE; EARLY GRAPE BAND; ASHBURTON WITH GRAPE BAND), goblet. Bryce, Walker and Co., ca. 1869. Extended table service including wine, cordials, egg cup, footed salt. *Ref. L-64; LEAPG-214; K1-8; Gob I-51; Metz 1-82; Unitt 1-224; Schroy-68; Jenks p. 253.*

GRAPE WITH SCROLL MEDALLION, creamer. Made ca. 1880 in extended table service. *Ref. K2-56; Metz 2-76.*

GRAPE AND FESTOON WITH SHIELD, creamer. Made by Sandwich early; Doyle and Co., 1870s. Extended table service including egg cup, mug. Crystal, blue. See below. *Ref. K1-13; Mugs p. 26.*

STIPPLED GRAPE AND FESTOON, goblet. Doyle and Co. #28, 1870; U. S. Glass Co., 1891. Extended table service including egg cup, wine, cordials. *Ref. L-63; Gob I-51; Metz 1-78; Unitt 1-224; Unitt 2-82.*

GRAPE AND FESTOON (WREATH), goblet. Portland Glass Co., 1860s; Steiner Glass Co., 1870; Boston and Sandwich, 1880s; U. S. Glass, 1891. Extended table service including wine, cordials. *Ref. L-65; Gob II-61; Metz 1-78; Metz 2-78; Jenks p. 252; Unitt 2-82.*

GRAPE AND FESTOON VARIATION, goblet. A variation of the preceding pattern.

GRAPE AND FESTOON WITH SHIELD, goblet. A variation of the Sandwich pattern, this one by Portland Glass. *Ref. L-65.*

BLACKBERRY SPRAY, mug. Probably Fenton Glass, ca. 1911. Crystal, colors, decorated. *Ref. K8-80; Mugs p. 24.*

BLACKBERRY BAND, goblet. *Ref. Gob II-62; Metz 2-78.*

RIBBED GRAPE (RAISIN), spoon holder. Boston and Sandwich Glass Co., ca. 1850 in extended table service including cordial, wine. *Ref. L-36; LEAPG-102; Metz 1-30; Gob I-16; Unitt 1-71; Jenks p. 438; Schroy-119.*

Grape Band

Grape w/Scroll Medallion

Grape and Festoon with Shield

Stippled Grape and Festoon

Grape and Festoon

Grape and Festoon Variation

Grape and Festoon w/Shield

Blackberry Spray

Blackberry Band

Ribbed Grape

PLATE 134. FRUIT

GRAPE BUNCH, goblet. Sandwich or Doyle, ca. 1870s. Extended table service including egg cup, wine. Crystal. *Ref. Metz 2-76; Hartley p. 49; H5-81B; Mugs-26.*

LOGANBERRY AND GRAPE (BLACKBERRY AND GRAPE), pitcher, both sides. Previously reported manufacturer (Dalzell, Gilmore and Leighton) is wrong; who made this pattern is not known. Extended table service including wine. *Ref. K1-45; Gob I-114; Metz 1-82; Metz 2-76; Unitt 1-236.*

GRAPE WITH VINE, creamer. Made ca. 1890s in extended table service including honey dish, berry bowl. Crystal, decorated. *Ref. K2-60; Metz 1-82.*

GRAPE WITH OVERLAPPING FOLIAGE, pitcher. Hobbs, Brockunier and Co., 1870. Extended table service. Crystal, milk glass. *Ref. K2-48; Metz 1-80; Hobbs p. 42.*

BEADED GRAPE MEDALLION, pitcher. Boston Silver Glass Co., 1869 – 1871. Extended table service including egg cup, wine, cordials. Variations in the pattern are found, some not banded, some with extra grapes, etc. My spoon holder has a row of ovals in the upper band of stippling. *Ref. L-66; Metz 2-76; Gob I-85; Unitt 1-229.*

MAGNET AND GRAPE, footed bowl. Boston and Sandwich, ca. 1870. Has stippled or frosted leaf. Extended table service including syrups, tumbler, wine, cordials, champagne. The wine has been reproduced. Flint glass. *Ref. L-63; Metz 1-78; Gob I-13, 98; Unitt 1-228; K1-17.*

GRAPE WITH HOLLY BAND, pitcher. Extended table service. *Ref. L-154 #16; Metz 1-91.*

GRAPE WITHOUT VINE, creamer. Federal Glass Co., 1913 – 1914. Extended table service. Crystal (only). *Ref. K4-73.*

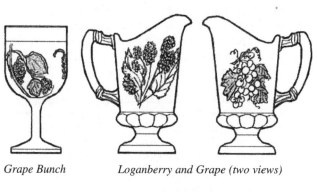

Grape Bunch   *Loganberry and Grape (two views)*

*Grape with
Vine*

*Grape
w/Overlapping
Foliage*

*Beaded Grape
Medallion*

Magnet and Grape

*Grape with
Holly Band*

*Grape Without
Vine*

PLATE 135. FRUIT

GRAPE AND GOTHIC ARCHES, goblet. Northwood Glass Co., ca. 1890. Extended table service. Crystal, milk glass, green. *Ref. K1-101; H4-33.*

CALIFORNIA (BEADED GRAPE; GRAPE AND VINE), creamer and pitcher. U. S. Glass Co. #15059 (Bryce; Ripley), 1899. A State Series pattern. Extended table service including cordial, round and square pitchers, 6" vase, wine, bread plate. The wine has been reproduced. Crystal, emerald green. *Ref. K4-94; Gob I-79; Metz 1-83; Unitt 2-215; HI-14; H5-39, 40; Jenks p. 101; Schroy-16.*

LATE PANELLED GRAPE (DARLING GRAPE), creamer and butter dish. Beatty-Brady Glass Co., 1890s; Indiana Glass Co. #154, 1913. Extended table service including wine. *Ref. K1-96; Gob I-120; LEAPG-208; Metz 1-80; Unitt 2-226; Welker p. 392.*

PANELLED GRAPE (MAPLE; HEAVY PANELLED GRAPE), spoon holder. Kokomo-Jenkins Glass Co. #507, after 1904. Extended table service including wine, cordials. Crystal, amber, other colors, milk glass. The goblet, wine, and cordial have been reproduced. *Ref. K3-61; K5-25; L-64; LEAPG-206; Gob I-95; Metz 1-78; Unitt 2-87; HIII-91, 96; Jenks p. 397.*

ARCHED GRAPE, pitcher. Boston and Sandwich, 1870s. Extended table service including cordial, wine, champagne. Crystal. *Ref. L-64; LEAPG-217; Gob I-51; Metz 1-80; Unitt 2-86; Schroy-7; Jenks p. 19.*

BRADFORD GRAPE (BRADFORD BLACKBERRY), pitcher. Boston and Sandwich Glass Co., 1860. Extended table service including champagne, cordial, wine, rare tumbler. *Ref. K5-25; Gob I-15; LV Pl. 22; Metz 1-83; Metz 2-78; Unitt 1-227.*

GRAPE WITH THUMBPRINT, pitcher. Made ca. 1890s in extended table service. Crystal, colors, milk glass. *Ref. L-164 #4; LEAPG-218; K5-96.*

Grape and
Gothic Arches

California (two examples)

Late Panelled Grape (two examples)

Panelled
Grape

Arched Grape

Bradford
Grape

Grape with
Thumbprint

PLATE 136. FRUIT

ASHBURTON WITH GRAPE BAND, tumbler. Only the tumbler is known.

RASPBERRY, pitcher. Made in the late 1870s in extended table service including tray. *Ref. K4-61.*

BLACKBERRY, pitcher. Hobbs, Brockunier and Co., 1870; Imperial Glass Co., 1914; Phoenix Glass Co., 1930s. Extended table service including rare celery vase, rare oval dish, single and double egg cups, wine, footed salt, champagne, lamps. The pitcher is rare but is being reproduced; Westmoreland is known to have reproduced this pattern, sometimes marked "WG." Crystal, milk glass. *Ref. K8-25; L-151; LEAPG-444; Metz 1-88; Gob I-132; Unitt 1-180; Schroy-22; Hobbs p. 43.*

APPLE AND GRAPE IN SCROLL, cruet. Fostoria Glass Co., 1898. Known in cruet and toothpick holder. Crystal, apple green. *Ref. HIII-54; HTP-48, 107; H6-18+.*

CURRANT, pitcher. Campbell, Jones and Co., ca. 1871. Extended table service including cordials, egg cup, wines, footed tumbler. *Ref. K8-8; L-153 #20; LEAPG-453; Gob I-59; Metz 1-88; Unitt 1-233; Jenks p. 141; Schroy-41.*

BERRY CLUSTER, pitcher. Extended table service. *Ref. K3-33; Metz 1-90.*

EARLY PANELLED GRAPE BAND, open salt. Made ca. 1870s in extended table service. *Ref. Gob II-21; Metz 1-80.*

BOHEMIAN GRAPE, pitcher. U. S. Glass Co., 1899. Made in juice pitcher and tumbler. Crystal, emerald green, rose-flashed. Scarce. *Ref. H5-40.*

PALM BEACH, cruet. U. S. Glass Co. #15119 (Glassport), 1909. Extended table service including wine. Crystal, decorated, carnival, opalescent. *Ref. LV-58; Metz 1-91; HII-22; H5-42, 151; H6-48; Schroy-106.*

*Ashburton
with Grape
Band*

Raspberry

Blackberry

*Apple and
Grape in
Scroll*

Currant

Berry Cluster

*Early Panelled
Grape Band*

*Bohemian
Grape*

Palm Beach

PLATE 137. FRUIT

GRAPEVINE WITH OVALS, mug. McKee and Brothers, 1870s. Crystal, amber, blue (rare). *Ref. Metz 2-202; Mugs p. 28; HTP-89.*

PINEAPPLE, pitcher. Hobbs, Brockunier and Co., 1886. Extended table service. Crystal, opalescent colors. *Ref. K8-21; LV Pl. 38; Metz 1-106; Metz 2-78.*

DEWBERRY, pitcher. Cooperative Glass Co. #375, ca. 1910. Crystal, teal blue, ruby-stained. *Ref. K7-11; H7-64+.*

LEAF AND GRAPE, mug. Made ca. 1900. *Ref. Mugs p. 28.*

GRAPEVINE WITH STARS, toy mug (author's name). Known in sapphire blue toy mug. This lovely pattern may be of English origin. Courtesy of Bob Burford.

GRAPEVINE, mug. King, Son and Co., 1870s. crystal, amber, cobalt. *Ref. Mugs p. 28.*

PANELLED GRAPE BAND (LATE PANELLED GRAPE BAND; GRAPE LEAF BAND), salt dish. King Glass Co., 1875; possibly Richards and Hartley Glass Co., 1875. Extended table service including egg cup, wine. *Ref. Gob I-29; Metz 1-80; Unitt 1-225; Salts p. 170.*

BARBERRY (OLIVE; BERRY McKEE; PEPPER BERRY), spooner. McKee Glass Co.; Boston and Sandwich; 1860s; 1880s. Extended table service including wine, cordials, egg cup, footed salt. There are several variations including one with oval berries and one with round. *Ref. K1-9; LEAPG-412; Gob I-59; Metz 1-90; Unitt 1-230; Schroy-13; Jenks p. 46.*

GRAPEVINE WITH THUMBPRINT BAND, mug. Jenkins Glass Co., ca. 1920. *Ref. Mugs p. 24.*

Grapevine with Ovals

Pineapple

Dewberry

Leaf and Grape

Grapevine with Stars

Grapevine

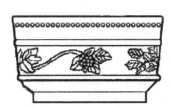

Panelled Grape Band

Barberry

*Grapevine with
Thumbprint Band*

PLATE 138. FRUIT

CHERRY AND FIG, pitcher. made in extended table service. *Ref. K1-45; Metz 1-87.*

NORTHWOOD PEACH, creamer. Northwood Glass Co., 1920. Extended table service including ruffled-edge bowl. Crystal, carnival glass. *Ref. K5-132.*

BALTIMORE PEAR (GIPSY; FIG; MARYLAND; TWIN PEAR), goblet and creamer. Adams and Co., 1874; U. S. Glass Co., 1891. Extended table service including open and covered sugar bowls. Crystal. *Ref. L-66; L-154 #10; LEAPG-455; Metz 1-84; K1-31; H5-69; Schroy-12.*

SWEET PEAR (SUGAR PEAR; AVOCADO), plate and creamer. Indiana Glass Co. #601 (Dunkirk factory), 1922 – 1933. Extended table service. Crystal, light green, canary, pink. *Ref. K4-111; Gob I-116; Metz 1-87.*

GOOSEBERRY, pitcher. Sandwich Glass, 1870s; Burlington Glass Works. Extended table service including handled tumbler, bar tumbler, wine. The wine has been reproduced. Crystal, opaque white. *Ref. L-166; LEAPG-460; Gob I-132; Metz 1-88; K4-66; Jenks p. 247; Schroy-67; Mugs p. 34.*

BARTLETT PEAR, bowl. Duncan Glass in extended table service. *Ref. LV Pl. 72; Metz 2-76.*

BOSC PEAR, pitcher. Indiana Glass Co. (Dunkirk), 1913. Extended table service. Crystal, flashed purple pears, gold leaves. *Ref. K7-27.*

STIPPLED PEPPERS, pitcher. Boston and Sandwich, 1870s. Extended table service included footed tumbler, egg cup. Crystal. *Ref. LEAPG-164 #9; Metz 1-106; Unitt 1-202; Gob I-139; Schroy-137.*

288

Cherry and Fig

Northwood Peach

Baltimore Pear (two examples)

Sweet Pear (two examples)

Gooseberry

Bartlett Pear

Bosc Pear

Stippled Peppers

PLATE 139. FRUIT

FRUIT BAND, salt shaker. *Ref. PetSal 29S.*

CHERRY, goblet. Bakewell, Pears and Co., ca. 1870. Extended table service including wine, champagne. Crystal, opalescent. *Ref. L-19, 66; LEAPG-457; Metz 1-90; Gob I-114; Schroy-34; Jenks p. 118.*

WREATHED CHERRY, toothpick holder (a reproduction) and creamer. Dugan Glass Co. Extended table service. Some pieces have cherries in relief on the inside of the bowl as well as the outside. Crystal, opalescent, slag. *Ref. K7-26; HTP-71, 72; HII-24, 92.*

CHERRY WITH THUMBPRINTS, pitcher. Jenkins Glass Co. (Kokomo), 1920s. Extended table service including lemonade, wine, mug. *Ref. K4-104; Gob I-132; Metz 1-90; Unitt 1-235.*

CHERRY AND CABLE (PANELLED CHERRY; CHERRY THUMBPRINTS), sugar bowl. Northwood Glass Co., 1880s. Extended table service. Crystal, decorated. *Ref. K5-63.*

STIPPLED CHERRY, pitcher. Lancaster Glass Co., probably in the 1880s. Extended table service. *Ref. K4-132; LEAPG-459; Metz 1-90.*

CHERRY SPRIG, creamer. Blown glass, not pressed. Made in extended table service. *Ref. K2-58.*

CHERRY LATTICE, creamer. Northwood Glass Co., 1880s. Extended table service. Crystal, pink/gold decoration. *Ref. Hartung, Northwood Pattern Glass – Clear, Colored, Custard and Carnival p. 12, 20. By author, 1969, Emporia, KS.*

GRAPE AND CHERRY, creamer. Westmoreland Glass Co. Made in a milk glass sugar and creamer set. *Ref. K1-94.*

Fruit Band   *Cherry*   *Wreathed Cherry (two examples)*

*Cherry with
Thumbprints*   *Cherry and Cable*   *Stippled Cherry*

Cherry Sprig   *Cherry Lattice*   *Grape and Cherry*

PLATE 140. HOBNAILS AND BEADS

HOBNAIL "PINEAPPLE," barber bottle. A novelty item.

PANELLED HOBNAIL, creamer. Bryce Brothers, ca. 1880; U. S. Glass after 1891. Extended table service including wine. Crystal, opaque white, canary, vaseline, blue. *Ref. K1-67; LEAPG-270; Gob I-33; Metz 1-186; Unitt 2-24; Mugs p. 70.*

DEWDROP AND ZIG ZAG (MITRED DEWDROP), pitcher. Challinor Glass Co., 1885; U. S. Glass Co. (Challinor #418), 1891. Known in pitcher, wine, and goblet. Crystal, purple slag, milk glass. *Ref. H5-94; Gob I-39; Metz 1-173; Unitt 1-292.*

HOBB'S HOBNAIL, creamer. U. S. Glass Co. (Hobbs), 1891. Made in water set: tumbler, pitchers, tray, finger bowl, butter dish, toy water set. All colors. The original Hobbs hobnail pattern was called "Dewdrop" and made in 1886. *Ref. H5-125; Hobbs p. 84.*

DEWDROP (HOBNAIL), creamer. Columbia Glass Co.; U. S. Glass Co., 1891. Advertised in the same set as Double-Eye Hobnail. Extended table service including sugar shaker, wine, cordial, castor set. *Ref. L-71; LEAPG-234; Gob I-77; Metz 1-190.*

HOBNAIL WITH BARS (HOBNAIL IN BIG DIAMOND), creamer. U. S. Glass Co. (Challinor #307), 1891. Extended table service including pieces with vertical bars not set into diamonds. See Plate 143 for the cruet that lacks diamond bars. *Ref. LV-66; H5-89; H6-30+.*

DOUBLE-EYE HOBNAIL WITH DECORATIVE BAND (HOBNAIL [POINTED] WITH ORNAMENTAL BAND; HOBNAIL DOUBLE-EYE; DEWDROP; COLUMBIA; DOT), cup and detail of Kamm's variation. Columbia Glass Co., 1889; U. S. Glass Co., 1891. Extended table service including open salt, ink stand. Crystal, blue, amber. *Ref. L-82; K1-57; Metz 1-187; Metz 2-100; Mugs p. 68; HTP-46.*

HOBNAIL, BALLFOOT, creamer. *Ref. L-81; Metz 187.*

BUTTON BAND (WYANDOTTE; UMBILICATED HOBNAIL), pitcher. Ripley and Co., 1880s; U. S. Glass Co., 1890s. Extended table service including castor set, cordial, wine. Crystal. *Ref. K3-111; Gob II-9; Metz 1-186; Schroy-29; Jenks p. 96.*

Hobnail Pineapple

Panelled Hobnail

Dewdrop and
Zig Zag

Hobb's Hobnail

Dewdrop

Hobnail with Bars

Double-Eye
Hobnail

Hobnail, Ballfoot

Button Band

PLATE 141. HOBNAILS AND BEADS

HOBNAIL BAND, pitcher. Made ca. 1890 in extended table service including cup and saucer, champagne, candlesticks, wine. *Ref. K2-131; Mugs p. 72 (no illus.); Schroy-75.*

GARTER BAND, goblet. Known in wine set. *Ref. Gob II-95; Metz 1-134.*

BEADED TRIANGLE, pitcher. Federal Glass Co., 1914. Clear, chocolate. Extended table service. *Ref. PetSal 154S.*

POPCORN, goblet. Boston and Sandwich, 1860s. Extended table service including cordial, goblet without the "ear of corn," wine. *Ref. L-25; Gob I-73; Metz 1-188; Unitt 1-97; K8-19.*

HOBNAIL WITH FAN, goblet. Adams and Co. #150. Extended table service. Crystal, ruby-stained. *Ref. L-71; H7-116+; Schroy-76.*

ACORN, syrup. Hobbs Glass Co.; Beaumont Glass Co. #220, 1890 – 1900. Made only in syrup, salt shaker, sugar shaker, mustard, and toothpick holder. *Ref. PetSal 21A.*

DEW AND RAINDROP, cup. Kokomo-Jenkins Glass Co., 1901 – 1905; Federal Glass Co., 1914. Extended table service including cordial, wine, sherbet. Crystal, ruby-flashed. The wine and cordial have been reproduced. *Ref. K4-113; Metz 1-188; Unitt 1-123; H7-103.*

RAINDROP, sauce dish. A flattened hobnail made by Doyle & Co., 1880s; U. S. Glass Co., 1891. Extended table service including wine, miniature lamp. Doyle's RAINDROP is also called "DOT" and is shown on Plate 25 with the similar "Thousand Eye" variations. Crystal, amber, blue, light green (rare). *Ref. L-61; H7-17.*

HOBNAIL, open salt dish. Beatty, New Brighton, McKee, Gillinder, others over many years. very extended table service including novelties, finger lamp, perfume bottles, lamp shades, trays, vases, soap dishes. Crystal, amber, canary blue. *Ref. L80-83; Metz 1-184; HII-91; H6-30+.*

FLATTENED HOBNAIL, goblet. Extended table service including wine, cordial. *Ref. L-71; LEAPG-268; Metz 1-186.*

HOBNAIL WITH THUMBPRINT BASE, salt shaker. Doyle and Co., 1880s; U. S. Glass Co., ca. 1895. Extended table service including toy set, toy tray. Crystal, amber, blue, ruby-stained (H5-52; but I own a ruby-red shaker that seems to be authentic.) *Ref. K1-70; K7-109; HTP-54; H7-36+; Metz 2-100; Mugs p. 70.*

Hobnail Band

Garter Band

Beaded Triangle

Popcorn

Hobnail
with Fan

Acorn

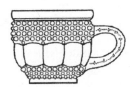

Dew and Raindrop

Raindrop

Hobnail

Flattened
Hobnail

Hobnail
w/Thumbprint
Base

PLATE 142. HOBNAILS AND BEADS

FEDERAL #2, quart jug. Federal Glass Co. *Ref. HGC4 p. 18.*

DOYLE'S #240, pitcher. Doyle and Co., 1870s; U. S. Glass Co. Made in water set: tumbler, pitchers, tray. *Ref. K7 Pl. 10.*

BANDED RAINDROPS (CANDLEWICK), pitcher. Made in the 1890s in extended table service including wine. Crystal, amber, milk glass, opalescent blue. *Ref. K2-31; Schroy-31; Mugs p. 66.*

DEWDROP WITH STAR, pitcher. Campbell, Jones and Co., 1877. A star is in the base. Extended table service including lamp, cheese dish, wine. *Ref. K2-31; K3-67/8; LEAPG-232; Gob II-9; Metz 1-188; Unitt 1-188, Unitt 2-207; Schroy-49.*

PANELLED DEWDROP, goblet. Campbell, Jones and Co., ca. 1878. Extended table service including cordial, champagnes, wine, jam jar. *Ref. LEAPG-242; K5-31; K7-11; Gob I-123; Metz 1-190; Unitt 1-126; Mugs p. 95.*

LOOP WITH DEWDROP, creamer. U. S. Glass Co. #15028, 1892. Extended table service including mug, wines, cordial. Crystal. *Ref. K1-72; L-79; Gob I-89; Metz 1-188; Schroy-92; Jenks p. 341; Mugs p. 76.*

TRIPLE FROSTED BAND, goblet. *Ref. Gob II-109; Metz 2-128.*

GRATED RIBBON (BEADED PANELS), goblet. Crystal Glass Co., 1877. Extended table service including wine. *Ref. K1-54; Gob II-96; Metz 1-190.*

PANELLED BEADS, creamer. Adams & Co., 1880s; U. S. Glass Co., 1891. Extended table service including wine. Compare with HOBNAIL-IN-SQUARE on Plate 51. *Ref. K8-33; Gob II-99; Metz 1-142.*

Federal #2

Doyle's #240

*Banded
Raindrops*

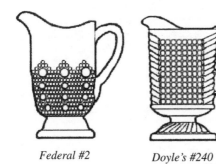

*Dewdrop
with Star*

*Panelled
Dewdrop*

*Loop with
Dewdrop*

*Triple Frosted
Band*

Grated Ribbon

Panelled Beads

PLATE 143. HOBNAILS AND BEADS

SEEDPOD (OLYMPIA), salt shaker. Riverside Glass Works Co., 1898. Extended table service including wine. Crystal, colors, ruby-stained. *Ref. PetSal 172F; Gorham p. 168; H7-73.*

PEAS AND PODS, wine goblet. U. S. Glass Co. (Bryce #5602), 1891. Made in wine set: decanter, wine, tray. Crystal, ruby-stained. *Ref. H5-73; H7-170+.*

BARRED HOBNAIL (WINONA), creamer. Brilliant Glass Works, 1888; Greensburg Glass Co., 1889. Extended table service including wine. Crystal, opalescent, colors, frosted. *Ref. K1-113; K8-162; LV-56; Gob II-82; Metz 1-186; Unitt 2-24; Welker p. 235; Mugs p. 70.*

PRINTED HOBNAIL, goblet. Made in the 1880s – 1890s in extended table service including water tray, wine. Crystal, green, amethyst, amber, canary, blue. Each hob has seven dots. No drawing can depict the true beauty of this wonderful pattern. *Ref. L-72; LEAPG-274; GobI-33; Metz 1-186; Unitt 2-24; Mugs p. 68.*

HOBNAIL WITH BARS, cruet. See Plate 140; this example lacks the identifying bars. Heacock shows a set of this pattern on page 91 of his book, U. S. GLASS FROM A TO Z; bowls shown have vertical bars, but the spooner, butter, sugar, and creamer have diamond bars. Finials look rather like spools of thread. *Ref. H5-91; H6-30+.*

GONTERMAN, pitcher. George Duncan and Sons, 1880s. Extended table service including tray. *Ref. Gob I; Metz 1-184; HPV #1-4; Jenks p. 245; Schroy-66.*

BEADED BLOCK, salt shaker. Eagle Glass and Mfg. Co. in milk glass. *Ref. W-135; PetSal 22-C.*

BEAD AND LOOP, salt shaker. *Ref. PetSal 154G.*

ZENITH, cruet. Made ca. 1905. Known in cruet and salt shaker. Crystal, pale blue (scarce). *Ref. HIII-57.*

Seedpod

Peas and Pods

Barred Hobnail

Printed Hobnail

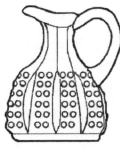
Hobnail with Bars

Gonterman

Beaded Block

Bead and Loop

Zenith

PLATE 144. HOBNAIL AND BEADS

GEORGIA GEM (LITTLE GEM), pitcher. Tarentum Glass Co., ca. 1900. Extended table service. Crystal, pink, green, custard glass, rare ruby-stained, gilded. *Ref. K7-60; HTP-50; HI-24; H4-44+; H6-28; H77-43+.*

LATE WASHINGTON (BEADED BASE), pitcher. U. S. Glass Co. #15074 (Ripley; King), 1904 – 1910. A State Series pattern. Extended table service including claret, wine, champagne, cordial, rectangular bowl. Crystal, ruby-stained, rose-flashed, painted. *Ref. H5-48; Unitt 2-249; H7-213.*

BEAD SWAG (BEADED BASE), pitcher. U. S. Glass Co. #1295, 1897 – 1905. Extended table service including rose bowl, mug, wine, cup and saucer. Crystal, ruby-stained, milk glass, emerald green, some custard and vaseline, decorated. *Ref. K2-75; Gob II-34; H7-73; Mugs p. 110; HTP-46, 49, 56; HI-14; H4-41; H6-19; Schroy-18.*

BEADED BULB, salt shaker. An opaque novelty. *Ref. PetSal-22F.*

BEAD COLUMN, creamer. Probably Kokomo Glass Co. (Heacock: *Pattern Glass Preview #1*), ca. 1905. Basic table service. *Ref. K7-12.*

DOUBLE BEADED BAND, goblet. Made ca. 1890 – 1892. A wine is known, courtesy of John Gregory. Crystal, ruby-stained. *Ref. Gob II-138; Metz 1-136; H7-106.*

SAWTOOTH BANDS (PLAIN BAND; BULGING BANDS), toothpick holder. A.H. Heisey Glass Co. #1225, ca. 1898 – 1910. Extended table service including sherbet, wine, champagne, claret. Crystal, ruby-stained, custard. See the pitcher in Plate 178. *Ref. HTP-53; K4-77; Burns p. 56; Metz 1-34; H7-67+.*

JEWEL AND FESTOON (LOOP AND JEWEL; BEADED FESTOON; QUEEN'S NECKLACE; VENUS), spoon holder. National Glass Co., 1903; Indiana Glass Co., 1906. Extended table service including master salt, sherbet, wine, champagne. *Ref K1-66; Metz 1-192; Gob 2-134; Schroy-92; Jenks p. 340.*

Georgia Gem

Late Washington

Bead Swag

Beaded Bulb

Bead Column

Double
Beaded
Band

Sawtooth Bands

Jewel and
Festoon

PLATE 145. HOBNAILS AND BEADS

BEADED RIB, salt shaker. The beads are sunken between panels. *Ref. PetSal 36S.*

CHAIN AND SWAG, syrup. Milk glass. *Ref. HIII-50.*

DOT AND DASH, creamer. Central Glass Co. #650, ca. 1880. Extended table service. *Ref. K5-11; Metz 2-126.*

BEAD AND PANEL (CHRISTMAS PEARLS), salt shaker. Opalescent-to-clear glass. *Ref. PetSal 154 H.*

SCALLOPED TAPE (JEWEL BAND), pitcher. Extended table service including tray, wine, egg cup. Crystal, amber, canary, blue, apple green. *Ref. K2-29; Metz 1-192; Gob I-24; Unitt 1-100; Jenks p. 469; Schroy-128.*

GARFIELD DRAPE, milk pitcher. See Plate 128.

BEAD AND SCROLL, pitcher and salt shaker. Possibly U. S. Glass, 1891 – 1899. Extended table service including toy table set (rare), wine. Crystal, frosted, ruby-stained, cobalt blue, green, gilded. Courtesy of John Gregory. *Ref. K2-112; PetSal 154; H1-74; H5-37, 51; H7-72.*

FOSTORIA'S PRISCILLA, syrup. Fostoria Glass Co. #1898 & #676, ca. 1900. Extended table service including scarce toothpick holder, two shapes salt shakers, wine, lamps, egg cup. Crystal, emerald green, gilded. *Ref. K8-200; K5-95; HI-50; HIII-36; H6-37; Schroy-116; Jenks p. 422.*

Beaded Rib   *Chain and Swag*   *Dot and Dash*

Bead and Panel   *Scalloped Tape*   *Garfield Drape*

Bead and Scroll (two examples)   *Fostoria's Priscilla*

PLATE 146. HOBNAILS AND BEADS

BEADED MEDALLION (BEADED MIRROR), pitcher. Boston and Sandwich Glass Co., late 1870s to early 1870s; Dalzell, Gilmore and Leighton in 1899. Extended table service including egg cup, open salt. *Ref. K1-39; Metz 1-180; H6-Cover; Jenks p. 55; Schroy-17.*

INDIANA (CORD DRAPERY), toothpick holder and syrup. National Glass Co. #350 (Greentown), 1899 – 1903; Indiana Glass after 1907. Extended table service including scarce syrup, wine. Crystal, amber, blue, green, opal, chocolate, ruby-stained. Do not confuse with U. S. Glass Co.'s INDIANA on Plate 52. This one should probably be called "Cord Drapery." *Ref. LV-39; PetSal 169J; Gob I-58; Metz 1-130; Jenks p. 130; Schroy-38; Mugs p. 62; Measell p. 37, 60; H7-132.*

NORTHWOOD-DUGAN BEADED CIRCLE, cruet. Northwood Glass Co., 1904; Dugan Glass Co. Extended table service including tumbler, berry set. Crystal, apple green, blue, amethyst (rare), custard (rare). *Ref. PetSal 154J; HIII-54; H6-19*

NESTOR, creamer. Northwood Glass Co. (National), 1903. Extended table service including cruet and tray, wine. The pattern is painted on; without it the pattern is hard to identify. Apple green, medium blue, amethyst. *Ref. K5-37; HTP-50; HI-30; HIII-59; H6-35; Schroy-102.*

BEADED OVAL AND SCROLL (DOT), pitcher. Bryce Brothers, 1870s. Made in extended table service including cordial, wine. Crystal. *Ref. L-77; LEAPG-245; K1-61; Gob I-119; Metz 1-188; Unitt 1-54.*

BEADED CIRCLE, goblet. Extended table service including egg cup, bud vase, jelly compote. *Ref. LV-34; Metz 1-181; Metz 2-126.*

OVAL AND FANS, salt shaker. Slag glass. *PetSal 1D.*

ST. LOUIS, mug. Westmoreland Specialty Co. in the early 1900s. Clear, rose-stained. *Ref. Mugs p. 70.*

FRAMED JEWEL (FANCY KING'S CROWN), pitcher. Canton Glass Co. #140, 1893. Extended table service including wine. Crystal, gilded, amethyst-stained, ruby-stained. *Ref. K5-77; K6 Pl. 27; Metz 1-157; Revi-106; Mugs p. 74; H7-119+.*

Beaded Medallion

Indiana (Cord Drapery) (two views)

*N.D. Beaded
Circle*

Nestor

*Beaded Oval
and Scroll*

Beaded Circle

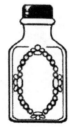

Oval and Fans

St. Louis

Framed Jewel

PLATE 147. HOBNAILS AND BEADS

TRIPLE BEAD BAND, goblet. *Ref. Gob II-139.*

BEAD AND CHAIN, creamer. Central Glass Co., 1880. Extended table service. *Ref. K7-57.*

SHERATON (IDA), pitcher. Bryce and Higbee, 1885. Extended table service including wine, berry set, bread tray. Crystal, amber, blue, green. *Ref. K3-38; K8-17; Gob I-127; Metz 1-136; Unitt 1-101; Jenks p. 477; Schroy-130.*

WELLINGTON (STAPLE), wine goblet. Westmoreland Glass Co., 1903 – 1912; Federal Glass Co. ca. 1914. Extended table service. Crystal, ruby-stained. *Ref. K5-74; PetSal 40G; HTP-85; HGC4-20; HPV #1-23; HPV #6-3; H7-213+.*

ALBION, butter dish. U. S. Glass Co., ca. 1891. An example of U. S. Glass Co.'s special butter dishes, sometimes with no matching pieces. They also made hen-on-basket butters, setting duck, and milk glass swans. *Ref. H5-176.*

EMPRESS (DOUBLE ARCH), creamer. Riverside Glass Works, 1898. Extended table service including oil lamps, mustard, rare breakfast sugar and creamer. Crystal, color, ruby-stained, gilded. *Ref. K7-59; HI-22; HIII-23; H6-26; H7-106; Jenks p. 191; Schroy-54.*

FEDERAL #1908, bowl. Federal Glass Co., 1914. *Ref. HGC4 p. 20.*

BEADED BAND AND PANEL, wine goblet. Imperial #582, 1915. *Ref. Archer p. 72, 77.*

HOOK, creamer. A mug hangs from the hook, and both sit on a fragile stand. *Ref. K6-18; Mugs p. 109.*

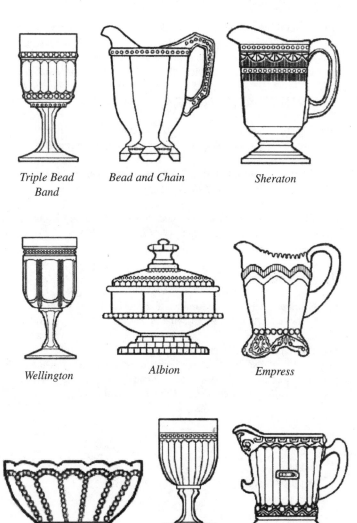

*Triple Bead
Band*

Bead and Chain

Sheraton

Wellington

Albion

Empress

Federal #1908

*Beaded Band
and Panel*

Hook

PLATE 148. HOBNAILS AND BEADS

LACY MEDALLION (JEWEL), tumbler. U. S. Glass Co., 1899 – 1920+. Souvenir ware including mugs, salt shaker, toothpick holder, wine, toy table set. Crystal, green, ruby-stained, cobalt blue (rare). *Ref. K1-106; Revi-314; H1-28; H5-149; H7-134.*

COLORADO, butter dish and creamer. U. S. Glass Co. #15057 (King; Richards and Hartley), 1898 – 1910. A State Series pattern. Very similar to LACY MEDALLION except most Colorado pieces have "feet." Extended table service including violet bowl, vase, perfume bottle (rare), wine, toy table service. Crystal, green, blue, ruby-stained, amethyst-flashed, gilded, decorated. *Ref. K2-115; Revi-314; HTP-47, 51, 56; HI-17; H5-166; H7-92+; Jenks p. 125; Schroy-36; Mugs p. 64.*

ABERDEEN, egg cup. Made in the early 1870s in extended table service including open and covered sugar bowls. Crystal. *Ref. Metz 1-128; Schroy-2; Jenks p. 3.*

FESTOON, pitcher. Portland Glass Co., 1860s. Extended table service including tray, pickle jar, wine. *Ref. L-166; LEAPG-548; K1-93; Jenks p. 207; Schroy-58; Metz 1-134.*

BEAD AND BAR MEDALLION (AEGIS), creamer. McKee and Brothers, ca. 1880. Extended table service including wine. *Ref. K1-60; Gob II-82; Metz 1-122; Unitt 1-328; Jenks p. 6; Schroy-3.*

GARLAND, goblet. *Ref. Gob II-131.*

BEADED PANEL, pitcher. Indiana Tumbler and Goblet Co.; later Jenkins Glass Co. Extended table service including egg cup, wine. *Ref. K1-54; K7-15; Measell p. 61.*

TORPEDO (FISH-EYE; PIGMY), creamer. Thompson Glass Co. 1889 – 1892. Extended table service including rose bowl, waste bowl, open flared bowl, wine, master salt, decanter, cup and saucer, lamp. Crystal, ruby-stained. In Montgomery Ward's catalog of 1894. *Ref. K2-107; Gob I-46; Metz 1-152; Unitt 1-78; Unitt 2-92; Schroy-145; Mugs p. 82; HIII-38; H7-204+.*

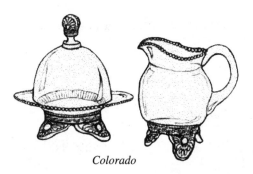

Lacy Medallion

Colorado

Aberdeen

Festoon

Bead and Bar
Medallion

Garland

Beaded Panel

Torpedo

PLATE 149. HOBNAILS AND BEADS

BEADED DART BAND, goblet. George Duncan and Sons #600, 1880s. Extended table service including pickle castor. Crystal, ruby-stained. *Ref. Gob II-7; Metz 1-190; H7-73, 74.*

BEADED DIAMOND BAND, creamer. George Duncan and Sons, 1890. Crystal, ruby-stained. *Ref. K2-37; H7-73, 74.*

PEACOCK FEATHER (GEORGIA), salt shaker. See Plate 22.

IMPERIAL #261, creamer. Imperial Glass Co., 1901. Extended table service including wine. *Ref. K7-10; Metz 2-164.*

BEADED OVAL, pitcher. Imperial Glass Co., 1904. Extended table service. *Ref. K7-32; Metz 1-181.*

BEADED ELLIPSE AND FAN, creamer. U. S. Glass Co., ca. 1905. *Ref. K2-94.*

CIRCLE AND SWAG, cup. Ohio Flint Glass Co., 1904. Extended table service. *Ref. HPV4 p. 6.*

BEADED RAINDROP, pitcher. U. S. Glass Co., ca. 1906. Extended table service. *Ref. K3-108; Metz 2-106.*

Beaded Dart Band

Beaded Diamond Band

Peacock Feather (Georgia)

Imperial #261

Beaded Oval

Beaded Ellipse and Fan

Circle and Swag

Beaded Raindrop

PLATE 150. HOBNAILS AND BEADS

LOOP WITH FISH EYE, goblet.

CONVENTIONAL BAND, creamer. Extended table service. *Ref. K1-17; Metz 1-98.*

KANSAS (JEWEL WITH DEWDROP), gilded pitcher. Cooperative Flint Glass Co., 1870s; U. S. Glass Co. #15072 (King), 1901; Kokomo-Jenkins, 1903; Federal Glass Co., 1914. A State Series pattern. Extended table service including wine, berry bowl, rare goblet, rare toothpick holder, cordial, bread plate. Crystal, color-stained, gilded. *Ref. K1-77; L-75; Gob I-47; Metz 2-106; Unitt 1-155; Unitt 2-235; HTP-84; Schroy-85; Jenks p. 306; Mugs p. 76.*

LACY DEWDROP (BEADED JEWEL), creamer. Cooperative Flint Glass Co., 1902; later production by Phoenix Glass #800 and Kemple #400, 1944. Extended table service. *Ref. K3-108; L-151; Gob I-79; Metz 1-192; Unitt 1-154.*

BEADED CHAIN (LOOPED CORD), goblet. Made ca. 1870s in extended table service. Flint glass. *Ref. Gob II-102; Metz 1-134.*

LOOP AND DART WITH ROUND ORNAMENT (LOOP AND JEWEL), goblet. Boston and Sandwich; Richards and Hartley; Portland Glass Co., ca. 1869. Extended table service including egg cup, butter pat, footed tumbler, cordial, wine, champagne. *Ref. L-149; LEAPG-437; Gob I-142; Metz 1-178; Unitt 1-150; Unitt 2-70; Jenks p. 338; Schroy-92.*

DRAPED JEWEL, creamer. Made ca. 1900 in extended table service. *Ref. K3-51.*

HEAVY JEWEL, tumbler. Fostoria Glass Co. #1225, ca. 1900. Extended table service. *Ref. L-137; LEAPG-549; Metz 2-102.*

DRAPERY (LACE), pitcher. Boston and Sandwich ca. 1865; Doyle and Co. #7, 1870s. Extended table service including egg cup. Has a pine cone finial. *Ref. L-108; LEAPG-549; K5-9; Gob I-133; Metz 1-180; Schroy-53; Jenks p. 186.*

WYOMING (ENIGMA), bowl. U. S. Glass Co. #15081 (Richards and Hartley; Gas City), 1903. A State Series pattern. Extended table service including wine, open and covered sugar bowls. Crystal. The funny little upper design may be early aviator hats and goggles; then again, maybe not. *Ref. K2-49; Gob I-140; Metz 2-102; Unitt 2-251; Schroy-157; Jenks p. 562; Mugs p. 91.*

Loop with
Fish Eye

Conventional
Band

Kansas

Lacy Dewdrop

Beaded Chain *Loop and Dart*

Draped Jewel

Heavy Jewel

Drapery

Wyoming

PLATE 151. HOBNAILS AND BEADS

RAY, celery vase. McKee Brothers, 1894. Extended table service. Crystal, ruby-stained. *Ref. K1-110; L-14; LEAPG-54; Metz 2-50; Mugs p. 104.*

WISCONSIN (BEADED DEWDROP), creamer and pitcher. U. S. Glass Co. #15079 (Gas City), 1903. A State Series pattern. Extended table service including mug, wine, two types salt shaker, master salt, cordial. Crystal. *Ref. 1-57; K7-46; Gob I-119; Metz 1-188; Unitt 2-250; LEAPG-242; H5-167; Jenks p. 559; Schroy-156; Mugs p. 62.*

CO-OP COLUMBIA, creamer. Cooperative Flint Glass Co., 1899. Extended table service including wine. Crystal, decorated. *Ref. K5-115; Revi-128.*

IDYLL, creamer. Jefferson Glass Co. #251, 1904. Extended table service including half-gallon jug, condiment set. Crystal, colors, opalescent. *Ref. K7-46; Schroy-29; HI-26; HII-214; H6-30.*

BEADED ELLIPSE (ALDINE), pitcher. McKee and Sons, 1900; Imperial Glass Co. #261, 1910. Extended table service including wine. *Ref. K3-106; K7-10; Metz 2-164.*

CHRYSANTHEMUM LEAF, toothpick holder. Boston and Sandwich, late 1880s; later ca. 1900 – 1903, probably National Glass Co. at the Northwood factory. *(Ref. HI-17.)* Extended table service. Crystal, chocolate, ruby-stained. *Ref. LV-52; Metz 2-66; HTP-83; HI-17; H7-15+.*

SCROLL WITH ACANTHUS, creamer. Central Glass Co.; Northwood in slag, 1904. Made in extended table service including jelly compote, open sugar. No goblet originally made. Crystal, apple green, amber, blue, slag. *Ref. K5-41; HI-40; HIII-23; H6-41; Schroy-128.*

FT. PITT CHAIN, pitcher. Ft. Pitt Glass Works, 1830s. Extended table service.

314

Ray

Wisconsin (two examples)

Co-op Columbia

Idyll

Beaded Ellipse

Chrysanthemum
Leaf

Scroll with
Acanthus

Ft. Pitt Chain

PLATE 152. HOBNAILS AND BEADS

DIAMONDS AND DEWDROPS, goblets. *Ref. Gob II-68; Metz 2-174.*

BEADS AND BARK, flower vase. Northwood Glass Co., 1902. A novelty in purple slag, and reportedly in green; also known in opalescent glass. This one has to be seen to be believed. *Ref. HII-63+.*

IMPERIAL #81, pitcher. Imperial Glass Co., after 1904. *Ref. K7-67.*

DOTS AND DASHES, goblet. Extended table service. *Ref. Gob II-123; Metz 2-126.*

BEADED BAND (THOUSAND EYE BAND), cordial. Made ca. 1890 in extended table service including wine. Crystal; rare in color. *Ref. L-61; LEAPG-247; Metz 1-136; Unitt 1-101; Schroy-15; Jenks p. 53.*

STIPPLED DART AND BALLS, pitcher. Made ca. 1890 in extended table service including wine. *Ref. K8-38; Gob II-33; Metz 1-182; Unitt 1-291.*

PANELLED HERRINGBONE (PRISM AND HERRINGBONE), salt shaker. Imperial Glass Co. #54, 1905. Extended table service including vase, cordial, wine. *Ref. K7-185; Metz 1-176; Gob II-137; Metz 2-150.*

POWDER AND SHOT, goblet. Boston and Sandwich; Portland Glass; possibly others. Extended table service including master salt, egg cup, castor bottle. *Ref. L-79; LEAPG-478; Jenks p. 414; Metz 1-114; Schroy-114.*

DEWDROP IN POINTS, pitcher. Greensburg Glass Co. #67, ca. 1875 – 1885. Extended table service including wine. *Ref. K3-13; LEAPG Pl. 87; Gob I-130; Metz 1-180; Unitt 1-123; Jenks p. 173; Schroy-49.*

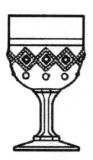

*Diamonds and
Dewdrops* *Beads and Bark* *Imperial #81*

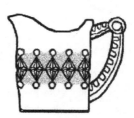

Dots and Dashes *Beaded Band* *Stippled Dart
and Balls*

*Panelled
Herringbone* *Powder and Shot* *Dewdrop in Points*

317

PLATE 153. HOBNAILS AND BEADS

ONE HUNDRED-AND-ONE (ONE-O-ONE; BEADED 1-0-1), goblet. George Duncan and Sons, 1885. Extended table service including lamp, platter, 6", 7", 8" plates, wine. Crystal, opaque white. *Ref. K1-71; LEAPG-238; Gob I-82; Metz 1-188; Schroy-105; Jenks p. 389; HI-30.*

ARCHAIC GOTHIC, creamer. Basic table service. *Ref. K2-20.*

ALABAMA (BEADED BULLS-EYE AND DRAPE), pitcher. The first State Series pattern by U. S. Glass Co. (#15062) in 1892 and 1899 (Glassport). Extended table service including tray, syrup, covered honey dish. Crystal, ruby-stained, green. *Ref. K1-81; HI-13; H7-65; Jenks p. 7.*

LOCKET ON CHAIN (STIPPLED BEADED SHIELD), cruet. A H. Heisey #160, 1896 – 1910. Extended table service including rare toothpick holder, rare cruet, rare wine. No syrup known. Crystal, ruby-stained, colors. *Ref. K8-186; Gob II-118; Unitt 2-119; K2-57; HI-50; HIII-56; H6-34; H7-143; Jenks p. 333; Schroy-91.*

TASSEL AND BEAD, salt shaker. Bryce Brothers Glass Co. *Ref. PetSal 175C.*

JEWELED HEART (SWEETHEART), salt shaker. Dugan Glass Co., 1898 – 1905. Extended table service including lamp, wine. Crystal, green, blue, scarce marigold carnival, opalescent. No goblets made originally, but repros are out there. *Ref. Unitt 2-220; K2-103; K5-41; HTP-46; HI-28; HII-22; HIII-29; H6-32.*

BEADED OVALS IN SAND, cruet. Dugan Glass Co., 1905. Extended table service. Blue, green, opalescent colors, decorated. *Ref. HI-14; HTP-50, 70; HII-13; HIII-54; H6-19.*

BEADED ARCH PANELS, mug. Burlington Glass Works, ca. 1890. Known in toys and goblet. Crystal, blue. *Ref. LV-79 #11; Metz 1-190.*

TEARDROP AND TASSEL (SAMPSON), pitcher. Indiana Tumbler and Goblet Co., 1890. Extended table service including wine, cordial, tumbler. Crystal, blue, amber; opaque colors of white, green, and yellow. *Ref. L-78; K1-95; Gob I-93; Metz 1-134; LEAPG-247; Schroy-139; Unitt 1-293.*

TENNESSEE (JEWELLED ROSETTES; JEWEL AND CRESCENT; SCROLLS WITH BULLS-EYE), salt shaker. U. S. Glass Co. (King) #15064, 1899. A State Series pattern. Extended table service including wine, jam jar, bread plate, and many other pieces. Crystal, stained. *Ref. K3-62; Gob II-5; Unitt 2-243; HTP-86; H5-147; Jenks p. 507; Schroy-140; Mugs p. 91.*

*One-Hundred-
and-One*

Archaic Gothic

Alabama

*Locket on
Chain*

Tassel and Bead

Jeweled Heart

*Beaded Ovals
in Sand*

*Beaded Arch
Panels*

*Teardrop and
Tassel*

Tennessee

319

PLATE 154. PANELS

FLARE TOP FLUTE, goblet. One of the many "Flute" type patterns. This one is shown in Millard's Goblets II, Plate 32.

COLONIAL PANEL, creamer. *Ref. K7-10.*

NAIL CITY, creamer. Central Glass #555, 1881. Extended table service. *Ref. K3-37.*

LATE COLONIAL, cup. Imperial Glass Co. Extended table service.

CHIPPENDALE, creamer. Ohio Flint Glass Co., 1907; Jefferson Glass Co., 1908; Central Glass Works, 1919; and even Geo. Davidson & Co. Teams Glassworks in England in 1933, which had purchased the original molds. Made in 147 items by Jefferson in 1908, who used the "Krys-tol" trademark. In time they produced 340 different Chippendale items including wines, cordials, champagnes, clarets, candlesticks, perfume bottles, pin trays, hair receivers, covered pomades, and ring holders. Crystal, ruby-stained. The main problem is that this pattern assumed every shape imaginable in a flute design — fat and round, tall and slim, large panelled, small panelled, square, and even footed. Kamm showed two creamers in Books 1 & 2, but neither was really Chippendale. Bill Heacock, in *Glass Collector 4*, p. 38 showed a large assortment of the pattern, and discussed it thoroughly. The English pieces were probably not marked "Krys-tol." In 1934 Queen Mary purchased several pieces of Chippendale at the British Industries Fair. Heacock believed that the pattern has never been reproduced in America. This is probably the hardest pattern of all to collect if it lacks the trademark or handle. *Ref. K1-107; K6-41; HGC4 p. 38; HGC5 p. 6; HII-76; H7-90+.*

ARCHED PANEL, creamer. *Ref. K1-105.*

FLUTE, goblet. Many companies made Flute, Bakewell, Pears and Co.; Adams and Co.; McKee Brothers; 1840 – 1870. Crystal, rare colors. *Ref. L-13; LEAPG-45; Metz 1-40; Schroy-63; Jenks p. 225; HI-23; HII-20; Mugs p. 40.*

CONNECTICUT FLUTE, goblet. This one has eight fluted panels. *Ref. Metz 1-41; Metz 2-82.*

BILIKEN FLUTE, goblet. The wine is known, courtesy of John Gregory. *Ref. Gob II-125.*

JANSSEN, goblet. *Ref. Gob II-125; Metz 1-204.*

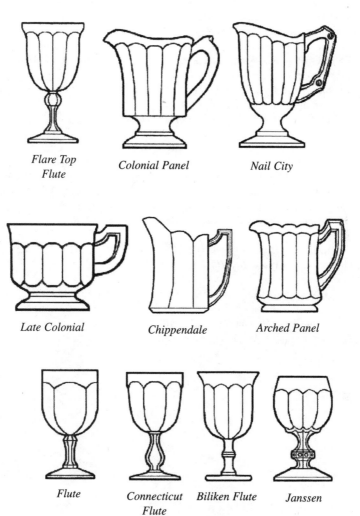

Flare Top
Flute

Colonial Panel

Nail City

Late Colonial

Chippendale

Arched Panel

Flute

Connecticut
Flute

Biliken Flute

Janssen

PLATE 155. PANELS

LOOP WITH KNOB STEM, goblet. *Ref. Gob II-16; Metz 1-38.*

RED FLUTE, goblet. *Gob II-21; Metz 1-41.*

LUCERE, creamer. Fostoria Glass Co. #1515, 1907. Extended table service including wine, champagne. (The name has been corrupted to "Lucerne," but this is the correct spelling, courtesy of John Gregory.) *Ref. K8-37.*

DUCHESS LOOP, goblet. Wine is also known. *Ref. Gob II-1; Metz 1-40; Metz 2-30.*

FLUTE, goblet. *Ref. L-13; LEAPG-45; Metz 1-40; Jenks p. 225; Schroy-63; HI-23; HII-20.*

GIANT FLUTE, goblet. *Ref. Gob II-132; Metz 1-41.*

JERSEY S, creamer. Jersey Glass Co., 1825. Known in open salt and creamer. *Ref. K4-67.*

HEISEY'S COLONIAL (PEERLESS), creamer. A. H. Heisey #300, ca. 1897. Extended table service including decanters, wines, cordials, champagnes, claret, brandy, water bottles, candlestick, bitters bottle, claret jug. Crystal, ruby-stained. Heisey #300½ is identical except for having plain rims, not scalloped. *Ref. K2-89; K8-189; Revi-176; H7-170.*

FT. PITT, creamer. U. S. Glass Co. #15123 (Glassport; Ripley), 1910. Extended table service including wine. Crystal. *Ref. H5-156.*

LATE COLONIAL VARIANT, creamer. Duncan and Miller #61, 1905. Extended table service including ice cream dishes, open salt, several shapes salt shakers, water tray, water bottle, candlesticks, claret, wine, cocktail, cordial, footed whiskey, champagnes, baskets, vases, decanter, fruit jar with lid. *Ref. K2-87.*

Loop with
Knob Stem

Red Flute

Lucere

Duchess Loop

Flute

Giant Flute

Jersey S

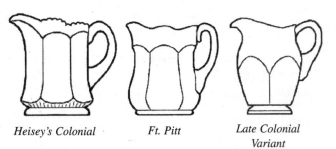

Heisey's Colonial

Ft. Pitt

Late Colonial
Variant

PLATE 156. PANELS

ROCKET BOMB, salt shaker. Usually found gilded. *Ref. PetSal 170N.*

WESTMORELAND COLONIAL (KEYSTONE COLONIAL), pitcher. Westmoreland Glass Co. #1776, ca. 1911. Extended table service including banana split dish, finger bowl, "Uneeda biscuit" holder, cordial, brandy, wine, claret, champagne, oil set, mustard set, iced tea, lazy susan. Crystal, ruby-stained. *Ref. Kovar, Westmoreland Glass Vol. IV p. 37; Schroy-154; H6-45; H7-67.*

TAPERING FLUTE, ale glass. *Ref. Gob II-81; Metz 1-41.*

DIAMOND STEM, pitcher. *Ref. K6-58; HII-65.*

HEISEY #339-2, salt shaker. A. H. Heisey Glass Co., ca. 1895. Their #339 was "Continental" on Plate 159.

PRETTY PANELS, syrup. Probably Hobbs, Brockunier and Co. #86, 1890 (Heacock). However, Hobbs #86 was exhibited at the Centennial Exposition in Philadelphia in 1876 and described as "a 10 inch bowl with 16 OG scallops." Extended table service. *Ref. K3-37; Hobbs p. 12; HIII-36.*

ESSEX, creamer. Fostoria Glass Co. #1372, 1905. Extended table service including claret, champagne, wine, cordial, cup, sugar shaker. *Ref. K8-32.*

PRESSED OCTAGON, syrup. Made ca. 1890 in crystal, milk glass, amber, and decorated. *Ref. HIII-36.*

PLAIN SCALLOPED PANEL (U. S. COLONIAL; COLONIAL), creamer. U. S. Glass Co. #15047 (Glassport), 1896. Extended table service including wine. Crystal, emerald green, cobalt blue (scarce). *Ref. K1-81; K3-51; Revi-316; Unitt 2-233; HI-36; H5-50, 143.*

DOUGLASS, toothpick holder. Cooperative Flint Glass Co., ca. 1903. Extended table service. Crystal, ruby-stained. *Ref. HI-27; H7-53+; HTP-52.*

BOUQUET, tumbler. Bakewell, Pears and Co., ca. 1875. Made in a water set in cased glass. *Ref. Schroy-23; Metz 1-66.*

Rocket Bomb   *Westmoreland Colonial*   *Tapering Flute*   *Diamond Stem*

Heisey #339-2   *Pretty Panels*   *Essex*   *Pressed Octagon*

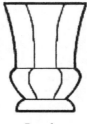
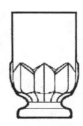

Plain Scalloped Panel   *Douglass*   *Bouquet*

PLATE 157. PANELS

DESPOT, goblet. *Ref. Gob II-81; Metz 2-178.*

HUBER, (FALMOUTH), celery vase. Cape Cod Glass Co., 1860s; Boston and Sandwich; New England Glass Co.; Bakewell, Pears and Co., ca. 1860s. Extended table service including tumblers, handled egg cup, bitters bottle, footed salt dip, quart jug, cordials, claret, decanters, wines, champagne, handled whiskey. Flint glass and crystal. *Ref. L-11; K4-56; Metz 1-34; LEAPG-49; Schroy-78; Jenks p. 285.*

BOHEMIAN, goblet. Bakewell, Pears and Co. *Ref. K6 Pl. 59; HI-15.*

LATE CRYSTAL, pitcher. O'Hara Glass Co., 1885; Richards and Hartley, 1888; McKee and Brothers, 1894; U. S. Glass Co., 1898. Extended table service including egg cup, wine. *Ref. K1-21.*

QUADRUPED, creamer. Indiana Glass Co., ca. 1920 – 1930s. Has been believed to be a part of Chippendale (see Plate 154) but it is not; believed to be made by Jefferson, but it is not. Extended table service. Crystal, ruby-stained. *Ref. K2-107; H7-180.*

BULBOUS BASE, syrup. Hobbs, Brockunier #311, ca. 1887; U. S. Glass Co., 1890s. Extended table service including tumbler with straight sides, finger bowl, sugar shaker. Crystal, cranberry glass. *Ref. HI-16; HIII-17; H5-31; H6-17.*

DOUBLE DONUT, pitcher. A Findlay, Ohio product, 1880s. Extended table service. *Ref. K2-32; Schroy-161.*

DUNCAN, spoon holder.

CRYSTALINA, sugar bowl and pitcher. Hobbs, Brockunier and Co. #334; U. S. Glass Co. (Hobbs), 1891 – 1920s. Extended table service including individual creamer with half-handle, bread plate, sherbet with saucer. Crystal, ruby-stained, amber-stained, emerald green, blue. See Plate 208. *Ref. H5-126; Schroy-40; Hobbs p. 116; H5-126; H7-97+.*

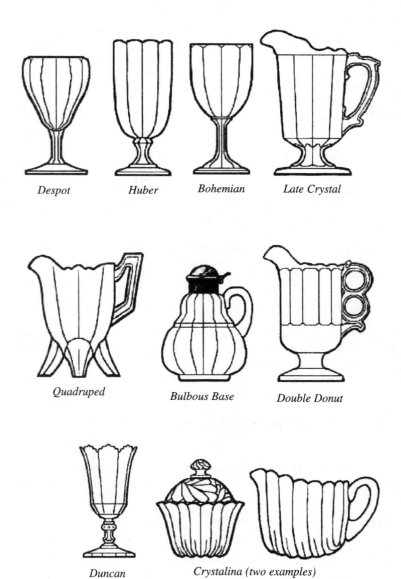

Despot   *Huber*   *Bohemian*   *Late Crystal*

Quadruped   *Bulbous Base*   *Double Donut*

Duncan   *Crystalina (two examples)*

PLATE 158. PANELS

MIOTON (PLAIN MIOTON), goblet. Possibly McKee, ca. 1880. Extended table service including wine, cordial, champagne. Crystal, ruby-stained. *Ref. Gob II-25; LEAPG-65; Gob I-4; Gob II-25; Metz 1-206; Unitt 1-17; H7-173.*

SPRIG WITHOUT SPRIG (ROYAL), wine goblet. Bryce, Higbee and Co. in the mid-1880s. Extended table service including bread plate, pickle jar, wine, cordial, champagne. This is the same pattern as SPRIG on Plate 194 without the flowers. *Ref. K8 Pl. 28; Gob I-126; Metz 1-58; Unitt 1-220.*

DUNCAN FLUTE, pitcher. George Duncan and Sons #2004, 1894. Extended table service. *Ref. K5-30.*

CHICK, sugar bowl. See Plate 7.

PETAL AND LOOP (O'HARA), plate. Boston and Sandwich, 1850s; O'Hara Glass Co. Extended table service including candlestick, wine, cordial, champagne. Flint glass. *Ref. L-4; LEAPG-26; Welker p. 423; Innes p. 364.*

EUREKA, egg cup. McKee and Brothers, 1866. Extended table service including footed tumbler, champagne, wine, cordial. Crystal, ruby-stained. *Ref. L-6; Gob I-147; Metz 1-20; LEAPG-69; Unitt 2-62; K3-17; Schroy-56; H6-26; H7-113.*

U. S. #5705, cruet. U. S. Glass Co., ca. 1909. Only the cruet is known. *Ref. HIII-88.*

CAMBRIDGE COLONIAL (NEARCUT COLONIAL), creamer. Cambridge Glass Co. #2750, ca. early 1900s. Extended table service including decanter, water bottle, vase, basket, punch bowl, wine. *Ref. K8-189; HTP-55.*

CROCUS, salt shaker. Milk glass. *Ref. PetSal 26D.*

OVOID PANELS, goblet. Made ca. 1860s; wine is also known. *Ref. Gob II-26; Metz 1-10; Unitt 2-62.*

PORTLAND PETAL (YUMA LOOP), spill holder and goblet. Portland Glass Co., ca. 1860s. Extended table service including wine. *Ref. Gob I-161; Metz 1-38; Unitt 1-20; K4-16.*

Mioton

Sprig without Sprig

Duncan Flute

Chick

Petal and Loop

Eureka

U.S. #5705

Cambridge Colonial

Crocus

Ovoid Panels

Portland Petal (two examples)

PLATE 159. PANELS

LOOP (O'HARA; SENECA LOOP), covered bowl. Boston and Sandwich; O'Hara Glass Co. #9, 1850s – 1860s; J. B. Lyon and Co., 1860s; McKee Glass Co., 1875; U. S. Glass Co., 1891. Extended table service including egg cup, master salt, wine, champagne, cordial, open and covered sugar bowls. Flint glass. *Ref. L-4; Gob 1-13; Metz 1-38; Unitt 1-21; K1-5; Schroy-91; Jenks p. 335.*

WIDE AND NARROW PANEL, creamer. Made ca. 1890. *Ref. K1-108.*

CHURCH WINDOWS (TULIP PETALS; COLUMBIA), pitcher. U. S. Glass #15082 (King; Richards and Hartley), 1903. Extended table service including sardine dish, open and covered sugar bowls, wines. Crystal, decorated. *Ref. K3-107; K4-115; Gob II-16; Metz 1-196; Unitt 2-65; H5-145; HTP-84.*

SANDWICH LOOP (FLUTE; EARLY LOOP), goblet. Another early flute type by Boston and Sandwich Glass Co., ca. 1860s, and others. Wine and champagne also known. *Ref. LV-84; Metz 1-24.*

HAIRPIN, goblet. Sandwich Glass, ca. 1850s. Extended table service including decanter, wine, champagne, egg cup, open and covered sugar bowls. crystal, milk glass. *Ref. Gob II-44; Metz 1-24; Jenks p. 255; Schroy-68.*

CONTINENTAL, pitcher. A. H. Heisey #339, 1903 – 1913. Extended table service including wine, two kinds of butter dishes, two kinds of creamers, two kinds of spooners, and two kinds of sugar bowls (flat, footed.) Crystal, ruby-stained. *Ref. K8-187; LEAPG-76; H7-93; Burns p. 10.*

NEARCUT #2692, creamer. Cambridge Glass Co., 1909. Extended table service including finger bowl, water bottle. *Ref. K7 Pl. 79.*

CHALICE, sugar bowl. Westmoreland Glass Co. #252, ca. 1896. Basic table service in milk glass. *Ref. K1-29.*

DELTA, syrup. Made ca. 1895; only the syrup known in amber and crystal. *Ref. HIII-23.*

U. S. #5701, cruet. U. S. Glass Co., ca. 1909. *Ref. HIII-88.*

ETCHED GRAPE, pitcher (etched.) U. S. Glass Co., 1900 – 1905. Extended table service. Crystal, emerald green. *Ref. K2-122.*

Loop

*Wide and
Narrow
Panel*

*Church
Windows*

*Sandwich
Loop*

Hairpin

Continental

Nearcut #2692

Chalice

Delta

U.S. #5701

Etched Grape

PLATE 160. PANELS

ASHLAND (SNOWDROP), goblet. Portland Glass Co., ca. 1880s. Extended table service including leaf-shaped dish, ice cream tray. *Ref. Gob II-31; Metz 1-138; Metz 2-123+.*

EVANGELINE, pitcher. U. S. Glass Co. #15131 (Gas City), 1909. Extended table service including wine. Crystal. *Ref. H5-168.*

FLAWLESS, butter tub and creamer. Duncan and Miller #72, ca. 1905 – 1910. Extended table service including punch bowl and cups, individual salts, vases, wine, claret, champagne, cordial. The butter and some other pieces lack the characteristic edge cutting of the pattern. Crystal, ruby-stained. *Ref. K6-15; Revi-149; H6-84; H7-101; Krause p. 159.*

STIPPLED LOOP, goblet. Wine is also known. *Ref. Gob II-27; Metz 1-213; Metz 2-154; Unitt 2-37.*

MARQUISETTE, spoon holder. Extended table service including wine, cordials, champagne. *Ref. L-159; Gob I-130; Metz 1-182; LEAPG-496; Schroy-96; Unitt 1-272; K3-70.*

U. S. GEORGIAN, syrup and pitcher. U. S. Glass Co. #15152 (Glassport; King), 1915. Extended table service including several style creamers, fruit jar with cover, sugar shaker, tray. There is much variation in this pattern. *Ref. H5-159.*

BANDED FLUTE, goblet. *Ref. Gob II-111.*

NEW ENGLAND FLUTE, goblet. *Ref. Gob II-142; Metz 1-40.*

PITTSBURGH FLUTE, goblet. Wine is also known. *Ref. Gob II-126; Metz 1-41; Metz 2-30; Unitt 1-18.*

U. S. PURITAN, creamer. U. S. Glass Co. #15155 (King), 1909. Extended table service. *Ref. H5-149.*

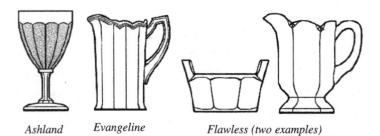

Ashland   Evangeline   Flawless (two examples)

Stippled Loop   Marquisette   U.S. Georgian (two examples)

Banded Flute   New England
Flute   Pittsburgh
Flute   U.S. Puritan

PLATE 161. PANELS

DOUBLE PETALLED FLUTE (DOUBLE PETAL TULIP), goblet. Wine is also known. *Gob II-33.*

THUMBNAIL (FLAT-TO-ROUND PANEL), cruet. Duncan and Miller Glass Co. #73. Extended table service. Crystal, ruby-stained, gilded. *Ref. PetSal 157S; H6-82; HTP-85; H7-41+.*

SPEARPOINT BAND (GOTHIC), cruet. McKee and Brothers, ca. 1904. Extended table service including wine, cordials, champagnes. Crystal, ruby-stained. *Ref. K7-31; HTP-54; HI-41; HIII-57; H7-123.*

GOLD BAND (RANSON), cruet. Riverside Glass Co., 1899. Crystal, vaseline, gilded. *Ref. K7-31; HI-25.*

BELTED PANEL, salt shaker. A. H. Heisey Co. #333. *Ref. PetSal 167R.*

COLONIS (45 COLONIS), pitcher. U. S. Glass Co. #15145 (Glassport), 1913. Extended table service including cordial, egg cup, tray. Most pieces lack the identifying horizontal rib. Crystal. *Ref. K5-146; H5-157.*

STIPPLED PANEL AND BAND, creamer. Made in the 1860s. *Ref. K1-16.*

LIGHTNING (CHAIN LIGHTNING), salt shaker. Tiffin Glass Co.; U. S. Glass Co. (Gas City), 1893. Extended table service including wine, cordial. Crystal. *Ref. K3-100; Gob I-108; Schroy-161; Metz 1-150.*

CAPSTAN, salt shaker. *Ref. PetSal 156J.*

BLOCKED THUMBPRINT BAND, syrup. Duncan Glass Co. #56, 1904 – 1913. Found in bar goods, shot glass, wine, toothpick holder. toy mug, cruet. Crystal, ruby-stained. *Ref HI-15; HIII-16; H6-47+; H7-79.*

*Double
Petalled Flute*

Thumbnail

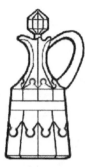

*Spearpoint
Band*

Gold Band

Belted Panel

Colonis

*Stippled Panel
and Band*

Lightning

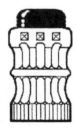

Capstan

*Blocked
Thumbprint Band*

PLATE 162. PANELS

MIOTON WITH PLEAT BAND, goblet. A wine is owned by John Gregory. *Ref. Gob II-131; Metz 1-52.*

REGINA, goblet and pitcher. Cooperative Flint Glass Co., 1902; Federal Glass Co. #1504, 1914. Extended table service including wine, cordial. *Ref. K5-103; HGC4 p. 20.*

PLEAT AND PANEL (DERBY), creamer. Bryce, Walker and Co., 1882; U. S. Glass Co., 1891. Extended table service including square plate, water tray, covered candy jar, wine, lamp, bread plate. Crystal, amethyst, canary, blue. *Ref. L-157; LEAPG-472; K2-24; Gob I-66; Metz 1-182; Unitt 1-146; H5-81; H6-37; Jenks p. 407; Schroy-112.*

LOOP WITH PRISM BAND, pitcher. Extended table service. *Ref. K2-121; Metz 1-147.*

PLEATED BANDS, goblet. *Ref. Gob II-66; Metz 1-136; Metz 2-198.*

CARTRIDGE BELT, goblet. The wine is also known. *Ref. Gob II-133; Unitt 1-248.*

X-RAY, pitcher. Riverside Glass Co. #462, 1896. Extended table service including wine, rare syrup, cloverleaf tray. Crystal, emerald green, amethyst (scarce), ruby-stained, usually gilded. Kamm remarks that there are deep grooves running down the sides with gilding alongside. *Ref. K5-136; HI-45; HIII-46, 57; H6-47; H7-17; Jenks p. 563; Schroy-157.*

PRISM AND FLUTE (PRISM; PRISM WARE), footed tumbler. Bakewell, Pears and Co., 1870s. Extended table service including egg cup, master salt, cordial, wine, champagne. Often engraved. *Ref. L-16; Gob I-126; Metz 1-146; LEAPG-71; Unitt 2-56.*

TRIPLE FINETOOTH BAND, goblet. *Ref. Gob II-108.*

ETCHED BAND, goblet. Portland Glass Co. Wine and cordial are known. *Ref. Swan p. 92.*

POGO STICK (CROWN), creamer. Lancaster Glass Co., ca. 1910. Extended table service. *Ref. K7-23; Schroy-113.*

*Mioton with
Pleat Band*   *Regina (two examples)*   *Pleat and Panel*

*Loop with
Prism Band*   *Pleated Bands*   *Cartridge Belt*   *X-Ray*

Prism and Flute   *Triple Fine-
Tooth Band*   *Etched Band*   *Pogo Stick*

PLATE 163. PANELS

PRISON STRIPE, creamer. A. H. Heisey #357, ca. 1904 – 1909. Extended table service including two creamers. Crystal, rare in opalescent. *Ref. K7-139; HTP-87.*

THREADING, creamer. George Duncan and Sons Glass Co., ca. 1904 – 1909. Extended table service including two creamers. Crystal, rare in opalescent. *Ref. K3-15; Metz 1-128.*

VENICE, pitcher. U. S. Glass Co. (Adams factory), 1891. Extended table service. *Ref. K4-105.*

HEISEY'S URN, salt shaker. A. H. Heisey #379, 1905 – 1907. Extended table service. *Ref. Burns p. 63.*

HEISEY'S BANDED FLUTE, toothpick holder. Heisey Glass Co., 1907 – 1932. Extended table service. Crystal. Note: Heacock calls this pattern #150, but Kamm (K4-90) shows a different pattern with that number which I show on Plate 46. *Ref. HTP-78.*

PLAIN TULIP, syrup. Made ca. 1850s in extended table service including wine. Flint glass. *Ref. L-50; Gob I-4; Metz 1-32; Metz 2-58.*

U. S. NIAGARA, creamer. U. S. Glass Co. #15162 (Glassport), 1915. Extended table service including cracker jar, mustard jar, wine. Crystal. *Ref. H5-161; Welker p. 413.*

PANELLED LADDER, goblet. *Ref. Gob II-3; Metz 2-152.*

MILLARD (FAN AND FLUTE; KENTUCKY WITH PLAIN PANELS; SOUVENIR), syrup (etched). U. S. Glass #15016 (Hobbs factory), 1893. Extended table service including wine. Crystal, amber-stained, ruby-stained, etched. *Ref. K5-60; K6-33; K8-63; LV-52; Gob II-55; Metz 2-142; Unitt 2-133; HI-50; HIII-33, 56; H5-49, 50; H7-26+; HTP-27.*

Prison Stripe *Threading* *Venice*

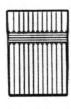

Heisey's Urn *Heisey's Band-* *Plain Tulip*
ed Flute

U.S. Niagara *Panelled Ladder* *Millard*

PLATE 164. PANELS

SCALLOPED LINES (SCALLOPED BAND), goblet. Extended table service including wine. *Ref. Gob II-14; Metz 1-132; Metz 2-126.*

THREAD BAND, creamer. Duncan and Miller Glass Co., 1900 – 1920s. Extended table service. Crystal, engraved.

FLUTED SCROLLS (FOGGY BOTTOM), salt shaker and creamer. Northwood Glass Co., late 1880s. Extended table service including epergne. Crystal, amber, sapphire blue, custard. *Ref. K2-119; Schroy-63; HIII-20; H6-28.*

SILVER QUEEN (ELMINO; FAYE), goblet and creamer. Ripley and Co., 1890; U. S. Glass Co., 1891. Extended table service including catsup, very plain tumbler, spooner with two handles, wine. Crystal, ruby-stained. *Ref. Gob II-104; K4-85; H5-121; Revi-234; Unitt 1-175; Unitt 2-51; H7-193+.*

RIPPLE (RIPPLE BAND; HERRINGBONE BAND), open salt and pitcher. Boston and Sandwich, late 1870s. Extended table service including compotes, champagne, claret, wine, cordial, lamp. *Ref. K3-20; Gob I-155; Metz 1-132; Unitt 1-103.*

MULTIPLE CIRCLE, goblet. *Ref. Gob II-39.*

TRIPLE LINE, creamer. *Ref. K7-2.*

NICKEL PLATE'S ROYAL, creamer. Nickel Plate Glass Co. #77, 1890; U. S. Glass Co., 1891. Extended table service including barrel-shaped tumbler. Crystal. *Ref. K5-35; H5-136.*

TRIPLE BAND, pitcher. The pitcher came with a pewter lid. *Ref. K4-126; Metz 1-50.*

Scalloped Lines   *Thread Band*   *Fluted Scrolls (two views)*

Silver Queen (two views)   *Ripple (two views)*

Multiple Circle   *Triple Line*   *Nickel Plate's Royal*   *Triple Band*

PLATE 165. PANELS

JEFFERSON COLONIAL, creamer. Jefferson Glass #270, 1903. Extended table service. Crystal, pale blue, green. *Ref. K8-28; HTP-55.*

ETRUSCAN, bowl and spoon holder. Bakewell, Pears and Co. Extended table service including egg cup. *Ref. L-20; LEAPG-78.*

PANELLED FINETOOTH, goblet. Extended table service including wine, relish dish with shield (scarce.) Flint glass. *Ref. Gob II-28; Metz 2-48.*

FOSTORIA #952, pitcher. Fostoria Glass Co., late 1880s. Extended table service. *Ref. Revi-162.*

REEDING (FOUR LINES), creamer. Cambridge Glass Co. #2960, 1916. Extended table service including wine, cordial. Courtesy of John Gregory. *Ref. K8-32.*

PHILADELPHIA, compote. New England Glass Co., 1869. Extended table service including egg cup, wine. Crystal, ruby-stained. *Ref. L-61; Metz 1-174; Unitt 1-126; LEAPG-195; H7-168.*

PLEATING (FLAT PANEL), pitcher. U. S. Glass Co. #15003 (Ripley; Bryce), 1891. Extended table service. Crystal, ruby-stained. The stain is applied by decal in fancy designs. *Ref. K8-70; LV-51; HTP-52; HI-36; H5-51, 81; H7-116+; Metz 1-148.*

Jefferson
Colonial

Etruscan (two examples)

Panelled Finetooth   *Fostoria #952*   *Reeding*

Philadelphia   *Pleating*

PLATE 166. PANELS

CLEAR RIBBON, spoon holder. George Duncan and Sons, 1880s. Extended table service including bread tray. *Ref. L-70; LEAPG-229; Metz 1-170; Schroy-36.*

FROSTED RIBBON (REBECCA AT THE WELL; BAKEWELL RIBBON), spooner and pitcher. Bakewell, Pears and Co., 1878; George Duncan and Sons #150, 1878; U. S. Glass, 1891. Extended table service including ale glass, wine, cordials, champagne, clarets, bitters bottle, waste bowl. The goblet has been reproduced. *Ref. L-69; Gob I-37; Metz 1-170; LEAPG-223; Unitt 1-119.*

FLUTED RIBBON (PANEL AND FLUTE), spoon holder. U. S. Glass #15022, 1891. Extended table service including decanter. *Ref. K3-95; L-67.*

FROSTED RIBBON, DOUBLE BARS, goblet. King Glass Co. #13, ca. 1875. Extended table service including wine. This pattern comes in a non-frosted version called KINGS RIBBON, which includes a toy table set. *Ref. Gob II-43; Revi-221; Unitt 1-18; Pine Press, Pennsylvania Glassware p. 40, 41; Metz 1-170.*

DOUBLE RIBBON, pitcher. King Glass Co., 1870s. Extended table service including bread plate, egg cup. Clear or frosted. *Ref. K1-53; L-67; LEAPG-227; Metz 1-170.*

RIBBON (REBECCA AT THE WELL; FROSTED RIBBON), spoon holder. Bakewell, Pears and Co., ca. 1870. Extended table service including rare wine, cordials, champagnes, dolphin-stemmed compote, covered cheese dish, water tray, waste bowl. See Plate 172, REBECCA AT THE WELL. *Ref. L-67; LEAPG-220; Schroy-120; Gob I-115; Metz 1-170; Metz 2-190; Unitt 1-118.*

CLEAR RIBBON VARIANT, creamer. Made ca. 1890. *Ref. K1-83.*

STIPPLED BAND (PANELLED STIPPLED BOWL), spoon holder. Made ca. 1870s in extended table service including footed salt. *Ref. L-107; LEAPG-220; Gob I-154; Gob II-41; K3-25; Metz 1-182; Unitt 1-444.*

344

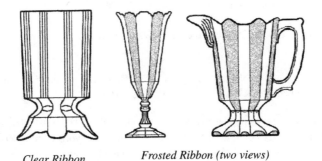

Clear Ribbon　　　　*Frosted Ribbon (two views)*

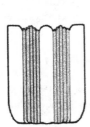  

Fluted Ribbon　　*Frosted Ribbon,*　　*Double Ribbon*
　　　　　　　　　　Double Bars

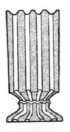  

　Ribbon　　*Clear Ribbon Variant*　　*Stippled Band*

PLATE 167. PANELS

FOSTORIA #551, pitcher. Fostoria Glass Co., 1898. Basic table service. *Ref. K8-28.*

FRANKLIN FLUTE, goblet. *Ref. Gob II-96.*

LOEHR FLUTE, goblet. *Ref. Gob II-135.*

SIDE WHEELER, creamer. Made in the mid-1880s in extended table service. *Ref. K5-31; Metz 2-154.*

STIPPLED BAR, spoon holder. U. S. Glass Co. #15044, 1895. Extended table service. Crystal, ruby-stained. *Ref. LV-63; Metz 1-173; Metz 2-108; H7-196+.*

OGLEBAY, engraved creamer. Hobbs, Brockunier Glass Co. #332, 1891. Extended table service including finger bowl, master salt. This pattern was reworked from WHEELING molds (see next entry), and all pieces are scarce. Crystal, plain, and engraved. *Ref. Hobbs p. 116.*

WHEELING, engraved creamer. Hobbs, Brockunier Glass Co. #115, 1887. Extended table service including toy tumbler, master salt, individual butter. Crystal, engraved, decorated. *Ref. LV-65; H6-58; Hobbs p. 102.*

TRIAD, creamer. Basic table service. Crystal, etched. *Ref. K4-39.*

THE JEFFERSON, pitcher. Jefferson Glass Co. #254, ca. 1907. Extended table service including spoon tray, finger bowl. Crystal, ruby-stained, opaque white. *Ref. K7-149.*

GATHERED KNOT, pitcher. Imperial Glass Co. #3, 1902. Extended table service including pickle jar, sugar shaker, cracker jar, vases, wine. *Ref. K7-181; Gob II-97, 104; Metz 2-154; Unitt 2-73.*

Fostoria #551

Franklin
Flute

Loehr Flute

Side Wheeler

Stippled Bar

Oglebay

Wheeling

Triad

The Jefferson

Gathered Knot

PLATE 168. PANELS

ORINDA, creamer. National Glass co. (Lancaster #1492), 1901. Extended table service. Crystal, ruby-stained. *Ref. K5-111; HI-34; H7-165.*

FLORIDA (GREEN HERRINGBONE; EMERALD GREEN HERRINGBONE; CLEAR HERRINGBONE; PANELLED HERRINGBONE), goblet and creamer. U. S. Glass Co. #15056 (Bryce), 1898. A State Series pattern. Extended table service including cordials, wide-mouthed vase, square berry bowls, plate, and sauce; wine. Crystal, emerald green, ruby-stained. *Ref. K1-46; L-161; Metz 1-176; Unitt 2-93; H5-38, 173; H7-6+; Jenks p. 222; Schroy-62.*

MITRED PRISMS (TRUMP), salt shaker. Extended table service including wine. *Ref. Gob I-68; Metz 1-172.*

CHAIN THUMBPRINTS, etched creamer. Made ca. 1885 – 1890 in extended table service. *Ref. K3-55; Metz 1-218.*

CUTTLEBONE, goblet. *Ref. Gob II-42.*

WASHBOARD (ADONIS; PLEAT AND TUCK), pitcher. McKee and Brothers, 1897; Lancaster Glass Co., 1898. Extended table service including wine, cordial. Crystal, blue, canary, green. *Ref. K6 Pl. 12; Metz 1-142.*

FINE FEATHER, salt shaker. *Ref. PetSal 28P.*

TREE, creamer. Paden City Glass Mfg. Co., ca. 1915 – 1920. Extended table service. Crystal, ruby-stained. *Ref. K8-31; H6-92; H7-133+.*

WINGED SCROLL (IVORINA VERDE), syrup. A. H. Heisey Glass Co., 1888 – 1905. Extended table service including smoker's set. Crystal, custard, and very rarely, milk glass. *Ref. K7-137; HTP-49; HI-44; HIII-46; H6-46.*

Orinda   *Florida (two examples)*

Mitred Prisms   *Chain*   *Cuttlebone*   *Washboard*
                Thumbprints

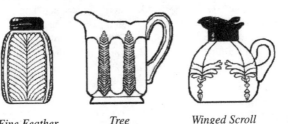

Fine Feather   *Tree*   *Winged Scroll*

PLATE 169. PEOPLE

ACTRESS (THEATRICAL; GODDESS OF LIBERTY; ANNIE; PINAFORE), spooner, creamer, pitcher, salt shaker, and goblet. Crystal Glass Co., ca. 1879; Adams and Co., 1880. Extended table service including covered cheese dish (Sanderson Moffit as "The Lone Fisherman," Stuart Robson and William Crane as "Two Dromios.") Romeo and Juliet were featured on a water pitcher; Fanny Davenport and Lillian Nielson on a butter dish; Kate Claxton and Lotta Crabtree on a goblet. Also made were trays, platter, and candlestick. Adams and Co. called their pattern "Opera." In the *News Journal of the Early American Pattern Glass Society*, Volume 5 Number 2 (Summer, 1998), a 1967 article by Edwin G. Warman was reprinted on pieces commemorating "H.M.S. Pinafore" by Gilbert and Sullivan. Mary Anderson is pictured on the spooner here, taken from a photo in the article. The marmalade jar is shown with Annie Pixley on one side and Maud Granger on the other. A celery vase shows deck scenes from the operetta and the name "Pinafore" is impressed near the top of the piece. Although Mr. Warman attributes the pattern to LaBelle Glass Co. of Bridgeport, Ohio, the latest word I have is that they did not manufacture "Actress." The pattern was made in crystal, ruby-stained, and etched. *Ref. PetSal 21E; K4-5; L-164 #11; Gob I-80; Metz 1-102; Schroy-2; Jenks p. 4; H7-10.*

VALENTINE (TRILBY), pitcher. U. S. Glass Co. (Glassport), 1895. Extended table service including cologne bottle, match holder. *Ref. L-164 #12; Metz 1-102; Jenks p. 537; Schroy-150.*

ACTRESS CHAIN (THREE-FACED MEDALLION), goblet. *Ref. L-154 #2; Gob II-8.*

BABY FACE (CUPID), spoon holder. George Duncan and Sons. Extended table service including knife rest, wine, cordial, champagne. All pieces are scarce. The wine has been reproduced (courtesy of John Gregory). *Ref. L-89; Gob I-149; Metz 1-102; Unitt 1-90; LEAPG-300; Jenks p. 37; Schroy-11.*

THREE FACE (THE SISTERS; THREE SISTERS; THREE GRACES; THREE FATES), champagne goblet. George Duncan and Sons #400, 1878; U. S. Glass Co., 1891; George Duncan's Sons and Co., 1892. Extended table service including oil lamp, claret, wines, champagnes, cordial, cracker jar, jam jar, salt dip. Has been extensively reproduced. At the Green Valley Auction in Pittsburgh in 1998, a rare hollow-stem champagne sold for $5,100. *Ref. L-89; LEAPG-291; K3-111; American Glass Volume II p. 168; Gob I-149; Metz 1-102; H5-106; Jenks p. 517; Schroy-143.*

Actress (three examples)

Actress (two examples)   *Valentine*

Actress Chain   *Baby Face*   *Three Face*

PLATE 170. PEOPLE

PSYCHE AND CUPID, pitcher. Made ca. 1880s in extended table service including jam jar, plate, platter, flat sauce, bread plate, wine. *Ref. L-75; LEAPG-347; Gob I-121; Metz 1-108; Unitt 1-258; K1-29; K4-3; Jenks p. 425; Schroy-117.*

CLASSIC, open sugar bowl and goblet. Gillinder and Sons, 1880s. Extended table service including plates for campaigns of Presidents Cleveland, Blaine, Hendricks, and Logan; and a warrior. Pieces with log feet are especially desirable. *Ref. L-97; LEAPG-298; Schroy-35; Metz 1-108.*

BELMONT'S ROYAL (ROYAL LADY), pitcher. Belmont Glass Co., 1881. Extended table service. Crystal. It features a woman's head on the rather oddly stippled background. *Ref. K4-109; K6 Pl. 90; Miller 4th Ed. p. 364; Schroy-125; Metz 2-188.*

CLASSIC MEDALLION (CAMEO), pitcher. Made ca. 1880s in extended table service. *Ref. K1-22; Metz 1-102; Schroy-35; Jenks p. 122.*

GIBSON GIRL, creamer. Kokomo Glass Co., 1904. Extended table service. *Ref. K2-26; Metz 2-184; Schroy-66.*

CUPID AND VENUS (GUARDIAN ANGEL; MINERVA), goblet. Richards and Hartley Flint Glass Co. #500, 1875 – 1884; U. S. Glass Co., 1891. Extended table service including wine, cordials, bread platter, jam jar, champagne, mugs, pickle castor. Crystal, scarce canary and amber. *Ref. L-70; LEAPG-346; Gob I-121; Metz 1-108; Unitt 1-258; K1-28; Mugs p. 8; Schroy-41; Jenks p. 140.*

CERES (CAMEO; GODDESS OF LIBERTY; MEDALLION), spoon holder. Atterbury and Co., ca. 1870. Extended table service including mug, covered candy jar. Crystal, opaque colors, amber. *Ref. K2-51; Schroy-161; Metz 1-108; Mugs p. 7/8.*

MINERVA (ROMAN MEDALLION), creamer. Boston and Sandwich Glass Co., 1870; others. Extended table service including wine, champagne, sherbet, jam jar, platter, bread plate. *Ref. K1-41; Gob I-54; Metz 1-108; Schroy-99; LEAPG-348.*

Psyche and Cupid   *Classic (two examples)*

Belmont's Royal   *Classic Medallion*   *Gibson Girl*

Cupid and Venus   *Ceres*   *Minerva*

PLATE 171. PEOPLE

HUMPTY DUMPTY, mug. Probably made in the 1880s, and in colors in the 1930s. Known in mug, tumbler, bowl, and plate. The reverse side features Tom Tom the Piper's Son. *Ref. Mugs p. 8/9; Metz 2-203; Miller p. 148.*

WESTWARD HO!, covered compote. See Plate 2.

BICYCLE GIRL, pitcher. Dalzell, Gilmore and Leighton, 1880s. Known only in the pitcher. *Ref. K5-126; Schroy-161.*

MAN'S HEAD, pitcher. Made ca. 1879 and seldom found. *Ref. K5-12.*

TREE OF LIFE WITH HAND, pitcher. Boston and Sandwich; Portland Glass Co.; George Duncan and Sons, 1885; all made Tree of Life. Extended table service including wine. However, the Bredehofts say that only Hobbs, Brockunier and Co. made pieces with the hand, their #98. Hobbs made their set in 1879 in extended table service including plate, finger bowl, lamp. Crystal, old gold, canary, sapphire, marine green. A cake stand without the Tree of Life design, but with the hand grasping its standard, is known. The Warren Glass Works Co. made an elaborate bouquet vase using the hand stem in 1882; it has about 12 flower holders sprouting from the hand. The goblet has been reproduced. *Ref. LV Pl. 11; Unitt 1-67; Jenks p. 526; Metz 1-138; Schroy-146; Hobbs p. 55.*

JAPANESE (GRACE), pitcher. George Duncan and Sons Glass Co., 1881. A variety of scenes appears on the pieces of this pattern, each with its own name from early glass researchers. See BIRD-IN-RING, Plate 7. Extended table service including jam jar, pickle jar in a silver frame. *Ref. K2-16; Metz 1-106; Jenks p. 299; Schroy-28.*

HAND, pickle jar. See Plate 44. The pattern HAND AND BAR on Plate 175, a very plain set, features a similar clenched fist as a finial.

BEARDED HEAD (VIKING; PROPHET; OLD MAN OF THE MOUNTAIN), pitcher. Hobbs, Brockunier and Co., 1876. Extended table service including egg cup, platter, vase, master salt, mug, apothecary jar, pickle jar with cover, covered mustard. No goblet or tumbler was originally made. Crystal, opal (very scarce), satin decoration, engraved. Some pitchers lack the head under the spout; and some sets have four feet instead of three. Contemporary trade journals called the figure a Roman Warrior. It must have taken a very special artist to design this bizarre pattern. *Ref. K1-81; Metz 1-7; Metz 1-6; Jenks p. 542; Hobbs p. 48.*

QUEEN ANNE (VIKING; BEARDED MAN; SANTA CLAUS; NEPTUNE; OLD MAN), creamer. LaBelle Glass Co., 1880s. QUEEN ANNE was their original company name. Extended table service including master salt. *Ref. K5 Pl. 26; K1-89; HTP-87; Jenks p. 428; Schroy-118.*

Humpty Dumpty *Westward Ho!* *Bicycle Girl*

Man's Head *Tree of Life with Hand* *Japanese*

Hand *Bearded Head* *Queen Anne*

PLATE 172. PEOPLE

SPHINX, salt shaker. A rare piece by the Imperial Glass Co. *Ref. PetSal 173A.*

CLEVELAND, plate. Probably a compaign item in 1884 featuring a Dewdrop border. *Ref. American Glass Vol. II p. 174.*

WASHINGTON CENTENNIAL (CENTENNIAL; CHAIN WITH DIAMONDS), oval plate. The handles are inscribed "Centennial 1876;" and around the bust, "First in War, First in Peace, first in the hearts of his countrymen." See Plate 59. A glass hatchet is also known bearing Washington's bust with an illegible inscription, probably a Centennial souvenir. *Ref. American Glass Vol. II p. 169; Gob II-20; Metz 1-112; Unitt 1-276; K2-124; Jenks p. 548; Schroy-152.*

BLAINE, plate. A campaign item for James G. Blaine in 1884 in the CLASSIC pattern. His running mate, John A. Logan (Black Jack Logan) was featured on a similar plate; not to be outdone, identical plates were issued with portraits of Cleveland and Hendricks, running in the same election. *Ref. American Glass Vol. II p. 172.*

GARFIELD, plate. This is probably a memorial to James A. Garfield issued in 1880 – 1881. *Ref. American Glass Vol. II p. 171.*

U. S. COIN, toothpick holder. U. S. Glass Co. #15005 (Central; Hobbs), 1891. Extended table service including wines, champagne, claret, open compotes with quarters, halves, and dimes; sauce with quarters, tumbler with dollar and dime, celery vase with halves and quarters, berry bowls with quarter and dollar. There are many reproductions. U. S. Glass also made COLUMBIAN COIN in 1893 in extended table service including champagne, wine. It used foreign coins in its design. *Ref. K3-80; Metz 1-113; Gob I-106; Unitt 1-73; Jenks p. 532; Schroy-148; HTP-89; H7-93.*

REBECCA AT THE WELL, compote. Bakewell, Pears and Co., ca. 1876. Part of the "RIBBON" pattern and of museum quality. See Plate 166. *Ref. Jenks p. 443; Schroy-120.*

LITTLE SAMUEL, compote. Hobbs Brockunier and Co., 1877. Made in compote, lamp, epergne, and candlestick in crystal and opal. The base may be crystal, opal or black. *Ref. Hobbs p. 137.*

Sphinx

Cleveland

*Washington
Centennial*

Blaine

Garfield

U.S. Coin

*Rebecca at the
Well*

Little Samuel

357

PLATE 173. PEOPLE

TEDDY ROOSEVELT, plate. Probably made in 1894, this is a piece of glass that began a lasting history of collectibles, but not in glass. Theodore Roosevelt was a Rough Rider in the Spanish-American War in 1898, and a well-known hunter of animals when it was thought to be the "manly" thing. But on one hunting expedition he refused to shoot a bear with cubs — rather a novel idea for the time — and the people took him to heart. This association of bears and Roosevelt led to naming toy bears "Teddy bears," a circumstance which he undoubtedly milked for political advantage. Today, one hundred years later, Teddy bears are one of our favorite items to collect, give, own, and love. Quite a feat, and our pattern glass had a big part in establishing that fun.

The plate is bordered with rustic branches, and Teddy's bears are depicted hunting, dancing, playing golf, tennis, and other games. One even plays a musical instrument. The American eagle and the "A Square Deal" motif are strictly American. The little bears actually become Roosevelt on the plate, showing his leisure activities in animation. It's a pity he wasn't the Clark Gable type, because his rather mediocre portrait belies its theme. Nonetheless, this plate could be the pinnacle of a pattern glass collection. Happy hunting!

Teddy Roosevelt Plate

PLATE 174. PEOPLE

HAND AND CORN, salt shaker. A novelty that Peterson said had been reproduced. *Ref. PetSal 30K.*

HAND AND FISHSCALE, salt shaker. A novelty that was also reproduced. *Ref. PetSal 30L.*

BILLIKEN, salt shaker. A rare novelty. *Ref. PetSal 156B.*

MAN IN HAT, salt shaker. A rare novelty. *Ref. PetSal 156B.*

MEPHISTOPHELES, ale glass. Known in ale glass, and possibly a goblet. A mug is known, probably not American, in crystal, frosted, and opaque colors. It has a dragon head handle. Another mug, similar in opaque white, has a plain handle. *Ref. Gob II (Front.); Metz 1-276; Schroy-161; Mugs p. 110.*

BASEBALL PLAYER, salt shaker. A rare novelty that would appeal to both glass lovers and sports fans. *Ref. PetSal 154C.*

LEAF ROSETTE, sugar bowl. Made in extended table service. The finial has a woman's head on it. *Ref. K7-56.*

SPANISH AMERICAN (ADMIRAL DEWEY; DEWEY), pitcher. Beatty-Brady Glass Co., 1890s. Extended table service including rare tumbler. *Ref. K2-123; Metz 2-184.*

Hand and Corn *Hand and Fishscale*

Billiken

Man in Hat

Mephistopheles

Baseball Player *Leaf Rosette* *Spanish American*

PLATE 175. PLAIN

ADAMS #329 (PLAIN TWO-MOLD), etched pitcher. U. S. Glass Co. (Adams), 1891. Extended table service including wine, cordial, claret, waste bowl. *Ref. K4-28; H5-71; Metz 1-72; Gob I-114; Unitt 1-210.*

HAND AND BAR (HAND), creamer. U. S. Glass Co. (Bryce), 1891. Extended table service. The finials in this pattern have a clenched fist holding a bar. See Plate 171, pattern HAND. Crystal. *Ref. H5-84; Metz 2-82.*

MONTANA, etched tumbler and etched pitcher. U. S. Glass Co. (Ripley), 1891. A State Series pattern. Heacock says on page 123 of *Victorian Colored Glass Book V* that this is not a State pattern; but on page 20 he says that it is a "little-known State pattern." Montana was the original manufacturer's name. Known in water sets: pitchers and tumblers. Crystal. *Ref. H5-123.*

INOMINATA, creamer. Made ca. 1875 – 1880. *Ref. K4-45.*

THE MIRROR, creamer. Greensburg Glass Co., early 1880s. Extended table service of many pieces including wine. Bowls have fine-cut pattern bases. *Ref. K8-26.*

BOSTON (PLAIN FLAT RING), creamer. New England Glass Co., 1868. Extended table service including wine, cordial, champagne. Plain or engraved. *Ref. K2-41; Wilson p. 338.*

LIBERTY BELL, mug. A Centennial Exposition souvenir in 1876. Milk glass. *Ref. Jenks p. 323; LEAPG-331; Metz 1-112; Schroy-89.*

CENTRAL #560, creamer. Central Glass Co., 1881. Extended table service. *Ref. K3-17.*

MARY JANE, pitcher. Made ca. 1890. *Ref. K2-33.*

Adams #329

Hand and Bar

Montana (two views)

Inominata

The Mirror

Boston

Liberty Bell

Central #560

Mary Jane

PLATE 176. PLAIN

DALZELL'S COLUMBIA, engraved pitcher. Dalzell, Gilmore and Leighton, 1893. Extended table service of sixty-two pieces. *Ref. K6 Pl. 43.*

IDAHO, goblet and etched pitcher. Ripley and Co., 1890; Bryce Brothers, 1891; U. S. Glass Co. (Ripley), after 1891. A State Series pattern. Extended table service including wine, tumbler, cup, tray. *Ref. H5-121.*

TAUNTON, etched salt shaker. Extended table service. *Ref. LV-50.*

CASCO, goblet. Portland Glass Co., 1870. Wine is also known. *Ref. Swan p. 50.*

DELOS, creamer. National Glass Co., 1900. Extended table service. *Ref. K5-67.*

U. S. BLOSSOM, creamer. U. S. Glass Co. #15045, 1895. Extended table service. Milk glass, decorated. *Ref. LV-40.*

URN, creamer. Heisey Glass Co. #379, ca. 1905 – 1907. Crystal. *Ref. K6-2; HTP-87.*

CROSSED DISKS, creamer. Made ca. 1890 in extended table service including egg cup. *Ref K4-35.*

NEVADA (THE UNITED STATES), decorated creamer. U. S. Glass Co. #15075, 1902. A State Series pattern. Formerly believed to be two different patterns, we now know that THE UNITED STATES is the same pattern as NEVADA. Featuring enamel decoration on frosted background, NEVADA was made in basic table service. Crystal. THE UNITED STATES was sold by Montgomery Ward in 1903 in a 34-piece set enamelled with white flowers. Crystal, decorated. *Ref. H5-28; K5-68; Jenks p. 380; Schroy-102.*

Dalzell's Columbia

Idaho (two examples)

Taunton

Casco

Delos

U.S. Blossom

Urn

Crossed Disks

Nevada

PLATE 177. PLAIN

SAWTOOTH BOTTOM, goblet. Crystal, ruby-stained. *Ref. Gob II-33; Metz 1-146; H7-161, 190.*

PLEAT BAND (PLAIN WARE), pitcher. Indiana Tumbler and Goblet Co. #137, 1897. Extended table service including milk pitcher, cordial, wine. *Ref. K5-139; Herrick p. 19; Measell p. 56.*

ADAMS SAXON, etched, ruby-stained cruet and creamer. Adams and Co., 1888; U. S. Glass Co., 1892. Extended table service including water tray, finger bowl, mug, wine, claret. Crystal, ruby-stained, etched. No drawing can do justice to this plain but beautiful pattern. *Ref. K3-11; H5-47, 50; H7-190+.*

ANGELSEY, creamer. Made ca. 1880. *Ref. K4-13.*

CROSSBAR HANDLE, creamer. *Ref. K6-9.*

FOSTORIA'S STERLING, creamer. Fostoria Glass Co. #141, 1888. Basic table service. *Ref. K5-33.*

HARMONY, etched creamer. *Ref. K8-1.*

ENGLISH COLONIAL, creamer. Riverside Glass Co., 1905; McKee Glass Co. #75, 1906 – 1927; Extended table service of forty-six pieces including wines, cordial, claret, punch bowl. Crystal, ruby-stained. *Ref. K3-138; H7-136.*

DOUBLE ZIG-ZAG (FRENCH), creamer. McKee Glass Co., 1880. Extended table service including wine set, champagnes, claret. *Ref. K3-11; Stout p. 68.*

Sawtooth Bottom Pleat Band Adams Saxon (two examples)

Angelsey Crossbar Handle Fostoria's Sterling

Harmony English Colonial Double Zig-Zag

PLATE 178. PLAIN

OHIO, salt shaker, cruet, and engraved pitcher. U.S. Glass #15050 (Ripley), 1897. A State Series pattern. Extended table service including sugar shaker, wine. Crystal, rare in ruby-stain, engraved. *Ref. K5-33; H5-149; H7-164.*

TRUNCATED CONE, salt shaker. *Ref. PetSal 42P.*

IONIC (ARABIAN), pitcher. McKee Glass Co., 1894. Marked "Pres-Cut." Extended table service including carafe, wine. *Ref. K5-75; Stout p. 121.*

SAWTOOTH BANDS, pitcher. See Plate 144.

VIGILANT, engraved creamer. Fostoria Glass Co. #403, 1894. Extended table service. *Ref. K5-82.*

McKEE's BERLIN, creamer. McKee Brothers, 1880. Extended table service including wine, champagne. Two types of goblet, one with stem like this and one with a stem tapering upward; the champagne and wine are similar. The celery has an elongated diamond stem. Dishes and nappies have scalloped edges. The only really identifiable pieces are the basic table service and one goblet. *Ref. Stout-54; H6-91 (courtesy of John Gregory).*

GRECIAN, creamer. Made in the 1890s. *Ref. K2-55.*

HOMESTEAD (CORDATE LEAF; LEAF WITH SPRAY), sugar bowl. Bryce, Higbee and Co., mid 1880s. Extended table service including 12" vase, open salts, individual salts, wine, and a celery vase that sometimes sells for a footed tumbler. The butter dish is footed with flanged horizontal handles. Frequently etched with a large leaf, hence its secondary names. *Ref. K8-2, 116; K2-17; H6-81.*

ATLAS (LITTLE BALLS), pitcher. This is the pitcher to the ATLAS pattern shown in Plate 11.

Ohio (three examples)

Truncated Cone	*Ionic*	*Sawtooth Bands*	*Vigilant*
McKee's Berlin	*Grecian*	*Homestead*	*Atlas*

PLATE 179. PLAIN

TEXAS STAR (SNOWFLAKE BASE), pitcher and base detail. The base features a "snowflake" design. See Plates 110 and 224.

SUNKEN TEARDROP, salt shaker and creamer. Extended table service. *Ref. K4-26; Pet-Sal 40T; Metz 2-136.*

SALOON, salt shaker. Made ca. 1888 and was actually used in saloons. *Ref. PetSal 171-i.*

V-BAND, creamer. *Ref. K6-27.*

EMPIRE, etched creamer. McKee Glass Co., 1896. Extended table service. *Ref. K3-40.*

ETCHED FERN (ASHMAN), etched goblet. Portland Glass Co., ca. 1880s. Extended table service including bread tray. *Ref. K1-89; Metz 1-164.*

WHEEL AND COMMA, etched creamer. Aetna Glass and Mfg. Co., 1881 – 1883. Extended table service. Found plain or acid-etched flower or leaf designs. *Ref. K3-5.*

IONA (PRISM RING), engraved creamer. George Duncan and Sons #415, 1879. Extended table service including claret, cordial, wine, champagne. *Ref. K3-10; K4-2; Duncan p. 55.*

Texas Star and detail   *Sunken Teardrop (two examples)*

Saloon   *V-Band*   *Empire*

Etched Fern   *Wheel and Comma*   *Iona*

PLATE 180. PLAIN

FLAT OVAL, engraved creamer. Extended table service. *Ref. K3-113; Metz 2-184.*

BIG TOP, compote. U. S. Glass Co. (Challinor #316-318), 1891. Made in several sizes of compotes only. Crystal. *Ref. H5-92.*

FROSTED EAGLE, pitcher. See Plate 10.

RIBBED DROPLET BAND (YELLOW VINTAGE, FROSTED), engraved goblet and pitcher. George Duncan and Sons #89, Dec., 1886 to 1890. Extended table service including tumblers with and without "feet." The butter dish does not have feet. Crystal, frosted, amber-stained, engraved. Goblet courtesy of Bob Burford. *Ref. Gob II-57; Duncan p. 93.*

ANGULAR, creamer. Made ca. 1880s. *Ref. K6-10; H6-47.*

CENTRAL #1879, creamer. Central Glass Co., 1879. Extended table service including lamps. *Ref. K6-3.*

CENTRAL #520, creamer. Central Glass Co., 1881. Extended table service. *Ref. K3-16.*

PANELLED RINGED STEM (PLAIN TWO-MOLD), creamer. Made ca. mid-1880s. *Ref. K2-18.*

IVY SPRAY, engraved creamer. *Ref. K2-11.*

Flat Oval

Big Top

Frosted Eagle

Ribbed Droplet Band (two examples)

Angular

Central #1879

Central #520

Panelled Ringed Stem

Ivy Spray

PLATE 181. PLANTS

EAR OF CORN, vase. Northwood-Dugan Glass Co., late 1890s. Extended table service including two types of creamer. Decorated crystal, opalescent. *Ref. K2-62.*

MAIZE, cruet. Libbey and Sons Co., 1889. Extended table service including sugar shaker, condiment set in holder, decanters, carafe, rose bowl, finger bowls. Opaque white, ivory, carnival, decorated. Imagine how pleased corn farmers in the heartland would be when discovering this pattern. See CORN WITH HUSK and BULGING CORN, below. *Ref. K5-92; HI-30; HIV-56; H6-34; HTP-45.*

CORN, sugar shaker. Dithridge and Co., ca. 1900. Made only in salt shakers and sugar shakers. Opaque colors. *Ref. PetSal 25N; HIII-21.*

CORN WITH HUSK, salt shaker. This piece is actually the salt shaker to the MAIZE pattern (above) by Libbey and Sons Co., 1889. *Ref. PetSal 25R; K5-92; HTP-62.*

CORN SPHERE, salt shaker. Opaque glass. *Ref. PetSal 25P.*

BULGING CORN, salt shaker. This is part of a condiment set in the MAIZE pattern (above) by Libbey and Sons Co., 1889. As each piece was discovered it received a name, and thus MAIZE is known by three names. *Ref. K5-92.*

HANGING LEAF, salt shaker. Milk glass. *Ref. W123; PetSal 32M.*

ARTICHOKE, salt shaker. See Plate 34.

Ear of Corn   *Maize*

Corn   *Corn with*   *Corn Sphere*
        Husk

Bulging Corn   *Hanging Leaf*   *Artichoke*

PLATE 182. PLANTS

MAPLE WREATH, pitcher. Jefferson Glass Co., Toronto, Canada, ca. 1918. Extended table service. Crystal, green. *Ref. HGCI p. 41.*

TREE STUMP, engraved compote. William Heacock reported that it was made by Portland Glass Co. in 1870, but later he wrote "probably Northwood." Known in footed sauce with handles, open and lidded large bowls, and a mug. *Ref. HII-85; Edwards p. 196.*

POND LILY, goblet. *Ref. Gob II-117.*

MAPLE LEAF (LEAF), open sugar bowl and pitcher. Gillinder and Sons, ca. 1885. Extended table service including large ice cream bowl, plates, bread plate, dolphin-based compote, platter, tray, vase, wine. The finial is a bunch of grapes, and the leaf is obviously a grape leaf. Crystal, vaseline, canary, blue, sapphire, amber. The goblet has been reproduced. *Ref. K4-143; LEAPG-414; Metz 1-72; Jenks p. 350; Schroy-95.*

STUMP, salt shaker. Peterson said it was part of a condiment set. *Ref. PetSal 40R.*

CABBAGE LEAF, celery vase and pitcher. Made ca. 1870s and 1880s in extended table service including rabbit plate, leaf-shaped pickle dish, cup, egg cup, covered cheese dish. Crystal, amber, frosted. *Ref. L-65; LEAPG-420; HII-64; Metz 1-107p; Metz 2-6.*

Maple Wreath *Tree Stump*

Pond Lily *Maple Leaf (two examples)*

Stump *Cabbage Leaf (two views)*

PLATE 183. PLANTS

IMPERIAL #79, pitcher. Imperial Glass Co., ca. 1902. *Ref. K7-187.*

MISSOURI (PALM AND SCROLL), goblet and creamer. U. S. Glass Co. #15058, 1899. A State Series pattern. Extended table service including wine, cordial. Crystal, emerald green, rare blue, rare amethyst, rare canary. *Ref. K2-133; Gob II-51; Metz 2-68; Unitt 1-212; Unitt 2-239; HIII-56; H6-35; Jenks p. 372; Schroy-100; Mugs p. 88.*

PARAGON, pitcher. Dalzell, Gilmore and Leighton, 1894. Extended table service. Crystal, ruby-stained. *Ref. K6-39; H7-127.*

PLUME, celery vase and pitcher. Adams and Co. #3, 1874; U. S. Glass Co., 1891 – 1898. Extended table service including two types of celery vase, cordial, square bowls, lamp, vase. Crystal, ruby-stained. Most of the pieces have the horizontal plume. The goblet has been reproduced. *Ref. K2-133; H5-62; Gob I-30; Metz 1-150; Unitt 2-91; Jenks p. 408; Schroy -112.*

BIG LEAF AND BUTTON, bowl. U. S. Glass Co. (Duncan #1002), 1891. Made in bowls only. Crystal, amber-stained. *Ref. H5-97.*

HEART, goblet. Bakewell, Pears and Co. Extended table service. *Metz 1-126.*

INVERTED FERN, goblet. Made ca. 1860s in extended table service including egg cup, wine, cordial, champagne, honey dish. Flint glass. *Ref. L-36; Metz 1-30; Gob I-66; LEAPG-121; Unitt 1-70; Unitt 2-76; Jenks p. 292; Schroy-81.*

STIPPLED PALM, pitcher.

Imperial #79   *Missouri (two examples)*

Paragon   *Plume (two examples)*

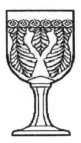

Big Leaf and Button   *Heart*   *Inverted Fern*   *Stippled Palm*

PLATE 184. PLANTS

LEAF AND RIB, salt shaker. Extended table service including salt dip. Crystal, amber, blue, canary. *Ref. PetSal 32E.*

FLORIDA PALM (TIDAL; PERFECTION), footed bowl and tumbler. Greensburg Glass Co., 1880s; Bryce, Higbee & Co., 1900. Extended table service including wine. *Ref. K3-110; K8-57; Gob I-95; Metz 1-74; Unitt 1-212.*

PANELLED PALM (BRILLIANT), syrup. U. S. Glass #15095 (Ripley factory), 1906. Extended table service including wine, tumbler. Crystal, rose-flashed, stained in yellow, rose, amethyst, and ruby. *Ref. Gob II-37; H5-43; Mugs p. 90/91; HTP-53; Unitt 2-76; Metz 2-68.*

PRESSED LEAF (N.P.L.), pitcher. McKee and Brothers, 1868; Central Glass Works, 1881. Extended table service including wine, cordial, champagne, egg cup, lamp. Some flint glass. *Ref. L-125; LEAPG-69; Metz 1-72; Gob I-44; Unitt 1-216; K3-20; Jenks p. 416.*

LONG MAPLE LEAF, pitcher. Made in the late 1880s in extended table service including mug. Crystal. *Ref. K4-144; Schroy-161; Metz 1-72.*

ARCHED LEAF, goblet. Made ca. 1870s in extended table service. *Ref. Metz 1-100; Metz 2-66.*

DIAMOND CUT WITH LEAF (FINECUT WITH LEAF), goblet. Windsor Glass Co., ca. 1890. Extended table service including mug, cordial, open and covered sugar bowls, wine. Crystal, canary, blue, green, light amber. The wine has been reproduced. *Ref. L-109; Gob I-89; Metz 1-160; LEAPG-337; Unitt 2-60; Mugs p. 23.*

PRESSED LEAF WITH CHAIN, goblet. *Ref. L-153 #16; Gob II-10; Metz 1-73; Metz 2-72.*

Leaf and Rib   *Florida Palm (two examples)*

Panelled Palm   *Pressed Leaf*   *Long Maple Leaf*

Arched Leaf   *Diamond Cut
with Leaf*   *Pressed Leaf
with Chain*

PLATE 185. PLANTS

STARS AND BARS WITH LEAF, pitcher. This version of Stars and Bars has a big molded, stippled leaf in addition to the main pattern. See Plate 96. *Ref. Miller 7th Ed. p. 553.*

LEAF BRACKET, cruet. Indiana Tumbler and Goblet Co., 1900. Extended table service. Crystal opalescent, chocolate, green. *Ref. K5-106; HI-28; H6-33.*

ACANTHUS LEAF, creamer. Extended table service. Milk glass, slag. *Ref. K2-53.*

ACANTHUS, miniature creamer. In the interest of being able to see it, this little jewel is shown the size of the others on this page, but it is mold-blown, and holds only ⅓ cup. Kamm didn't think it was a toy creamer, but thought it might be a salesman's piece. Although not part of a set, this one would be prized by anyone who collects any pattern of pressed glass. *Ref. K7-63.*

MEDALLION SPRIG (STYLISTIC LEAF), salt shaker. West Virginia Glass Co., ca. 1894. Extended table service including lemonade set. All pieces are scarce. Crystal, colors, opaque, decorated. *Ref. L-102; HTP-46, 62; HI-30; HIII-32; PetSal 33S.*

LEAF-IN-OVAL (PENELOPE), creamer. Extended table service including punch bowl. Crystal, ruby-stained. *Ref. K8-53; H7-6+.*

LEAF UMBRELLA, salt shaker. Northwood Glass Co. #263 (Martin's Ferry), ca. 1889. Extended table service including rare butter dish (looks like a covered candy bowl, Heacock), sugar shaker, finger bowl, covered powder jar with metal top. Cased colors of pink, blue, yellow; cranberrry, cranberry spatter; sometimes satin finished. *Ref. PetSal 32S; HI-29; HIII-31; H6-33; HTP-54.*

ARROWHEAD (ANDERSON), creamer. Made ca. 1900 in extended table service. *Ref. K3-64.*

LATTICE LEAF (CO-OP #323), creamer. Cooperative Flint Glass Co., 1906. Extended table service including wine, cordial. Crystal, gilded, stained. *Ref. K5 Pl. 3; Gob II-122; H7-140+.*

*Stars and Bars
with Leaf*

Leaf Bracket

Acanthus Leaf

Acanthus

*Medallion
Sprig*

Leaf-in-Oval

Leaf Umbrella

Arrowhead

Lattice Leaf

PLATE 186. PLANTS

BLOCK AND PALM (EIGHTEEN-NINETY), goblet. Beaver Falls Glass Co., ca. 1890s. Extended table service including coke stand. Crystal, milk glass. *Ref. K5-58; Metz 1-74.*

PANELLED ANTHEMION, pitcher. Made ca. 1885 in extended table service. *Ref. K4-59; Metz 1-77.*

ANTHEMION, pitcher. Model Flint Glass Co., 1890. Extended table service. Crystal. *Ref. L-58; LEAPG-466; Metz 1-76; Schroy-6; Jenks p. 16; K5-137.*

STAR AND PALM, goblet. *Ref. Gob II-26; Metz 1-118.*

SUNRISE IN ARCH, mug. *Ref. Mugs p. 90.*

RIBBED PALM (SPRIG; ACANTHUS), pitcher. McKee and Brothers, 1863. Extended table service including wines, champagne, cordial, egg cup, three types of lamp. The glass sometimes has a pink hue. The wine has been reproduced. Crystal. *Ref. K4-55; Metz 1-30; Gob I-3; LEAPG-119; Unitt 1-71; Jenks p. 442.*

GARDEN OF EDEN, goblet. See Plate 6.

ATTERBURY'S LEAF, mug. Atterbury and Co., 1878 (patent). Crystal, colors. *Ref. Mugs p. 36.*

PANELLED FERN (HAMMOND; PANELLED LEAF), pitcher. Made ca. 1878 in extended table service including wine. Opaque white and blue. *Ref. K5-43; Gob II-39; Metz 1-70; Metz 2-56; Unitt 1-210.*

Block and Palm

Panelled Anthemion

Anthemion

Star and Palm

Sunrise in Arch

Ribbed Palm

Garden of Eden

Atterbury's Leaf

Panelled Fern

PLATE 187. PLANTS

FALLING LEAVES, pitcher. Federal Glass Co., ca. 1910. Extended table service. Leaves are impressed on the inside of the bowl. Crystal. *Ref. K4-132; Schroy-161.*

ROYAL OAK, syrup. Northwood Glass Co., 1889 – 1890. Extended table service including water set, pickle castor, sugar shaker. Frosted crystal, rubina. *Ref. K5-86; HIII-40; HI-39; H6-40; Metz 1-69; Jenks p. 459; Schroy-125.*

FEATHER BAND, pitcher. U. S. Glass Co. #15122 (Bryce), after 1910. Extended table service including both flat and footed sugar bowls. Crystal. *Ref. K4-134; H5-156.*

RIBBED ACORN, bowl. Boston and Sandwich. Extended table service including honey dish. *Ref. L-39; Metz 2-74.*

FROSTED LEAF (STIPPLED LEAF), decanter. Portland Glass Co., ca. 1850s; Boston and Sandwich, 1860s. Extended table service including wine, cordial, egg cup, decanter, rare champagne. Flint glass. The wine has been reproduced. *Ref. L-94; Metz 1-26; Metz 2-118; Gob I-114; Gob II-26; LEAPG-320; Unitt 1-210; Jenks p. 233; Schroy-64.*

BIRCH LEAF (N.P.L.; ROSE LEAF; PRESSED LEAF), compote. Cape Cod Glass Co., 1860s. Extended table service including egg cup, master salt, wine, champagne. Crystal, milk glass. *Ref. Gob I-44; Gob II-65; Metz 1-72; Metz 2-72; Unitt 1-217.*

MURANO (LEAF AND FAN), salt shaker. Greensburg Glass Co., 1894. Extended table service including castor bottle, wine. John Gregory has a wine with hatched leaves. Crystal, ruby-stained. *Ref. PetSal 167B; PetPat 221; H7-57, 153+.*

NETTED ACORN (ACORN; NETTED ROYAL OAK), sugar shaker. Northwood Glass Co., ca. 1895 – 1905. Extended table service including water set. Crystal, milk glass, apple green, amethyst, blue. *Ref. HIII-33.*

OAK WREATH (OAK LEAF WREATH), pitcher. Central Glass Co., 1880s; U. S. Glass after 1891. Extended table service. Crystal; colors (U. S. Glass.) *Ref. K6-5; Metz 2-72; Mugs p. 36.*

Falling Leaves   *Royal Oak*

Feather Band

Ribbed Acorn   *Frosted Leaf*   *Birch Leaf*

Murano   *Netted Acorn*   *Oak Wreath*

PLATE 188. PLANTS

SWAG WITH BRACKETS, creamer. Jefferson Glass Co., ca. 1903. Extended table service. Crystal, opalescent, vaseline, other colors. *Ref. K1-86; HI-42; HIII-31; H6-43; Schroy-139.*

MARSH FERN, salt shaker and pitcher. Riverside Glass Co. #327, 1889. Extended table service. *Ref. K3-143; Metz 1-70; Schroy-96.*

STIPPLED LOOP WITH VINE BAND, goblet. *Ref. Gob II-50.*

HOPS BAND (MAPLE; PRESSED LEAF BAND), creamer. King Glass Co., ca. 1871. Extended table service including wine. *Ref. K3-19; Gob I-31; Metz 1-76.*

LONG FAN WITH ACANTHUS LEAF (FAN WITH ACANTHUS LEAF; BIJOU), pitcher. Greenburg Glass Co., mid-1880s. Extended table service. *Ref. K2-125; K8-62.*

LEAF ROSETTE, salt shaker. See Plate 174.

BEADED ACORN (BEADED ACORN MEDALLION), egg cup. Boston Silver Glass Co., ca. 1869. Extended table service including wine, champagne, footed and flat sauces. Thanks to Charles Marlin for sending me rubbings of this fine old pattern. *Ref. L-65; LEAPG-422; K8-7; Gob I-85; Metz 1-72; Unitt 1-142.*

CACTUS (PANELLED AGAVE), syrup. Indiana Tumbler and Goblet Co., 1900 – 1903; National Glass Co. Extended table service including mug, cracker jar, mustard jar, flat and stemmed butter dishes. Crystal, chocolate; other colors are rare. Fenton reproduced items in 1979 – 1980; so did St. Clair Glass Co. *Ref. K1-78; H2-95 (repro); HI-17; HIII-18; H6-21; Mugs p. 23; HTP-54; Schroy-30.*

Swag with Brackets

Marsh Fern (two views)

*Stippled Loop
with Vine
Band*

Hops Band

*Long Fan with
Acanthus Leaf*

Leaf Rosette

Beaded Acorn

Cactus

PLATE 189. PLANTS

LEAFY SCROLL, creamer. U. S. Glass Co. #15034 (Gillinder factory), 1896. Extended table service. Crystal. *Ref. K4-91; H5-172.*

RIPLEY'S WYOMING, tumber and pitcher. U. S. Glass Co. (Ripley factory), 1891. Extended table service. Crystal. (Not a State Series pattern; for Wyoming it is ENIGMA on Plate 150.) *Ref. H5-121.*

CIRCLED SCROLL, creamer. Dugan Glass Co., ca. 1903. Extended table service, but no toothpick holder or celery vase. Crystal, colors, opalescent; and later molds in carnival colors. *Ref. K4-70; HII-19; HIII-54; H6-22; Metz 2-68.*

PANELLED IVY, pitcher. Kamm noticed similarities to U. S. Glass patterns in this one; I have read that U. S. Glass made it. However, Heacock does not show it in his *U. S. Glass Book.* Extended table service. *Ref. K3-69; Metz 1-69.*

SANDWICH VINE, goblet. An early pattern known only in the goblet. Charles Marlin reports that at the Green Valley Auction on Oct. 3, 1998, this goblet with gilt highlights sold for $10,500. If more people know about the pattern, other pieces may appear, and, as Charles says, "What a discovery that would be!" *Ref. Metz 1-3; Metz 2-60.*

SPIRALLED IVY, pitcher. Made in the mid-1880s in extended table service. Crystal. *Ref. L-147; LEAPG-430; Metz 1-69; Metz 2-74.*

BASKETWEAVE WITH FROSTED LEAF, pitcher. Made ca. 1890 – 1900 in extended table service including egg cup, water tray. Crystal, canary, blue, green. See other basketweave patterns on Plate 234. *Ref. Miller 7th Ed. p. 371.*

Leafy Scroll   *Ripley's Wyoming (two examples)*

Circled Scroll   *Panelled Ivy*

Sandwich Vine   *Spiralled Ivy*   *Basketweave with Frosted Leaf*

PLATE 190. PLANTS

STIPPLED IVY, footed salt dish. Extended table service including wine. Like BUDDED IVY without little buds. *Ref. L-119; Gob I-47; LEAPG-444; Metz 1-69; Unitt 1-224; Unitt 2-82; K5-7.*

RIBBED LEAVES, mug and sherbet cup. Federal Glass Co., 1914. Crystal. *Ref. HGC4-22; Metz 2-206; Mugs p. 33.*

RIBBED IVY, goblet. Made ca. 1850s in extended table service including champagne, wines, cordials, whiskey tumbler (scarce), castor bottle, decanter, open salt, egg cup, hat. *Ref. L-39; Metz 1-30; Metz 2-190; Unitt 1-70; Jenks p. 441; Schroy-120.*

IVY IN SNOW (FORREST WARE), pitcher. Cooperative Flint Glass Co., 1880s; Phoenix Glass Co. in 1937 from original molds. Extended table service including tumbler, wine, cordial, champagne, claret, jam jar, cup and saucer. Crystal, amber, ruby-stained; white was reproduced only by Phoenix. *Ref. L-119; LEAPG-427; Gob I-146; Metz 1-68; Unitt 1-180; K3-97; Jenks p. 295; Schroy-82; H7-118.*

SOUTHERN IVY, pitcher. Made ca. 1880s in extended table service including egg cup, tumbler. Crystal. *Ref. L-166; LEAPG-124; Metz 1-69; Metz 2-74; Schroy-133.*

ROYAL IVY, sugar shaker. Northwood Glass Co., ca. 1889. Extended table service including pickle castor, jam jar, lamp, tumbler. Frosted crystal, plain and frosted rubina, cased rainbow, rainbow cracquelle (also frosted); amber-stained, opaline, and other experimental colors that would be very scarce. *Ref. K5-87; HI-38+; HIII-40; Metz 1-69; Schroy-1225; Jenks p. 458.*

BUDDED IVY, goblet. Made in 1870 in extended table service including wine. *Ref. L-119; LEAPG-428; Schroy-26; Jenks p. 86; Gob I-47; Metz 1-68; K8-6.*

HAMILTON WITH LEAF, pitcher. Cape Cod Glass Co., 1860s; Boston and Sandwich Glass Co., 1870s; others later. Extended table service including tumbler, wine, cordial, egg cup, footed salt, two sizes lamps. Crystal, clear, and frosted; a 9" blue lamp is known. *Ref. L-57; LEAPG-178; Schroy-69; Jenks p. 258; Metz 1-26; Gob I-117; Gob II-155; Unitt 2-90; K4-18.*

Stippled Ivy   *Ribbed Leaves (two examples)*

Ribbed Ivy   *Ivy in Snow*   *Southern Ivy*

Royal Ivy   *Budded Ivy*   *Hamilton with Leaf*

PLATE 191. PLANTS

PANELLED ACORN BAND, pitcher. Boston and Sandwich early; other companies later. Extended table service including egg cup. *Ref. L-125; Metz 1-72; Metz 2-6.*

ACORN BAND 2 (ACORN VARIANT), goblet. Portland Glass Co. Extended table service including rare wine, egg cup, flat and footed sauces. *Ref. L-125; Gob I-114; Gob II-46; Metz 1-72; LEAPG-439; Unitt 1-210; Schroy-2.*

ACORN BAND 1 (ACORN VARIANT), goblet. A variation of the above pattern also by Portland Glass. *Ref. L-125.*

ACORN, goblet. Made ca. 1870s in extended table service including egg cup. The goblet has been reproduced. *Ref. L-125; LEAPG-114; Metz 1-72; HI-13; HIII-14.*

OAK LEAF BAND WITH MEDALLION (BEADED ACORN WITH LEAF BAND), goblet. Portland Glass Co. *Ref. Gob II-10; LV Pl. 79 #4; Batty p. 147.*

OAK LEAF BAND, goblet. Portland Glass Co. Extended table service. *Ref. Metz 2-72.*

WHITE OAK, creamer. *Ref. K2-65; Metz 1-73.*

PANELLED OAK, creamer. Lancaster Glass Co., 1911. Extended table service. *Ref. K7-41.*

OAK LEAVES, goblet. *Ref. L-153 #4.*

CHESTNUT OAK (OLD ACORN), pitcher. Made in the early 1870s in extended table service. *Ref. K1-86; L-125; Schroy-160; Metz 1-73.*

Panelled Acorn Band   *Acorn Band 2* *Acorn Band 1*

Acorn   *Oak Leaf*   *Oak Leaf Band*   *White Oak*
           Band with
           Medallion

Panelled Oak   *Oak Leaves*   *Chestnut Oak*

PLATE 192. PLANTS

HOLLY, goblet. Boston and Sandwich Glass Co., 1860s – 1870s. Extended table service including wine, egg cup. Flint glass. *Ref. L-116; Metz 1-74; Gob I-83; LEAPG-436; Unitt 2-75; Jenks p. 277; Schroy-76.*

HOLLY BAND, pitcher. Made ca. 1870s in extended table service. *Ref. K6-64; Metz 1-75.*

TWIN LEAVES, creamer. Made in basic table service. *Ref. K7-1.*

HOLLY CLEAR, two creamers. Indiana Tumbler and Goblet Co. (National Glass Co. #450), 1903. Extended table service including toothpick holder on pedestal, vase, rare mug. Crystal, ruby-stained, amber opalescent (which is called HOLLY AMBER.) This pattern had been produced for about five months when the factory burned. *Ref. K5-81; H1-26; HIII-28; H6-30; Mugs p. 30; HTP-71; H7-15; Metz 1-75.*

HOLLY AMBER, syrup. See above (HOLLY CLEAR). Probably the most gorgeous piece of pattern glass ever made, with prices to match.

LEAF MEDALLION (REGENT), cruet. Northwood Glass Co., ca. 1904. Extended table service including cruet, salt and pepper on a matching tray; water set, berry set. Crystal, very dark green, deep amethyst, cobalt blue. *Ref. K5-122; Schroy-88; HIII-56; H6-33, 85.*

CROSSED FERN, creamer. Made in extended table service including family-sized butter with four feet. Crystal, opaque white, opaque turquoise. *Ref. K3-111.*

PANELLED HOLLY (PANELLED HOLLY AND DIAMOND), creamer. Northwood Glass Co., ca. 1905. Extended table service but no toothpick, celery vase or cruet. Crystal, carnival, opalescent, white, blue, green, painted decorations. *Ref. K2-59; HII-22; Metz 1-75; Schroy-109.*

Holly

Holly Band

Twin Leaves

Holly Clear (two examples)

Holly Amber

Leaf Medallion

Crossed Fern

Panelled Holly

PLATE 193. PLANTS

WHEAT AND BARLEY (DUQUESNE; HOPS AND BARLEY; OATS AND BARLEY), pitcher. Bryce Brothers, late 1870s; U. S. Glass, 1891. Extended table service. Crystal, amber, blue. *Ref. K1-41; L-50; LEAPG-498; H5-81; Jenks p. 553; Metz 1-84; Schroy-154.*

THREE LEAF CLOVER, spill holder.

CLOVER, pitcher. Extended table service. *Ref. Metz 2-6.*

STIPPLED CLOVER, butter dish. Extended table service including cordial, wine. *Ref. L-141; LEAPG-500; Metz 1-77; Metz 2-6.*

PANELLED SPRIG, syrup. Northwood Glass Co., 1895 – 1905. Extended table service including sugar shaker, pickle castor set, jam jar. Crystal, milk glass, rubina, cranberry, apple green, amethyst, blue, and clear with opalescent lattice design, very rare with speckled finish; decorated. Wright has reproduced cruets and salt shakers. *Ref. HI-41; HII-44; HIII-34; H6-36+; HTP-50; Metz 1-58.*

TREE OF LIFE WITH SPRIG, creamer. Portland Glass Co., 1870s. Extended table service. Not all pieces have the little wheels. *Ref. K2-27.*

LEAF AND STAR (TOBIN), creamer. New Martinsville Glass Co. #711, 1909. Extended table service including wine. Crystal, ruby-stained, marigold-flashed. *Ref. K6-17; Gob II-136; Metz 1-218; Unitt 1-156; HI-28; HCG1-13; HPV1-24; H7-141+; Jenks p. 321; Schroy-88 .*

FERN SPRAYS, vase.

BARLEY (SPRIG; INDIAN TREE), pitcher. Made in the late 1870s in extended table service including cordials, jam jar, wine. *Ref. K1-34; L-116; Gob I-97; Metz 1-84; Unitt 2-18; LEAPG-342.*

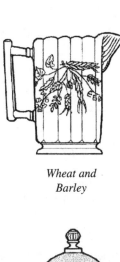

Wheat and Barley

Three Leaf Clover

Clover

Stippled Clover

Panelled Sprig

Tree of Life with Sprig

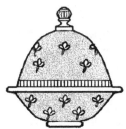

Leaf and Star

Fern Sprays

Barley

PLATE 194. PLANTS

SEASHELL (BOSWELL), engraved creamer. Made in basic table service in the 1870s. The finials are spiral shells. *Ref. Gob II-66; K4-1; LV Pl. 20; Metz 1-142; Unitt 1-90; Jenks p. 472; Schroy-129.*

SCROLLED SPRAY, creamer. Westmoreland Glass Co.; known only in pitcher, salt shaker, vase, sugar and creamer. *Ref. K2-91.*

HOLLAND (OAT SPRAY), pitcher. McKee Glass Co., 1894. Extended table service. *Ref. K4-37.*

FERN SPRIG, goblet. *Ref. Metz 1-71; Metz 2-60.*

FERN, goblet. Union Glass Co., ca. 1880. Known in goblets. *Ref. K8-66.*

SPRIG (ROYAL), pitcher. Bryce, Higbee and Co.; McKee and Brothers, 1880s. Extended table service including scarce wine. Crystal, ruby-stained. Bryce also produced this pattern without the sprig, see SPRIG WITHOUT SPRIG, Plate 158. *Ref. L-78; LEAPG-425; Gob I-126; Metz 1-58; Unitt 1-220; K8-3; H7-6.*

PANELLED WHEAT (WHEAT), pitcher. Hobbs, Brockunier and Co., 1871. Extended table service including egg cup, "jug," sugar and cover with spoon rack, wine. Crystal, opal, light blue opaque. *Ref. K1-40; Hobbs p. 44.*

ORIENTAL, pickle jar. Made in extended table service. *Ref. K7-77; Metz 1-110.*

BAMBOO, pitcher. LaBelle Glass Co., 1883. Extended table service. Crystal, engraved, ruby-stained. *Ref. K5 Pl. 2; Metz 1-141; Metz 2-71; Jenks p. 41; H7-28+.*

BARRED FISHSCALE, creamer. Made ca. 1875 – 1885 in opaque colors. *Ref. K5-59.*

Seashell   *Scrolled Spray*   *Holland*

Fern Sprig   *Fern*   *Sprig*   *Panelled Wheat*

Oriental   *Bamboo*   *Barred Fishscale*

PLATE 195. RIBS AND COLUMNS

CAMBRIDGE #2625, butter dish. Cambridge Glass Co., 1910 – 1915. Courtesy of Bob Burford.

RIBBED WARE (BAR AND BEAD), pitcher. U. S. Glass Co. (Gillinder), 1891. Extended table service. Crystal. *Ref. K4-65; K8-169.*

INSIDE FLUTE, pitcher. *Ref. K5-140.*

PRISM, egg cup. McKee Glass Co., 1864. Extended table service including decanter, wine, champagne, cordial, claret. *Ref. L-13; LEAPG-71; Unitt 2-56; Gob I-75; Metz 1-146.*

HEISEY'S COARSE RIBBING, creamer. A. H. Heisey Glass Co., 1902. *Ref. K8-51.*

HEAVY RIB, creamer. This beauty was made by Jeannette Glass Co. in **1947**. Kamm described it in 1953 — so, beware. *Ref. K7-62.*

INSIDE RIBBING (PRESSED OPTIC), creamer. Beaumont Glass Co. #101, 1900. Extended table service. Crystal, ruby-stained. *Ref. K8-37; HII-21; H7-133, 176.*

U. S. RIB, creamer. U. S. Glass Co. #15061 (Glassport), 1899. Extended table service of many pieces. Crystal, emerald green, gilded. *Ref. K7-42; HI-43; HIII-57; H5-38; H6-45.*

REX, creamer. McKee Glass Co. #136, 1894. Extended table service including plate, finger bowl, straw jar, soda glasses, sundae, fruit bowl with lid, wine, footed sherbet. *Ref. K5-101; K8-38.*

PRISM BARS, creamer. Made in the early 1890s in extended table service. *Ref. Gob II-54; K4-42.*

Cambridge #2625

Ribbed Ware

Inside Flute

Prism

Heisey's Coarse Ribbing

Heavy Rib

Inside Ribbing

U.S. Rib

Rex

Prism Bars

PLATE 196. RIBS AND COLUMNS

BEATTY RIB (RIBBED OPAL), pitcher. A. J. Beatty Glass Co. #87, 1888; U. S. Glass Co., 1891. Extended table service including two sizes toothpick holder, banana boat, cracker jar, sugar shaker, wine. Opalescent white, blue, and canary (scarce). *Ref. L-147; K6-54; HI-15; HII-18; HIII-16; Schroy-19; Metz 1-100.*

RIBBING, creamer. Made ca. 1875. *Ref. K7-1.*

SUNKEN ARCHES, creamer. See Plate 34.

YOKED LOOP (SCALLOPED LOOP), goblet. Extended table service. Crystal, ruby-stained. *Ref. Gob II-54; H7-199+; Metz 1-26.*

FINE RIB (REEDED), footed salt dish. New England Glass Co.; Union Glass Co.; 1860s. Extended table service including champagne, cordial, claret, wine. *Ref. L-36; LEAPG-111; Jenks p. 213; Schroy-60; Gob I-148; Metz 1-50; Unitt 1-70.*

PALMER PRISM (SCALLOPED FLUTE), goblet. Portland Glass Co., 1868. *Ref. Swan p. 60; Revi-282.*

CELTIC CROSS, engraved creamer. George Duncan and Sons #771, 1883. Extended table service. *Ref. K2-111; Metz 1-50.*

TRIANGULAR PRISM, goblet. Made in 1855 in extended table service including whiskey tumbler, wine, master salt. Flint glass. *Ref. Gob II-29; Metz 2-34.*

LOOPS AND OVALS, goblet. *Ref. Gob II-26.*

LOOP AND PETAL, goblet. See Plate 34.

RIBBED BANDS, creamer. Made ca. 1880s. *Ref. K7-7.*

Beatty Rib   *Ribbing*   *Sunken Arches*

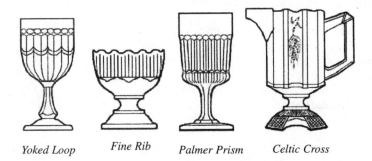

Yoked Loop   *Fine Rib*   *Palmer Prism*   *Celtic Cross*

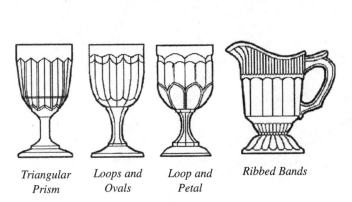

Triangular   *Loops and*   *Loop and*   *Ribbed Bands*
Prism   *Ovals*   *Petal*

PLATE 197. RIBS AND COLUMNS

TEARDROP, pitcher. Dalzell, Gilmore and Leighton Glass Co., late 1890s. Extended table service including candlestick, wine. *Ref. K7-18; Metz 1-144.*

CLIMAX (BULLET BAND; LITTLE BULLET), etched pitcher. U. S. Glass Co. (Columbia factory), 1891. Extended table service. Crystal, blue. *Ref. K7-44; H5-130.*

DOUBLE BEETLE BAND (SMOCKING BANDS), pitcher. Columbia Glass Co., 1880s. Extended table service including wine. Crystal, yellow, amber, blue. *Ref. K3-47; Metz 1-136; Unitt 1-248; Unitt 2-99.*

OLD COLUMBIA (COLUMBIA), creamer. Columbia Glass Co., 1890; U. S. Glass Co. (Columbia), 1891. Extended table service including wines. Crystal. *Ref. HPV #1, 16; H5-131; Mugs p. 98; Gob II-77; Unitt 2-57; Revi-125; HCG1 p. 11.*

ADAMS #52, creamer. U. S. Glass Co. #329 (Adams), 1891. Crystal. *Ref. H5-72.*

BELLE, creamer. Ohio Flint Glass Co., 1897. Extended table service of sixty items. Crystal, ruby-stained, etched, engraved. *Ref. K5-64; H7-16.*

FULTON (MARTHA'S TEARS; TEARDROP BANDS), salt shaker. Brilliant Glass Co., 1889; Greensburg Glass Co., 1890. Extended table service including tray, finger bowl, wine. *Ref. K3-129; K4-117; K8-166; Gob I-103; Metz 1-149; Unitt 1-107.*

VULCAN, creamer. National Glass Co. (McKee factory), 1900; Ohio Flint Glass Works, 1902. Extended table service including wine. Crystal, ruby-stained. *Ref. K5-101; HTP-86; H6-76; H7-7.*

FOOTED PANELLED RIB, creamer. U. S. Glass Co. (Challinor #308), 1891. Basic table service. Crystal. *Ref. LV-59; Metz 1-170; H5-90.*

Teardrop

Climax

Double Beetle
Band

Old Columbia

Adams #52

Belle

Fulton

Vulcan

Footed Panelled Rib

PLATE 198. RIBS AND COLUMNS

ICICLE, sugar bowl. Bakewell, Pears and Co., ca. 1870s. Extended table service including individual butter dish, flat and footed butter dishes, master salt, 5" lamp. *Ref. L-19, 20, 22; LEAPG-87; Jenks p. 288; Metz 1-53; Schroy-161.*

BANDED ICICLE, pitcher. Bakewell, Pears and Co., 1870s. Extended table service. Crystal. *Ref. Gob II-137; Metz 1-52.*

WAVE, creamer. Made ca. 1880s. *Ref. K7-14.*

LATE BANDED ICICLE, goblet. A wine is known. *Ref. Gob II-137; Metz 1-52.*

RIBBED DRAPE, toothpick holder. Jefferson Glass Co. #250, 1907. Extended table service. Crystal, rare electric blue, rare apple green, custard, decorated with flowers. The cruet is very rare in blue or green. *Ref. K7-150; HI-37; H4-48+; H7-39; HTP-46.*

BLAZE, sugar bowl. New England Glass Co., ca. 1869. Extended table service including plates, wine, cordial, champagne, egg cup. Flint glass. *Ref. L-13; Gob I-76; Metz 1-53; LEAPG-63; Batty p. 23; Jenks p. 70; Schroy-22.*

BELTED ICICLE (LATE ICICLE), pitcher. Fostoria Glass Co. #162, 1889. Extended table service including wine. *Ref. K8-63; Gob I-102; Gob II-137; Metz 1-52; Revi-158; Unitt 1-110.*

TRANSVERSE RIBS, salt shaker. Extended table service. *Ref. Gob II-42; Metz 1-50.*

RIB AND BEAD (NAOMI), creamer. National Glass Co. (McKee factory), ca. 1901. NAOMI was the original manufacturer's name. Extended table service including both rounded and square salt shakers, 6" fluted top vase. Crystal, ruby-stained. *Ref. K8-60; HI-37; H6-72; H7-155.*

STEDMAN, syrup. McKee and Brothers, 1864. Extended table service including champagne, decanter, cordial, wines, egg cup. Flint glass. *Ref. L-13; Gob I-13, 76, 88; Metz 1-52; LEAPG-63; Unitt 1-111; Unitt 2-147.*

Icicle   *Banded Icicle*   *Wave*

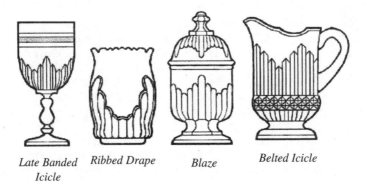

Late Banded Icicle   *Ribbed Drape*   *Blaze*   *Belted Icicle*

Transverse Ribs   *Rib and Bead*   *Stedman*

PLATE 199. RIBS AND COLUMNS

PORTLAND, goblet and cruet. U. S. Glass Co. #15121 (Glassport; Ripley; Central), 1910. Extended table service including pomade jar, puff box, decanter, vases, water bottle, sugar shaker, wines, cordial. Crystal. *Ref. K1-107; Gob I-96; Metz 1-196; Metz 2-124; Unitt 1-36; H5-155; H7-175; Schroy-114; Jenks p. 413.*

THE BEDFORD (LONG PUNTY), creamer. Fostoria Glass Co. #1000, 1901 – 1905. Extended table service including wine, claret. Crystal. *Ref. K3-81; HTP-83; Revi-157; Measell p. 22.*

CORDOVA (PRISM BUTTRESS; POINTED THUMBPRINT AND PANEL), goblet. O'Hara Glass Co., 1890; U. S. Glass Co., 1891 (lengthy production.) Extended table service including inkwell, handled lamp, egg cup, wine. Crystal, ruby-stained, green. *Ref. K1-105; K6 Pl. 2; LV-66; Metz 2-168; HI-18; H5-162; H7-95; Jenks p. 132; Schroy-38.*

ELEPHANT TOES, creamer. U. S. Glass Co. (Richards and Hartley factory), 1905. Extended table service. Crystal, gilded, amethyst or green stain on the base thumbprints. *Ref. H5-28; HTP-53.*

PITTSBURGH (PRISM AND GLOBULES), creamer. Bryce Brothers, 1890; Bellaire Goblet Co.; U. S. Glass Co. (Bryce), 1891. Extended table service including cake baskets, individual salt, wine, champagne, decanters, pickle castor set, fan-shaped vase, sugar shaker. The celeries come in two variations, one with straight lip, the other panelled and flared. The cake basket has curved raised sides on a tall pedestal. Crystal. *Ref. K4-63; LV-63; H5-77; Gob II-140; Metz 2-138.*

TRUNCATED CUBE (THOMPSON #77), salt shaker. Thompson Glass Co., 1894. Extended table service including wine, rare syrup. Crystal, ruby-stained. *Ref. K5-82; Gob II-35; H6-45; Metz 2-142; Unitt 2-138; H7-56+; Schroy-146.*

LONG BUTTRESS, sugar bowl. Fostoria Glass Co. #1229, ca. 1904. Extended table service including individual creamer and sugar, pickle jar, vases. Crystal, ruby-stained. *Ref. K7-46; HTP-82; H7-87, 143.*

BARRED OVAL (OVAL AND CROSSBAR), pitcher. U. S. Glass Co. #15004 (Duncan), 1891. Extended table service including water bottle. Crystal, scarce in ruby-stained. *Ref. K6-25; LV-41; H5-97; H7-37+; Schroy-15; Metz 1-154; Jenks p. 48.*

Portland (two examples)   *The Bedford*

Cordova   *Elephant Toes*   *Pittsburgh*

Truncated   *Long Buttress*   *Barred Oval*
Cube

PLATE 200. RIBS AND COLUMNS

DOUBLE ARCH (INTERLOCKING CRESCENTS), creamer. King Glass Co.; U. S. Glass Co. #15024 (Columbia), 1892. Extended table service. Crystal, ruby-stained. *Ref. K5-73; HI-21; H7-106+; Metz 1-150.*

CHELSEA, tumbler. Cambridge Glass Co., ca. 1906. Extended table service including soda glasses, ten sizes goblets, several sizes tumblers, punch bowl, nut cup, vases, baskets, syrup jug with plate. Marked "Near Cut" after 1906. Crystal. *Ref. K8-65.*

BALL (NOTCHED BAR), salt shaker and cruet. McKee Glass Co. #492, 1894; Belmont Glass Co. #492, 1889. Extended table service including wine. Crystal, amber-stained. *Ref. K5-62; K7-17; Gob II-160; Metz 1-196; H6-78.*

FAN BAND (SCALLOPED FLOWER BAND, BRYCE YALE), goblet. Bryce Higbee and Co., 1887; U. S. Glass Co. (Higbee), 1907; New Martinsville Glass Co., 1916. Extended table service including tray, finger bowl, wine. *Ref. K4-14; K8-115; Gob II-25; Metz 1-136; Unitt 1-103.*

CUT LOG (PIONEER #15; CAT'S EYE AND BLOCK; ETHOL; WESTMORELAND #15), handled nappy and creamer. Bryce Higbee and Co., ca. 1891; Westmoreland Specialty Co. in 1899, their #15. Heacock discovered a rare error by Kamm, in that she read some old ads incorrectly and believed CUT LOG to be by Greensburg Glass Co. The stranger than fiction truth is that CUT LOG is the same pattern as PIONEER #15, one having plain notches, and the other with ridged notches, but neither is by Pioneer, which was a decorating firm. The nappy shown here is by Bryce, Higbee, the creamer by Westmoreland. Westmoreland made a cruet; Bryce did not. Items to be found include mug, wine, "canoe," vase, finger bowl. Crystal; ruby-stained would be rare. *Ref. K1-118; K8-61; LV-53; Unitt 1-252; Metz 1-140; HCG1 p. 88; H7-214+; Jenks-146; Schroy-42.*

EUREKA, wine goblet. See Plate 158.

BROKEN COLUMN (IRISH COLUMN; NOTCHED RIB; RATTAN AND BAMBOO), pitcher and ruby-stained syrup. Columbia Glass Co., 1887; U. S. Glass Co. #15021 (Richards and Hartley; Columbia), 1893 – 1900. Very extended table service including banana dish, handled basket, pickle castor, cracker jar, water bottle, rare 7" plate, rare sugar shaker, rare covered compote, wine, cordial, champagne, claret. Being reproduced. Crystal, ruby-stained, cobalt blue. *Ref. K4-116; LV-71; Gob II-69; Metz 1-140; Unitt 1-26; Jenks p. 80; Schroy-25; HIII-16; H5-47; H7-83.*

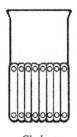

Double Arch   *Chelsea*   *Ball (two examples)*

Fan Band   *Cut Log (two examples)*

Eureka   *Broken Column (two examples)*

PLATE 201. RIBS AND COLUMNS

BRYCE #160, salt shaker. Bryce Brothers; U. S. Glass Co., ca. 1891. Extended table service including sugar shaker, tray. *Ref. H5-82.*

TRIPLE BAR (SCALLOPED PRISM; U.S. #84), creamer. Doyle and Co. #84, 1880s; U. S. Glass Co., 1895. Extended table service including wine. Crystal. *Ref. K3-91; K8-103; Unitt 2-29; Metz 1-162; LV Pl. 59.*

TRIPLE BAR AND LOOP, creamer. Made during the 1880s. Milk glass. *Ref. K2-80.*

FISHBONE BOW, salt shaker. *Ref. PetSal 161B.*

PANELLED FISHBONE, salt shaker. *Ref. PetSal 28V.*

FISHBONE, salt shaker. Extended table service. *Ref. PetSal 28U; Metz 1-140.*

FLORIDA, salt shaker. (A State Series Pattern.) See Plate 168.

WINDOW AND DRAPE, salt shaker. This was originally a snuff bottle. *Ref. PetSal 177E.*

HERRINGBONE BUTTRESS (HERRINGBONE RIB; COLUMBIAN), goblet. Indiana Tumbler and Goblet Co. #140, 1899. Extended table service including wine, cordial, cracker jar. Crystal, chocolate glass, green. Some pieces have the added detail of a "ribbon" with beads and a fan, similar to CACTUS (Plate 188.) *Ref. K5-123; Gob II-18; Metz 2-1-62; Unitt 2-28; Measell p. 58; H6-29.*

PARIS (ROUGHNECK; ZIPPER CROSS), creamer. Bryce, Higbee and Co., 1898; J. B Higbee, 1907; New Martinsville, 1918. Extended table service including wine, cake basket. Crystal, ruby-stained. *Ref. K5-40; PetSal 171B; H6-96; H7-10; NM p. 30.*

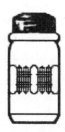

Bryce #160   *Triple Bar*   *Triple Bar and Loop*

Fishbone Bow   *Panelled Fishbone*   *Fishbone*   *Florida*

Window and Drape   *Herringbone Buttress*   *Paris*

415

PLATE 202. RIBS AND COLUMNS

PALING (BANDED PALING), pitcher. Made ca. 1880s in extended table service. *Ref. K3-24; Gob II-14.*

PUFFED BANDS (SNOW BAND), creamer. Made ca. 1880s in extended table service including wine. Crystal, blue. *Ref. K2-45; Metz 1-182.*

PRISM COLUMN (BEADED COARSE BARS), creamer. U. S. Glass #15023, 1892. Extended table service including wine, ice tub, mustard can, water bottle. Crystal, light green. *Ref. K2-45; K6-15; Gob II-15; Metz 1-182; Unitt 1-147.*

FLUTE AND CROWN, pitcher. Westmoreland Glass Co., 1896. Extended table service. Milk glass. *Ref. K2-118.*

EDGEWOOD, creamer. Fostoria Glass Co. #375, 1899. Extended table service including carafe. *Ref. K5-103.*

GROOVE AND SLASH (HEISEY'S #1250), pitcher. A. H. Heisey and Co. #1250, ca. 1897. Extended table service including cracker jar, pickle jar, bonbon. A similar pattern is MARDI GRAS on Plate 102. *Ref. K7-136.*

PICKET BAND (STAVES WITH SCALLOPED BAND; PEN), goblet. Doyle and Company, ca. 1870s. Extended table service including wine. Crystal, blue. *Ref. K3-33; Gob II-49; Metz 1-132.*

FOSTORIA'S #1231, creamer. Fostoria Glass Co., ca. 1903. Extended table service including vases, finger bowl, rose bowl, pickle jar, punch bowl. *Ref. K8-40.*

THE PRIZE (BEADED COARSE BARS), creamer. National Glass Co. (McKee #500), 1900 – 1904. Extended table service including wine, cordial, water bottle. Crystal, emerald green, ruby-stained. *Ref. K5-67; H7-176.*

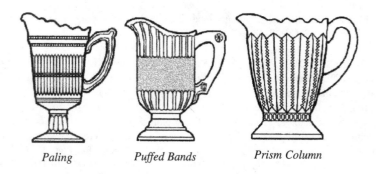

Paling   *Puffed Bands*   *Prism Column*

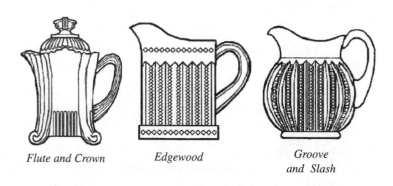

Flute and Crown   *Edgewood*   *Groove and Slash*

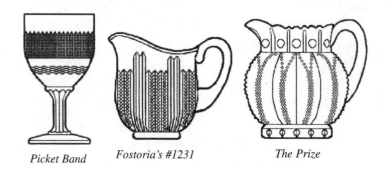

Picket Band   *Fostoria's #1231*   *The Prize*

417

PLATE 203. RIBS AND COLUMNS

WELLSBURG, creamer. National Glass Co. #681 (Dalzell factory), 1901. Extended table service. Crystal, ruby-stained. *Ref. K5-63; H7-214.*

ZIPPER BORDERS, etched syrup. Made ca. 1898, but only syrup known. Crystal, ruby-stained, etched. *Ref. HIII-47; H7-219.*

MICHIGAN (LOOP AND PILLAR; PANELLED JEWEL; BULGING LOOPS; DESPLAINES), plate. U. S. Glass Co. #15077 (Glassport), 1902. A State Series pattern. Extended table service including vases, rare ruby-stained toothpick holder, wine, toy table set, mug, handled lemonade. Crystal, rose-flashed (maiden's blush), green-flashed, decorated, vaseline-stained, green-stained. The toothpick has been reproduced in all colors including carnival glass. A four-piece set (sugar with cover, creamer, spoon holder, and covered butter) was sold for $7.50 in 1909. See the insert just after Plate 12. *Ref. K1-106; Gob II-44; Unitt 1-242; Unitt 2-237; Mugs p. 76; H3-56, 79; HI-50; HIII-56; H5-35; HTP-53, 54; H7-150; Jenks p. 366; Schroy-99.*

SERRATED SPEAR POINT, goblet. The wine is known (courtesy of John Gregory.) *Ref. Gob II-74.*

SERRATED PANELS, bowl. U. S. Glass Co. #15089 (Gas City), 1904. Extended table service. Crystal. *Ref. H5-164.*

NELLY (SYLVAN; FLORENCE; PRISM AND BROKEN COLUMN), creamer. McKee Glass Co., 1894. Extended table service including vase, wine, cordial. Crystal, ruby-stained. *Ref. K5-39; Revi-240; Unitt 2-54; H6-31, 48; HTP-49; H7-135.*

IRIS WITH MEANDER (IRIS), pitcher. Jefferson Glass Co., 1904. Extended table service. Crystal, blue, green, amethyst. It was also made in opalescent colors of white, blue, canary and green; amber opalescent is rare. *Ref. K6-63; HI-27; HII-22; H6-31+; Schroy-81.*

NATIONAL PRISM, celery vase. National Glass Co., 1900. Known also in a 10" tray and a sugar bowl (or cracker jar, it is unclear which.) Crystal. *Ref. HCG1 p. 77.*

McKEE'S UNION, creamer. McKee Glass Co., 1901. Extended table service. Crystal, ruby-stained. *Ref. H6-70; H7-45.*

Wellsburg

Zipper Borders

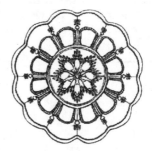

Michigan

*Serrated Spear
Point*

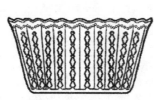

Serrated Panels

Nelly

*Iris with
Meander*

*National
Prism*

*McKee's
Union*

PLATE 204. RIBS AND COLUMNS

ZIPPER SLASH, pitcher. George Duncan's Sons and Co. #2005, 1894. Extended table service including wine, champagne, banana dish. Crystal, frosted, ruby-stained. *Ref. K3-83; Metz 1-198; HTP-52; HI-45; H7-218.*

SERRATED PRISM (NOTCHED PANEL; BANDED SERRATED PRISM), creamer. Tarentum Glass Co., 1902. Extended table service. Crystal, ruby-stained. *Ref. PetSal 34H; Gob II-17; Metz 1-170; HTP-82.*

IMPERIAL #77, pitcher. Imperial Glass Co., ca. 1902. *Ref. K7-66.*

ZIPPER IN DIAMOND, cruet. Possibly an unlisted Riverside pattern, ca. 1895 – 1905 in crystal and ruby-stained. *Ref. H6-47.*

SERRATED RIB, salt shaker. In this one the surfaces of the panels protrude more than the zippers. *Ref. PetSal 37G.*

PANELLED PLEAT (ROBINSON'S LADDER), goblet. Robinson Glass Co., 1893. Basic table service and goblet are known. See a similar goblet on Plate 163, PANELLED LADDER. *Ref. Gob II-42; K6 Pl. 37; Metz 1-198.*

ZIPPER (COBB; LATE SAWTOOTH), pitcher. Richards and Hartley Flint Glass Co., 1885. Extended table service including wine, covered jam jar, toy banana stand, sugar shaker. Crystal, blue, *Ref. K2-19; Gob I-105; Jenks p. 565; Schroy-158; Metz 1-34.*

LADDERS (LOOP AND PYRAMID), cup. Tarentum Glass Co. #292, 1901. Extended table service including vase, wine. Crystal, gilded, rare in ruby-stained. The cruet is square with the ladders on each corner. *Ref. K5-79; Gob II-79; Metz 2-150; PetPat-190; HPV2-17, 18; Lucas p. 331; Mugs p. 86/87; Unitt 1-242; H7-7.*

LACY VALANCE (PERSIAN SHAWL), creamer. Made ca. 1890s in extended table service including bread tray, flat-sided honey dish. It features a triangular medallion with scrolls in the end panels. *Ref. K2-34.*

ZIPPERED BLOCK (CRYPTIC), creamer. Duncan Glass Co., 1890; U. S. Glass Co., 1891. Extended table service including water bottle. Crystal, ruby-stained (scarce). *Ref. K3-131; H5-102; H7-37+; Jenks p. 566; Schroy-158; Metz 2-162.*

Zipper Slash   Serrated Prism   Imperial #77

Zipper in Diamond   Serrated Rib   Panelled Pleat   Zipper

Ladders   Lacy Valance   Zippered Block

PLATE 205. RIBS AND COLUMNS

STRIGIL, pitcher. Tarentum Glass Co. #1644, ca. 1902. Extended table service including egg cup, wine. Crystal. *Ref. K2-83; K5-39; Schroy-138; Jenks p. 501.*

FISHSCALE (CORAL), pitcher. Bryce Brothers, 1880s; U. S. Glass Co., 1891. Extended table service including tray, finger bowl. Crystal, ruby-stained. *Ref. K1-58; LEAPG-481; H5-79; H7-94.*

FILE (RIBBED SAWTOOTH), pitcher. Columbia Glass Co., 1888; Imperial Glass Co. #256, 1904; U. S. Glass Co.; 1891. Extended table service including wine, cordial, vases. Crystal. *Ref. K2-30; Metz 1-142.*

ALASKA (LION'S LEG), cruet and pitcher. Northwood Glass Co., 1897 – 1910. Extended table service including jewel tray, rose bowl. No toothpick holder known. Crystal, emerald green, opalescent white, blue and green; decorated. *Ref. K1-83; HII-18; H6-18.*

IOWA (PANELLED ZIPPER), cruet. U. S. Glass Co. #15069 (Glassport), 1900. A State Series pattern. Extended table service including wine. Crystal, rose-flashed. *Ref. PetSal 164D; Gob II-136; Unitt 1-165; Metz 1-198; HI-46; HV-180; H6-31; Schroy-81.*

TRIPLE PRISM GRID, salt shaker. Imperial Glass Co. #256½, ca. 1915. Extended table service. *Ref. K7-208.*

BROKEN PILLAR AND REED, toothpick holder. Model Flint Glass Co. #909 (Albany), ca. 1900. Extended table service. Crystal, amethyst-flashed, color-stained (scarce). *Ref. Bond p. 30.*

SANDWICH HEART, pitcher. A very early Boston and Sandwich pattern, made in other pieces but not common. Museum quality. *Ref. K7-16.*

Strigil

Fishscale

File

Alaska (two examples)

Iowa

*Triple Prism
Grid*

*Broken Pillar
and Reed*

*Sandwich
Heart*

PLATE 206. ROPES

ROPE AND RIBS, sugar shaker. Central Glass Co., ca. 1890. Extended table service. Crystal, amber, blue, canary. *Ref. HIII-59.*

BUTTRESSED ARCH, creamer. *Ref. K3-109.*

CORD AND TASSEL, pitcher. LaBelle Glass Co., 1872; Central Glass Co., 1876. Extended table service including wine, mug, cordial, egg cup, lamp. Crystal. The wine has been reproduced. *Ref. L-116; Metz 1-130; LEAPG-550; Unitt 1-276; Mugs p. 109.*

LOOP HERRINGBONE, syrup. U. S. Glass Co., 1901. Crystal syrup known. *Ref H5-173.*

CABLE VARIANT, goblet. *Ref. L-164 #2.*

ROPE BANDS (ARGENT; CLEAR PANELS WITH CORD BAND), pitcher. Bryce Brothers, 1884; U. S. Glass Co. (Bryce), 1891. Extended table service including wine, platter. Crystal. *Ref. K5-14; Gob I-154; Metz 1-130; Unitt 2-35; Schroy-122; H5-85.*

BEADED ROPE PANEL, salt shaker. Extended table service. *Ref. PetSal 37S.*

CORD AND BARS, goblet. Gillinder and Sons #3, 1880s. A wine is known. *Ref. Gob II-87; Unitt 2-28; Welker p. 235.*

TRIPLE BAR WITH CABLE (PENTAGON), creamer. King Glass Co., ca. 1880s; George Duncan and Sons, ca. 1880 – 1885. Extended table service. *Ref. K2-115; LV-43.*

Rope and Ribs   *Buttressed*
                       Arch   *Cord and Tassel*

Loop Herringbone   *Cable Variant*   *Rope Bands*

Beaded Rope   *Cord and Bars*   *Triple Bar with Cable*
Panel

PLATE 207. ROPES

ROPE PANEL, salt shaker. Extended table service. Milk glass. *Ref. PetSal 37S.*

CABLE (ATLANTIC CABLE; CABLE CORD), goblet and plate. Boston and Sandwich, 1859. Extended table service including rare creamer, rare water pitcher, egg cup, lamps, rare footed tumbler, wine, champagne, cordials, decanters, master salt. Crystal; rare in opaque white, blue, and green. *Ref. L-36; Gob I-37; Metz 1-130; LEAPG-180; Unitt 1-267; Unitt 2-28; Jenks p. 99; Schroy-30.*

LOOPED ROPE, syrup. Extended table service. Opaque white. *Ref. K7-19.*

CABLE WITH RING, creamer. Boston and Sandwich Glass Co., 1860s. Extended table service including honey dish, lamp. No goblet or tumbler known. Crystal. *Ref. K1-5.*

ROPED DIAMOND, goblet. *Ref. Gob II-109; Metz 2-170.*

RETICULATED CORD (DRUM), goblet. O'Hara Glass Co. #600, 1885; U. S. Glass Co. (O'Hara), 1891. Extended table service including open-handled plate, wine. Crystal, color (scarce). *Ref. Gob I-130; Gob II-139; Metz 1-130; Unitt 1-290.*

PANELLED CABLE, creamer. U. S. Glass Co. (Bryce), 1891. Extended table service. Crystal. *Ref. K6-14; H5-84.*

Rope Panel   *Cable (two examples)*

Looped Rope   *Cable with Ring*

Roped Diamond   *Reticulated Cord*   *Panelled Cable*

PLATE 208. SHELLS

ARGONAUT SHELL (NAUTILUS), pitcher. Northwood Glass Co., 1898 – 1910. Extended table service. Custard, opalescent blue and white; some novelties in canary opalescent; carnival. The toothpick holder was made only in custard. Reproduced by L. G. Wright, 1970 – 1971 in crystal, blue, opalescent in a number of pieces. *Ref. K4-32; HI-13; H2-25, 90; H4-16; H6-18; Schroy-7.*

U. S. COMET (DRAPED FAN), wine and pitcher. Doyle and Co., ca. 1880s; U. S. Glass Co., 1895. Extended table service. Crystal, amber, vaseline. *Ref. K3-82; K7 Pl. 13, 14; Gob II-41; Metz 1-154; Unitt 2-225.*

SCALLOP SHELL, creamer. Made in extended table service including wine. The base is circular, the body square. *Ref. K2-38.*

CRYSTALINA, plate. See Plate 157.

TRIPLE SHELL, salt shaker. Eagle Glass and Mfg. Co., 1898. Milk glass. *Ref. PetSal 172J.*

SHELL (JEFFERSON SHELL), creamer. Northwood-Dugan Glass Co. at Indiana, Penn. ca. 1900 – 1910. Extended table service, but no syrup made. A mug was made and has been reproduced with an "N" on the base. Note: This was called "Jefferson Shell" until William Heacock discovered its true manufacturer. Crystal, blue, apple green; opalescent blue, green, and white; ruby-stained, limited carnival. *Ref. K7-58; HI-40; HII-23; HIII-56; H6-42; H7-192.*

SHELL ON RIBS (SHELL), creamer. U. S. Glass Co. (Columbia), 1891. Basic table service. Crystal. *Ref. H5-129.*

SHELL AND SCALE, salt shaker. Made in extended table service including cake stand. *Ref. PetSal 172H.*

SHELL AND JEWEL (VICTOR), tumbler. Westmoreland Glass Co.; Fostoria Glass Co.; 1893. Extended table service. No goblet made. Crystal, blue, green. *Ref. K1-68; Metz 1-216; Metz 2-102; Jenks p. 474; Schroy-129.*

GENEVA (SHELL AND SCROLL), toothpick holder. National Glass Co. (McKee), 1900. Extended table service. Crystal, emerald green, custard, decorated, ruby-stained, rare in chocolate. *Ref. K2-117; HI-24; HIII-25; H6-28; H7-122.*

BEADED SHELL (NEW YORK), mug. Dugan Glass Co., 1904. Extended table service. Crystal, green, blue, gilded, clear opalescent, light green and blue opalescent. Later they made amethyst, blue, rare white, and marigold colors in carnival glass. Reproduced in custard by L. G. Wright; has a "lazy N" on the bottom. *Ref. Edwards p. 20; Mugs p. 63.*

Argonaut Shell *U.S. Comet (two views)* *Scallop Shell*

Crystalina *Triple Shell* *Shell* *Shell on Ribs*

Shell and Scale *Shell and Jewel* *Geneva* *Beaded Shell*

PLATE 209. SQUARES AND RECTANGLES

CHANDELIER (CROWN JEWELS), salt shaker. O'Hara Glass Co., 1888; U. S. Glass Co., 1891. Extended table service including wine. Crystal. *Ref. K2-114; Gob I-163; Metz 1-49; Metz 2-180, 218; Unitt I-244; Jenks p. 117; Schroy-34.*

BLOCK BAND SQUARES (BLOCK BAND), tankard pitcher. Crystal, ruby-stained. *Ref. K7-20; H7-79.*

HIDALGO (FROSTED WAFFLE), etched creamer. U. S. Glass Co. (Adams), 1891. Extended table service including cup and saucer, tray, finger bowl, many odd-shaped relish dishes and bowls. Crystal, frosted, ruby-stained, etched. *Ref. K3-56; LV-49; H5-68; H7-129; Schroy-74; Jenks p. 273; Metz 1-168.*

NORTHWOOD'S REGAL BLOCK (BLOCK MIDRIFF), salt shaker. Northwood Glass Co. Crystal, amber-stained, Francesware. *Ref. PetSal 155-i; HII-33, 34.*

TWIN PANELS (PRISM AND CLEAR PANELS), goblet. Extended table service including wine. *Ref. K8-71; Gob I-24; Metz 1-206.*

RIB AND BLOCK, goblet. *Ref. Gob II-128; Metz 1-206.*

BLOCK ON STILTS, goblet. The wine is also known. *Ref. Gob II-32; Unitt 1-252.*

CHECKERBOARD BAND, creamer. U. S. Glass Co. (Challinor #82), 1891. Basic table service. Crystal. *Ref. K7-60; Metz 2-186.*

SAXON, creamer. Bakewell, Pears and Co., 1875. Extended table service including wine, claret, egg cup, covered jar. Crystal, ruby-stained. *Ref. L-20; Gob II-12; Metz 1-52; LEAPG-76; LV-188; HTP-42; HI-39; HIII-57; H6-41; H7-190; Schroy-127.*

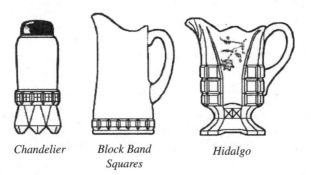

Chandelier   Block Band   Hidalgo
                     Squares

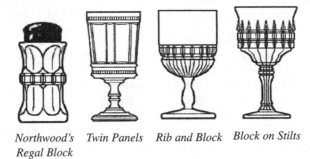

Northwood's   Twin Panels   Rib and Block   Block on Stilts
Regal Block

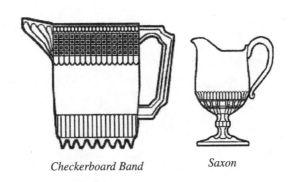

Checkerboard Band   Saxon

PLATE 210. SQUARES AND RECTANGLES

WAFFLE AND BAR, miniature creamer. Duncan Glass. *Ref. K1-115.*

PRESSED BLOCK, compote. See Plates 11 and 19.

BLOCK AND BAR, creamer. *Ref. K5-45; Metz 2-16.*

BEADED THUMBPRINT BLOCK, mug. See Plate 19.

PRISM CUBE, goblet. *Ref. Gob II-58.*

HERCULES PILLAR – LATE, syrup. Hobbs, Brockunier and Co., 1890. Goblet, wine, champagne, cordial, and syrup known in crystal, blue, amber, apple green, and scarce canary. *Ref. Gob I; Hobbs p. 156; Gob I-3; Metz 1-24; HIII-27.*

HOOPED BARREL, salt shaker. *Ref. PetSal 21V.*

BLOCK WITH THUMBPRINT, salt shaker. Made ca. 1876 in extended table service including footed tumbler, wine. *Ref. l-101; Gob I-117, 126; Metz 1-24; LEAPG-35; Unitt 2-46; K4-21.*

SQUARE BLOCK, salt shaker. Crystal, ruby-stained. *Ref. PetSal 173B; H7-195.*

THUMBPRINT BLOCK (ROUND), etched creamer. This is part of a pattern called THUMBPRINT BLOCK (BANQUET), shown on Plate 211. One might not realize that they are in the same set, which U. S. Glass called BANQUET. Columbia Glass Co., 1886; U. S. Glass Co., 1891. Extended table service including rose bowl, wine. Crystal. *Ref. K5-57; Revi-125, 127; H5-129, 130.*

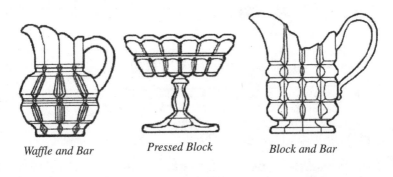

Waffle and Bar   Pressed Block   Block and Bar

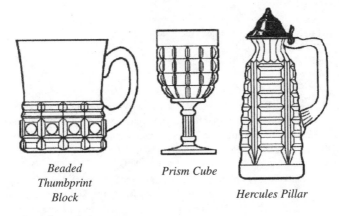

Beaded
Thumbprint
Block

Prism Cube

Hercules Pillar

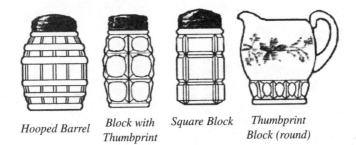

Hooped Barrel   Block with
Thumbprint   Square Block   Thumbprint
Block (round)

PLATE 211. SQUARES AND RECTANGLES

BLOCK AND RIB, creamer. Opaque white. *Ref. K3-48.*

SPLIT WAFFLE, individual creamer. U. S. Glass Co. (O'Hara), ca. 1891. Known in individual creamer and sugar, and syrup in crystal, blue, and amethyst. Probably made in amber also. *Ref. HGC3 p. 21.*

GREENSBURG #130 (BLOCK BARREL), creamer. Greensburg Glass Co., 1889. Extended table service including basket, wine. *Ref. K5 Pl. 7; K7-62.*

BLOCK, spoon holder. Extended table service including cup, wine, covered cracker jar. Crystal, color-stained. *Ref. H7-108.*

SECTIONAL BLOCK, goblet. *Ref. Gob II-109.*

DUNCAN #46, cruet. George Duncan and Sons, ca. 1900. Two sizes of cruet are known. *Ref. Bones-110.*

THUMBPRINT BLOCK, creamer. See Plate 210.

TACKLE BLOCK, goblet. Known in two types of flint goblet, ca. 1840s. *Ref. Gob II-49; Metz 1-8.*

WAFFLE, tumbler. Boston and Sandwich; Bryce, Walker and Co., early 1860s. Extended table service including egg cup, champagne, claret, wine, water and whiskey tumblers, cordials, decanters, rare quart creamer, rare water pitcher, castor bottle. Flint glass. *Ref. L-46; K6-7; Metz 1-18; LEAPG-139; Jenks p. 543; Schroy-151.*

McKEE'S PILLOW, toy creamer. This was **not** made by McKee (!) but by A. J. Beatty and Sons and U. S. Glass Co. One of the joys of pattern glass is coping with the wrong name. It was made in the 1890s. See other "pillow" patterns on Plate 53. *Ref. K7-48.*

ELSON'S BLOCK, creamer. Elson Glass Co. #150, 1891. Extended table service. Crystal, ruby-stained. *Ref. K5-12; H7-114.*

Block and Rib   Split Waffle   Greensburg #130

Block   Sectional   Duncan #46   Thumbprint
            Block   Block

Tackle Block   Waffle   McKee's Pillow   Elson's Block

435

PLATE 212. SQUARES AND RECTANGLES

"PRISON WINDOW" (INDIANA), salt shaker. This is the State Series pattern for Indiana, a shaker given the name of "Prison Window," an amusing name that should not be lost. See INDIANA on Plate 52.

BERLIN (REEDED WAFFLE), pitcher. Adams and Co., 1874; Bryce Brothers #87, 1880s; U. S. Glass Co., 1891. Extended table service including wine, covered cracker jar. Crystal, color-stained. *Ref. K1-98; Mugs p. 100; H5-72 (in the tumbler section).*

WAFFLE WITH POINTS (WAFFLE WITH SPEARPOINTS; BLOCK CUT), creamer. Elson Glass Co. #99, 1887; U. S. Glass Co., 1891. Extended table service including wine. *Ref. K4-27; Gob I-96; Metz 1-166; Unitt 1-114.*

DUNCAN BLOCK (DUNCAN'S LATE BLOCK; WAFFLE BLOCK; WAFFLE VARIANT), creamer, individual creamer, and syrup. Duncan and Miller Glass Co., 1887; U. S. Glass Co. (Duncan #331), 1891. Extended table service including parlor lamp, square and triangular bowls, 7" and 8" trays; mustard jar, punch bowl, ice tub, sugar shaker, rose bowls, basket, water bottle, two sizes sugar bowls, covered cheese dish, carafe, wine. In the ads, this syrup was called "hotel molasses can ewer, mouth plated." Crystal, ruby-stained. *Ref. K1-118; LV-117; H5-46, 100; H7-77, 108; Mugs p. 101; Metz 2-142; Jenks p. 187; Schroy-53.*

BLOCK AND PILLAR, salt shaker. *Ref. PetSal 23D.*

WAFFLE WINDOW, salt shaker. *Ref. PetSal 176S.*

WAFFLE OCTAGON, salt shaker. Has a rotary agitator and top patented Christmas, 1877. *Ref. PetSal 43D.*

BANDED BARREL, syrup. Made ca. 1895 and known only in the syrup. Crystal, amber, green. *Ref. HIII-15.*

Prison Window

Berlin

*Waffle with
Points*

Duncan Block (three examples)

Block and Pillar *Waffle Window* *Waffle
Octagon* *Banded Barrel*

PLATE 213. SQUARES AND RECTANGLES

GRILLE, creamer. This is square with the handle and spout on the corners. *Ref. K7-16.*

OVERALL LATTICE (MOESSER), creamer. Indiana Tumbler and Goblet Co. #38, 1897; Indiana Glass Co., 1904 – 1908. Extended table service including cordial, wine, ruffled bowl. Crystal, vaseline, ruby-stained. *Ref. K2-43; Gob II-107; Metz 2-152; H7-166+.*

PLAID, pitcher. Made ca. 1880s in extended table service including wine. Crystal. *Ref. L-76; LEAPG-164; Metz 1-163.*

WAFFLE KEG, salt shaker. A. H. Heisey Co. #1425. *Ref. PetSal 43C.*

CUBE, goblet. Boston and Sandwich Glass Co. Extended table service. Flint glass. *Ref. L-26; Metz 1-166.*

BEATTY HONEYCOMB (BEATTY WAFFLE), sugar shaker and cruet. Beatty and Sons Glass Co., ca. 1888; U. S. Glass Co., 1895. Extended table service including water set, rare perfume bottle. White and blue opalescent. Reproductions include rose bowl, covered sugar, pulled vase, and baskets in blue and green opalescent by Fenton in the late 1950s. *Ref. LV-69; HI-15; HII-18; HIII-16, 54; H6-19; Schroy-19; Mugs p. 102.*

SCREEN, salt shaker. *Ref. PetSal 171-0.*

ZENITH BLOCK, goblet. *Ref. Gob II-71; Metz 2-116.*

POINTED CUBE, wine goblet. Made ca. 1880s in a water set: decanter, tray, wine. *Ref. Metz 2-158.*

OPEN BASKETWEAVE (OPEN PLAID), creamer. Central Glass Co. #861, 1880s; U. S. Glass Co., 1891. Extended table service including cordial, plate, wine. Crystal. *Ref. K1-30; Gob I-127; Metz 1-162; Unitt 2-32.*

Grille

*Overall
Lattice*

Plaid

Waffle Keg

Cube

Beatty Honeycomb (two examples)

Screen

Zenith Block

Pointed Cube

*Open
Basketweave*

PLATE 214. SQUARES AND RECTANGLES

U. S. SHELL (DOYLE'S SHELL; SHELL; KNIGHT; CUBE AND FAN), creamer. Doyle and Co. in the 1880s; U. S. Glass Co., 1891 – 1898. Extended table service including waste bowl, water tray, mug, wine. Crystal, amber, ruby-stained, and possibly blue. The mug has only one row of squares-in-diamond. Heacock said this pattern was "similar to" Doyle's Shell; Dr. Charles Marlin points out that Kamm found the pattern "Shell" in a U. S. Glass Co. catalog, Doyle factory. They are obviously one and the same pattern. *Ref. K3-76; Mugs p. 88; H5-24 (no illustration); Gob II-84; Unitt 2-23; K3-76; K8-20; Schroy-53; H7-192.*

SKILTON (OREGON), goblet and covered compote. Richards and Hartley Flint Glass Co., 1888; U. S. Glass Co., 1891. Heacock says this was not the State Series for Oregon, although the original catalog names it "Oregon." U. S. Glass's "Beaded Loop" was the State Series pattern for Oregon. Extended table service including wine. Crystal, ruby-stained. *Ref. Gob II-59; LV-44; Metz 1-154; Unitt 1-252; H5-115; H7-164+; Schroy-132; Jenks p. 482.*

BLOCK AND FAN (ROMEO; BLOCK WITH FAN; BORDER), tumbler. Richards and Hartley #544, 1885; U. S. Glass Co., 1891; Extended table service including plates, lamp, wine, cordial, sugar shaker, castor set, cracker jar, ice tub. Crystal, ruby-stained, milk glass. *Ref. K3-75; LV-85; Gob I-57, 135; Metz 1-154; Revi-286; H5-108; H7-78.*

WAFFLE AND STAR BAND (BLOCK AND STAR SPEAR POINT; VERONA), creamer. Tarentum Glass Co., ca. 1910. Extended table service including punch bowl, wine. Crystal, ruby-stained. *Ref. K1-113; Gob II-110; Metz 1-118; Unitt 2-131; HTP-82; H7-209; Jenks p. 73; Schroy-23.*

COLUMN BLOCK (PANEL AND STAR), creamer. O'Hara Glass Co. #500, ca. 1890. Extended table service including rare toothpick holder. Crystal, vaseline. *Ref. K3-75; HIII-54; H6-23; Metz 1-156.*

SWAG BLOCK, creamer. U. S. Glass Co. (Duncan #326), 1891. Extended table service. Crystal, ruby-stained. *Ref. K3-130; H5-101; H7-37; Metz 2-142.*

CRADLED PRISMS, creamer. Challinor, Taylor, 1885. Extended table service including wine. *Ref. K4-112; Metz 2-174; Unitt 2-163.*

BLOCK AND SUNBURST, creamer. George Duncan and Sons, 1880s. Extended table service including wine, mug, tankard creamer. *Ref. K1-102.*

U.S. Shell

Skilton (two views)

Block and Fan

Waffle and
Star Band

Column Block

Swag Block

Cradled Prisms

Block and Sunburst

PLATE 215. SQUARES AND RECTANGLES

FANCY LOOP, spoon tray. A. H. Heisey #1205, 1898 – 1909. Extended table service including punch bowl and cups, cracker jar, bar tumbler, claret, champagne, sherry, wines. Crystal, colors, gilded. Compare this pattern with NEW JERSEY on Plate 85, and CRYSTAL QUEEN on Plate 91. *Ref. K2-97; HTP-50, 53; H7-115; Burns p. 16.*

RING AND BLOCK, etched tankard pitcher. U. S. Glass Co. (King), 1891. Extended table service. Crystal. *Ref. K4-128.*

REWARD, creamer. National Glass Co. (Riverside), 1901. Extended table service. Crystal, ruby-stained. *Ref. K5-109; HTP-83; H6-38; H7-185.*

STARRED BLOCK, creamer. Dalzell, Gilmore and Leighton, ca. 1896. Montgomery Ward sold a tankard-type pitcher in this pattern in 1896. Similar patterns are on Plates 52 and 77. *Ref. K4-114.*

CLARK, creamer. Extended table service. *Ref. LV-68.*

SANDWICH PLAID, plate. Made 1835 – 1845 in extended table service. All pieces are uncommon.

CO-OP BLOCK, etched creamer. Cooperative Flint Glass Co., 1899. Extended table service including wine. Crystal, ruby-stained. *Ref. K5-93; K6 Pl. 18; H6-24; H7-52+.*

Fancy Loop

Ring and Block

Reward

Starred Block

Clark

Sandwich Plaid

Co-op Block

PLATE 216. SQUARES AND RECTANGLES

DOYLE'S #80, creamer. Doyle and Co., ca. 1880; U. S. Glass Co., 1891. Extended table service. Crystal, colors, ruby-stained. *Ref. K8-48; H7-108.*

CUBE AND BLOCK, pitcher. U. S. Glass Co. (Richards and Hartley #401), 1891. Extended table service. Crystal, ruby-stained. *Ref. H5-180; H7-98.*

PICTURE WINDOW, etched pitcher. Central Glass Co. #870. Extended table service. *Ref. K4-139.*

THREE STORIES (BLOCK AND PLEAT; BRYCE PERSIAN), creamer. Bryce, Higbee and Co., 1885. Extended table service of over 35 different pieces including candy jar, mug, tray, wine. Crystal, amber, blue. *Ref. K5-36; K8-18; LEAPG-511; Metz I-159; Gob 1-24; Unitt 1-296; Mugs p. 103.*

PLUME AND BLOCK (FEATHER AND BLOCK), creamer. U. S. Glass Co. (Hartley #189), 1891. Extended table service. Crystal, ruby-stained. *Ref. K3-74; H7-98+.*

LATIN CROSS, creamer. Kamm says the stippled background contains scattered short raised bars "like crystalline spicules." *Ref. K3-35.*

KLONDIKE (ENGLISH HOBNAIL CROSS; AMBERETTE; ALASKA), creamer. Dalzell, Gilmore and Leighton #75, 1899. (Earlier attributions of A. J. Beatty and Sons and Hobbs, Brockunier were mistaken.) Extended table service including pickle boat, square tray, bud vase, champagne. Crystal, frosted, ruby-stained, amber-stained. *Ref. K2-100; K6 Pl. 15; Unitt 1-80; HI-28; H6-32; H7-136; Jenks p. 315; Schroy-87. (The Bredehofts discuss KLONDIKE, Hobbs, Brockunier and Co. Glass p. 165.)*

QUARTERED BLOCK, creamer. Duncan and Miller Glass Co. #55, 1903; Union Stopper Co., 1911. Extended table service including wine, champagne. *Ref. K2-90; K3-96; HTP-83; Metz 2-138; Jenks p. 426; Schroy-117; H7-167+.*

PILLOW BANDS, pitcher. Extended table service. *Ref. K2-77.*

Doyle's #80

Cube and Block

Picture Window

Three Stories

Plume and Block

Latin Cross

Klondike

Quartered Block

Pillow Bands

445

PLATE 217. SQUARES AND RECTANGLES

CROSSED BLOCK (ROMAN CROSS), goblet and detail. Made in the late 1800s in extended table service. *Ref. Gob II-31.*

PANELLED ENGLISH HOBNAIL (PANELLED STAR AND SQUARE; NOTCHED FINECUT), goblet and detail. Tarentum Glass Co., 1901. A wine is known. Crystal, ruby-stained. *Ref. L-86; Gob I-145; Metz 1-168; Unitt 1-164; Unitt 22-128; H7-168+.*

HOBBS' BLOCK (DIVIDED SQUARES), pitcher. Hobbs, Brockunier and Co. #330, 1889; U. S. Glass Co., 1891. Extended table service including water bottle, rose bowl, tankard ½-gallon. Crystal, Frances decoration, amber rims; flashed, decorated. Hobbs probably reworked molds from a pattern called Quartered Block with Stars, which is essentially the same except for little "stars" in some of the squares. Fenton Art Glass Co. reproduced Hobbs' Block in opaque colors. *Ref. K3-95; HIII-67; H5-19; Jenks p. 276; Schroy-75; Hobbs p. 113.*

BEADED BLOCK, IMPERIAL'S, jelly compote. Imperial Glass Co., 1927 – 1930s. Depression glass in large table service in many colors. Very similar to the next pattern except for the "frosted" blocks.

FROSTED BLOCK, creamer. Imperial Glass Co., 1913 – 1930s. Late ware was colored in "Depression Glass" pink, chartreuse, and apple green. Extended table service. Crystal, many colors, vaseline opalescent. *Ref. K1-98; K3-26; Metz 1-230.*

MALTESE CROSS, pitcher. U. S. Glass Co. (Duncan #1003), 1891. Extended table service including water tray, finger bowl, pickle jar. Crystal. *Ref. Gob I-35; K5-31; H5-104; H6-88.*

TAPPAN, toy creamer. McKee Glass Co., 1894. Toy basic table service. Crystal, amber. *Ref. K3-127; HTP-54.*

BASKETWEAVE (PLAID), syrup. Possibly Columbia Glass Co., ca. 1885 in extended table service including egg cups, lamp, mug, 12" tray, wine, cordials. Crystal, amber, blue, canary, vaseline, apple green, opaque white. *Ref. L-104; K5-51; Gob I-127; Metz 1-162; LEAPG-526; Unitt 2-27; Schroy-15; Jenks p. 50; Mugs p. 102.*

Crossed Block

Panelled Eng.
Hobnail

Hobbs' Block

Beaded Block,
Imperial's

Frosted Block

Maltese Cross

Tappan

Basketweave

PLATE 218. SQUARES AND RECTANGLES

ROMAN KEY (FROSTED ROMAN KEY; GREEK KEY; ROMAN KEY WITH RIBS), celery vase. Boston and Sandwich; Union Glass Co. Extended table service including champagne, wines, cordial. Flint glass. *Ref. L-94; LEAPG-302; Gob I-72; Gob II-150; Metz 1-36; Schroy-121; Jenks p. 448.*

VICTORIAN JUBILEE, pitcher. Made ca. 1897 in extended table service. The open compote bears a medallion portrait of Queen Victoria. *Ref. K3-59.*

PLAIN ROMAN KEY (CLEAR ROMAN KEY), creamer. Boston and Sandwich Glass Co. Extended table service including cordial, wine, champagne, master salt. *Ref. K3-18; Metz 1-36; Gob I-17; Unitt 1-65.*

HEISEY'S GREEK KEY (GRECIAN BORDER), creamer. A. H. Heisey Glass Co. #433, #433½, 1911. Extended table service including very rare toothpick holder, sundae dish, sherbet, banana split dish, wine, cordial, claret, champagne. Crystal, pinkish crystal. *Ref. K8-51; HI-50; HTP-87.*

GREEK KEY, master salt. Portland Glass Co. Extended table service including ice tub, lamp, sherbet, wine, cordial. *Ref. Swan p. 89.*

U. S. SHERATON (GREEK KEY), creamer. U. S. Glass Co. #15144, 1912. Extended table service including miniature lamp, mustard jar, jam jar, several sugar bowls, dresser set and tray, ring stand, toothpick holder, pin tray, "sanitary" toothpick holder shaped rather like a matchbox. Crystal, light green, gilded with gold or platinum. *Ref. K5-100; Schroy-148; H5-158; HTP-91; Mugs p. 100, 101.*

ROMAN KEY BASE, salt shaker. Milk glass. *Ref. PetSal 37M.*

ROMAN KEY COLLAR, salt shaker. Extended table service. Milk glass. *Ref. PetSal 37N.*

PANELLED ROMAN KEY, salt shaker. Extended table service. *Ref. PetSal 37O; K3-18.*

ROMAN KEY, FROSTED BAND, goblet. Extended table service including champagne. *Ref. Gob II-150.*

Roman Key

Victorian Jubilee

Plain Roman Key

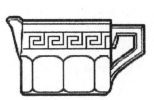

Heisey's Greek Key

Greek Key

U.S. Sheraton

*Roman Key
Base*

*Roman Key
Collar*

*Panelled
Roman Key*

*Roman Key,
Frosted Band*

PLATE 219. STARS

WHEAT AND BURR, goblet. Made ca. 1895 in extended table service including wine, mug. Courtesy of Bob Burford. *Ref. Ware, Glass Collector's Digest Vol. VII #4 (Dec. 1993 – Jan. 1994) p. 86, 87; Heacock, Rare & Unlisted Toothpick Holders (1984) p. 55 #1289.*

STAR AND LINES, mug. Possibly by Westmoreland, ca. 1900. *Ref. Mugs p. 108.*

STAR AND PUNTY, pitcher. Boston and Sandwich Glass Co., early. Known pieces include lamp, cologne bottle, creamer, pitcher, sugar bowl. Scarce. *Ref. K5-86.*

STAR AND CIRCLE, goblet. Extended table service including 5½" compote, rare flint goblet. Flint glass. *Ref. Gob II-8; Metz 1-14.*

DOYLE'S #400 (BANDED PRISM BAR), spoon holder. Doyle and Co.; U. S. Glass Co., 1891. Extended table service. Crystal, amber. *Ref. Gob II-53; K7-73; Metz 1-120.*

SANDWICH STAR AND BUCKLE, pitcher. Boston and Sandwich Glass Co., early. Pieces known include spill holder, syrup, cologne bottles. *Ref. K2-9.*

HEXAGON STAR, salt shaker. Made ca.1900 and known also in toothpick holder and spooner. Its name refers to the six sides of the whole shaker. *Ref. PetSal 173K; HTP-83; Heacock showed the spooner in a July 8, 1981 article in the Antique Trader.*

DAGGER, salt shaker. Extended table service. Crystal, ruby-stained. *Ref. PetSal 26Q; H7-63+.*

STAR WITH ZIPPERS, salt shaker. Federal Glass Co., 1914. *Ref. HGC4 p. 22.*

Wheat and Burr

Star and Lines

Star and Punty

Star and Circle

Doyle's #400

*Sandwich Star
and Buckle*

Hexagon Star

Dagger

*Star with
Zippers*

PLATE 220. STARS

STAR AND BAR, salt shaker. (Do not confuse with **"Stars and Bars"** on Plate 96.) *Ref. PetSal 173C.*

STAR AND DART, butter dish. Made ca. 1850s in basic table service. Flint glass. *Ref. Metz 1-14.*

STARLYTE, pitcher. Lancaster Glass Co., 1910. Extended table service. Crystal. *Ref. K3-101.*

STAR-OF-BETHLEHEM (NEARCUT STAR; CUT STAR; CAMBRIDGE STAR), toilet bottle and pitcher. Cambridge Glass Co. #2656, 1907. Extended table service including water bottle, champagne, claret, wine, cordial, soda glass. Crystal, ruby-stained. *Ref. K7-178; Revi-96; H7-158; Barret p. 14.*

STARGLOW, pitcher. U. S. Glass Co. #15120 (Gas City), 1910. Extended table service including wine, castor set, vase. *Ref. H5-155.*

QUEEN'S JEWELS (QUEEN'S NECKLACE; CROWN JEWELS), salt shaker. Bellaire Goblet Co. #101, 1889; U. S. Glass Co., 1891. Extended table service including cologne bottle, pickle jar, wine. No goblet was made. Crystal. *Ref. K3-78; Revi-66, Unitt 2-185; H5-22 (no illustration).*

BETHLEHEM STAR (BRIGHT STAR; STARBURST), toothpick holder. Indiana Glass Co., 1910 – 1920. Extended table service including wine. Crystal. *Ref. K3-78; Gob II-104; Unitt 1-289; HTP-91; Jenks p. 63; Schroy-21.*

ZANESVILLE, squat syrup. Robinson Glass Co. #122; McKee Glass Co., 1901. Extended table service including tall syrup, blown and pressed shakers. Crystal, ruby-stained. *Ref. HI-45; H6-66; H7-17+.*

Star and Bar

Star and Dart

Starlyte

Star-of-Bethlehem (two views)

Starglow

Queen's Jewels

Bethlehem Star

Zanesville

PLATE 221. STARS

AMERICAN SHIELD (SHIELD), goblet. Made ca. 1876. Kamm thought it might be a Pennsylvania product because of the star in a keystone on the shield, the emblem of that state. Between the two shields is an outline of a keystone with the inscription "1776, July 4, 1876." Crystal, ruby-stained. *Ref. K7-72; Metz 1-120; H7-192.*

BANDED STAR, creamer and detail of rim. King, Son and Co., ca. 1880. Extended table service. *Ref. K4-110; Metz 1-120.*

CENTENNIAL SHIELD (FLAG), pitcher. Extended table service. *Ref. K3-58; Metz 1-120.*

STAR AND SWAG, bowl. *Ref. L-190.*

JEWELLED MOON AND STAR (MOON AND STAR VARIATION; MOON AND STAR WITH WAFFLED STEM; LATE MOON AND STAR; COOP IMPERIAL), goblet. Wilson Glass Co., ca. 1890; Cooperative Flint Glass Co., 1896. Extended table service including egg cup, bread tray, individual open salt, wine. Crystal, frosted "moons," ruby-stained, decorated. The original name was "Imperial." The wine has been reproduced. *Ref. K1-131; Metz 1-210; Unitt 1-305; Gob II-62; HIII-48, 84; H7-241.*

DEWDROP AND STAR, goblet. Extended table service. *Ref. L-154 #4; K7-71; Metz 2-104.*

STAR AND THUMBPRINT (OLD MOON AND STAR), open sugar bowl. New England Glass Co., ca. 1840s. Extended table service including spill holder, lamp. All pieces are rare. Crystal, canary. *Ref. K8-72.*

TWINKLE STAR VARIANT, goblet. Only this piece known. The stars are six-pointed, and pressed from the outside, author's name.

STAR AND IVY, cup. Model Flint Glass Co., 1890s. Has a saucer without the star. Crystal, light and dark amber, blue. *Ref. Mugs p. 108.*

American Shield   *Banded Star*   *Centennial Shield*

Star and Swag   *Jewelled Moon and Star*   *Dewdrop and Star*

Star and Thumbprint   *Twinkle Star Variant*   *Star and Ivy*

455

PLATE 222. STARS

UTAH (TWINKLE STAR; STARLIGHT; FROST FLOWER), salt shaker, goblet, pitcher. U. S. Glass Co. #15080 (Gas City), 1903; Federal Glass Co., ca. 1914. A State Series pattern. Extended table service including wine. Crystal, frosted. The stars are impressed on the inside of each piece. *Ref. K4-122; Gob I-38; Metz 2-104; Unitt 1-286; Unitt 2-247; H5-166; Jenks p. 534; Schroy-149.*

STIPPLED SANDBUR (STIPPLED STAR VARIANT; COCKLE BURR), goblet. Beatty-Brady Glass Co., 1903. Extended table service including wine. Crystal. *Ref. Gob II-41; K1-103; Metz 1-117; Unitt 1-286.*

SHUTTLE (HEARTS OF LOCH LAVEN), mug. Indiana Tumbler and Goblet Co. #329, 1896; Indiana Glass Co., 1898. Extended table service including punch cups, champagne, wine, cordial. Crystal, chocolate, caramel. *Ref. K8-24; Gob I-30; Metz I-310; Jenks p. 481; Schroy-132; Unitt 2-78; Mugs p. 73.*

EFFULGENT STAR (STAR GALAXY; ALL OVER STARS), mug. Central Glass Co. #876, 1880. Extended table service including wine. Crystal, amber, blue. *Ref. K8-78; Gob II-122; Metz 1-117; Metz 2-104; Mugs p. 110; HPV3 p. 9.*

STAR ROSETTED (SNOWFLAKE; GENERAL GRANT), goblet and detail. McKee and Brothers, 1875. Extended table service including wine, 10" plate featuring the motto "A Good Mother." Crystal. *Ref. K5-10; L-98; LEAPG-529; Gob I-38; Metz 1-116; Unitt 1-97; Jenks p. 491; Schroy-135.*

STAR AND PILLAR (PARIS; STARS AND BARS), creamer. McKee Glass Co., 1880. Extended table service including wine, champagne. Crystal. *Ref. L-154; #17; Gob I-122; Metz 2-104; K8-14.*

STIPPLED STAR, pitcher. Gillinder and Sons, 1870s. Extended table service including egg cup, bread plate, wine. Crystal. The goblet and wine have been reproduced, as have other pieces in color. *Ref. L-147; Gob I-38; Metz 1-117; Unitt 1-286; LEAPG-479; Jenks p. 498; Schroy-137.*

Utah (Twinkle Star) (three examples)

Stippled Sandbur   *Shuttle*   *Effulgent Star*

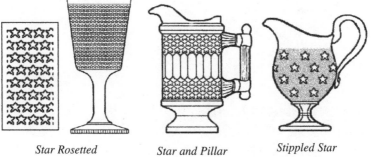

Star Rosetted   *Star and Pillar*   *Stippled Star*

PLATE 223. STARS

FEDERAL #1609 (CO-OP #294), wine goblet. Cooperative Flint Glass Co., 1900; Federal Glass Co., ca. 1914. The wine and cordial are also known, courtesy of John Gregory. *Ref. HGC4 p. 20; Welker p. 342.*

SHRINE (JEWEL WITH MOON AND STAR; JEWELLED MOON AND STAR; ORIENT), mug. Beatty-Brady Glass Co., 1896; Indiana Glass Co., 1904; Extended table service including two sizes of salt shaker, wine, champagne. Crystal, frosted. *Ref. K1-101; LV-35; Metz 1-116; Unitt 1-155; HPV1-19; PGP 3-6; Schroy-131; Jenks p. 480; Mugs p. 317.*

BOXED STAR, pitcher. Jenkins Glass Co., ca. 1908; Federal Glass Co. Extended table service. *Ref. K7-12; HGC3 p. 17.*

DIAMOND, vase. Ohio Flint Glass Co., 1896. Extended table service. Crystal, ruby-stained. *Ref. K6 Pl. 67; H7-6+.*

FESTOONED STARS, goblet. *Ref. Gob II-112.*

STAR IN HONEYCOMB (LA VERNE), pitcher. Bryce Brothers #80, late 1880; U. S. Glass, 1891. Extended table service including wine. Crystal. *Ref. K2-122; K8-62; Gob I-168; Metz 1-118; Unitt 1-132.*

FEATHERED STAR, pitcher. Union Stopper Co., ca. 1908. Extended table service. *Ref. HPV #2 p. 4.*

Federal #1609

Shrine

Diamond

Boxed Star

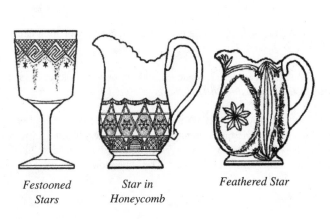

Festooned
Stars

Star in
Honeycomb

Feathered Star

PLATE 224. SWIRLS

TEXAS STAR, salt shaker. See Plates 110 & 179.

CYCLONE (GRECIAN SWIRL), butter dish. O'Hara Glass Co., 1880s; U. S. Glass, 1891. Extended table service including champagne, wine. *Ref. LV-207; Metz 2-110.*

LEANING PILLARS, syrup. Syrup and sugar shaker known, made ca. 1895. Crystal, amber, pale blue, amethyst. *Ref. HIII-31.*

NICKEL PLATE #26, pitcher. Nickel Plate Glass Co., 1890; U. S. Glass Co., 1891. Extended table service including covered cheese dish, mustard pot. *Ref. K5-102.*

FOSTORIA'S SWIRL, creamer. Fostoria Glass Co. #175, 1890. Extended table service including vase, castor set, water bottle. *Ref. K5-90.*

RIGHT SWIRL, goblet. *Ref. Gob II-154.*

PINWHEEL, plate. Extended table service including child's punch set. *Ref. L-44; Metz 1-194.*

NARROW SWIRL, creamer. George Duncan and Sons. This was a sales container for mustard, horseradish, honey, etc. and had a metal lid. *Ref. K1-109.*

BLOWN SWIRL (FRANCESWARE SWIRL; WINDOWS), sugar shaker. Hobbs, Brockunier and Co. #326, 1889. Extended table service including mustard jar, finger bowl, waste bowl, castor set in metal frame, covered cheese dish, sugar shaker, lamp shades. The "Windows" name applies to an opalescent line with "dots." Crystal, amber-stained, frosted. Fenton has reproduced the covered sugar, but without a lid finial; also the cruet and salt shaker in colors including an opaque powder blue and ruby opalescent. *Ref. K6-68; Hobbs p. 108.*

BANDED SWIRL, goblet. A wine is also known, courtesy of John Gregory. *Ref. Gob II-105; Metz 1-200; Metz 2-105.*

RIDGE SWIRL, sugar shaker. Made ca. 1900 in only this piece. Crystal, cobalt, amber, emerald green. *Ref. Taylor Pl. 1; HIII-38.*

PARIAN SWIRL (PARIAN RUBY), syrup. Northwood Glass Co., 1894. Extended table service including sugar shaker, night lamp. Montgomery Ward sold it in 1894. It has an artichoke-shaped finial on covered pieces. Satin camphor, cranberry, blue satin, light green opaque, decorated. Not made in crystal. The same molds were used for "Royal Ivy." *Ref. K5-89; HI-35; HIII-35; H6-36.*

Texas Star   Cyclone   Leaning Pillars   Nickel Plate #26

Fostoria's Swirl   Right Swirl   Pinwheel   Narrow Swirl

Blown Swirl   Banded Swirl   Ridge Swirl   Parian Swirl

PLATE 225. SWIRLS

LUTZ (SWIRL AND BALL VARIANT), pitcher. McKee and Brothers, 1894. Extended table service including mustard jar, pickle jar. Crystal. *Ref. K2-106; Mugs p. 104, 105.*

BALL AND SWIRL (SWIRL AND BALL; RAY; SWIRL BAND; BALL AND SWIRL BAND; FROSTED BALL AND SWIRL), goblet, tankard creamer and etched creamer. McKee Brothers, 1894; made into the 1930s. Extended table service including cordial set, 6" plate, candlestick, wine. A two-ringed stemmed wine is also known. Crystal. *Ref. K1-110; K3-49; Gob II-32; Metz 1-145; Mugs p. 104, 105; Jenks p. 38; Schroy-12.*

DOUBLE LINE SWIRL, goblet. The wine is known, courtesy of John Gregory. *Ref. Gob II-20; Metz 2-112.*

PRESSED SWIRL, cruet. U. S. Glass Co. (Central), 1891. Only cruet known in crystal, amber, blue. The stopper is a ball with swirls. *Ref. HIII-56; H5-33; H6-37.*

SWIRL BAND, etched mug and creamer. Probably by Burlington Glass Works, 1880s (Adams/Mordock). There was at least a basic table service made plus goblet and mug. Crystal, etched. *Ref. K2-12; Mugs p. 104, 105.*

SWIRL WITH BEADED BAND (NOVA SCOTIA BUTTONS AND BOWS), goblet. Wine or champagne is known. *Ref. Gob II-147; Metz 1-200; Unitt 1-134.*

SPOOL STEM SWIRL, goblet. *Ref. Gob II-154.*

EAST LIVERPOOL, etched creamer. East Liverpool Glass Co. of East Liverpool, Ohio, 1882 – 1883. Extended table service including cordial, wine, 10" plate. This company had barely started production when the factory burned, so this pattern is limited. *Ref. K4-69.*

SWIRL AND CABLE, creamer. Dalzell, Gilmore and Leighton, shown in a Butler Brothers catalog in spring, 1893. (Butler Brothers was a distribution company, not a manufacturer.) The sugar, creamer, and celery are known for sure, courtesy of Dr. Charles Marlin. Crystal. *Ref. K2-85; Mugs p. 106.*

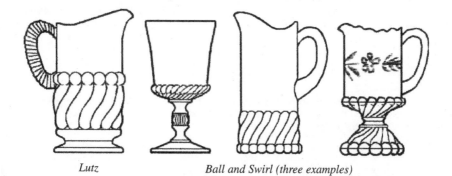

Lutz   *Ball and Swirl (three examples)*

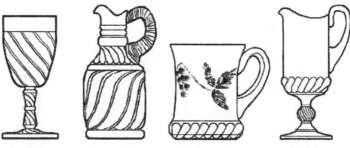

Double Line   *Pressed Siwrl*   *Swirl Band (two examples)*
Swirl

Swirl with   *Spool Stem*   *East Liverpool*   *Swirl and Cable*
Beaded Band   *Swirl*

463

PLATE 226. SWIRLS

ORINOCO, creamer. A. J. Beatty and Co., 1888. Extended table service. *Ref. K5-111.*

FLAME (SERRATED RIBS), bowl and castor bottle. Duncan Glass Co. #1000, ca. 1884; U. S. Glass Co., ca. 1898. Known in castor sets, pickle jar, mustard, salt shaker, bowls with silver frames. Courtesy of Bob Burford. *Ref. Krause, Glass Review, May 1984 p. 14; Duncan p. 89.*

WIDE SWIRL, salt shaker. *Ref. PetSal 41M.*

TWO PLY SWIRL, syrup. George Duncan and Son #51, 1902. Extended table service. An early ad stated that there were 75 to 100 pieces in this line in crystal and color-stained. *Ref. PetSal 41J; H7-39, 206.*

SLASHED SWIRL (SWIRL AND DIAMOND; AMERICA; SWIRL AND SAWTOOTH; SWIRL AND DIAMOND WITH OVALS), pitcher. American Glass Co., 1890; Riverside Glass Works #348, 1891; U. S. Glass Co., 1891. Extended table service including wine, carafe. Crystal, ruby-stained. Some pieces in this set could be entirely different patterns; see Plate 231 for the tumbler which has diamond point around the swirls, and has been known as "Swirl and Diamond," or "America." *Ref. K1-112; K2-106; K6 Pl. 11, 33 & p. 32; Gob II-131; Metz 1-212; H7-199, 219.*

BAR AND SWIRL, goblet. *Ref. Gob II-79; Metz 2-110.*

PECAN SWIRL, tankard pitcher. *Ref. K4-102.*

SWIRL WITH FAN, tankard pitcher. *Ref. K3-95.*

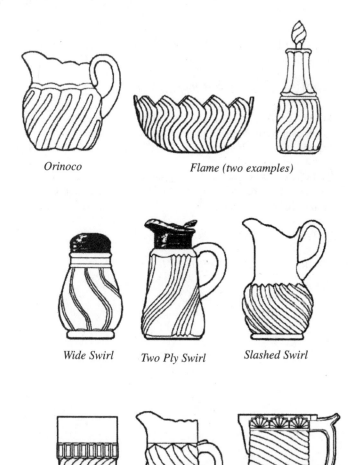

Orinoco   *Flame (two examples)*

Wide Swirl   *Two Ply Swirl*   *Slashed Swirl*

Bar and Swirl   *Pecan Swirl*   *Swirl with Fan*

PLATE 227. SWIRLS

RIB AND SWIRL, salt shaker. milk glass. *Ref. PetSal 170B.*

DIAGONAL BAR BAND, salt shaker and creamer. Made ca. 1880s in extended table service. *Ref. K2-12.*

DIAGONAL FROSTED RIBBON, goblet. Duncan Glass Co., ca. 1880s. Extended table service including oil lamp, square plate. *Ref. Gob II-23; Metz 1-171; Metz 2-42.*

PEBBLED SWIRL, goblet. *Ref. Gob II-20; Metz 2-110.*

CLEAR DIAGONAL BAND (CALIFORNIA), creamer. Ripley & Co., 1879. Extended table service including wine, cordial, jam jar, "Eureka" bread plate. Crystal. *Ref. K1-44; L-156; LEAPG-558; Gob I-112; Metz 1-172; Revi-294; Schroy-35; Jenks p. 123.*

SLASHED SWIRL BORDER, goblet. Possibly the Burlington factory in Canada. Extended table service including footed sauces and bowls, footed creamer. Crystal, engraved. Courtesy of Bob Burford. *Ref. Unitt 1-77.*

FISHSCALE SWIRL, goblet. *Ref. Gob II-51; Metz 2-112.*

RING AND SWIRL, goblet. *Ref. Gob II-139; Metz 2-168.*

Rib and Swirl   *Diagonal Bar Band (two examples)*

Diagonal   *Pebbled*   *Clear*
Frosted   *Swirl*   *Diagonal*
Ribbon   *Band*

Slashed Swirl   *Fishscale*   *Ring and Swirl*
Border   *Swirl*

PLATE 228. SWIRLS

PILGRIM BOTTLE, salt shaker. Belmont Glass Co., ca. 1882; Central Glass Co. Extended table service. Crystal, amber, blue, vaseline. Kamm couldn't believe that the creamer she found was part of a set; she thought it might have been a whiskey container. The creamer's swirls are not as pronounced as the salt shaker, being more like a thick rope. *Ref. K6-21; HIII-35.*

SWIRLED COLUMN (BEADED SWIRL), creamer and mug. George A. Duncan and Sons #335, 1890; U. S. Glass Co. #15085, 1904. Extended table service including sugar shaker, tankard creamer, wine, cordial. Crystal, light green, dark green, ruby-stained, gilded. *Ref. LV-41; K3-113; Gob II-79; Metz 2-110; H5-45; H7-74; Mugs p. 104; Jenks p. 56; Schroy-18.*

BEADED SWIRL AND DISC, mug. East Liverpool Glass Co., ca. 1890s; U. S. Glass Co. #15085 (Bryce), 1904. Extended table service. Crystal, blue, green, and stained "discs" of amber, yellow, fuchsia. *Ref. K8-36; HI-14; H5-164 & 177; Mugs p. 104.*

FLICKERING FLAME (ZANZIBAR), creamer. Westmoreland Glass Co., 1896. Basic table service plus rare syrup. Sometimes painted red in the grooves. Milk glass, opaque colors. *Ref. K2-92; Schroy-161; HTP-56.*

WAVEY (WAVE), tankard creamer. Probably a container for mustard, jelly, honey, pickles, etc. *Ref. K7-44.*

CHALLINOR #27, pitcher. U. S. Glass Co. (Challinor), 1891. Opaque glass with painted flowers. *Ref. H5-55.*

PURITAN, mug. Westmoreland Specialty Co., ca. 1900. Known in three sizes mug, creamer. Crystal, blue, amethyst, yellowish green, and dark brown; ruby-stained, gilded. *Ref. HCGI p. 82; H77-178+; Mugs p. 104.*

BEADED SWIRL AND LENS, creamer. Crystal, colored "lens." *Ref. K3-95; H6-19; H7-74+.*

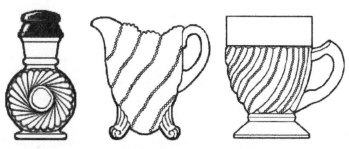

Pilgrim Bottle   *Swirled Column (two examples)*

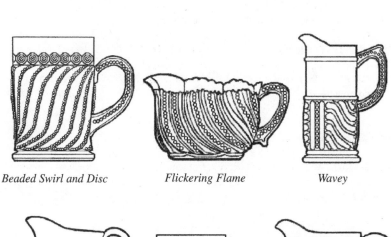

Beaded Swirl and Disc   *Flickering Flame*   *Wavey*

 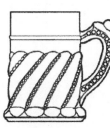 

Challinor #27   *Puritan*   *Beaded Swirl and Lens*

PLATE 229. SWIRLS

RUFFLES, salt shaker. U. S. Glass Co. #15008 (Gillinder), 1891. Extended table service. Crystal, ruby-stained. *Ref. K6 Pl. 36; H7-189.*

HEAVY DRAPE, pitcher. Fostoria Glass Co. #1300, 1904. Extended table service including egg cup, wine, cordial, egg cup. Crystal, ruby-stained. *Ref. K7-39; K8-91; HTP-83; H7-126+.*

COOLIDGE DRAPE, oil lamp. A lamp like this was in the room where Calvin Coolidge took the oath of office after President Harding's death. Found in crystal, cobalt blue. *Ref. Schroy-161; Metz 1-13.*

SCALLOPED SWIRL (YORK HERRINGBONE), salt shaker. Ripley and Co., 1885; U. S. Glass Co. #15026, 1892. Extended table service including wine. Crystal, ruby-stained, green (scarce), blue (scarce). *Ref. K6 Pl. 32; Gob I-45; Gob II-141; Schroy-128; Metz 2-141; HI-39; H5-51; H7-191.*

CURTAIN AND BLOCK, salt shaker. *Ref. PetSal 26L.*

SWIRL AND DOT, celery vase. Extended table service. *Ref. LV-63; Metz 2-112.*

DIAMOND PRISMS, goblet. Indiana Tumbler and Goblet Co., 1900. Extended table service including wine. *Ref. Gob II-58; Metz 1-156; Unitt 1-248; Metz 2-116; H7-65; Measell p. 51.*

KOKOMO, etched spooner. See Plate 42.

CURTAIN (SULTAN), celery vase. Bryce Brothers, 1875 – 1885. Extended table service including waste bowl, square plate. Crystal; rare in amber; possibly made in blue. *Ref. K3-118; L-85; LEAPG-322; Jenks p. 144; Schroy-41; Metz 1-130; Mugs p. 106.*

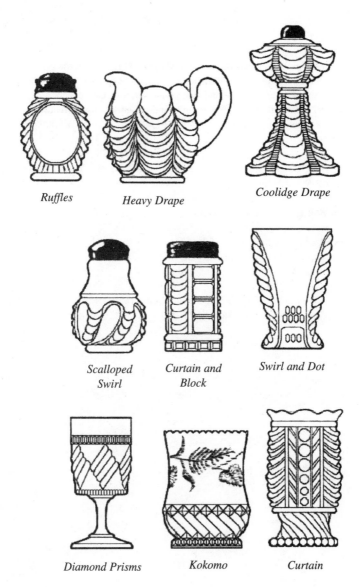

Ruffles *Heavy Drape* *Coolidge Drape*

Scalloped Swirl *Curtain and Block* *Swirl and Dot*

Diamond Prisms *Kokomo* *Curtain*

PLATE 230. SWIRLS

KING'S #500 (PARROT; BONE STEM; SWIRL AND THUMBPRINT), syrup. King Glass Co., 1890; U. S. Glass Co.; 1891 – 1910. Extended table service including rare oil lamp, rare salt shaker, cologne bottle, wine. Crystal, cobalt blue, ruby-stained, gilded. *Ref. K5-71; K8-72; Metz 2-116; Unitt 1-316; HIII-29; H5-37, 42; H6-32; H7-137; Jenks p. 309; Schroy-86*

S-REPEAT, toothpick holder (reproduction), and syrup. Operators of the Northwood Glass Co., ca. 1900; National Glass Co., 1903; Dugan-Diamond Glass Co., 1904. Extended table service including rare jelly compote, decanter, wine set, tray. Goblets are new; also reproduced were large wines, toothpick holders. Crystal, amethyst, light green, sapphire blue; limited colors of blue opalescent and carnival glass. *Ref. K4-115; HPV4 p. 9; HI-41; HIII-41, 59; H6-40+.*

FOSTORIA'S VICTORIA, tumbler and creamer. Fostoria Glass Co. #183, 1890. Extended table service. *Ref. K5-73.*

DOUBLE SCROLL, pitcher. See Plate 32.

WEDDING BELLS, cruet. Fostoria Glass Co. #789, ca. 1901. Extended table service including egg cup, punch bowl, wine. Crystal, rose-flashed. *Ref. K4-113; K6-Pl. 91; HIII-45; H6-45.*

DOUBLE SNAIL, pitcher. George Duncan and Sons, 1890 – 1891. Known in four sizes of pitchers. Crystal, ruby-stained. *Ref. K5 Pl. 30; Metz 1-209; Metz 2-168; H7-107, 194.*

IDAHO (SNAIL), goblet. See Plate 15.

King's #500

S-Repeat (repro)

S-Repeat

Fostoria's Victoria (two views)

Double Scroll

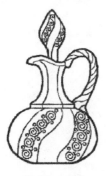

Wedding Bells

Double Snail

Idaho

PLATE 231. SWIRLS

SLASHED SWIRL, tumbler. See Plate 226.

FEATHER, salt shaker and tumbler. See Plate 74.

SWIRLED STAR, spoon holder. Jefferson Glass Co. (Canadian plant), ca. 1885 – 1895. *Ref. K7-75.*

FOSTORIA #1641, toothpick holder. Fostoria Glass Co., 1909 – 1913. Extended table service including molasses can with silver or nickel top, cracker jar, sugar shaker, tumblers. Some pieces were reproduced in 1969, called "Sovereign" as part of the Centennial II collection. Courtesy of Bob Burford of the Early American Pattern Glass Society. *Ref. Kerr p. 125.*

JERSEY SWIRL (SWIRL; WINDSOR SWIRL; SWIRL AND DIAMONDS), tumbler. Windsor Glass Co., 1886. Extended table service including wines, bread plate, two sizes of goblet, salt dip. Crystal, amber, blue, canary. The goblet and wine have been reproduced. *Ref. K3-49; L-69; Metz 1-200; Unitt 1-136; Gob I-28; Unitt 2-216; Jenks p. 301; Schroy-83.*

DIAMOND SWIRL (ZIPPERED SWIRL AND DIAMOND), sugar bowl. U. S. Glass Co. #15042, 1895. Extended table service including wine, cordial. Crystal, ruby-stained. *Ref. K4-93; K6 Pl. 33; H5-51; Batty p. 144.*

SWIRL AND PANEL, salt shaker. Made ca. 1900 in extended table service including toothpick holder, egg cup. *Ref. PetSal 40X.*

SPIRALLED DIAMOND POINT, sugar bowl or pickle jar (4 inches high.) *Ref. K8-75.*

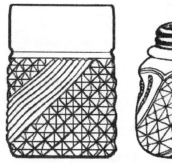

Slashed Swirl

Feather (two examples)

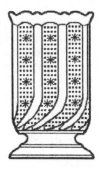

Swirled Star

Fostoria #1641

Jersey Swirl

Diamond Swirl

Swirl and Panel

Spiralled Diamond
Point

PLATE 232. ODDS AND ENDS

LOG CABIN, creamer and covered compote. Central Glass Co., 1875. Extended table service including rare pitcher, covered vegetable bowl. Crystal. *Ref. K8-59; L-106; LEAPG-477; Schroy-91; Metz 1-6; Jenks p. 334.*

BRANCHED TREE, pitcher. Dalzell, Gilmore and Leighton, 1890s. Extended table service. Crystal, amber, blue. *Ref. K4-124.*

THE TOWN PUMP (PUMP AND TROUGH), creamer. Northwood Glass Co., 1907. It came in a set of sugar and creamer. The sugar bowl is an oblong hollowed-out log on little feet, a trough. Opalescent colors of white, blue, and canary; emerald green. Some pieces are signed "Northwood" in script. There are reproductions. *Ref. K2-108; HII-38.*

LEGGED TROUGH, creamer. Under the base there is a spray of berries. *Ref. K7-56.*

WOODEN PAIL (OAKEN BUCKET; BUCKET SET), creamer. Bryce Brothers, 1880s; U. S. Glass Co., 1891. Extended table service including jelly buckets, ice bucket, toy set. Crystal, amber, blue, canary, amethyst (rare). *Ref. K1-55; H5-36, 44, 81; Jenks p. 561.*

PICKET (PICKET FENCE; FENCE; LONDON), pitcher. King Glass Co., late 1880s. Extended table service including jam jar, wine, water tray, match holder (collected as a toothpick holder.) Crystal, blue, apple green, amber, frosted; plain, stippled. *Ref. K1-88; L-107; LEAPG-484; Gob I-175; Metz 1-132; Schroy-111; Jenks p. 404; Unitt 1-146; HI-35.*

LOG HOUSE, creamer. Adams and Co., 1871 – 1872. Basic table service. *Ref. K5-41.*

TREEBARK, pitcher. Extended table service. Crystal, amber. *Ref. K1-48; Metz 1-87.*

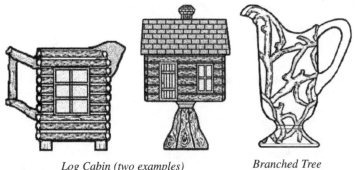

Log Cabin (two examples)   *Branched Tree*

   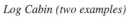   

The Town Pump   *Legged Trough*   *Wooden Pail*

Picket   *Log House*   *Treebark*

PLATE 233. ODDS AND ENDS

ORANGE PEEL BAND, goblet. A variation on the next pattern. *Ref. Gob II-94; Metz 2-108.*

ORANGE PEEL, goblet. Wine is also known. *Ref. Gob I-64; Metz 1-183; Metz 2-108; Unitt 2-37.*

SNAKESKIN (OVERSHOT), goblet and plate. Extended table service. *Ref. L-135; LEAPG-238.*

CAPE COD, goblet. Boston and Sandwich, 1870s. The pattern is much like CANADIAN except for scenes, which show shorelines with tree, sailboat, lighthouse, etc. Extended table service including jam jar, four sizes plates, cordials, wine, cup and saucer. Crystal. *Ref. L-115; LEAPG-328; Jenks p. 107; K8-68; Gob I-176; Metz 1-110; Unitt 1-137.*

LITTLE RIVER, pickle jar. The scenes on this piece show water views with a large mill wheel on the water, an arched bridge with a church building on rocks with tall trees, a stream with a man in a row boat, etc. Kamm doesn't show the windmill pictured here, which appeared in a Wallace-Homestead Price Guide some years ago. A pickle castor is also known. *Ref. K8-74; Schroy-161.*

CANADIAN, pitcher. Burlington Glass Works in Ontario, Canada, 1870s. Extended table service including jam jar, bread tray, wine, cordial. Crystal. *Ref. L-112; LEAPG-327; K1-40; Gob I-35; Schroy-30; Jenks p. 103; Metz 1-110.*

SHELL AND TASSEL SQUARE, tray. See Plate 5.

TREE OF LIFE, goblet. Boston and Sandwich; Portland Glass; Beatty-Brady Glass Co., 1898. Duncan Glass; U. S. Glass (1891), Hobbs, Brockunier & Co., 1879; 1868; 1873. Extended table service including egg cup, wines, cordials, champagne, lamp shade, ice cream tray. One very unique piece has a pitcher that fits on a stand and has a hook on it from which hangs a mug. Hobbs used satin finishes on finials and feet. Crystal, amber, light and dark blue, green, cranberry, canary, amethyst. The colors are not common. There has been some reproduction, particularly a leaf-shaped dish in copper or red, and the wine. *Ref. K3-120; LV-11, 12; L-52; Metz 1-138; Metz 2-120; Gob I-80; Jenks p. 524; Schroy-145; Hobbs p. 56; Mugs p. 109.*

CANTON HOUSE, creamer. The creamer is also seen without the house. *Ref. K5-16.*

Orange Peel Band

Orange Peel

Snakeskin (two examples)

Cape Cod

Little River

Canadian

Shell and Tassel Square

Tree of Life

Canton House

PLATE 234. ODDS AND ENDS

BAMBOO BEAUTY, creamer. U. S. Glass Co. (Columbia), 1891; Basic table service. Crystal. *Ref. H5-128.*

TILE (OPTICAL CUBE), goblet and pitcher. Thompson Glass Co. #19, 1890. Extended table service of 75 items in all. *Ref. K6-22; Gob II-70.*

BELLAIRE BASKETWEAVE, cruet. Bellaire Goblet Co., ca. 1890. Novelty items were made including toothpick holder, cruet tray. Crystal, amber, blue. *Ref. Smith p. 50; HI-14; HIII-54, 58; H6-20, 96.*

FINDLAY #19, creamer. Flindlay Glass Co., 1891. Extended table service including wine, mug. *Ref. K5-72; Unitt 2-22; Bred p. 23.*

BASKETWEAVE WITH CABLE, pitcher. Atterbury and Co., ca. 1874. Opaque glass. *Ref. K7-24.*

GYRO, covered jar. National Glass Co. (McKee), 1901. This strange pattern is an opalescent novelty.

RING-HANDLED BASKET, salt shaker. Milk glass. *Ref. PetSal 37K; W-26; HII-70.*

BRICKWORK, creamer. Indiana Tumbler and Goblet Co., ca. 1900. Extended table service. Crystal, caramel slag. *Ref. K4-58.*

Bamboo Beauty   *Tile (two examples)*

Bellaire   *Findlay #19*   *Basketweave*
Basketweave   *with Cable*

Gyro   *Ring-Handled*   *Brickwork*
                  Basket

PLATE 235. ODDS AND ENDS

DRAPED WINDOW, goblet. *Ref. Gob II-152; Metz. 1-131; Metz 2-116.*

BELL, salt shaker. Made ca. 1876 in extended table service including toy table set. *Ref. PetSal 165H.*

CENTENNIAL 1876 (LIBERTY BELL), mug and goblet. Adams and Co., 1875. Extended table service of over 35 items including platter, bread plate, wine, champagne. (Was mistakenly thought to be by Gillinder.) Crystal, opaque white. *Ref. Mugs p. 61; L-117, 118; LEAPG-331; K1-25; Gob I-29; Metz 1-112; LV-156; Schroy-89.*

HAYES (HAYES AND WHEELER), mug. Adams and Co., 1876. It was made for the presidential campaign of 1876 and has Wheeler's name on the other side. The base is signed "Adams & Co. Glass Works." Crystal, opaque white; rare. *Ref. Mugs p. 60.*

BALLOON, creamer. Made ca. 1850s in Ohio. Other pieces are known. It shows a hot air balloon, a heart, and a harp. All pieces are rare. *Ref. K3-76; Metz 1-6; Metz 2-175; Schroy 161.*

DRUM, mug. Bryce, Higbee and Co., ca. 1880. Known in toy table service, mustard, and mug. It has tiny cannons for finials. Crystal, blue (scarce). *Ref. K7-47; HTP-79; Schroy-161; Mugs p. 108.*

FINE RIBBED ANCHOR AND SHIELD (RHODE ISLAND; SHIELD AND ANCHOR), goblet. Only the flint goblet is known in crystal; very scarce. *Ref. Hartley/Cobb, The State Series, Early American Pattern Glass p. 60; Gob 1-143; Gob 2-7; Metz 1-110, Unitt 1-160.*

HARP (LYRE), spill holder. Bryce Brothers, 1840s or 1850s. Extended table service including two sizes butter dishes, two types of goblet, two types of whale oil lamps. Crystal, green. The goblet is rare. *Ref. L-14; Schroy-70; Jenks p. 263; Metz 1-14.*

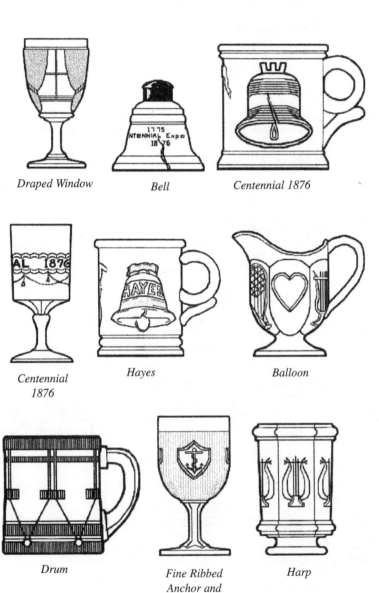

Draped Window

Bell

Centennial 1876

Centennial 1876

Hayes

Balloon

Drum

Fine Ribbed Anchor and Shield

Harp

GLASS COMPANIES

Adams and Co., Pittsburgh, PA, ca. 1851 – 1891. Joined U. S. Glass Co. in 1891 as Factory A.

Aetna Glass and Manufacturing Co., Bellaire, OH, 1880 – 1891.

American Flint Glass Works, Wheeling, VA, 1840s.

American Glass Co., ca. 1889 – 1891.

Anchor-Hocking Glass Co., ca. 1904 to present. Began as Hocking Glass Co., and in 1906 Ohio Flint Glass Co. merged with it.

Atterbury and Co., Pittsburgh, PA, 1859 – 1894.

Bakewell and Co., Pittsburgh, PA. Began as Bakewell, Payn and Page Co. (Pittsburgh), 1808. Still operating in the 1870s.

Bartlett-Collins Glass Co., 1915 – 1982, successor to Pioneer Glass Co.

Beatty, Alexander J. and Sons, Steubenville, OH, 1879. Moved to Tiffin, OH, and joined U. S. Glass Co. in 1892 as Factory R.

Beatty-Brady Glass Co., Steubenville, OH, 1850; Dunkirk, IN, 1898. Joined National Glass in 1899.

Beaumont Glass Co., Martins Ferry, OH, 1895. In 1905 joined Hocking Glass Co., which became Anchor-Hocking Glass Co. In 1906 became Tygart Valley Glass Co. until 1926.

Beaver Falls Cooperative Glass Co., Beaver Falls, PA, 1879. Became Beaver Falls Glass Co., 1887.

Beaver Valley Glass Co., 1904 – 1925.

Bellaire Goblet Co., Bellaire, OH, 1879; Findlay, OH, 1888. Joined U. S. Glass in 1891 as Factory M.

Belmont Glass Co., Bellaire, OH, 1866 – 1890.

Boston and Sandwich Glass Co., Sandwich, MA, 1825 – 1888.

Brilliant Glass Works, Brilliant, OH, 1880. Moved to LaGrange in 1880 and merged with Novelty Glass Works, 1889.

Bryce, McKee and Co., Pittsburgh, PA, 1850; became Bryce, Walker and Co. in 1854.

Bryce, Walker and Co., Pittsburgh, PA, 1855; became Bryce Brothers in 1882.

Bryce Brothers, Pittsburgh, PA, 1882. Moved to Hammondsville, PA, 1889; joined U. S. Glass in 1891 as Factory B. Moved to Mt. Pleasant, PA in 1896 and was still operating in 1911.

Buckeye Glass Co., Wheeling, WV, 1849; moved to Bowling Green, OH in 1888. Closed in 1906. See Excelsior Glass Works for their other factory.

Burlington Glass Works in Canada.

Cambridge Glass Co. (National Glass Co.), Cambridge, OH, 1901; still operating in 1953.

Campbell, Jones and Co., Pittsburgh, PA, 1865. Became Jones, Cavitt and Co., 1883.

Canton Glass Co., Canton, OH, ca. 1883; Marion, IN, 1883; joined National Glass in 1899.

Cape Cod Glass Co., 1858 – 1900.

Central Glass Co., Wheeling, WV, 1863; joined U. S. Glass in 1891 as Factory O; became Central Glass Works later.

Central Glass Co., Summitsville, IN. Joined National Glass in 1899; survived and was still operating in 1924.

Cumberland Glass Co., Cumberland, MD. Joined National Glass Co. in 1899.

Challinor, Taylor and Co. (Challinor, Hogan Glass Co.), Pittsburgh, PA, 1866; Tarentum, PA, 1884. Joined U. S. Glass as Factory C in 1891.

Columbia Glass Co., Findlay, OH, 1886; joined U. S. Glass in 1891 as Factory J.

Consolidated Lamp and Glass Co., 1893 – 1964.

Cook, T. G. and Co., 1873.

Cooperative Flint Glass Co., Beaver Falls, PA, 1879 – 1937.

Crystal Glass Co., Pittsburgh, PA, 1879; Bridgeport, OH, 1882. Burned in 1884. Moved to Bowling Green, OH, 1888. Joined National Glass Co. in 1899; reorganized by 1906; closed in 1908.

Curling, R. B. and Sons (Curling, Price and Co.), Pittsburgh, PA 1827; became Dithridge and

Sons, 1860.

Dalzell, Gilmore and Leighton Glass Co. (Dalzell Brothers and Gilmore), Brilliant, OH, 1883; went to Wellsburg, WV in 1884; joined National Glass, 1899.

Dithridge and Co. (Ft. Pitt Glassworks), Pittsburgh, PA, 1860. To Martins Ferry, OH in 1881; New Brighton, PA in 1887 and became Dithridge and Sons.

Doyle and Company, Pittsburgh, PA, 1866. Joined U. S. Glass in 1891 as Factory P.

Dugan Glass Co. (Indiana Glass Co.), Indiana, PA, 1904 – 1931.

Dugan Glass Co. (Lonaconing), 1914 – 1918.

Duncan, George and Sons, Pittsburgh, PA, 1874. Became George A. Duncan and Sons; and George Duncan's Sons; joined U. S. Glass in 1891 as Factory D. Became Duncan and Miller Glass Co., 1903 – 1955.

Eagle Glass and Mfg. Co., Wellsburgh, WV.

East Liverpool Glass Co., East Liverpool, OH, 1882 – 1883. In 1889 Specialty Glass Co. started there.

Elson Glass Works, Pittsburgh, PA, 1882 – 1893.

Evansville Glass Co., 1903 – 1907.

Excelsior Glass Works (Buckeye Glass Co.), Wheeling, WV, 1849; moved to Martins Ferry, OH, 1879. Burned in 1894.

Fairmont Glass Co. joined National Glass in 1899.

Federal Glass Co., 1900 – 1980.

Fenton Art Glass Co., Martins Ferry, OH, and Williamston, WV, 1906 to present.

Findlay Flint Glass Co., Findlay, OH, 1888 – 1900.

Fostoria Glass Co., Fostoria, OH, 1887; Roundsville, WV, 1891. Added factory at Miles, OH in 1910. Still producing.

Franklin Flint Glass Co., Philadelphia, PA, 1861. Operated by Gillinder and Sons.

Gillinder and Sons, Philadelphia, PA, 1861. Moved to Greensburgh, PA, in 1888. Joined U. S. Glass as Factory G in 1891.

Greensburg Glass Co, Greensburg, PA,1889; joined National Glass in 1899.

Hazel Atlas Glass Co, 1885 – 1982+.

Heisey, A. H. Glass Co, Newark, OH, 1895 – 1958.

Higbee, J. B. Glass Co, Bridgeville, PA, 1907 – 1918.

Hobbs, Brockunier and Co. (Hobbs, J. H. Glass Co.), Wheeling, WV, 1845. Joined U. S. Glass as Factory H in 1891; dismantled shortly thereafter.

Huntington Glass Co., 1892 – 1932.

Ihmsen, C., 1836 – 1895.

Imperial Glass Co, Dunkirk, IN, 1901 – 1982.

Indiana Glass Co., Dunkirk, IN, 1898 – 1982+.

Indiana Tumbler and Goblet Co., Greentown, IN, 1853. Joined National Glass in 1899; burned in 1903.

Jeannette Glass Co., 1898 – 1982+.

Jefferson Glass Co, Steubenville, OH, 1901; to Follansbee, WV in 1907; still operating in 1920s.

Jenkins Glass Co., Greentown, IN, 1894.

Jones, Cavitt and Co., Limited, Pittsburgh, PA, 1885 – 1891.

Kemple, John E. Glass Co., Kenova, WV; East Palestine, OH, 1945 – 1980. Reproduced McKee patterns from old molds.

Keystone Tumbler Works, Rochester, PA, 1897; joined National Glass in 1899.

King, Son and Co., Pittsburgh, PA, 1864 as Johann, King and Co.; became King Glass Co., ca. 1879.

King Glass Co., Pittsburgh, PA, ca. 1879; became U. S. Glass Factory K in 1891.

Kokomo (Jenkins) Glass Co., Kokomo, IN, 1899 – 1932.

LaBelle Glass Co., Bridgeport, OH, 1872; burned in 1887; sold in 1888 to Muhleman Glass Works, LaBelle, OH.

Lancaster Glass Co., Lancaster, OH, 1908 – 1924.

Libbey, W. H. And Sons Co., Toledo, OH, ca. 1899.

Lyon, J. B. and Co., 1827 – 1875.

McKee and Brothers, Pittsburgh, PA, 1850; moved to Jeannette, PA, 1889; joined National Glass in 1899. Was McKee Glass Co. by 1904.

Millersburg Glass Co., 1908 – 1912.

Model Flint Glass Co., Findlay, OH, 1888; to Albany, IN between 1891 and 1894. Joined National Glass in 1899; failed 1902.

Mosaic Glass Co., 1891 – 1894.

Mt. Washington Glass Works, 1837 – 1871; Mt. Washington Glass Co, 1871 – 1983+.

National Glass Co. (Bellaire), 1869 – 1981+.

National Glass Co., Pittsburgh, OH, 1898 – 1910.

New England Glass Co. (New England Glass Works), Cambridge, MA, 1817. Became W. L. Libbey and Sons in 1880.

Nickel Plate Glass Co, Fostoria, OH, 1888. Joined U. S. Glass as Factory N in 1891.

Northwood Glass Co., Indiana, PA (became part of Dugan Glass Co., ca. 1896). Joined National Glass in 1899. Became Harry Northwood Glass Co. in 1910 at Wheeling, WV. Failed in 1924.

Novelty Glass Co., LaGrange, OH, 1880. Moved to Brilliant, OH, 1882. Joined U. S. Glass in 1891 as Factory T. Moved to Fostoria, OH, in 1892 and burned in 1893.

O'Hara Glass Co., Limited, 1875 – 1891.

Ohio Flint Glass Co., Lancaster, OH, 1890; joined National Glass in 1899.

Paden City Glass Manufacturing, Co., 1916 – 1951.

Pioneer Glass Co., 1903 – 1915.

Pittsburgh Glass Work, Pittsburgh, PA, 1798 – 1852. Became James B. Lyon Glass Co. Associated with O'Hara Glass Co., Pittsburgh. Joined U. S. Glass in 1891.

Portland Glass Co., Portland, ME, 1863 – 1873.

Richards and Hartley Flint Glass Co., Pittsburgh, PA, 1865; Tarentum, PA, 1884. Joined U. S. Glass in 1891.

Ripley and Co., Pittsburgh, PA, 1866; became U. S. Glass Factory F in 1891.

Ripley and Co., Connellsville, 1910 – 1918.

Riverside Glass Works, Wellsburgh, WV, 1879; joined National Glass in 1899.

Robinson Glass Co., Zanesville, OH, 1893; joined National Glass in 1899; burned in 1906.

Rochester Tumbler Co., Rochester, PA, 1872; joined National Glass in 1899.

Royal Glass Co., Marietta, OH, 1897; joined National Glass in 1899; burned Thanksgiving Day, 1903. (Their machinery came from Huntington, WV Glass Co.)

Specialty Glass Co., East Liverpool, OH, 1888 – 1898.

Steiner Glass Co., Buckhannon, WV, 1870s.

Sweeney, McCluney and Co., 1830 – 1877.

Tarentum Glass Co., Tarentum, PA was operating in 1893 – 1931.

Thompson Glass Co., Uniontown, PA, 1888 – 1895.

Tygart Valley Glass Co., 1906 – 1926.

Union Flint Glass Works, Pittsburgh, PA, 1854. Moved to Bellaire, OH in 1880; sold to Dithridge Flint Glass Works in 1882. New plant at Martins Ferry; to Ellwood, PA, in 1895. Became Northwood Co. in 1896.

Union Stopper Co., 1902 – 1916.

Westmoreland Glass Co. (Westmoreland Specialty Co.), Grapeville, PA, 1889 – 1985.

West Virginia Glass Co., Martins Ferry, OH, 1861; joined National Glass in 1899.

Windsor Glass Co., 1886 – 1890.

Wright, L. G. Glass Co., ca. 1930 on.

INDEX

45 Colonis 334
Aberdeen **308**
Acanthus **382**, 384
Acanthus Leaf **382**
Acanthus Scroll **158**
Acme 20
Acorn 274, **294**, 386, **394**
Acorn Band 1 **394**
Acorn Band 2 **394**
Acorn Diamonds **124**
Acorn Variant **394**
Actress **350**
Actress Chain **350**
Ada **228**
Adams 128, 204
Adams #52 **406**
Adams #329 **362**
Adams Diamond **86**
Adams Saxon **366**
Admiral 216
Admiral Dewey 360
Adonis 348
Aegis 308
Aetna **164**
Aetna #300 **162**
Aetna's #335 112
Aida **210**
Akron Block 100
Alabama **318**
Alaric 20
Alaska **422**, 444
Alba Blossoms **258**
Albany 118, **126**
Albion **306**
Alden 146
Aldine 314
Alexis 184
Alligator **12**
Alligator Scales **78**
Alligator Scale w/Spearpoint 78
All-Over Diamond **100**
All Over Stars 456
Almond 54
Almond Thumbprint **54**
Alpha 194
Amazon **88**
Amber Block 172
Amberette 444
Amboy **98**
Amelia 180
America 464
American Beauty **248**
American Shield **454**
Amulet 192
Anderson 382
Andes 272
Angelsey **366**
Angelus **30**
Angora **124**
Angular **372**
Annie 350
Anona 118
Anthemion **384**
Antwerp **144**
Apollo **38**
Apple and Grape in Scroll **284**
Apple Blossoms **258**
Aquarium **20**
Arabesque **132**
Arabian 368
Archaic Gothic **318**
Arch and Forget-Me-Not Bands **246**
Arch and Sunburst 188
Arched Cane and Fan 182
Arched Diamond Point 180
Arched Fleur-de-Lis **76**
Arched Grape **282**
Arched Leaf **380**
Arched Ovals **32**
Arched Panel **320**
Arched Tripod **114**
Arctic 18
Argent 424
Argonaut Shell **428**
Argus **36**
Argyle 54, 106
Arizona 148
Arrowhead **382**
Arrowhead in Oval 182
Arrowsheaf **196**
Art **100**
Artichoke **78**
Art Novo **258**
Ashburton **32**
Ashburton w/Grape Band 278, 284
Ashland **332**
Ashman 370
Aster and Leaf **254**
Athenia 270
Atlanta 14, **220**
Atlantic Cable 426
Atlas **30**
Atterbury's Leaf **384**
Aurora **126**
Austrian **94**
Avocado 288
Aztec **234**
Aztec Sunburst 234
Baby Face **350**
Baby Thumbprint 36
Bag Ware 160, 162
Bakewell Block **108**
Bakewell Ribbon 344
Balder 200
Balky Mule 11
Ball **412**
Ball and Bar **92**
Ball and Swirl **462**
Ball and Swirl Band 462
Ballfoot Hobnail **292**
Balloon **482**
Baltimore Pear **288**
Bamboo **400**
Bamboo Beauty **480**
Band **80**
Banded Barrel **436**
Banded Buckle **82**
Banded Diamond Point 84
Banded Fine Cut **186**
Banded Fleur-de-Lis **76**
Banded Flute **332**
Banded Icicle **408**
Banded Paling 416
Banded Portland 124
Banded Prism Bar 450
Banded Raindrops **296**
Banded Serrated Prism 420
Banded Star **454**
Banded Swirl **460**
Banner 264
Banquet 432
Bar and Bead 402
Bar and Block 100
Bar and Diamond 94
Bar and Flute **36**
Bar and Swirl **464**
Barberry **286**
Barley **398**
Baroque **76**
Barred Fishscale **400**
Barred Forget-Me-Not **268**
Barred Hobnail **298**
Barred Oval **410**
Barred Star **106**
Barrel Ashburton 32
Barrel Excelsior **42**
Barrelled Block 172
Barrelled Thumbprint **60**
Bars and Buttons 100
Bartlett Pear **288**
Baseball Player **360**
Basketweave **446**
Basketweave Rose 274
Basketweave with Cable **480**
Basketweave with Frosted Leaf **390**
Bassettown 218
Beacon Light **152**
Bead and Bar Medallion **308**
Bead and Chain **306**
Bead and Loop **298**
Bead and Panel **302**
Bead and Scroll **302**
Bead Band 56
Bead Column **300**
Bead Swag **300**
Beaded 1-0-1 318
Beaded Acanthus **270**
Beaded Acorn **388**
Beaded Acorn Medallion 388
Beaded Acorn w/Leaf Band 394
Beaded Arch Panels **318**
Beaded Band **316**
Beaded Band and Panel **306**
Beaded Base 300
Beaded Block **298**
Beaded Block, Imperial's **446**
Beaded Bottom **260**
Beaded Bulb **300**
Beaded Bulls-Eye and Drape 318
Beaded Chain **312**
Beaded Circle **304**
Beaded Coarse Bars 416
Beaded Dart Band **310**
Beaded Dewdrop 314
Beaded Diamond **82**
Beaded Diamond Band **310**
Beaded Ellipse **314**
Beaded Ellipse and Fan **310**
Beaded Fan **148**
Beaded Festoon 300
Beaded Finecut **158**
Beaded Flower **256**
Beaded Flower and Leaf 274
Beaded Grape 282
Beaded Grape Medallion **280**
Beaded Jewel 312
Beaded Lobe **30**
Beaded Loop 162
Beaded Medallion **304**
Beaded Mirror 304
Beaded Oval **310**
Beaded Oval and Fan 182
Beaded Oval and Scroll **304**
Beaded Oval Band **52**
Beaded Ovals 162
Beaded Ovals in Sand **318**
Beaded Oval Window 54
Beaded Panel **210**
Beaded Panel and Sunburst **210**
Beaded Panels 296
Beaded Raindrop **310**
Beaded Rib **302**
Beaded Rope Panel **424**
Beaded Shell **428**
Beaded Star 208
Beaded Swirl 468
Beaded Swirl and Disc **468**
Beaded Swirl and Lens **468**
Beaded Thumbprint Block **48**
Beaded Triangle **294**
Beaded Tulip **272**
Beads and Bark **316**
Bean 58
Bearded Head **354**
Bearded Man 354
Bear with Book **12**
Beatty Honeycomb **438**
Beatty Rib **404**
Beatty Waffle 438
Beaumont's Columbia **124**
Beaumont's Flora **254**
Beautiful Lady **150**
Beauty **92**
Beaver Band **10, 16**
Belfast **40**
Bell **482**
Bellaire #2 **70**
Bellaire Basketweave **480**
Belle **406**
Bellflower, Double Vine **252**
Bellflower, Single Vine **252**
Belmont **166**
Belmont Diamond **140**
Belmont's Reflecting Fans **140**
Belmont's Royal **352**
Belt Buckle 156
Belted Icicle **408**
Belted Panel **334**
Bent Buckle 190
Berkeley **50**
Berlin **436**
Berry Cluster **284**
Berry McKee 286
Bethlehem Star **452**
Bevelled Buttons **172**
Bevelled Diagonal Block **100**
Bevelled Diamond and Star **118**
Bevelled Star **204**
Bevelled Windows **64**
Bicycle Girl **354**
Big Diamond **88**
Big Leaf and Button **178**
Bigler **36**
Big Block 172
Big Button 172
Big Star **204**
Big Top **372**
Big X **186**
Bijou 388
Biliken Flute **320**
Billiken **360**
Birch Leaf **386**
Bird and Fern 24
Bird and Strawberry **24**
Bird and Tree **24**
Bird-in-Ring **22**, 354
Birds and Insects **24**
Birds at Fountain **24**
Bismarc Star 220
Blackberry **284**
Blackberry and Grape 280
Blackberry Band **278**
Blackberry Spray **278**
Blaine **356**
Blaze **408**
Blazing Cornucopia **202**
Blazing Pinwheels 152

Patterns in this index are listed by page numbers; numbers in bold face indicate illustrated patterns.

Blazing Star 152
Bleeding Heart **238**
Block 172, **434**
Blockade 140, 172
Block and Bar **432**
Block and Circle 50
Block and Dent **184**
Block and Diamond 94
Block and Double Bar 100
Block and Fan 168, **440**
Block and Honeycomb **62**
Block and Lattice **172**
Block and Palm **384**
Block and Panel **110**
Block and Pillar **436**
Block and Pleat 444
Block and Rib **434**
Block and Rosette **155**
Block and Star 158
Block and Star Spear Point 440
Block and Sunburst **440**
Block and Triple Bars **174**
Block Band 430
Block Band Diamond **112**
Block Band Squares **430**
Block Barrel 434
Block Cut 436
Blocked Arches **50**
Blocked Thumbprint **152**
Blocked Thumbprint Band **334**
Blockhouse 156
Block Midriff 430
Block on Stilts **430**
Block with Fan 440
Block with Thumbprint **432**
Block with Thumbprint, Late **48**
Block w/Stars 156
Blooms and Blossoms 238
Blown Swirl **460**
Bluebird 24
Blue Heron **26**
Boar **18**
Bogalusa 64
Bohemian 260, **326**
Bohemian Grape **284**
Boling **140**
Bone Stem 472
Bontec **228**
Border 440
Bordered Ellipse **196**
Bosc Pear **288**
Boston **362**
Boswell 400
Bosworth 114
Bouquet **324**
Bowline **56**
Bow Tie **66**
Boxed Star **458**
Box-in-Box **184**
Box Pleat **114**
Boylan 194
Bradford Blackberry 282
Bradford Grape **282**
Branched Tree **476**
Brazen Shield **218**
Brazil 244
Brazilian **222**
Brickwork **480**
Bridle Rosettes 168
Bright Star 452
Brilliant 92, 170, **206**, 380
Bringing Home the Cows **16**
Britannic **204**
Broken Bands **120**
Broken Bar and Thumbprint **82**
Broken Column **412**
Broken Pillar and Reed **422**
Brooch Band **100**
Brooklyn **42**
Broughton 116
Bryce **32**
Bryce #160 **414**
Bryce Elipse **58**
Bryce Persian 444
Bryce Yale 412
Bucket Set 476
Buckingham **224**
Buckle **82**
Buckle and Diamond **126**
Buckle and Shield **98**
Buckle and Star **182**
Buckle with English Hobnail **80**
Budded Ivy **392**
Bulbous Base **326**
Bulbous Bulls-Eye 56
Bulging Bands 300
Bulging Corn **374**
Bulging Loops 418
Bulle-Eye and Bar 42
Bullet 28, 30
Bullet Band 406
Bullet Emblem **28**
Bulls-Eye **44**
Bulls-Eye and Arrowhead 66
Bulls-Eye and Bar **42**
Bulls-Eye and Broken Column **42**
Bulls-Eye and Buttons **98**
Bulls-Eye and Daisy **52**
Bulls-Eye and Diamond Quilted **102**
Bulls-Eye and Fan **216**
Bulls-Eye and Loop 58
Bulls-Eye and Princess Feather 46
Bulls-Eye and Prism **42**
Bulls-Eye and Rosette **212**
Bulls-Eye and Spearhead 56
Bulls-Eye and Star 212
Bulls-Eye and Waffle 68
Bulls-Eye and Wishbone **80**
Bulls-Eye Band 80
Bulls-Eye Diamond 176
Bulls-Eye in Diamond **98**
Bulls-Eye in Heart 68
Bulls-Eye Variant 46
Bulls-Eye w/Diamond Point 80, 176
Bulls-Eye w/Diamond Points **80**
Bulls-Eye with Fleur-de-lis 46
Butterfly **20**
Butterfly Ears **20**, **126**
Butterfly Handles **20**
Butterfly with Spray **20**
Button and Button **174**
Button and Star **180**
Button and Star Panel **216**
Button Arches **190**
Button Band **292**
Button Block **176**
Button Panel **178**
Button Panel with Bars **178**
Buttressed Arch **424**
Buttressed Loop **72**
Buttressed Sunburst **216**
Buzz Saw in Parenthesis 234
Buzz Star **230**
Cabbage Leaf **376**
Cabbage Rose **248**
Cable **426**
Cable Cord 426
Cable Variant **424**
Cable with Ring **426**
Cactus **388**
Cadmus **94**
Caledonia 232
California **282**, 466
Cambridge #2504 **144**
Cambridge #2511 **118**
Cambridge #2579 **218**
Cambridge #2625 **402**
Cambridge #2626 202
Cambridge #2700 **106**
Cambridge Colonial **328**
Cambridge Curly **72**
Cambridge Feather 160
Cambridge Ribbon 168
Cambridge Star 452
Cameo 352
Canadian **478**
Canadian Drape 268
Canadian Horseshoe 32, 38
Candlewick 296
Candy Ribbon 32
Cane **176**
Cane and Cable **176**
Cane and Fan **176**
Cane and Rosette **176**
Cane and Sprig 264
Cane and Star Medallion 212
Cane Column **170**
Cane Horseshoe **200**
Cane Insert **182**
Cane Medallion **80**
Cane Pinwheel **230**
Caneshield 222
Cane Variant 180
Cannonball **30**
Cannonball Pinwheel **232**
Canton House **478**
Cape Cod 110, **478**
Capital **72**
Capstan **334**
Cardinal Bird **24**
Carltec **224**
Carmen **104**
Carnation **238**
Carolina **36**
Cartridge Belt **336**
Casco **364**
Cathedral 50
Cat's-Eye **36**
Cat's Eye and Block 412
Cat's-Eye and Fan **66**
Cavitt **140**
Celtic **36**, 128
Celtic Cross **404**
Centennial 356
Centennial 1876 **482**
Centennial Shield **454**
Centipede **198**
Central #438 122
Central #520 **372**
Central #560 **362**
Central #1879 **372**
Ceres **352**
Chain **40**
Chain and Shield **70**
Chain and Swag **302**
Chain, Early **70**
Chain Lightning 334
Chain Thumbprints **348**
Chain w/Diamonds 356
Chain with Star **40**
Chalice **330**
Challinor #27 **468**
Challinor #314 **96**
Challinor Double Fan **140**
Challinor's Tree of Life **268**
Challinor Thumbprint 60
Champion **148**
Chandelier **430**
Checkerboard **168**
Checkerboard Band **430**
Checkers **110**
Chelsea **412**
Cherry **290**
Cherry and Cable **290**
Cherry and Fig **288**
Cherry Lattice **290**
Cherry Sprig **290**
Cherry Thumbprints 290
Cherry with Thumbprints **290**
Chesterfield 108
Chestnut **178**
Chestnut Oak **394**
Chevroned Diamonds **108**
Chick **22**, **328**
Chickenwire 62
Chilson **214**
Chimo 198
Chippendale **320**
Christmas Pearls 302
Chrysanthemum 210
Chrysanthemum Leaf **314**
Church Windows **330**
Cincinnati Honeycomb 64
Circle and Swag **310**
Circled Scroll **390**
Circle X **150**
Circular Saw **232**
Clarissa 222
Clark **442**
Class Act 152
Classic **352**
Classic Medallion **352**
Clear Block 172
Clear Diagonal Band **466**
Clear Herringbone 348
Clear Lily 266
Clear Lion Head **14**
Clear Panels w/Cord Band 424
Clear Ribbon **344**
Clear Ribbon Variant **344**
Clear Roman Key 448
Clear Stork **26**
Clematis **240**, 264
Cleveland **356**
Climax **92**
Clio **164**
Clover **164**, **398**
Coachman's Cape **102**
Coarse Cut and Block **178**
Coarse Zig-Zag **134**
Coat of Arms 188
Cobb 420
Cockle Burr 456
Coin and Dewdrop **58**
Coin Spot 58
Collins 32
Colonial 324
Colonial and Mitre 64
Colonial Panel **320**
Colonial with Diamond Band **80**
Colonial with Garland 240
Colonis **334**
Colorado **308**
Colossus 134
Columbia 292, 330, 406
Columbian 414
Columbia Radiant 190
Column Block **440**
Columned Thumbprints **184**
Comet **42**, 82, 230
Comet in the Stars **234**
Compact 40
Concave Ashburton 36
Concave Circle 56
Concaved Almond 32
Concaved Arrowheads **78**
Connecticut **120**
Connecticut Flute **320**
Continental **330**
Conventional Band **312**
Coolidge Drape **470**
Co-op #190 100
Co-op #294 458
Co-op #295 142
Co-op #296 104
Co-op #323 382

Patterns in this index are listed by page numbers; numbers in bold face indicate illustrated patterns.

Co-op 20th Century ... 78
Co-op Block ... **442**
Co-op Columbia ... **314**
Coop Imperial ... 454
Co-op Rex ... **218**
Co-op's Royal ... **56**
Coral ... 422
Coral Gables ... **98**
Corcoran ... 214
Cord and Bars ... **424**
Cord and Tassel ... **424**
Cordate Leaf ... 368
Cord Drapery ... 304
Cordova ... **410**
Coreopsis ... **258**
Corn ... **374**
Cornell ... **116**
Corn Sphere ... 374
Cornucopia ... 216, **276**
Corn with Husk ... **374**
Corona ... 62
Corrigan ... **56**
Corset and Thumbprint ... 36
Cosmos ... **256**
Cottage ... **204**
Cradled Diamonds ... 196
Cradled Prisms ... **440**
Crane ... 26
Cranesbill ... **238**
Crazy Patch ... **214**
Creased Hexagon Block ... 62
Crescent ... 80, 192
Crescent and Fan ... 206
Criss-Cross Band ... **104**
Crocus ... **328**
Croesus ... **74**
Cromwell ... 212
Crosby ... 224
Cross Bands ... **120**
Crossbar ... 100
Crossbar and Cane ... **186**
Crossbar Handle ... **366**
Crossed Block ... **446**
Crossed Disks ... **364**
Crossed Fern ... **396**
Crossed Shield ... **196**
Cross in Diamond ... **112**
Crowfoot ... 60
Crown ... 336
Crown and Shield ... 150
Crown Jewel ... 184
Crown Jewels ... 430, 452
Crusader Cross ... 112
Cryptic ... 420
Crystal ... 104
Crystal #12 ... **60**
Crystal Anniversary ... 32
Crystal Ball ... 30
Crystalina ... **326, 428**
Crystal Queen ... **194**
Crystal Rock ... **262**
Crystal Wedding ... **32**
Cube ... **438**
Cube and Block ... **444**
Cube and Daisy ... 186
Cube and Diamond ... 136, 186
Cube and Double Fan ... 142
Cube and Fan ... 440
Cube with Fan ... 136
Cupid ... 350
Cupid and Venus ... **352**
Curled Leaf ... **238**
Curling Colonial ... 42
Currant ... **284**
Currier and Ives ... **11, 168**
Curtain ... **470**
Curtain and Block ... **470**
Curtain Tie-back ... **214**
Cut Block ... **90**
Cut Block and Daisy ... 186
Cut Log ... **412**
Cut Star ... 452
Cuttlebone ... **348**
Cyclone ... **460**
Czar ... 18
Czarina ... **136**
Dagger ... **450**
Dahlia ... **248**
Dahlia and Leaf ... **254**
Daisies in Oval Panels ... 216
Daisy ... 60
Daisy and Bluebell ... 244
Daisy and Button ... **164**
Daisy and Button "V" ... **166**
Daisy and Button w/Almond Band ... 164
Daisy and Button with Narcissus ... **266**
Daisy and Button w/Oval Panels ... 158
Daisy and Button w/Rimmed Panel ... 164
Daisy and Button w/Scroll Panel ... 164
Daisy and Cane ... **236**
Daisy and Cube ... 204
Daisy and Cube w/Oval Panels ... 158
Daisy and Palm ... **254**
Daisy and Scroll ... **234**
Daisy Co-op ... 266
Daisy in Diamond ... **188**
Daisy in Oval ... **204**
Daisy in Panel ... 162
Daisy-in-Square ... 162, **174**
Daisy Medallion ... **272**
Daisy Pleat ... **268**
Daisy Square ... 60
Daisy w/Amber Stripes ... 160
Daisy Whorl with Diamond Band ... 250
Daisy Whorl ... **250**
Dakota ... **35, 36**
Dalton ... **196**
Dalzell's Columbia ... **364**
Dancing Goat ... **16**
D & B Band ... **164**
D & B Oval Medallion ... 164
D & B Petticoat ... 166
D & B "V" ... 166
D & B w/Clear Stripes ... 160
D & B with Crossbar ... **166**
D & B with Crossbar, Pointed ... **166**
D & B with Prisms ... **166**
D & B with Thin Bars ... **164**
D & B with Thumbprint ... **164**
D & B w/V Ornament ... 166
Dandelion ... **242**
Darby ... 142
Darling Grape ... 282
Dart ... **130**
Deep Star ... **106**
Deer Alert ... **12**
Deer and Doe ... 12
Deer and Dog ... **18**
Deer and Oak Tree ... **12**
Deer & Pine Tree ... **10, 12**
Deer, Dog and Hunter ... 18
Deer Racing ... 12
Deer with Lily-of-the-Valley ... **12**
Delaware ... **254**
Delos ... **364**
Delta ... 262, **330**
Derby ... 336
Desplaines ... 418
Despot ... **326**
Dew and Raindrop ... **294**
Dewberry ... **286**
Dewdrop ... **292**
Dewdrop and Fan ... 148
Dewdrop and Star ... **454**
Dewdrop and Zig Zag ... **292**
Dewdrop in Points ... **316**
Dewdrops and Flowers ... **268**
Dewdrop with Star ... **296**
Dewey ... 274, 360
Diadem ... 210
Diagonal Band ... **152**
Diagonal Band with Fan ... **134**
Diagonal Bar Band ... **466**
Diagonal Bead Bands ... 106
Diagonal Block and Fan ... 152
Diagonal Frosted Ribbon ... **466**
Diagonal Rosettes ... **256**
Diamond ... 110, 112, **458**
Diamond and Long Sunburst ... 148
Diamond and Sunburst ... **144**
Diamond and Sunburst, Early ... **138**
Diamond and Sunburst Variant ... 144
Diamond and Sunburst Zippers ... 144
Diamond and Teardrop ... 142
Diamond and Thumbprint Crossbar ... 166
Diamond Band ... **84**
Diamond Band with Panels ... **190**
Diamond Bar ... 122
Diamond Bar and Block ... 100, 106
Diamond Beaded Band ... 146
Diamond Block ... 86, 100, 172
Diamond Block and Fan ... 136
Diamond Block with Fan ... **172**
Diamond Bridges ... **94**
Diamond Crystal ... 178
Diamond Cut with Leaf ... **380**
Diamond Fan ... **146**
Diamond Flute ... **222**
Diamond Gold ... 180
Diamond Horseshoe ... 126
Diamond in Diamond ... **110**
Diamond in Points ... **96**
Diamond in Space ... **112**
Diamond Lace ... **228**
Diamond Lattice ... **108**, 122
Diamond Medallion ... 112
Diamond Mirror ... **140**
Diamond Panels ... **98**
Diamond Point ... **96**
Diamond-Point and Punty ... **98**
Diamond Point Band ... 88
Diamond Point Discs ... **80**
Diamond Point Loop ... **104**
Diamond Point w/Flutes ... 96
Diamondpoint w/Panels ... 84
Diamond Prisms ... 118, **470**
Diamond Quilted ... **108**
Diamond Ridge ... **122**
Diamond Rosettes ... **104**
Diamonds and Crossbars ... **140**
Diamonds and Dewdrops ... **316**
Diamond Side ... **92**
Diamonds in Oval ... 118
Diamond Spearhead ... **122**
Diamond Splendor ... 80, 100
Diamond Stem ... **324**
Diamond Sunburst ... **138**
Diamond Swag ... **96**
Diamonds w/Double Fans ... **138**
Diamond Swirl ... **474**
Diamond Wall ... 106
Diamond w/Dual Fan ... 136
Diamond Web ... **100**
Diamond Whirl ... **234**
Diamond with Circle ... **82**
Diamond with Diamond Point ... **104**
Diamond with Fan ... **110**
Diamond with Peg ... **190**
Diapered Flower ... **270**
Dice and Block ... **114**
Dickinson ... **82**
Dinner Bell ... 204
Dithridge #25 ... **260**
Divided Block w/Sunburst ... 142
Divided Diamonds ... 78
Divided Hearts ... **46**
Divided Medallion w/Diamond Cut ... 150
Divided Squares ... 108, 446
Divided Star ... 212
Dixie Belle ... **206**
Dog and Deer ... 18
Dog Hunting ... **18**
Dogwood ... 258
Doll's Eye ... 186
Dolly Madison ... **244**
Dolphin ... **20**
Doltec ... **272**
Dominion ... 110
Doric ... 160
Dot ... 246, 292, 304
Dot and Dash ... **302**
Dots and Dashes ... **316**
Dotted Loop ... **206**
Double Arch ... 306, **412**
Double Band Forget-Me-Not ... **252**
Double Beaded Band ... **300**
Double Beetle Band ... **406**
Double Blaze ... 134
Double Circle ... **40**
Double Crossroads ... **186**
Double Dahlia with Lens ... **244**
Double Daisy ... **250**
Double Diamond Panel ... **98**
Double Donut ... **326**
Double-Eye Hobnail ... **292**
Double Fan ... **140**
Double Flute ... 32
Double Greek Key ... **40**
Double Icicle ... 134
Double Line Swirl ... **462**
Double Loop ... 32, **132**
Double Loop and Dart ... **132**
Double Petalled Flute ... **334**
Double Petal Tulip ... 334
Double Pinwheel ... **230**
Double Prism ... 86
Double Red Block ... 62, 172
Double Ribbon ... **344**
Double Scroll ... **74**
Double Snail ... **472**
Double Spear ... **108**
Double Thumbprint Band ... **36**
Double Wedding Ring ... 40
Double Y's ... **28**
Double Zig-Zag ... **366**
Douglass ... **324**
Doyle ... **130**
Doyle's #80 ... **444**
Doyle's #240 ... **296**
Doyle's #400 ... **450**
Doyle's Shell ... 440
Dragon ... **22**
Draped Fan ... 428
Draped Garland ... **76**
Draped Jewel ... **312**
Draped Red Block ... 128
Draped Red Top ... 128
Draped Top ... 128
Draped Window ... **482**
Drapery ... **312**
Drapery Variant ... 132
Dropped Diamonds ... **122**
Drum ... 426, **482**
Duchess ... **152**
Duchess Loop ... **322**
Duncan ... **326**
Duncan #40 ... **218**

Patterns in this index are listed by page numbers; numbers in bold face indicate illustrated patterns.

489

Duncan #46 ... **434**
Duncan #77 ... **64**
Duncan #904 ... **78**
Duncan #2001 ... **84**
Duncan Block ... **436**
Duncan Flute ... **328**
Duncan Homestead ... **224**
Duncan Mirror ... **82**
Duncan Panel ... **54**
Duncan's Clover ... **168**
Duncan's Late Block ... 436
Duquesne ... 398
Dynast ... 190
Eagle and Arms ... 28
Eagle's Fleur-de-Lis ... **76**
Earl ... 120
Early Colonial ... 42
Early Grape Band ... 278
Early Loop ... 330
Early Panelled Grape Band ... **284**
Ear of Corn ... **374**
East Liverpool ... **462**
Edgerton ... **138**
Edgewood ... **416**
Effulgent Star ... **456**
Egg and Dart ... 42, 88
Egg Band ... **58**
Egg in Sand ... **58**
Egyptian ... **16**
Eighteen-Ninety ... 384
Eight-O-Eight ... **46**
Eleanor ... 156
Electric ... **30**
Elephant ... **10**, 14, **20**
Elephant Toes ... **410**
Elite ... 116
Ellipse and Star ... **208**
Ellipse One ... **50**
Ellipses ... **48**
Ellipse Two ... **66**
Ellrose ... 164
Elmino ... 340
Elson's Block ... **434**
Emerald Green Herringbone ... 348
Empire ... 148, 216, **370**
Empire Colonial ... 42
Empress ... **306**
English ... **94**, 104
English Cane ... **174**
English Colonial ... **366**
English Hobnail ... **110**
English Hobnail and Thumbprint ... **134**
English Hobnail Cross ... 444
English Quilting ... **88**
English Walnut Variant ... 108
Enigma ... 312
Era ... 70, 156
Essex ... **324**
Estate ... 72
Esther ... **72**, 92
Etched Band ... **336**
Etched Fern ... **370**
Etched Fern and Waffle ... 110
Etched Grape ... **330**
Ethol ... 412
Etruria ... 44
Etruscan ... **342**
Etta ... **208**
Euclid ... 194
Eugenie ... **52**
Eulalia ... 11
Eureka ... **328**, **412**
Evangeline ... **332**
Excelsior ... 38, 56
Excelsior Early ... **42**
Excelsior Variant ... 42
Excelsior w/Double-Ringed Stem ... 42
Eye Band ... **44**
Eyebrows ... 30
Eyelet ... **38**
Eyewinker ... **30**
Faceted Flower ... **246**
Faceted Rosette Band ... 184
Fagot ... **192**
Fairfax Strawberry ... 276
Falling Leaves ... **386**
Falmouth ... 326
Falmouth Strawberry ... 276
Famous ... **68**
Fan and Feather ... **136**
Fan and Flute ... 338
Fan and Star ... **114**
Fan Band ... **412**
Fancy Arch ... **184**
Fancy Cut ... **218**
Fancy Diamonds ... **106**, 122
Fancy Fans ... 250
Fancy King's Crown ... 304
Fancy Loop ... **442**
Fandango ... 98
Fan w/Acanthus Leaf ... 388
Fan w/Crossbars ... 148
Fan with Diamond ... 124
Fan with Split Diamond ... **146**
Fashion ... **206**
Faye ... 340
Feather ... 114, **160**, **474**
Feather and Block ... 444
Feather and Quill ... 160
Feather Band ... **386**
Feather Cut ... 198
Feather Duster ... **184**
Feathered Ovals ... **150**
Feathered Points ... **214**
Feathered Star ... **458**
Feather Swirl ... **160**
Federal #2 ... **296**
Federal #102 ... **148**
Federal #1605 ... **66**
Federal #1607 ... **104**
Federal #1608 ... **142**
Federal #1609 ... **458**
Federal #1908 ... **306**
Federal #1910 ... **218**
Federal's Imperial ... **146**
Fence ... 476
Fentec ... **226**
Fern ... **400**
Fern Burst ... **208**
Fernette ... 234
Fern Garland ... **250**
Fernland ... 226
Fern Sprays ... **398**
Fern Sprig ... **400**
Fern Wheel ... 230
Fern Whirl ... 230
Ferris Wheel ... **224**
Festoon ... **308**
Festooned Stars ... **458**
Festoons and Sunbursts ... 202
Fickle Block ... 146
Field Thistle ... **262**
Fig ... 288
Figure Eight ... 32
File ... **422**
Filigree ... 72
Filley ... 46
Findlay #19 ... **480**
Findlay's Pillar ... 178
Finecut ... **162**
Finecut and Block ... 106, **144**
Finecut and Diamond ... 112
Finecut and Fan ... **66**
Fine Cut and Feather ... 160
Fine Cut and Panel ... **170**
Fine Cut and Rib ... **158**
Fine Cut and Ribbed Bars ... 92
Fine Cut Band ... **200**, 204
Fine Cut Bar ... 148
Finecut Medallion ... 94, 112
Finecut w/Leaf ... 380
Fine Feather ... **348**
Fine Rib ... **404**
Fine Ribbed Anchor and Shield ... **482**
Fingerprint ... 54
Fish ... **18–20**
Fishbone ... **414**
Fishbone Bow ... **414**
Fish-Eye ... 318
Fishnet and Poppies ... **256**
Fishscale ... **422**
Fishscale Swirl ... **466**
Five-Footed Oval ... 204
Flag ... 454
Flambeaux ... 216
Flamboyant ... 222
Flame ... **464**
Flamingo ... **26**
Flare Top Flute ... **320**
Flat Diamond ... **96**
Flat Diamond and Panel ... **102**
Flat Diamond Box ... **102**
Flat Iron ... **118**
Flat Oval ... **372**
Flat Panel ... 342
Flat Panelled Star ... **168**
Flattened Diamond and Sunburst ... **146**
Flattened Fine Cut ... **162**
Flattened Hobnail ... **294**
Flattened Sawtooth ... **88**
Flat-to-Round Panel ... 334
Flawless ... **332**
Fleur-de-Lis ... **76**
Fleur-de-Lis and Drape ... 76
Fleur-de-Lis and Tassel ... **76**
Flickering Flame ... **468**
Floradora ... **260**
Floral Diamond ... 152
Floral Diamond Band ... **120**
Floral Oval ... **264**
Florence ... 418
Floricut ... **262**
Florida ... **242**, **348**, **414**
Florida Palm ... **380**
Florida Pineapple ... 276
Flower and Bud ... **238**
Flower and Diamond ... **264**
Flower and Honeycomb ... **238**
Flower and Panel ... 256
Flower and Pleat ... **238**
Flower and Quill ... **240**
Flower Band ... **252**
Flower Band Barrel ... **256**
Flower Band, Warman's ... **250**
Flower Basket ... **270**
Flowered Oval ... **56**
Flowered Scroll ... **258**
Flower Fan ... 208
Flower Flange ... **274**
Flower in Square ... 162
Flower Medallion ... 264
Flower Panelled Cane ... 176
Flower Pot ... **246**
Flower Spray w/Scrolls ... 260
Flower Windows ... **242**
Flower with Cane ... **180**
Flute ... **322**, 330
Flute and Cane ... **176**
Flute and Crown ... **416**
Flute and Split ... 36
Fluted ... 186
Fluted Diamond Point ... 84
Fluted Ribbon ... **344**
Fluted Scrolls ... **340**
Flying Birds ... **24**
Flying Robin ... 24
Flying Stork ... **26**
Flying Swan ... **28**
Foggy Bottom ... 340
Footed Panelled Rib ... **406**
Forget-Me-Not ... **240**
Forget-Me-Not in Scroll ... **252**
Forget-Me-Not in Snow ... 246
Formal Daisy ... **204**
Forrest Ware ... 392
Fostoria ... 78
Fostoria's #226 ... **120**
Fostoria #551 ... **346**
Fostoria's #600 ... **220**
Fostoria #952 ... **342**
Fostoria #956 ... **192**
Fostoria #1008 ... **72**
Fostoria's #1231 ... **416**
Fostoria #1641 ... **474**
Fostoria's Priscilla ... **302**
Fostoria's Rococo ... **46**
Fostoria's Sterling ... **366**
Fostoria's Swirl ... **460**
Fostoria's Victoria ... **472**
Four Lines ... 342
Four Petal ... **116**
Four Petal Flower ... 254
Four Thumbprints ... **38**
Fox and Crow ... **18**
Framed Circles ... **44**
Framed Jewel ... **304**
Francesware Swirl ... 460
Franklin Flute ... **346**
French ... 366
Fretted Vault ... 48
Fringed Drape ... **192**
Frisco ... **78**
Frontier ... **64**
Frost Crystal ... **214**
Frosted Ball and Swirl ... 462
Frosted Block ... **446**
Frosted Chain ... 40
Frosted Circle ... **214**
Frosted Crane ... 26
Frosted Dog ... 18
Frosted Eagle ... **28**, **372**
Frosted Festal Ball ... 38
Frosted Fleur-de-Lis ... 76
Frosted Leaf ... **386**
Frosted Magnolia ... 242
Frosted Medallion ... **204**
Frosted Ribbon ... **344**
Frosted Ribbon, Double Bars ... **344**
Frosted Roman Key ... 448
Frosted Stork ... **26**
Frosted Waffle ... 430
Frost Flower ... **256**
Fruit Band ... **290**
Ft. Pitt ... **322**
Ft. Pitt Chain ... **314**
Fuchsia ... **240**
Fuchsia w/Diamond Band ... 264
Fulton ... **406**
Funnel Rosette ... **168**
Gaelic ... **264**
Gala ... 114
Galloway ... **126**
Garden of Eden ... **20**, **384**
Garden Pink ... **264**
Garfield ... **356**
Garfield Drape ... **268**, **302**
Garland ... **308**
Garland of Roses ... **248**
Garter Band ... **294**
Gathered Knot ... **346**
Gem ... 100, 172, 236
Gem Star ... **124**
General Grant ... 456
Geneva ... 180, **428**
Georgia ... **54**, 116, 310
Georgia Belle ... **210**

Patterns in this index are listed by page numbers; numbers in bold face indicate illustrated patterns.

Georgia Gem 300
Giant Bulls-Eye 56
Giant Flute 322
Giant Prism w/Thumbprint
    Band 42
Giant Sawtooth 86
Gibson Girl 352
Gipsy 288
Giraffe 14
Gladiator 198
Glentec 194
Globe and Star 166
Gloria 184
Gloved Hand 188
Goddess of Liberty 350, 352
Gold Band 334
Golden Jewel 202
Gonterman 298
Good Luck 246
Gooseberry 288
Gothic 50, 78, 334
Gothic Windows 158
Grace 22, 354
Granby 102
Grand 112
Grand Republic 192
Grape and Cherry 290
Grape and Festoon 278
Grape and Festoon
    Variation 278
Grape and Festoon
    with Shield 278
Grape and Gothic Arches . .282
Grape and Vine 282
Grape Band 278
Grape Bunch 280
Grape Leaf Band 286
Grapevine 286
Grapevine with Ovals 286
Grapevine with Stars 286
Grapevine with
    Thumbprint Band 286
Grape with Holly Band . . .280
Grape Without Vine 280
Grape with Thumbprint . . .282
Grape with Vine 280
Grape w/Overlapping Foliage .280
Grape w/Scroll Medallion . .278
Grasshopper 22
Grasshopper Without Insect . .246
Grated Diamond and Sunburst . .144
Grated Ribbon 296
Grecian 368
Grecian Border 448
Grecian Swirl 460
Greek 134
Greek Cross Band 156
Greek Key 448
Green Herringbone 348
Greensburg #130 434
Greensburg's Flora 88
Greensburg's Pillar 168
Greentown #11 148
Grenade 194
Grille 438
Grogan 156
Groove and Slash 416
Guardian Angel 352
Gyro 480
Hairpin 330
Halley's Comet 44
Hamilton 110
Hamilton with Leaf 392
Hammond 46, 384
Hand 98, 354, 362
Hand and Bar 362
Hand and Corn 360
Hand and Fishscale 360
Hanging Basket 246
Hanging Leaf 374

Hanover 156
Harmony 366
Harp 482
Hartford 68, 96
Hartley 158
Harvard 126
Harvard Yard 104
Hawaiian Lei 114
Hayes 482
Hayes and Wheeler 482
Heart 378
Heart Band 190
Heart in Sand 68
Heart Plume 118
Hearts and Spades 196
Hearts of Loch Laven 456
Heart Stem 252
Heart with Thumbprint 68
Heavy Diamond 86
Heavy Drape 470
Heavy Finecut 162
Heavy Gothic 192
Heavy Jewel 312
Heavy Panelled Fine Cut . .160
Heavy Panelled Grape 282
Heavy Rib 402
Heck 86
Heisey #150 102
Heisey #339-2 324
Heisey #343½ 204, 220
Heisey's #1250 416
Heisey's Banded Flute 338
Heisey's Coarse Ribbing . . .402
Heisey's Colonial 322
Heisey's Greek Key 448
Heisey's Panelled Cane . . .170
Heisey's Pineapple and Fan .142
Heisey's Plantation 276
Heisey's Sunburst .168, 204, 220
Heisey's Urn 338
Helene 118
Henrietta 172
Hercules Pillar 432
Hero (etched) 116
Heron 26
Herringbone 134
Herringbone Band 340
Herringbone Buttress 414
Herringbone Rib 414
Hexagonal Block 158, 172
Hexagonal Block Band 172
Hexagonal Bulls-Eye 62
Hexagon Block 62
Hexagon Star 450
Hickman 148
Hidalgo 430
High Hob 80
Highland 134
Hinoto 84
Hobbleskirt 166
Hobbs' Block 446
Hobbs Diamond and Sunburst .138
Hobb's Hobnail 292
Hobnail 294
Hobnail Band 294
Hobnail Double-Eye 292
Hobnail in Big Diamond . . .292
Hobnail-in-Square 112
Hobnail Pineapple 292
Hobnail with Bars 292
Hobnail with Fan 294
Hobnail w/Ornamental Band .292
Hobnail w/Thumbprint Base .294
Hobstar 188, 202
Hob Star 208
Hobstar Band 180
Holbrook 136
Holland 400
Hollis 100
Holly 396

Holly Amber 396
Holly Band 396
Holly Clear 396
Home 120
Homestead 368
Honeycomb 64
Honeycomb and Zipper . . .64
Honeycomb Obi 64
Honeycomb with
    Flower Rim 256
Hook 306
Hooped Barrel 432
Hops and Barley 398
Hops Band 388
Horn and Fruits 276
Horn of Plenty 82, 214
Horsehead Medallion 12
Horseshoe 246
Horseshoe Curve 226
Hourglass 42, 88
Huber 326
Huckabee 176
Huckle 184
Hummingbird 24
Humpty Dumpty 354
Hundred Eye 60
Hundred Leaved Rose 248
Hungarian 94
Iceberg 18
Icicle 408
Icicle with Chain Band 114
Icicle with Star 214
Ida 306
Idaho 40, 364, 472
Idyll 314
IHC 106
Ilex 138
Illinois 222
Imperial #4 90
Imperial #9 150
Imperial #77 420
Imperial #79 378
Imperial's #80 94
Imperial #81 316
Imperial #261 310
Imperial's Candlewick 30
Imperial Star 208
Indiana . . . . . . .46, , 114, 436
Indiana (Cord Drapery) . . .304
Indiana Swirl 160
Indian Sunset 228
Indian Tree 398
Inna 152
Inominata 362
Inside Flute 402
Inside Ribbing 402
Intaglio 260
Intaglio Daisy 262
Intaglio Sunflower 272
Interlocked Hearts 196
Interlocking Crescents 412
Inverness 36
Inverted Feather 198
Inverted Fern 378
Inverted Loops and Fan . . .142
Inverted Prism and
    Diamond Band 122
Inverted Prisms 178
Inverted Round 58
Inverted Strawberry 276
Inverted Thistle 262
Inverted Thumbprint 58
Inverted Thumbprint Oval . .58
Inverted Thumbprint
    w/Daisy Band 256
Iona 370
Ionic 368
Iowa 422
Iris 418
Irish Column 412

Iris with Meander 418
Iron Kettle 130
Isis 220
Ivanhoe 126
Iverna 202
Ivorina Verde 348
Ivy in Snow 392
Ivy Spray 372
Jabot 144
Jacob's Coat 134
Jacob's Ladder 134
Jam Jar 50
Janssen 320
Japanese 22, 354
Japanese Iris 242
Jasper 158
Jeanette 222
Jefferson #271 244
Jefferson Colonial 342
Jefferson Shell 428
Jersey 190
Jersey S 322
Jersey Swirl 474
Jewel 170, 176, 308
Jewel and Crescent 318
Jewel and Festoon 300
Jewel and Flower 274
Jewel Band 302
Jeweled Heart 318
Jewelled Diamond and Fan . .140
Jewelled Moon
    and Star 454, 458
Jewelled Rosettes 318
Jewel w/Dewdrop 312
Jewel w/Moon and Star . . .458
Job's Tears 54
Josephine's Fan 148
Jubilee 220
Jumbo 10, 14
Juno 230
Kalonyal 54
Kamm's Mirror 82
Kamoni 200
Kansas 35, 312
Kayak 118
Kenneth 206
Kentucky 35, 136
Kentucky w/Plain Panels . .338
Keystone 202, 216
Keystone Colonial 324
King Arthur 126
King's #29 128
King's #500 472
King's Block 168
King's Breast Plate 222
King's Crown 38
King's Curtain 140
King's Floral Ware 238
Kirkland 266
Klondike 444
Knight 440
Knobby Bottom 30
Knobby Bulls-Eye 212
Knob Stem Colonial 42
Kokomo 94, 470
Lace 312
Lace Band 90
LaClede 148
Lacy Cable 226
Lacy Daisy 174
Lacy Daisy, New Martinsville .174
Lacy Dewdrop 312
Lacy Floral 254
Lacy Heart 118
Lacy Medallion 118, 308
Lacy Spiral 134
Lacy Valance 420
Ladders 420
Ladders and Diamonds
    w/Star 212

Ladder to the Stars **92**
Ladder with Diamonds **92**
Lady Hamilton **112**
La France 248
Lakewood **124**
Large Stippled Chain **70**
Large Thumbprint 32
Late Banded Icicle **408**
Late Buckle 156, 182
Late Butterfly **20**
Late Colonial **320**
Late Colonial Variant **322**
Late Crystal **326**
Late Diamond Point Band **96**
Late Fleur-de-Lis 76
Late Icicle **408**
Late Lion 14
Late Mirror 82
Late Moon and Star 454
Late Panelled Grape **282**
Late Panelled Grape Band 286
Late Rosette **250**
Late Sawtooth 84, 420
Late Strawberry Variant 276
Late Swan **28**
Late Thistle **262**
Late Washington **300**
Late Way Colonial 42
Latin Cross **445**
Lattice **122**
Lattice and Lens **122**
Lattice and Oval Panels 102
Lattice Leaf **382**
Lattice with Bars **96**
La Verne 458
Lawrence 44
Leaf 376
Leaf and Dart **132**
Leaf and Fan 386
Leaf and Flower **240**
Leaf and Grape **286**
Leaf and Rib **380**
Leaf and Star **398**
Leaf Bracket **382**
Leaf-in-Oval **382**
Leaflets **120**
Leaf Medallion **396**
Leaf Rosette **360**
Leaf Umbrella **382**
Leaf with Spray 368
Leafy Panel and Thumbprint 48
Leafy Scroll **390**
Leaning Pillars **460**
Lee **44**
Lee's Lily-of-Valley **240**
Legged Trough **476**
Lenox **214**
Lens and Block **88**
Lens and Star **204**
Liberty **216**
Liberty Bell **482**
Lightning **334**
Lilly 72
Lily 274
Lily-of-the-Valley **240**
Lincoln Drape **46**
Lincoln Drape with Tassel **46**
Lined Diamonds **110**
Lined Panel **38**
Lion **14**
Lion and Baboon **14**
Lion's Head 14
Lion's Leg 422
Lion with Cable 14
Lippman 96
Little Balls 368
Little Band **164**
Little Bullet 406
Little Daisy **270**
Little Flower **258**
Little Gem 300
Little Owl **22**
Little River **478**
Little Samuel **356**
Locket 188
Locket on Chain **318**
Locust 22
Loehr Flute **346**
Loganberry and Grape **280**
Log and Star **186**
Log Cabin **476**
Log House **476**
London 476
Lone Star 236
Long Buttress **410**
Long Fan with Acanthus Leaf **388**
Long Maple Leaf **380**
Long Optic **58**
Long-Petalled Thumbprint 42
Long Punty 410
Long Spear 22
Long Star **106**
Long Teardrop and Thumbprint **32**
Loop **330**
Loop and Block **128**
Loop and Block with Waffle Band **126**
Loop and Chain Band **70**
Loop and Dart 132
Loop and Dart with Diamond Ornament **132**
Loop and Dart with Round Ornament **132**
Loop and Diamond 142
Loop and Fan 142
Loop and Honeycomb **64**
Loop and Jewel 98, 132, 300, 312
Loop and Moose Eye 58
Loop and Petal **404**
Loop and Pillar 418
Loop and Pyramid 420
Looped Cord 312
Looped Rope **426**
Loop Herringbone **424**
Loops and Drops 182
Loops and Ovals **404**
Loops w/Stippled Panels 136
Loop with Dewdrop **296**
Loop with Elk **12**
Loop with Fish Eye **312**
Loop with Knob Stem **322**
Loop with Prism Band **336**
Lotus 20, **212**
Lotus and Serpent 20
Louise **214**
Louisiana **102**
Louis XV **260**
Lovers 68
Lower Manhattan **32**
Lozenges **124**
Lucere **322**
Lutz **462**
Lyre 482
Madeira **244**
Madison **38**
Madora 182
Magic 274
Magna **150**
Magnet and Grape **280**
Magnolia **242**
Maiden's Blush 124
Maine **254**
Maize **374**
Majestic **142**
Majestic Crown **186**
Majestic Kin **142**
Maltese 134
Maltese Cross **446**
Malvern **150**
Manhattan **32**
Man in Hat **360**
Man's Head **354**
Many Diamonds 138
Maple 282, 388
Maple Leaf **376**
Maple Wreath **376**
Mardi Gras **216**
Mario **38**
Marlboro 118
Marquisette **332**
Marsh Fern **388**
Marsh Pink **242**
Martec **200**
Martha's Tears 406
Mary Jane **362**
Maryland **142**, 288
Mascotte **110**
Masonic **178**
Massachusetts **180**
Mayflower 36, 240
Maypole **134**
McKee Hobnail **176**
McKee's Berlin **368**
McKee's Comet **160**
McKee's Pillow **434**
McKee's Stars and Stripes **206**
McKee's Sunburst **234**
McKee's Union **418**
McKee's Virginia **48**
Medallion **196**, 352
Medallion Fan 182
Medallion Sprig **382**
Medallion Sunburst **224**
Mellor **50**
Melrose **146**
Melton **48**
Memphis **186**
Menagerie 22
Mephistopheles **360**
Merrimac **112**
Michigan **418**
Midget Thumbprint **60**
Midway 116
Midwestern Pomona 238
Mikado 20, 166
Mikado Fan 140
Millard **338**
Milton 186
Milton Cube and Fan 136
Minerva **352**
Minnesota **35**, **200**
Minor Block 110
Mioton **328**
Mioton with Pleat Band **336**
Mirror 126
Mirror and Fan **66**
Mirror and Loop **42**
Mirror Punty 36
Mirror Star **156**
Missouri **35**, **378**
Mitered Bars 130
Mitered Diamond 170
Mitered Diamond Points 130
Mitred Dewdrop 292
Mitred Diamond **128**, 170
Mitred Prisms **348**
Mobile 92
Model Gem 172
Model Peerless **180**
Modiste 190
Moesser 438
Monkey **14**
Monkey Under Tree 14
Monroe **46**
Montana **362**
Moon and Star **212**
Moon and Star Variation 454
Moon and Star with Waffled Stem 454
Moon and Stork **26**
Morning Glory **262**
Mosiac Scroll **74**
Mt. Vernon **128**
Muchness 200
Multiple Circle **340**
Multiple Scroll **72**
Murano **386**
Nail **155**
Nail City **320**
Nailhead **100**
Naomi 408
Napoleon **148**
Narcissus Spray **244**
Narrow Swirl **460**
National Prism **418**
National's Eureka **150**
National Star **152**
Nautilus 428
Navarre **210**
N.D. Beaded Circle 304
Nearcut **198**
Near Cut #2260 198
Near Cut #2651 198
Nearcut #2692 **330**
Nearcut #2697 **232**
Nearcut #2508 38
Nearcut Colonial 328
Nearcut Star 452
Nebraska 220
Nebraska Star 220
Nellie 220
Nelly **418**
Nemesis 148
Neptune 354
Nestor **304**
Net and Scroll **82**
Netted Acorn **386**
Netted Royal Oak 386
Nevada **364**
New Century 254
New England Flute **332**
New England Pineapple **98**
New Era **156**
New Floral 238
New Grand 112
New Hampshire **190**
New Jersey **182**
New Martinsville 128
New Martinsville Carnation **242**
New Mexico 234
Newport 52, **156**
New York 428
New York Honeycomb **64**
Niagara **62**
Nickel Plate #26 **460**
Nickel Plate's Richmond **100**
Nickel Plate's Royal **340**
Nogi 192
Nonpareil **112**
Nortec 198
North Pole 18
Northwood Nearcut **188**
Northwood Peach **288**
Northwood's Regal Block **430**
Nostalgia 260
Notched Bar 412
Notched Bull's-Eye 46
Notched Finecut 446
Notched Panel 420
Notched Rib 412
Nova Scotia Buttons and Bows 462
Nova Scotia Diamond **174**
N.P.L. 380, 386
N.S. Starflower 268
Nucut #526 **218**
Oaken Bucket 476

Patterns in this index are listed by page numbers; numbers in bold face indicate illustrated patterns.

Oak Leaf 274
Oak Leaf Band **394**
Oak Leaf Band with Medallion **394**
Oak Leaf Wreath 386
Oak Leaves **394**
Oak Wreath **386**
Oasis **14**
Oats and Barley 398
Odd Fellow **268**
Oglebay **346**
O'Hara 328, 330
O'Hara Diamond **94**
O'Hara's Crystal Wedding 114
Ohio **368**
Oklahoma **146**
Old Acorn 394
Old Colony 250
Old Columbia **406**
Old Glory 156
Old Man 354
Old Man of the Mountain 354
Old Moon and Star 454
Old Quilt 168
Olive 286
Olympia 298
Omnibus 202
Oneata **198**
One-Hundred-and-One **318**
One-O-One 318
Open Basketweave **438**
Open Plaid 438
Open Rose **248**
Opposing Icicle 134
Opposing Pyramids **88**
Optic 32
Optical Cube 480
Optic Flute **90**
Orange Peel **478**
Orange Peel Band **478**
Orbed Feet 30
Oregon **35, 162**
Orient 182, 458
Oriental **400**
Orinda **348**
Orinoco **464**
Orion 162
Orion Thumbprint **58**
Ornate Star **212**
Ostrich Looking at the Moon 26
Oval and Crossbar 410
Oval and Fans **304**
Oval Diamond Panel **102**
Oval Lens 82
Oval Loop 32
Oval Medallion **54**
Oval Mitre **44**
Oval Panel **54**, 102
Oval Panelled Daisy and Button 164
Ovals and Fine Pleat **72**
Oval Sett 54
Oval Star **196**
Oval Thumbprint **38**
Oval Thumbprint Band **30**
Oval Windows **50**
Overall Diamond **108**
Overall Hob **172**
Overall Lattice **438**
Overshot 478
Ovoid Panels **328**
Owl **22**, 26, 176
Owl and Fan 22
Owl and Possum **18**
Owl and Stump **26**
Owl Head **12**
Oxford **222**
Paddles and Stars **220**
Paddlewheel **154**
Paddlewheel Shield **230**
Paisley with Purple Dots 202
Palace 68, 212
Paling **416**
Palm and Scroll 378
Palm Beach **284**
Palmer Prism **404**
Palmette **118**
Palm Leaf Fan **198**
Pampas Flower **238**
Panama **148**
Panegyric 48
Panel and Cane **122**
Panel and Flute 344
Panel and Rib **98**
Panel and Star 440
Panelled 44 **270**
Panelled Acorn Band **394**
Panelled Agave 388
Panelled Anthemion **384**
Panelled Apple Blossom 258
Panelled Beads **296**
Panelled Cable **426**
Panelled Cane **170**
Panelled Cardinal **24**
Panelled Cherry 290
Panelled Daisy 164, **244**
Panelled Daisy and Button **164**, 166
Panelled Dewdrop **296**
Panelled Diamond 160
Panelled Diamond and Flower **274**
Panelled Diamond Blocks **146**
Panelled Diamond Cross **146**, 160
Panelled Diamond Cut and Fan 158
Panelled Diamond Point **104**
Panelled Diamonds and Finecut 104
Panelled Diamonds and Rosettes **134**
Panelled Dogwood **258**
Panelled English Hobnail 216, **446**
Panelled Fern **384**
Panelled Fine Cut **158**
Panelled Finetooth **342**
Panelled Fishbone **414**
Panelled Flattened Sawtooth **92**
Panelled Flower and Fern **254**
Panelled Flowers 260
Panelled Flower Stippled 254
Panelled Forget-Me-Not 264
Panelled Grape **282**
Panelled Grape Band **286**
Panelled Heather **244**
Panelled Herringbone **316**, 348
Panelled Hexagons **62, 172**
Panelled Hobnail **292**
Panelled Holly **396**
Panelled Holly and Diamond 396
Panelled Honeycomb **274**
Panelled Iris 264
Panelled Ivy **390**
Panelled Jewel 418
Panelled Ladder **338**
Panelled Lattice **128**
Panelled Leaf 384
Panelled Oak **394**
Panelled Oval **82**
Panelled Oval Finecut 94
Panelled Palm **380**
Panelled Pleat **420**
Panelled Primula **244**
Panelled Ringed Stem **372**
Panelled Roman Key **448**
Panelled "S" **30**
Panelled Sagebrush **246**
Panelled Sawtooth **84**
Panelled Smocking **90**
Panelled Sprig **398**
Panelled Star and Button 178
Panelled Star and Square 446
Panelled Stippled Bowl 344
Panelled Strawberry **276**
Panelled Strawberry Cut **160**
Panelled Sunburst 210
Panelled Sunbursts and Daisy **264**
Panelled Sunflower **272**
Panelled Swan **28**
Panelled Thistle **262**
Panelled Thousand Eye **60**
Panelled Thumbprint 68
Panelled Wheat **400**
Panelled Zipper 422
Panel, Rib and Shells **50**
Panel w/Diamond Point Band **88**, 96
Pannier **54**
Pansy 240, **242**, 258
Pansy and Moss Rose **240**
Pantagraph Band **124**
Parachute **142**
Paragon 160, 200, **378**
Parian Ruby 460
Parian Swirl **154**
Paris **414**, 456
Parrot **22**, 472
Parrot and Fan 22
Parrot Pitcher 22
Parthenon 16
Pathfinder 202
Pattee Cross **116**
Pattern F **106**
Pavonia **90**
Peacock and Palm 22
Peacock at the Fountain **22**
Peacock Eye 54
Peacock Feather 54
Peacock Feather (Georgia) **310**
Peacock Tail 82
Pearl Flowers **256**
Peas and Pods **298**
Pebbled Swirl **466**
Pecan Swirl **464**
Pecorah 150
Peerless 214, 322
Pen 416
Pendant **192**
Pendleton **42**
Penelope 382
Pennsylvania 98, **200**
Pennsylvania Hand 98
Pentagon **204**, 424
Pepper Berry 286
Pequot **102**
Perfection 380
Periwinkle **256**
Persian **150**
Persian Shawl 420
Pert Set 246
Petal 78
Petal and Loop **328**
Petalled Medallion 206
Petticoat **114**
Philadelphia **342**
Picket **476**
Picket Band **416**
Picket Fence 476
Picture Window **444**
Pig and Corn **16**
Pigmy 308
Pilgrim **142**
Pilgrim Bottle **468**
Pillar **58**, 96
Pillar and Cut Diamond 90
Pillar Bulls-eye **30**
Pillow and Sunburst **116**
Pillow Bands **444**
Pillow Encircled **116**
Pillow-in-Oval **116**
Pillows **116**
Pimlico 222
Pinafore 350
Pineapple **286**
Pineapple and Fan **136**
Pineapple Stem 90
Pins and Bells **268**
Pinwheel 232, **460**
Pinwheels 152
Pioneer 12
Pioneer #15 412
Pioneer #21 **66**
Pioneer's Victoria **90**
Pittman **128**
Pittsburgh **410**
Pittsburgh Daisy 264
Pittsburgh Fan **138**
Pittsburgh Flute **332**
Plaid **438**, 446
Plain Band 300
Plain Flat Ring 362
Plain Miotin 328
Plain Roman Key **448**
Plain Scalloped Panel **324**
Plain Tulip **338**
Plain Two-Mold 362, 372
Plain Ware 336, 366
Pleat and Panel **336**
Pleat and Tuck 348
Pleat Band **366**
Pleated Bands **336**
Pleated Medallion **274**
Pleated Oval **148**
Pleating **342**
Plume **378**
Plume and Block **444**
Plume and Fan **112**
Plutec **186**
Plytec **198**
Pogo Stick **336**
Poinsettia **266**
Pointed Arches **126**
Pointed Bulls-Eye 88
Pointed Cube **438**
Pointed Fingerprint 54
Pointed Gothic **192**
Pointed Jewel **192**
Pointed Panel 166
Pointed Thumbprint 54
Pointed Thumbprint and Panel 410
Polar Bear **18**
Polka Dot 58
Pond Lily **376**
Popcorn **294**
Portland 170, **410**
Portland Petal **328**
Portland w/Diamond Point Band 124
Posies and Pods **270**
Postscript **210**
Potted Plant 246
Powder and Shot **316**
Prayer Mat 246
Prayer Rug 246
Pressed Block **30, 48, 432**
Pressed Diamond **94**
Pressed Leaf **380**, 386
Pressed Leaf Band 388
Pressed Leaf with Chain **380**
Pressed Octagon **324**
Pressed Optic 402
Pressed Spray **238**
Pressed Swirl **462**
Pretty Band 240
Pretty Panels **324**
Pride 132, 202
Primrose **248**

Patterns in this index are listed by page numbers; numbers in bold face indicate illustrated patterns.

Primrose and Pearls **258**
Prince Albert **210**
Prince of Wales Plumes ...**216**
Prince's Feather **160**
Princess Feather **118**
Princeton **142**
Printed Hobnail **298**
Priscilla **184**
Prism **128, 336, 402**
Prism and Broken Column ..**418**
Prism and Clear Panels **430**
Prism and Crescent **48**
Prism and Daisy Bar **156**
Prism and Diamond **92**
Prism and Diamond Band ..**122**
Prism and Flattened Sawtooth ..**84**
Prism and Flute **336**
Prism and Globules **410**
Prism and Herringbone ...**316**
Prism and Sawtooth **84**
Prism Arc **118**
Prismatic **120**
Prism Bars **402**
Prism Buttress **410**
Prism Column **416**
Prism Cube **432**
Prism Ring **370**
Prism w/Diamond Points ..**92**
Prism w/Double Block Band ..**178**
Prism Window **114**
Prison Stripe **338**
Prison Window **114, 436**
Prophet **354**
Prosperity **224**
Pseudo-Czarina **136**
Psyche and Cupid **352**
Puffed Bands **416**
Pump and Trough **476**
Punty and Diamond Point ...**68**
Puritan **142, 260, 468**
Pyramid and Shield **228**
Pyramids **170**
Quadruped **326**
Quantico **268**
Quartered Block **146, 444**
Quatrefoil **124**
Queen **166**
Queen Anne **354**
Queen's Jewels **452**
Queen's Necklace **300, 452**
Question Mark **32, 238**
Quilt and Flute **100**
Quilted Fan Top **136**
Quilted Phlox **270**
Quintec **236**
Quixote **126**
Rabbit in Tree **16**
Rabbit Tracks **142**
Racing Deer **12**
Radiant **62, 166, 190, 220**
Radiant Daisy **202, 206**
Radiant Petal **198**
Radium **202**
Rainbow **170**
Rainbow Variant **178**
Raindrop **60, 294**
Raisin **278**
Rambler **234**
Ramona **98, 182**
R & H Swirl **94**
Ranson **334**
Raspberry **284**
Rattan and Bamboo **412**
Ray **314**
Rayed Divided
    Diamond Heart **118**
Rayed Flower **180**
Rayed with Loop **54**

Rebecca **242**
Rebecca at the Well ...**344, 356**
Recessed Ovals **48**
Recessed Pillar **50**
Red Block **154**
Red Block and Lattice ...**172, 180**
Red Flute **322**
Red Loop and Finecut **182**
Red Sunflower **266**
Red Top **190**
Reeded Waffle **436**
Reeding **342**
Regal Block **100**
Regent **396**
Regina **336**
Reticulated Cord **426**
Reverse 44 ....**270**
Reverse Torpedo **80**
Reward **442**
Rex **218, 402**
Rexford **194**
Rhode Island **482**
Rib and Bead **408**
Rib and Block **430**
Rib and Swirl **466**
Ribbed Acorn **386**
Ribbed Bands **404**
Ribbed Drape **408**
Ribbed Droplet Band **372**
Ribbed Ellipse **216**
Ribbed Forget-Me-Not **246**
Ribbed Grape **278**
Ribbed Ivy **392**
Ribbed Leaves **392**
Ribbed Oval **404**
Ribbed Palm **384**
Ribbed Pineapple **84**
Ribbed Sawtooth **422**
Ribbed Thumbprint **32**
Ribbed Ware **402**
Ribbing **404**
Ribbon **344**
Ribbon Band with Pendants ..**130**
Ribbon Candy **32**
Richmond **84**
Ridge Swirl **460**
Right Swirl **460**
Ring and Block **442**
Ring and Swirl **466**
Ring-Handled Basket **480**
Ripley's Wyoming **390**
Ripple **340**
Ripple Band **340**
Rising Sun **200**
Riverside **142**
Riverside's Aurora **208**
Riverside's Victoria **128**
Roanoke **84**
Roanoke Star **208**
Robin **10**
Robin Hood **40**
Robinson's Ladder **420**
Robinson's Puritan **206**
Rochelle **118**
Rock Crystal **260**
Rocket **194**
Rocket Bomb **324**
Rococo **76**
Roman **66**
Roman Cross **446**
Roman Key **448**
Roman Key Base **448**
Roman Key Collar **448**
Roman Key, Frosted Band ..**448**
Roman Key w/Ribs **448**
Roman Medallion **352**
Roman Rosette **250**
Romeo **440**
Romola **50**
Rope and Ribs **424**

Rope and Thumbprint **58**
Rope Bands **424**
Roped Diamond **426**
Rope Panel **426**
Rosby **236**
Rose **248**
Rose and Sunbursts **248**
Rose-in-Snow **248**
Rose Leaf **386**
Rose Point Band **264**
Rose Sprig **248**
Rosetta **232**
Rosette **274**
Rosette and Palms **212**
Rosette Bands **250**
Rosette Medallion **184**
Rosette Row **256**
Rosette with Pinwheels **266**
Rose Windows **216**
Rose Wreath **260**
Rotec **182**
Roughneck **414**
Round **18**
Royal **232, 328, 400**
Royal Crystal **142**
Royal Ivy **392**
Royal Lady **352**
Royal Oak **386**
Ruby **130**
Ruby Bar and Flute **36**
Ruby Crown **38**
Ruby Diamond **122**
Ruby Rosette **116**
Ruby Star **94**
Ruby Talons **244**
Ruby Thumbprint **38**
Ruffled Eye **272**
Ruffles **470**
Running Bulls-Eye **44**
Rustic **132**
Rustic Rose **274**
Saloon **370**
Sampson **318**
Sanborn **130**
Sandwich Heart **422**
Sandwich Loop **330**
Sandwich Plaid **442**
Sandwich Star **156**
Sandwich Star and Buckle ..**450**
Sandwich Vine **390**
Santa Claus **354**
Sawtooth **84, 86**
Sawtooth and Star **94**
Sawtooth and Window **86**
Sawtooth Band **88**
Sawtooth Bands **300**
Sawtooth Bottom **366**
Sawtoothed Honeycomb **62**
Saxon **430**
Scalloped Band **340**
Scalloped Daisy **190**
Scalloped Diamond Point ...**96**
Scalloped Flower Band **412**
Scalloped Flute **404**
Scalloped Lines **340**
Scalloped Loop **404**
Scalloped Prism **414**
Scalloped Six-Point **150**
Scalloped Swirl **155**
Scalloped Tape **302**
Scallop Shell **428**
Screen **438**
Scroll **72**
Scroll and Chain **74**
Scroll and Dots **134**
Scroll Band **74**
Scrolled Spray **400**
Scrolled Sunflower **272**
Scroll in Scroll **74**
Scrolls w/Bulls Eye **318**

Scroll with Acanthus **314**
Scroll with Cane Band **176**
Scroll with Flowers **268**
Scroll with Star **40**
Seagirt **148**
Seashell **400**
Sectional Block **434**
Sedan **178**
Seedpod **298**
Seely **78**
Semi-Oval **114**
Seneca Loop **330**
Sequoia **160**
Serrated Block and Loop **62**
Serrated Panels **418**
Serrated Prism **420**
Serrated Rib **420**
Serrated Rib and Finecut ...**96**
Serrated Ribs **464**
Serrated Spear Point **418**
Serrated Teardrop **36**
Sextec **210**
Sharp Oval and Diamond ...**102**
Shasta Daisy **250**
Sheaf and Block **146**
Sheaf and Diamond **144**
Shell **124, 428**
Shell and Jewel **428**
Shell and Scale **428**
Shell and Scroll **428**
Shell and Tassel **18**
Shell and Tassel Square ...**478**
Shell on Ribs **428**
Shelton Star **220**
Shepherd's Plaid **136**
Sheraton **306**
Shield **226, 454**
Shield and Anchor **482**
Shield and Chain **70**
Shield and Spike **132**
Shield Band **38**
Shield in Red, White, and Blue ..**28**
Shields **70**
Shimmering Star **208**
Shining Diamonds **142**
Short Teasel **136**
Shoshone **152**
Shrine **458**
Shuttle **456**
Siamese Necklace **216**
Side Wheeler **346**
Silver Band **158**
Silver Queen **340**
Silver Sheen **134**
Singing Birds **24**
Single Rose **258**
Sister Kate **124**
Six Panel Fine Cut **160**
Six Pansy **258**
Skilton **440**
Slashed Swirl **464**
Slashed Swirl Border **466**
Slewed Diamond **104**
Slewed Horseshoe **202**
Small Comet **40**
Smocking **78**
Smocking Bands **406**
Smooth Diamond **134**
Snail **40, 472**
Snakeskin **478**
Snakeskin with Dot **52**
Snow Band **416**
Snowdrop **332**
Snowflake **226, 456**
Snowflake and Starburst ...**226**
Snowflake Base **232, 370**
Snowflower **208**
Snowshoe **118**
Solar **232**
Southern Ivy **392**

Patterns in this index are listed by page numbers; numbers in bold face indicate illustrated patterns.

Souvenir ... 338
Spades ... 196
Spanish American ... **360**
Spartan ... 106
Spearheads ... **78**
Spear Point ... 192
Spearpoint Band ... **334**
Spearpoint w/Daisy Band ... 90
Specialty ... **56**
Specialty #6 ... **90**
Specialty Pattern E ... **90**
Sphinx ... **356**
Spider Fans ... **142**
Spinner Daisy ... 234
Spinning Star ... **232**
Spiral and Maltese Cross ... **74**
Spiralled Diamond Point ... **474**
Spiralled Ivy ... **390**
Spiralled Triangle ... **128**
Spirea Band ... **120**
Split Waffle ... **434**
Spool Stem Swirl ... **462**
Spotted Box ... **270**
Spray and Cane ... 264
Sprig ... 384, 398, **400**
Sprig in Snow ... **252**
Sprig without Sprig ... **328**
Square and Diamond Band ... 112
Square and Diamond Bands ... 120
Square and Dot ... 120
Square Block ... 168, **432**
Squared Daisy and Diamond **106**
Squared Dot ... 120
Squared Fine Cut ... **158**
Squared Star ... **88**
Squared Sunburst ... **196**
Square Fuchsia ... 242
Square in Diamond Point ... 90
Square Lion's Head ... 14
Squat Pineapple ... **236**
Squirrel ... **16**
Squirrel-in-Bower ... **16**
Squirrel with Nut ... **16**
S-Repeat ... **472**
Staple ... 306
Star ... 112, 208
Star and Bar ... **452**
Star and Circle ... **450**
Star and Crescent ... **202**
Star and Dart ... **452**
Star and Diamond ... **106**, 122
Star and Diamond Point ... **184**
Star and Fan ... **210**
Star and Feather ... **158**
tar and Ivy ... **454**
tar and Ladders ... **224**
tar and Lines ... **450**
tar and Notched Rib ... **210**
tar and Oval ... 204
tar and Palm ... **384**
tar and Pillar ... **456**
tar and Punty ... 212, **450**
tar and Rib ... **188**
tar and Swag ... **454**
tar and Thumbprint ... **454**
tar Band ... **114**
ar Base ... **192**
arburst ... 452
tardust ... **224**
arflower Band ... 242
ar Galaxy ... 456
arglow ... **452**
ar in Bulls-Eye ... **212**
ar in Diamond ... **106**
ar in Honeycomb ... **458**
ar in Octagon ... **218**
ar-in-Square ... **114**
arlight ... 456
arlyte ... **452**
ar Medallion ... 180
Star Octad ... **220**
Star-of-Bethlehem ... **452**
Star of David ... **222**
Star of the East ... 222
Starred Block ... **442**
Starred Cosmos ... **266**
Starred Jewel ... 214
Starred Loop ... **208**
Starred Scroll ... **206**
Star Rosetted ... **456**
Stars and Bars ... **204**, 456
Stars and Bars with Leaf ... **382**
Stars and Stripes ... **92**
Startec ... **190**
Star Whorl ... 230
Star-with-Handle ... **188**
Star with Zippers ... **450**
Staves w/Scalloped Band ... 416
Stayman ... 132
St. Bernard ... **18**
Stedman ... **408**
Steele ... 184
Stellar ... 196
Stemless Daisy ... 256
Stepped Diamond Point ... **84**
Sterling ... **152**
Stippled Band ... **344**
Stippled Bar ... **346**
Stippled Beaded Shield ... 318
Stippled Chain ... **70**
Stippled Cherry ... **290**
Stippled Clover ... **398**
Stippled Daisy ... **272**
Stippled Dart and Balls ... **316**
Stippled Diamond Band ... **130**
Stippled Diamonds ... **86**
Stippled Double Loop ... 132
Stippled Fans ... **236**
Stippled Fleur-de-Lis ... 76
Stippled Fleur-de-Lis Diamond Band ... 76
Stippled Flower Band ... **252**
Stippled Forget-Me-Not ... **86**
Stippled Grape and Festoon ... **278**
Stippled Ivy ... 392
Stippled Leaf ... 386
Stippled Leaf and Flower ... 20
Stippled Leaf, Flower and Moth ... 20
Stippled Loop ... 332
Stippled Loop with Vine Band ... **388**
Stippled Medallion ... **76**
Stippled Oval ... 58
Stippled Palm ... **378**
Stippled Panel and Band ... **334**
Stippled Peppers ... **288**
Stippled Primrose ... 248
Stippled Sandbur ... **456**
Stippled Scroll ... 72
Stippled Star ... 274, **456**
Stippled Starflower ... **252**
Stippled Star Variant ... 456
Stippled Strawberry ... **276**
Stippled Violet ... 268
Stippled Woodflower ... **240**
St. Louis ... **304**
Stork ... 26
Stork Looking at the Moon ... 26
Stratford ... **84**
Strawberry ... **276**
Strawberry and Cable ... **276**
Strawberry and Currant ... **276**
Strawberry and Fan Variant **174**
Strawberry with Checkerboard ... **276**
St. Regis ... 64
Strigil ... **422**
Strutting Peacock ... **22**
Stump ... **376**
Style ... **182**
Stylistic Leaf ... 382
Stylized Flower ... **256**
Sugar Pear ... 288
Sultan ... 260, 470
Summit ... 210
Sun and Star ... 184
Sunbeam ... **194**
Sunburst ... **206**
Sunburst and Bar ... **94**
Sunburst and Star ... **236**
Sunburst Diamond ... 180
Sunburst in Oval ... **204**
Sunburst Medallion ... 272
Sunburst on Shield ... **210**
Sunburst Rosette ... 204
Sunflower ... **274**
Sunflower Patch ... **262**
Sunk ... 166
Sunk Daisy ... **266**
Sunk Diamond and Lattice ... **104**
Sunken Arches ... **78, 404**
Sunken Buttons ... **170**
Sunken Primrose ... 242
Sunken Teardrop ... **370**
Sunk Honeycomb ... **62**
Sunk Jewel ... 214
Sunk Prism ... **102**
Sunrise ... 200
Sunrise in Arch ... **384**
Sunshine ... 200
Superior ... **88**
Swag Block ... **440**
Swag with Brackets ... **388**
Swan ... **28**
Swan on Pond ... **28**
Swan Two ... 28
Swan with Tree ... **28**
Sweetheart ... 318
Sweet Heart ... **182**
Sweet Pear ... **288**
Swirl ... 160, 474
Swirl and Ball ... 462
Swirl and Ball Variant ... 262
Swirl and Cable ... **462**
Swirl and Diamond ... 464
Swirl and Diamonds ... 474
Swirl and Diamond w/Ovals ... 464
Swirl and Dot ... **470**
Swirl and Panel ... **474**
Swirl and Sawtooth ... 464
Swirl and Thumbprint ... 472
Swirl-Atop-Diamond ... 104
Swirl Band ... 94, **462**
Swirled Block ... 108
Swirled Column ... **468**
Swirled Star ... **474**
Swirl with Beaded Band ... **462**
Swirl with Fan ... **464**
Sydney ... **116**
Sylvan ... 108, 418
Tackle Block ... **434**
Tacoma ... **140**
Tandem Diamonds and Thumbprint ... **122**
Tape Measure ... **70**
Tapered Vine ... 254
Tapering Flute ... **324**
Tappan ... **446**
Tarentum's Atlanta ... **142**
Tarentum's Ladder with Diamonds ... **92**
Tarentum's Manhattan ... **122**
Tarentum's Victoria ... **238**
Tarentum's Virginia ... **138**
Tarentum Thumbprint ... **38**
Target ... **52**
Tassel and Bead ... **318**
Taunton ... **364**
Teardrop ... **406**
Teardrop and Cracked Ice ... 48
Teardrop and Tassel ... **318**
Teardrop and Thumbprint ... **32**
Teardrop Bands ... 406
Teardrop Flower ... **244**
Teardrops and Diamond Block ... 100
Teasel ... **136**
Teddy Roosevelt ... **358**
Teepee ... 130, 148
Tennessee ... 34, 318
Tennis Racquet ... **32**
Ten-Pointed Star ... **188**
Tepee ... **148**
Teutonic ... 106
Texas ... **136**
Texas Bulls-Eye ... **46**
Texas Star ... **232, 370, 460**
Theatrical ... 350
The Bedford ... **410**
The Jefferson ... **346**
The Kitchen Stove ... **190**
The Mirror ... **362**
The Mosaic ... **244**
The Prize ... **416**
The Sisters ... 350
The States ... **212**
The Summit ... **270**
The Town Pump ... **476**
The United States ... 364
Thistle ... 30, 274
Thistle and Clover ... **250**
Thistle and Fern ... **262**
Thistleblow ... **264**
Thompson #77 ... 410
Thousand Diamonds ... **112**
Thousand Eye ... **60**
Thousand Eye Band ... **56**, 316
Thousand Faces ... 64
Thousand Hexagons ... **62**
Thread Band ... **340**
Threading ... **338**
Three Deer ... **12**
Three Face ... **350**
Three-Faced Medallion ... 350
Three Fates ... 350
Three Fruits ... 276
Three Graces ... 350
Three-in-One ... **122**
Three Leaf Clover ... **398**
Three Panel ... **170**
Three Ply Panel ... **110**
Three Sisters ... 350
Three Stories ... **444**
Thrush and Apple Blossoms ... 24
Thumbnail ... **334**
Thumbprint ... 36, 58
Thumbprint and Diamond ... **130**
Thumbprint and Prisms ... 38
Thumbprint Block ... **434**
Thumbprint Block (round) ... **432**
Thumbprint on Spearhead ... 36
Thumbprint on Spearpoint ... **48**
Thumbprint Panel ... 68
Thumbprint Row ... **48**
Thumbprint Serrated Bar ... 68
Thumbprint Windows ... **38**
Thunderbird, Hummingbird and Fern ... 24
Tidal ... 380
Tidy ... **132**
Tieback ... **74**
Tile ... **480**
Tiny Finecut ... **160**
Tiny Lion ... **14**
Tiny Thumbprint ... 38
Tippecanoe ... 12
Tiptoe ... **98**
Tobin ... 398
Togo ... 220
Tokyo ... **52**

Patterns in this index are listed by page numbers; numbers in bold face indicate illustrated patterns.

Toltec **188**
Tong **44**
Tooth and Claw 72
Toothed Medallion **82**
Top and Bottom Scroll 72
Torpedo **308**
Tossed Scrolls 74
Transverse Ribs **408**
Tree **348**
Treebark **476**
Tree of Life **478**
Tree of Life with Hand **354**
Tree of Life with Sprig **398**
Tree Stump **376**
Trellis Scroll 74
Tremont **184**
Triad **346**
Triangular Medallion **268**
Triangular Prism **404**
Trilby **350**
Triple Band **340**
Triple Bar **414**
Triple Bar and Loop **414**
Triple Bar with Cable **424**
Triple Bead Band **306**
Triple Bulls-Eye 68
Triple Fine-Tooth Band . . .**336**
Triple Frosted Band **296**
Triple Line **340**
Triple Prism Grid **422**
Triple Shell **428**
Triple Thumbprints 68
Triple Triangle **90**
Triple X **110**
Tripod Stem 114
Trump **348**
Truncated Cone **368**
Truncated Cube **410**
Truncated Prisms 88
Tulip **90**
Tulip and Honeycomb **64**
Tulip and Oval **42**
Tulip Band **252**
Tulip Petals **330**
Tulip w/Sawtooth **90**
Turtle **20**
Tuxedo **170**
Twin Crescents **234**
Twin Feathers **220**
Twinkle Star **456**
Twinkle Star Variant **454**
Twin Ladders **68**
Twin Leaves **396**
Twin Panels **430**
Twin Pear 288

Twin Snowshoes **194**
Twin Sunbursts **226**
Twin Teardrops **118**
Two Band **70**
Two Flower **262**
Two Handle **52**
Two Panel **162**
Two Ply Swirl **464**
Tycoon 58
Umbilicated Hobnail **292**
Union **176**
Unique **116**
Urn **364**
U.S. #84 . . . .**414**
U.S. #156 . . . .**56**
U.S. #341 . . . .**62**
U.S. #5701 . . . .**330**
U.S. #5705 . . . .**328**
U.S. Blossom **364**
U.S. Coin **356**
U.S. Colonial **324**
U.S. Comet **428**
U.S. Georgian **332**
U.S. Niagara **338**
U.S. Peacock **202**
U.S. Puritan **332**
U. S. Regal **236**
U.S. Rib **402**
U.S. Shell **440**
U.S. Sheraton **448**
U.S. Thumbprint 36
U.S. Victoria **234**
Utah (Twinkle Star) **456**
Valencia 78
Valencia Waffle **158**
Valentine **350**
Valtec **198**
V-Band **370**
Venice **338**
Venus **300**
Vera **192**
Vermont **256**
Vermont Honeycomb **256**
Vernon 64
Verona **440**
Vesta **112**
Victor **152**, 428
Victoria **82**
Victorian Jubilee **448**
Vigilant **368**
Viking **148**, 354
Vincent's Valentine 68
V-in-Heart **196**
Virginia **124**, 126
Vulcan **406**

Wading Heron **26**
Waffle **434**
Waffle and Bar **432**
Waffle and Fine Cut 162
Waffle and Star Band **440**
Waffle and Thumprint **68**
Waffle Block **436**
Waffle Keg **438**
Waffle Octagon **436**
Waffle Variant **436**
Waffle Window **436**
Waffle with Points **436**
Waffle w/Spearpoints **436**
Ward's New Era **78**
Washboard **348**
Washington Centennial .**128**, 356
Washington Early **48**
Waterfall **160**
Waterfowl 28
Waterlily **242**, 264
Waterlily and Cattails **242**
Wave **408**, 468
Waverly **120**
Wavey **468**
Webb **218**
Wedding Bells **472**
Wedding Ring **40**
Wellington **306**
Wellsburg **418**
Western Star **208**
Westmoreland **108**
Westmoreland #15 412
Westmoreland #500 168
Westmoreland Colonial **324**
Westmoreland's Priscilla 146
Westward Ho! 12
Wetzel **222**
Wheat **206**, 400
Wheat and Barley **398**
Wheat and Burr **450**
Wheat Sheaf **198**
Wheel and Comma **370**
Wheel in Band **214**
Wheeling **346**
Wheeling Block **174**
Wheel of Fortune **236**
Whirled Sunburst in Circle .**232**
Whirligig **230**
Whirlwind **232**
White Oak **394**
Whitton **192**
Wide and Narrow Panel **330**
Wide Swirl **464**
Wigwam **130**, 148
Wildflower **264**

Wild Rose **258**
Wild Rose w/Bow Knot **260**
Wild Rose w/Scrolling **154**
Willow Oak **274**
Wiltec **230**
Wimpole **128**
Windflower **262**
Window and Drape **414**
Windows **460**
Windsor 32
Windsor Swirl **474**
Winged Scroll **348**
Winking Eye **30**
Winona 30, 298
Wisconsin **314**
Wishbone **196**
Wooden Pail **154**
Woodrow **126**
World's Pattern **100**
Wreath **274**, 278
Wreath and Bars **250**
Wreathed Cherry **290**
Wreathed Sunburst **272**
Wyandotte **292**
Wycliff 40
Wyoming **312**
X-Bull's Eye **210**
XLCR 38
X Logs **118**
X-Ray **336**
Yale **60**
Yellow Vintage **372**
Yoke and Circle **70**
Yoked Loop **404**
York Colonial **42**
York Herringbone **470**
Yuma Loop **328**
Yutec **236**
Zanesville **452**
Zanzibar **468**
Zenith **298**
Zenith Block **438**
Zephyr **94**
Zig-Zag **130**
Zig-Zag Band **130**
Zipper **420**
Zipper Borders **418**
Zipper Cross **414**
Zippered Block **420**
Zippered Heart **196**
Zippered Swirl **94**
Zippered Swirl and Diamond .**474**
Zipper in Diamond **420**
Zipper Slash **420**

Patterns in this index are listed by page numbers; numbers in bold face indicate illustrated patterns.